CAREERS
with
Dogs

CAREERS
with
Dogs

The **Comprehensive Guide**
to Finding Your Dream Job

By Kim Campbell Thornton

BOWTIE
PRESS

Irvine, California

Lead Editor: Jarelle S. Stein
Senior Editor: Amy Deputato
Assistant Editor: Elizabeth L. McCaughey
Art Director: Cindy Kassebaum
Production Supervisor: Jessica Jaensch
Production Coordinator: Tracy Burns
Publishing Coordinator: Karen Julian
Indexer: Melody Englund

Vice President, Chief Content Officer: June Kikuchi
Vice President, Kennel Club Books: Andrew DePrisco
BowTie Press: Jennifer Calvert, Amy Deputato, Lindsay Hanks,
Karen Julian, Elizabeth L. McCaughey, Roger Sipe, Jarelle S. Stein

Library of Congress Cataloging-in-Publication Data

Thornton, Kim Campbell.
  Careers with dogs : the comprehensive guide to finding your dream job /
by Kim Campbell Thornton.
     p. cm.
  Includes bibliographical references and index.
  ISBN 978-1-933958-19-4
  1. Dog industry--Vocational guidance. I. Title.
  SF426.55.T46 2010
  636.70023--dc22
                         2010031138

BowTie Press®
A Division of BowTie, Inc.
3 Burroughs
Irvine, California 92618

Printed and bound in China
14 13 12 11 10   1 2 3 4 5 6 7 8 9 10

To Mordecai Siegal,
a dear friend who will always be
the dean of the dog writers.

You are missed.

CONTENTS

Introduction

When most of us think of occupations that involve working with dogs, veterinarian, veterinary technician, dog groomer, and dog trainer immediately spring to mind. Those are certainly the best known of the dog-focused careers, but as many people have learned, to their delight, a number of other professions, occupations, and pursuits can focus on dogs. Whether your interest in dogs lies in behavior; canine health, well-being, welfare, and advocacy; human health, welfare, assistance, and protection; sports; or some other area, there's a good chance that your passion can become your life's work.

If you're interested in a dog-related health career, you may have thought you were limited to being a veterinarian or veterinary technician, but did you know that you could pursue a career as a pet rehabilitation therapist, pet massage practitioner, or pet EMT (emergency medical technician)? If you do pursue veterinary medicine, you can specialize in anesthesiology, behavior, cardiology, dentistry, dermatology, emergency and critical care, epidemiology, immunology, internal medicine, neurology, nutrition, oncology (cancer), ophthalmology, radiology, surgery, theriogenology (reproduction), or toxicology (poisonous substances). You can serve as a veterinarian for the military or work as a veterinary consultant for a pet-food company. You can open a general small-animal practice, study diseases at a university, or extract the secrets of the canine genome at the National Institutes of Health. Those are just a few of the options for veterinarians.

There are ways other than practicing medicine to ensure a dog's physical well-being. Dog groomers don't just make dogs look nice and smell good. They're keen observers of the canine condition. A groomer can be a dog's first line of defense, alerting owners to the presence of external parasites, ear infections, and skin problems. Groomers help dogs in poor condition regain their beauty and self-esteem (yes, dogs have it, too!).

Animal-control officers, shelter employees, and humane educators help dogs in need. Animal-control officers ensure that dogs are licensed, mediate barking-dog disputes, and investigate cruelty cases. Shelter employees evaluate dogs and interview potential adopters to help make the best match for all involved. Humane educators visit schools and teach students about kind and appropriate pet care. Other advocates for dogs include lawyers who focus on pet-related legal issues and employees at dog- or animal-related organizations. The latter includes dog registries such as the American Kennel Club and the United Kennel Club and pet-health institutions such as the Morris Animal Foundation, the Canine Eye Registration Foundation, and the Orthopedic Foundation for Animals.

The human health field also has a place for dog lovers. Animal-assisted therapy (AAT) involves more than just taking dogs to visit nursing homes and children's hospitals. Health and human services professionals with specialized training provide AAT to clients with the goal of improving their physical, social, and reasoning skills as well as their emotional well-being. Therapists who practice AAT may work with clients individually or in a group setting. Medical doctors work in tandem with veterinarians to find treatments and cures for diseases that affect both people and animals, and psychologists help people overcome their fear of dogs or work out pet-related relationship problems with the goal of creating a happier home for people and their pets.

Dogs assist people by tracking criminals; detecting bombs, drugs, and other contraband; searching for injured people after disasters; indicating the presence of termites; and much more. They don't work alone, however. They and their handlers form close-knit teams. Dog handlers may work for the military, the police, a federal or local disaster agency, or private businesses.

All dogs need training, and with some 74 million of them in the United States, there's plenty of work for people who understand how dogs think and how to motivate them. Dog trainers and behaviorists are employed in many different fields, from entertainment, where they train dogs for film and television work, to animal shelters, where they help homeless dogs acquire the skills they need to successfully adapt to a new family. Behaviorists and trainers teach obedience classes, train guide and assistance dogs, and help people solve their pets' behavior problems. They may work for an organization or set up their own businesses.

If you have an entrepreneurial mindset, you'll find the pet field rich in possibilities. You can open a pet boutique, become a pet detective, start a dog-walking business, or design pet products. Starting a business that caters to doting dog lovers can be a satisfying and lucrative way to include dogs in your work life.

The pet industry itself is a multibillion-dollar business. Pet-food, pet-pharmaceutical, pet-supply, and pet-insurance companies need product developers, account managers, salespeople, event planners, marketing professionals, public-relations people, and many other types of employees to run their businesses. These jobs may or may not bring you in contact with dogs on a daily basis, but they do allow you to become immersed in a specialized field in which you have a strong interest.

Creative types needn't feel left out. Writers, photographers, and artists can all find a niche involving dogs. Artists create portraits of dogs, immortalizing them on canvas. Dog photographers work not with supermodels such as Heidi Klum but with the beauties of the dog world. They take photos for dog magazines or calendars and every weekend can be found photographing the winners at dog shows. Writers and editors fill staff positions at companies that publish dog magazines and books or work as freelancers for print and digital media.

If your interests lie in the realm of science, there's a place for you as well. Genetics is big business these days, and that includes dog genetics. The unraveling of the canine genome is helping to unlock the secrets of dog diseases, history, and even behavior as well as to find links between human and canine illnesses. Have an interest in wild dogs? Consider a career in wildlife biology.

You may have thought that showing dogs in conformation—at dog shows ranging from those of the local kennel club to the prestigious Westminster Kennel Club show in New York City—was merely a hobby, but some people do make a living in show-related occupations. Professional handlers, judges, and show superintendents are all essential to the smooth running of a show. Although breeding dogs is more of a hobby than a profession, without breeders there would be no dog shows, no assistance dogs, no working dogs—no purebred dogs of any kind, for that matter. That would be a great loss, because when we look at purebred dogs or train them to carry out the tasks they were traditionally bred to complete, such as hunting or herding, we see history come to life and experience the bond that has linked people and dogs for more than 15,000 years.

The desire to work with dogs can take you in almost any direction. Let this book serve as your roadmap to the ideal dog-related career for you.

The Pet Industry and Dog-Related Careers

It's no secret that we love our pets. We pamper them with soft beds, interactive toys, and special diets. We take them on vacation with us or board them at kennels with spa facilities. We give them gifts at holidays such as Hanukkah; we hang stockings filled with organic treats for them at Christmas. We refer to our pets as our "kids." Even when the economy goes south, we readily spend money on caring for our companion animals. It's no wonder that a thriving pet industry has sprung up to cater to animals and their people. And that thriving industry offers plenty of employment opportunities.

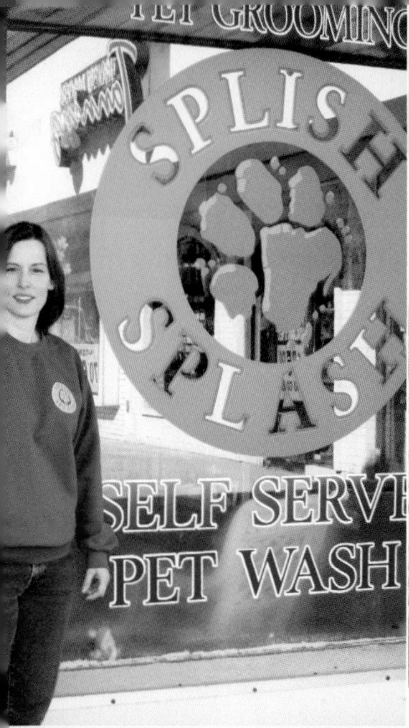
SPLISH SPLASH
SELF SERVE
PET WASH

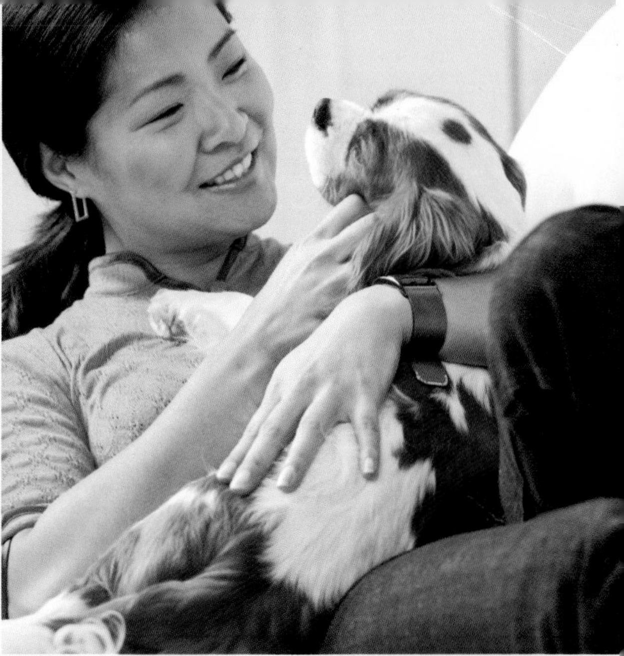

Oust

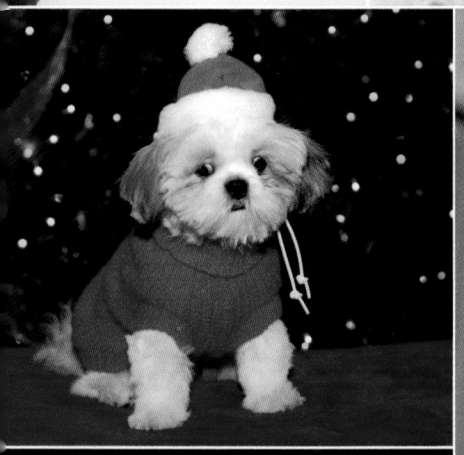

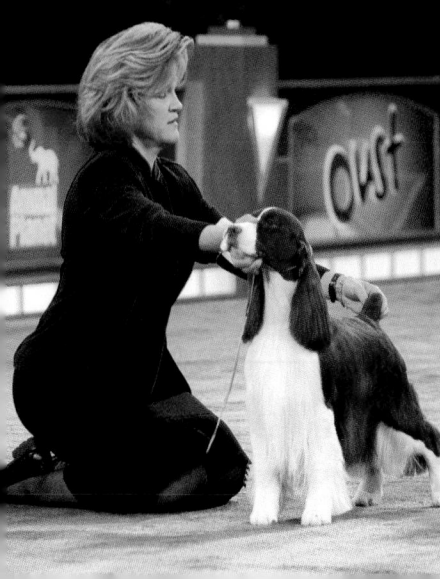

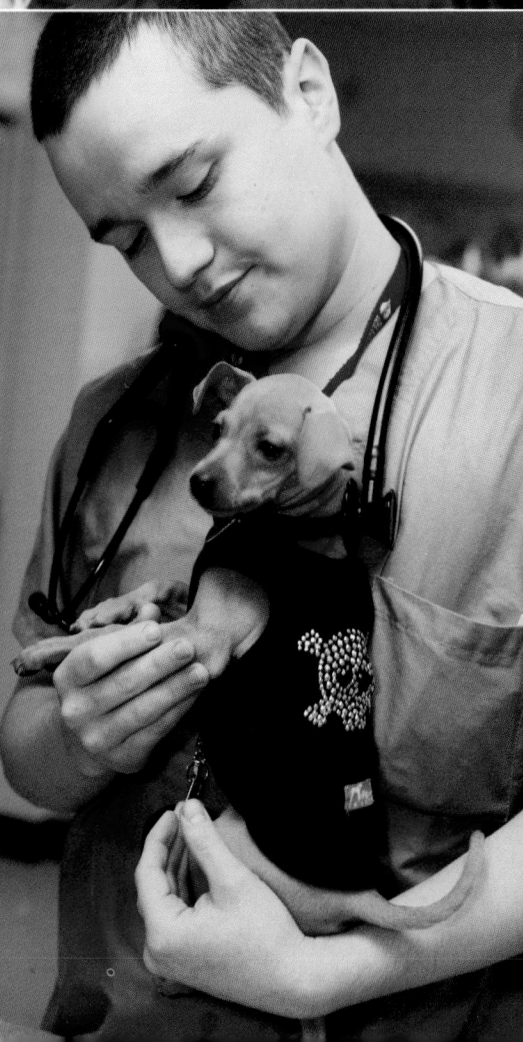

CHAPTER 1

The Pet Industry in America

The rise of the pet industry started in the 1960s, when dogs and cats began making their way into our hearts as more than mere animals on whom we spent only what we had to. Signs of this cultural change included the advent of mass-merchandised convenience foods and premium diets for animals, the introduction of more advanced training techniques, and the emergence of publications dedicated to pets and their care. Pet-related companies that got their start in the 1960s were at the forefront of what would become a multibillion-dollar industry.

Today, the pet industry encompasses food, veterinary care, supplies, nonprescription medications, and pet services such as grooming and boarding. Researchers estimate that pet owners spent $45.4 billion on their animals in 2009, up from $43.2 billion in 2008 and $17 billion in 1994. All this recent spending occurred during one of the biggest recessions this country has ever seen. According to the U.S. Census Bureau, the pet industry is now the seventh-largest retail segment in the country, ahead of the toy industry and the candy industry. Pet-supply sales are increasing—5 to 7 percent annually—while sales of baby supplies are decreasing.

What's Fueling the Growth?

What's fueling the explosion in the buying of pet services and products among consumers? Several factors, including the time constraints that

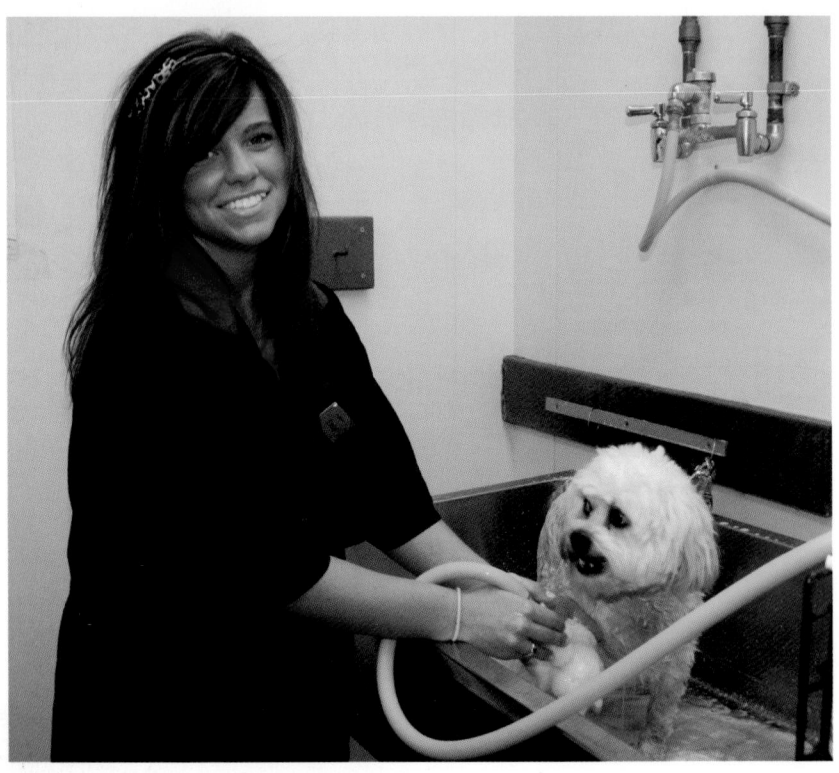

At the PetSmart grooming salon in Woodhaven, Michigan, Emily Meadows bathes a customer. Grooming and other pet services are in high demand among dog owners.

are experienced by two-income families, more disposable income among empty nesters and childless couples, and a desire for high-tech and high-end products and better animal health care.

Less Time, More Disposable Income

Baby boomers with empty nests and young married professionals with no kids and lots of disposable income drive the spending on pets. Dual-career couples have a two-pronged motivation for their pet-spending habits.

First, purchasing treats, toys, or other special items for their animals brings the owners pleasure. Second, many of them work long hours and are not able to spend as much time with their pets as they would like, so they pay other professionals—such as pet sitters and dog walkers—to ensure that their animals get the necessary exercise and companionship. Dog owners also spend their money on services such as grooming, boarding, massage, and yoga.

High-Tech Gadgets and High-End Products

Thanks to pet owners' interest in and concern for the well-being of their animals, products for companion animals now extend far beyond traditional necessities. Among the high-tech items for pets are computerized ID tags, GPS tracking devices for lost pets, and programmable feeding and drinking systems. High-end pet supplies include decorator daybeds and designer collars and clothing by such companies as Coach and Burberry. Companies known for catering to people—Paul Mitchell, Omaha Steaks, Origins, Harley-Davidson, and Old Navy, for instance—also offer lines of pet products that include shampoo, treats, clothing, and toys.

These brands don't slap their names on just anything. The Omaha Steaks Steak Treats for Dogs and Cats, which resemble the beef jerky the company produces for people, are made from the same premium Midwestern beef as the human version, minus the high levels of sodium and certain spices that might not agree with a dog's or cat's digestive system. The John Paul Pet company, which was created by the cofounder of the Paul Mitchell line of hair-care products, tests its shampoos and conditioners on people first to ensure that they won't irritate the sensitive skin of pets. Harley-Davidson's pet collection includes denim and leather jackets, riding goggles, bandanas, and spiked leather collars for dogs who ride shotgun in a sidecar or a motorcycle dog carrier.

A canine biker sports a Harley-Davison jacket and cap. People are clamoring for high-end brand-name pet apparel.

The most stylish pets—or at least the ones with the most stuff—have carryalls for their paraphernalia, which can include a blanket, a folding water dish, a water bottle, and poop-pickup bags. Coat wipes and air fresheners keep pets and cars (as well as homes) smelling clean. Some automobile manufacturers even design optional dog-safety features for their cars and SUVs. Car harnesses, seatbelts, and car seats for dogs have proliferated.

The Best Animal Health Care

Many dog owners want to ensure that their animals get the best health care available, from high-end diagnostics to pain relief to complementary therapies such as acupuncture and chiropractic. To help pay for it, they're turning to pet health insurance.

Online veterinary pharmacies meet pet owners' needs by providing home delivery of medications, usually at lower prices. With these trends in mind, more and more veterinary practices offer levels of care approaching that for people.

Pet-Friendly Environments

Businesses not traditionally pet-related are getting into the act, as well. Hotels across the country, including luxury resorts, not only have adopted pet-friendly policies but also are actively courting pet owners. They are offering special meals, dog walking, pet sitting, and spa services for the animals of guests. Similar trends in pet-friendly environments include restaurants with outdoor seating areas for people with pets, walk-up windows at Starbucks so dog lovers don't have to leave their pets outside when they order, and shopping centers that welcome animals, such as Stony Point Fashion Park in Richmond, Virginia, and Fashion Island in Newport Beach, California.

More Sources for Pets and Products

The growth in sales of specialty foods, toys, luxury items, and convenience accessories comes from passionate pet people who seek selection, style, and originality in the items they choose for their animals. They want products as good as those they'd purchase for themselves and ones that will match the style and décor of their homes, whether they live in a Colonial saltbox, a California bungalow, or a New York high-rise exuding global chic. No wonder pet products can be found not only in traditional pet-supply stores but also in discount, warehouse, home improvement, and lawn and garden stores as well as in freestanding independent pet boutiques that sell specialty items and treats.

The dot-com bust of the 1990s was a mere bump in the road for online pet suppliers. They include not only the major players, such as PETCO and PetSmart, but also small businesses that focus on one product or a collection of unique products. The Web sites of these suppliers have increasingly sophisticated design and usability.

Bill and Jack Kelly:
Brothers with a Passion for Nutrition

Two brothers and World War II army vets, Bill and Jack Kelly of Medina, Ohio, established Bil-Jac Foods in 1947. The first product the company introduced was Bil-Jac Frozen Dog Food, which boasted fresh meat sources and little processing. For more than sixty years, the company has remained family-owned and -operated, and the company's credo remains "making pet food is our only business, our life's work, and our passion." Bil-Jac has built its business on investing in putting more quality ingredients in the bag and fewer dollars into marketing. The company claims to have revolutionized the dog-food industry with its "exclusive nutrient protection technology," which involves how high-quality proteins are pasteurized and vacuum-dried to preserve the integrity of the amino acids needed for proper nutrition and digestion.

As pet adoptions have increased, so too have the avenues for acquiring a pet. Prospective pet owners are no longer limited to breeders or to animal shelters in their immediate areas. With the advent of pet-adoption Web sites and rescue Web sites for individual breed and all-breed rescue groups, as well as informative Web sites created by breed clubs, people have more alternatives and opportunities for acquiring a dog.

It's much easier now to find a good breeder through a breed-club Web site or to find exactly the type of dog you'd like to adopt because of the greater access provided by the Internet to many different shelters and rescue groups.

What does all of this mean? It means that pets are more than companions; they're big business. Target, Wal-Mart, Costco, and IKEA are among the big-box retailers catering to pet owners by expanding their selections of pet products and offering products stamped with their own labels. Colgate-Palmolive and Nestlé entered the field by purchasing pet-food manufacturers Hill's and Ralston-Purina, respectively. Industry analysts expect the amount of money spent on pets to increase.

Saturation will happen at some point in time, but experts believe that the pet industry is still at the low end of the growth curve. This means that opportunities abound for people who are interested in careers in this wide-open field.

CHAPTER 2

Forecast for Animal-Related Jobs

G iven the prediction of continued growth in the pet industry, employment opportunities appear bright. The service industry as a whole is growing rapidly in the United States; pet services can fill a niche in many well-to-do communities as well as in middle-class areas. The growth in unique pet products is also a sign of future job opportunities in areas such as sales and promotion.

Want an edgy and challenging job? Seek out positions in law enforcement or the military. If you're interested in veterinary medicine or scientific research, you can find plenty of opportunity.

Individuals with an artistic flair can put their talents to good use as photographers, artists, and writers. Dog shows also provide interesting career opportunities. Other fields that offer the potential for animal-related job opportunities include the law, public relations and communications, and sales.

It's clear that dogs are our best friends in more ways than one. We can do more than share our home life with them. We can work for them and with them in many different ways to help improve their lives as well as the lives of others.

Pet Services

Dog lovers with an entrepreneurial bent face a bright future, especially those with an interest in starting pet-related businesses such as dog walking,

Doctor of physical therapy and certified canine rehab practitioner Amy Kramer works with a patient at California Animal Rehabilitation, the care business she founded in Santa Monica with veterinarian Jessica H. Waldman. They have been nonstop busy since opening in 2007.

sitting, grooming, and training. Service industries are expected to account for approximately 18.7 million of the 18.9 million new wage and salary jobs generated through 2014. The American Pet Products Association (APPA) estimates that owners spent $3.4 billion on pet services in 2009, up from $2.4 billion in 2005. Two-income families, in particular, have the money but not the time to spend on their dogs. The state of the economy is also important, as pet owners tend to spend even more on animal services when the economy is strong.

If you want to help animals, consider shelter work. The job outlook for animal-care workers, such as kennel attendants and shelter workers, is promising. While it's not good news for animals, the U.S. Bureau of Labor Statistics (BLS) predicts that jobs in animal shelters will be plentiful. Although this type of work is rewarding in some ways, it can also be demanding and stressful. Shelter workers may deal with people who are sad about giving up their pets as well as those who callously abandon their animals when they are tired of them. Shelter workers also see pets who have been mistreated, are sick, or are difficult to work with because they are untrained. Because of the various stresses of the job, many shelter employees switch careers eventually, thereby creating opportunities for other people who wish to enter the field.

The *Occupational Outlook Handbook* published by the Bureau of Labor Statistics predicts that employment of animal-care and service workers such as kennel attendants, groomers, pet sitters, animal-control and shelter employees, and trainers will grow by 18 to 26 percent through 2018. Advantages of these jobs include not only direct involvement with dogs but also generally flexible work schedules. In addition, such jobs usually don't require a college degree. The work can be backbreaking, however, especially for groomers and kennel attendants, and anyone working in this field risks being bitten by the animals they work with.

Trainers with good communication and self-promotion skills can find work teaching assistance or service dogs, training dogs for the entertainment industry, or as a broadcast personality, such as Victoria Stilwell of the Animal Planet television show *It's Me or the Dog*.

Pet Products and Public Relations

The APPA estimates that American pet owners spent $10.2 billion on pet supplies in 2009, an increase of $200 million from 2008. One of the trends in this area is automated products such as self-cleaning litter boxes and programmable food and water dishes. Dog lovers with engineering or design skills may well find a place in the pet-product industry.

Careers in various facets of the pet industry include retail sales and management, promotions, public relations management, and event planning. There's always a place for a good salesperson, especially one who has in-depth knowledge about the products. If you love dogs and are knowledgeable about their care, you'll be better able to help customers choose the products that meet their needs. Retail sales positions are expected to grow by approximately 8 percent through 2018, reflecting the increase in consumer spending by a growing population.

Other pet-industry sales jobs include being a sales representative for a pet-food manufacturer, veterinary pharmaceutical company, or pet-product manufacturer or wholesaler. These jobs are also expected to grow between 7 and 13 percent through 2018. With pet owners spending $26 billion per year on food and supplies, this area holds many opportunities.

Promotions managers or specialists direct programs that combine advertising with purchase incentives to increase sales. They seek to reach

Sarah Carey, who manages public relations efforts for the University of Florida College of Veterinary Medicine and the UF Veterinary Hospitals, spends a day on the beach with Katie.

dealers, distributors, and consumers through direct mail, telemarketing, television or radio advertising, catalogs, exhibits, inserts in newspapers, Internet advertisements or Web sites, in-store displays, product endorsements, and special events. Purchasing incentives may include discounts, samples, gifts, rebates, coupons, sweepstakes, and contests. Promotions managers may publish newsletters that provide information of interest to their target audiences. Related jobs include account manager, public relations specialist, advertising manager, and marketing manager.

Creative Arts

The creative arts—photography, painting, writing, and editing—offer a wide scope of opportunities for dog lovers. If you have a creative skill and would like to use it in a career with dogs, consider a career as a dog-show photographer, a pet portrait photographer or painter, a dog magazine editor, or a freelance writer.

In the fields of writing, editing, photography, and art, employment is expected to grow about as fast as the average for all occupations through

2018. The increasing specialization of magazines, as well as the growth of online publications and business Web sites and newsletters, means that writers, editors, and photographers have many more outlets for their work. Unfortunately, the increase in digital media is affecting the amount of money these professionals can make—and not in a good way. Print media salaries are decreasing because of the upsurge in digital media, and the new jobs in digital publications pay less than those in print media. In addition, although creative fields offer many opportunities, they're also highly competitive.

Craft artists and fine artists work primarily on commission and may require some other source of income to pay their bills, at least until their talents are recognized and they develop a regular clientele. Art directors may find employment not only at pet magazines but also at pet-related companies, in advertising or public relations.

Many people want to work in fashion design, and some want to specialize in creating clothing and accessories that either feature dogs or are for dogs. The best opportunities for these people may be as entrepreneurs, selling their creations to apparel and pet-product wholesale firms. Haute couture for pets is popular and gets lots of press when worn by the dogs of celebrities, but stylish and affordable designs that appeal to middle-income consumers will be most in demand.

If you've ever been to a dog show, especially a prestigious one such as the Westminster Kennel Club show, you've seen the trove of jewelry sold by vendors there: gold, silver, and bejeweled necklaces, rings, bracelets, earrings, and cufflinks—all in the forms of different dog breeds. People who love their purebred dogs also love to wear jewelry fashioned in the breed's image. A jeweler who can create such designs will have a ready-made clientele. Jewelers who specialize in this type of work are usually

Barkworthy INSIGHT

EVENT PLANNING

Event planners or public relations managers may be involved in special events, such as the sponsorship of dog shows, parties to introduce new products, or other pet-related promotions. Tie-ins with special events help pet-industry companies gain public attention without advertising directly. Competition is keen for these jobs, but employment in the fields of advertising, marketing, promotion, public relations, and sales management is expected to increase by 16 percent through 2018.

entrepreneurs who sell their wares at dog shows or through catalogs or on Web sites.

Jewelry for dogs themselves, primarily charms that can be worn on collars, is becoming popular as well, creating another market for designers in this field. Thanks to the rise in nontraditional jewelry marketers—discount stores, mail-order and catalog companies, television shopping networks, and Internet retailers—as well as increasing numbers of affluent people (including working women who like to buy their own baubles and people age forty-five and older), jewelry sales are expected to remain strong in the recovering economy.

Dog Shows

Unsurprisingly, some of the most hands-on careers involving dogs are those in the dog-show world. You thought showing dogs was just a hobby? Think again. Professional handlers are paid to take dogs into the show ring to earn their conformation championships or to achieve a certain standing within their breed or Group, such as number-one English Springer Spaniel or number-one Sporting Dog. And someone has to judge those dogs. Dog-show judges travel all over the world to evaluate show dogs, determining which ones will become champions and, more than likely, pass on their genes to the next generation of dogs. Who runs those dog shows? The show superintendent is the one who handles entries, determines when and where a show will take place, prints judging programs and catalogs, and much more. The Bureau of Labor Statistics doesn't track these specialized dog-show jobs, but with the thousands of dog shows that take place each year—the largest U.S. ones drawing more than 3,500 entries—there's definitely room for growth in this field.

Law Enforcement

Want to combine your interest in law enforcement with your love of dogs? Consider becoming a police- or military-dog handler, U.S. customs inspector, or arson-dog handler. Police dogs and their handlers track missing people, help control crowds, search for explosives or illegal drugs, chase criminals, and guard prisoners. In the military, dogs and their handlers are responsible for guarding bases and aircraft hangars, locating land mines and other explosives, and searching for casualties. Customs dogs and their handlers work at seaports and airports to seek out contraband such as drugs and food products being brought into the country illegally. Arson-dog handlers determine whether fires were set deliberately. Dog handlers may also patrol and guard property or provide security at events.

A U.S. Customs and Border Protection officer at the Canine Enforcement Training Center teaches a detector dog to search a car trunk.

Although these jobs can be dangerous, they're also challenging and exciting, which can make them attractive. They may or may not require a college degree, but all require at least a high-school diploma. Competition for dog-handling jobs may be high, but the growth of employment for police in general is expected to grow as fast as the average, approximately 10 percent, through 2018. Layoffs are rare in this industry, and trained law-enforcement officers are always in demand, especially if they have a skill such as dog handling. Opportunities are best in local police departments rather than in state police or federal law-enforcement agencies. Applicants with a college education in law enforcement will be most desirable.

Veterinary Medicine and Science

According to the APPA, pet owners spent an estimated $12.2 billion on veterinary care in 2009. The BLS expects employment for veterinarians to increase 33 percent through 2018. Do you have a more analytical mind and an interest in research? Scientists have decoded the canine genome, but there's still much to learn from it about what makes dogs tick. Studying the genetic underpinnings of the canine species is only one of the opportunities available to someone with an interest in biology.

Veterinary Care

The median annual earnings of veterinarians in 2008 were $79,050. Veterinarians who practice in East or West Coast cities or who specialize in a particular field will probably earn the most, but they are also more likely to have higher overhead costs and higher living expenses. Becoming a veterinarian also requires an investment of time and education. Veterinarians must complete four years of college plus several more years of veterinary school.

If you are not sure that you are cut out to be a veterinarian, but you are still interested in the field of pet health, you may want to train as a veterinary technician or a veterinary technologist. Employment in this field is expected to grow by 36 percent—that is a much faster rate than average for all occupations—through the year 2018. Specializing in advanced veterinary services, such as dental care and surgery, can create additional opportunities.

Besides working in a veterinary practice, veterinary technicians and technologists can seek jobs at biomedical facilities, diagnostic laboratories, wildlife facilities, humane societies, animal-control facilities, boarding kennels, drug- or food-manufacturing companies, and food-safety inspection facilities.

Charles Cruft: The P.T. Barnum of Dog Shows

A young Charles Cruft began his association with canines as an employee of Spratt's dog food company. It was as a Spratt's representative that Cruft visited Paris to assist with a dog show at the World Exhibition in 1879. From this experience, Cruft decided to start his own dog shows in London and soon became the Barnum of the European dog-show world. Naming the show after himself, the publicity-hungry entrepreneur hailed Cruft's Dog Show "the greatest show on earth" and attracted thousands of entries, including the Collies and Pomeranians of the reigning monarch Queen Victoria. Crufts quickly became the most prestigious show in the United Kingdom—and perhaps the world. After Cruft's death in 1938, the show was sold to the English Kennel Club, which continues to produce the show each winter, still attracting thousands of purebred dogs from around the world.

Scientific Research

Biologists with an interest in dogs and wildlife might study the origin, behavior, diseases, and life processes of wild canids, such as wolves in Yellowstone National Park or endangered African wild dogs. The findings of these professionals help us understand more about our own domestic dogs. Ecologists study the relationships among organisms and between organisms and their environments. In wild dogs, that might involve observing the effects of such factors as population size, the abundance or absence of prey, or the encroachment of humans into the dogs' territory.

Other biologists work in research and development of new veterinary drugs, treatments, and diagnostic tests. Research using techniques such as recombining DNA has led to the production of new and safer vaccines for dogs. Biotechnology researchers isolate genes and determine their function. This work leads to the discovery of genes associated with specific diseases and inherited traits, such as certain types of cancer. Biological research can have commercial applications in the pet-food industry, as well. A career in biology may lead to managerial or administrative positions, such as planning and overseeing programs for testing pet foods and drugs or directing activities at municipal zoos.

National Park Service wildlife biologist Doug Smith carries a tranquilized wolf in Yellowstone National Park.

CHAPTER 3

Your Career Path and Education

Know thyself. This admonition from the ancient Greeks may be the best career advice ever given. Being aware of and honest about your interests and abilities is the first step in finding the career that's right for you, whether you are a high-school or college student or someone seeking a career in a new field.

One of the advantages of working with dogs is the variety of backgrounds that can lead to a rewarding position. Depending on your career interest, the educational requirements for working with dogs range from a high-school diploma (sometimes not even that) to years of graduate study. Take into account your learning style and level of interest in higher education when deciding which job will be right for you.

Discovering Your Path

In deciding on a career path, consider your skills and your personality. People have different types of skills, some that are natural and some that they acquire through school, work, and life experiences. Skills you may learn in school include meeting deadlines, working under pressure, problem solving, presenting ideas verbally or in writing, speaking a foreign language, and working as a member of a team. Skills learned on the job may include human-resource management, project administration, and research or design techniques. The abilities to relate to people and to

Questions to Ask

To find the career that will match your talents and bring you the most satisfaction, begin by asking yourself the following questions:

Personality Traits

- How do I enjoy spending my days?
- What do I like thinking, learning, and talking about?
- Do I enjoy talking to people or am I the quiet type?
- Do I like asking people questions?
- What kind of people do I enjoy being around?
- Do I like being the center of attention, or do I prefer the background?
- Would I rather live in the city or in the country?
- Do I like to travel, or am I a homebody?
- What are my favorite volunteer activities, hobbies, or sports?

Skills

- Am I analytical or creative?
- Do I have artistic abilities in writing, photography, or art?
- Do I excel in science and mathematics classes?
- Am I good at selling things or persuading people to my way of thinking?

Work Environment

- Would I rather work for a big corporation, a small company, or myself?
- Do I prefer to be part of a team or to work on my own?
- Do I like being busy all the time, or do I need plenty of time to spend with friends and family to be at my best?
- How much money would I like to make?

Animal Specifics

- What animal-related activities do I enjoy?
- Am I good at teaching my pet tricks or behaviors?
- Do I enjoy spending time making sure my pet is clean and beautiful?

Kris Parlett, Procter & Gamble Pet Care External Relations team member, poses with actress Betty White during a media junket to support the Morris Animal Foundation.

pay attention to detail often come through day-to-day living but may be learned in school or the workplace.

Personal traits such as patience, reliability, risk taking, resourcefulness, and innovation can also affect your choice of careers. Sometimes these are learned through life experiences, but often they are innate. For instance, patience often develops naturally with experience, but it can be difficult for a timid or withdrawn person to become a gregarious risk taker. It can happen, but it requires a lot of desire, willpower, and practice. People willing to make that effort can be successful at risk taking, but they often need a lot of down time to recharge their energy. To discover your skills and traits, answer the questions in the box "Questions to Ask" (*opposite*).

Matching Skills and Traits with Careers

Studying the answers to the questions in "Questions to Ask" and making a list of your traits and skills, as well as your preferences in work environment and pet activities, can help you clarify your interests. You will start to see a pattern emerge, indicating whether you prefer to work with people or with information, whether you'd like a demanding career with lots of travel or a quiet one in which you work alone or with only one or two other people, and whether a high salary or job satisfaction is more important to your happiness and well-being.

Recognizing and accepting these factors is essential to choosing the right career. For instance, if you have a scientific mind and like the idea of becoming a veterinarian, but the thought of talking to dozens of dog owners every day makes you shudder, you might instead consider a career in veterinary research, studying the causes of canine diseases or contributing to the development of a new vaccine or drug. Or suppose you enjoy meeting people and traveling and you have a persuasive personality, but hitting the books for seven or more years isn't your idea of a good time. Rather than becoming a veterinarian, you may want to consider a career in sales, marketing, or public relations for a pet-food manufacturer, pharmaceutical firm, or pet-product company in a position that would allow you to attend dog shows, veterinary conferences, and other animal-related events.

Are you on the planning committee for your high-school prom or your city's annual Fourth of July parade? You probably have good organizational and communication skills, which can lead you to careers as disparate as event manager for a pet-food company or director of an animal-welfare foundation.

These are just a few examples of how you can evaluate your skills and personality to plan your future. You'll also want to consider various facets of job satisfaction. Study the following list of factors and number them in order of importance from 1 to 12, with 1 being the most important. The answers will help you refine your choices.

- Contributing to society
- Financial rewards
- Helping others
- Intellectual challenge
- Interacting with the public
- Job security
- Potential for advancement
- Professional status
- Recognition
- Supervising or managing others
- Working as part of a team
- Working independently

Exploring More Sources

Once you have an idea of the type of career you want to pursue, you need to gather as much information about it as you can. In addition to reading the chapters on specific careers in this book, you should look for information in various other books and periodicals and on Web sites. Then arrange to talk with a professional in the field.

Books, Periodicals, and Web Sites

Books that can help you explore and define yourself include the latest editions of *Do What You Are: Discover the Perfect Career for You Through the Secrets of Personality Type*, by Paul D. Tieger and Barbara Barron-Tieger (Little Brown) and *What Color Is Your Parachute? A Practical Manual for Job Hunters and Career Changers*, by Richard Bolles (Ten Speed Press). *Do What You Are*, whose authors have decades of experience training career counselors, outplacement consultants, and human-resource specialists, is a guide to

Libraries such as this one are great sources for information on occupations, on technical schools and colleges, on careers opportunities, and on other aspects of job hunting.

Financial Considerations

You may or may not make a lot of money in your chosen career. Sometimes, working in a field you love re-  quires financial sacrifices. This is not always the case, but it's definitely something you should be prepared for. Lots of people have an interest in working with animals, which means that employers often have their pick of the best people and can set their own terms. You have to consider whether working with animals or in a pet-related field balances out the possibility that you won't be rolling in dog biscuits. That's especially important if you're thinking about making a career change.

Answering the following questions will help you decide if a career is right for you financially and whether it is feasible for you to make a career change:

○ What income level can I reasonably expect from this career?

○ What benefits (health insurance, paid vacation, sick leave, retirement plan) can I expect from this career?

○ If benefits are not included, can I afford to pay for them myself or do I have another source of coverage?

○ Would I rather work directly with dogs or would I be satisfied with a higher-paying position in a pet-related industry?

○ How much money do I need for personal expenses (housing, food, medical costs, utilities, transportation, child or pet care)?

○ If I am starting a business, how much will I need for start-up costs?

○ Is my credit good enough to get a loan for educational or start-up expenses?

○ Am I organized and disciplined enough to pay quarterly estimated taxes and keep track of my expenses? If not, can I afford to pay a bookkeeper to do those things for me?

MIND YOUR MANNERS
Remember what you learned in kindergarten: Always say please and thank you. If someone spends a great deal of time with you for an informational interview or gives you a great lead or piece of advice, write a thank-you note. Not only is it the polite thing to do, but it's also a way for you to stand out.

personality type and can help you determine how you process information, make decisions, and interact with people. It links personality types with occupations and uses case studies to help readers tailor their job searches to their strengths or get the most out of a chosen career.

Once you have a handle on your personality type, *What Color Is Your Parachute?* described by *Fortune* magazine as "the gold standard of career guides," offers practical job-hunting advice not only for people new to the workforce but also for career changers, victims of layoffs, and people reentering the job market after taking time off to care for dependents or to go back to school. Neither book is pet oriented, but together they provide a foundation for finding the right job in any field.

Exploring your career options is the next step. To supplement the career information in this book, check your library or a bookstore for books about your chosen career. Look beyond the typical career guide. For instance, aspiring veterinarians may enjoy reading Nick Trout's *Tell Me Where It Hurts: A Day of Humor, Healing, and Hope in My Life as an Animal Surgeon* (Broadway, 2008). Want to be a wildlife biologist who studies wild canids? Look for *Swift and Enduring* (E.P. Dutton, 1981), by George and Lory Frame, about their time in Africa spent tracking the endangered painted dogs. Read books by trainers and behaviorists, people who show dogs, and animal-welfare advocates. Their experiences can give you an idea of the highlights as well as the problems these types of work.

For more information about the training and education needed for a specific career, earning prospects, job outlook, working conditions, and job-search tips, consult the *Occupational Outlook Handbook*, published by the U.S. Bureau of Labor and Statistics. You can find it in your library in the reference section or online at www.bls.gov/OCO. It provides an excellent overview of most careers, from animal-control officer to veterinarian, as well as seven- to ten-year job projections in each field.

Don't forget to check consumer magazines and trade journals, such as *Dog World* magazine, *Pet Product News International*, and the *Journal of the*

American Veterinary Medical Association. You can subscribe to them or find them at newsstands as well as at libraries. If your library doesn't carry a publication, talk to the librarian about obtaining a copy.

The Internet is another great source of both objective and subjective information. Lots of trainers, veterinarians, and other pet professionals have blogs, for instance. Reading them can give you a window into their work life and the issues they face in their fields.

Information Interviews

Reading books and magazines and surfing the Web are useful for acquiring background information, but there's nothing like talking to people who work in a field. This is the best way to learn how to become established in a given career and what's actually involved in a job on a day-to-day basis, and it will help you develop and refine your career goals.

Set up what's known as an "information interview" with people in your desired field. It will probably be easy to find people who work in your hometown or nearby as animal-control officers, dog trainers, groomers, or veterinarians. Look in the phone book or talk to the people who care for your pets. Professional organizations, such as the National Dog Groomers Association, the American Pet Products Association, the Pet Care Services Association, and the Public Relations Society of America, can also help you find people in pet-related jobs. The *Occupational Outlook Handbook* lists organizations as resources for different careers, so look for leads there.

Once you've identified someone in the field, call to make an appointment to speak to that person by phone or at his or her place of business. Explain that you are not seeking a job interview but would like to learn more about the field as a possible career. Some busy people may prefer to answer your questions by e-mail, so be sure to give them that option.

For a phone call or personal meeting, write your questions down in advance, be on time, and take good notes. Don't forget to send a thank-you note afterward. Such a gesture of courtesy can pay off when you need a reference for a college or graduate-school application or for an apprenticeship. Even if you just speak casually to your veterinarian, groomer, or another pet professional about his or her job, be sure to thank that person.

Try to talk to more than one person in a given field. For instance, if you want to be a dog groomer, speak to one who owns his or her own business, one who works for a veterinarian or a pet-supply store, and one who runs a mobile grooming van or do-it-yourself dog wash. If you are interviewing veterinarians, talk to a general-practice one and an emergency-room one as well as a couple with specialty practices in fields such as cardiology or dentistry. If you're interested in a career in pet products, interview the owner of a pet boutique and the manager of a pet-supply superstore.

If you're not sure where your interests lie, do as many different information interviews as you can. Think, too, about where you'd like to live, the lifestyle you want, what salary you need, and what type of organization you'd like to work for. These factors affect such decisions as where you choose to go to school or apply for a job. As you review interview notes and compare them with notes about career desires and skills, knowledge, and needs, you'll start to develop a picture of what career to pursue.

Pursuing Education and Acquiring Experience

If you're not academically inclined, you may prefer to get your training on the job, apprenticing with a professional. If you do want formal education in a particular field, research as many different educational programs as possible to make sure you choose the best for your purposes. Professional organizations often have their own requirements for members, including certification and licensing.

In addition to on-the-job training or formal education, make the effort to learn on your own. Spend as much time as possible watching dogs, studying their behavior, reading about them, and viewing them in works of art. Your self-study, along with your education in the fundamentals of your career, will help train your eye and give you a firm foundation as you pursue your chosen field.

Learning about dogs starts with observing and interacting with your own pet.

On-the-Job Training

Not every dog-related career requires formal education. Often, the best way to gain experience is to learn on the job. Groomers, dog trainers, and professional handlers have a long history of serving in apprenticeships to people established in their field to learn the trade.

Working in retail isn't exactly an apprenticeship, but it is the type of job that's frequently open to people with little or no experience in pet-supply sales. A friendly, helpful attitude toward customers and a strong work ethic will go a long way in the pet-supply business, and it doesn't hurt to be knowledgeable about the products the store carries.

Careers in the arts also allow you to get your education on the job. Many artists and photographers never take a course; they learn by doing.

Are you planning to work in the field of human welfare but want to incorporate dogs into your job? Police- and military-dog handlers often learn the dog-handling aspect on the job, but prior experience through personal ownership, volunteer work for a search-and-rescue organization, or formal study at a dog-training school can help as well.

Lead cashier and accredited pet trainer Kayla Barett stocks the shelves at PetSmart in Woodhaven, Michigan. Working at a pet-supply store can be a good way to learn more about dogs and pet products.

Formal Education

Groomers and trainers may also attend schools that specialize in educating future canine hairstylists and dog whisperers. People who plan to be trainers, whether they apprentice or attend a dog-training school, can benefit from college courses in animal behavior and human psychology. Because trainers teach the owner to teach the dog, it can be immensely helpful to understand the psychology of learning and learn what

Profiles of Bachelor's Degree Programs

Students at Pennsylvania's Bucknell University can earn a bachelor of arts or bachelor of science degree in animal behavior. The interdisciplinary major combines the study of biology and psychology. Coursework includes chemistry, math, physics, biology, and psychology, plus electives in the humanities, social sciences, languages, and cultures. Classes cover animal behavior, behavioral ecology, and organic evolution, to name just a few. Students have the opportunity to perform research with faculty and study abroad in environments as diverse as Asia, Africa, and Australia.

Canisius College, located in Buffalo, New York, says it offers more undergraduate courses in animal behavior than does any other four-year college or university. Students have access to internships at the Buffalo Zoo and the Aquarium of Niagara, as well as at other, more distant animal facilities such as Chicago's Brookfield Zoo and the Dolphin Research Center in Florida. Its minor in animal behavior has six required courses: comparative animal behavior is required for everyone, and students choose the other five classes from a range that includes social organization of mammals; sex, evolution, and behavior; animal learning; behavioral neuroscience; reproductive biopsychology; and vertebrate zoology.

At Purdue University (*above*) in Indiana, through its Center for the Human-Animal Bond, undergraduates with any major can study the issues surrounding the role of animals in society and earn a certificate in animal welfare and societal concerns. The interdisciplinary undergraduate program, which requires sixteen to eighteen credit hours, is designed to educate students about the sociology, ethics, biology, behavior, and economics of animal care and use; provide a scientific and philosophical basis of animal care and use; teach students how to resolve conflicts concerning the humane use of animals; develop leaders in animal policy development; and inspire research to improve human and animal well-being. Required courses include biology, animal welfare and human interaction, companion-animal management, evolution of behavior, applied small-animal behavior, and ethics and animals as well as a research project related to human-animal interactions.

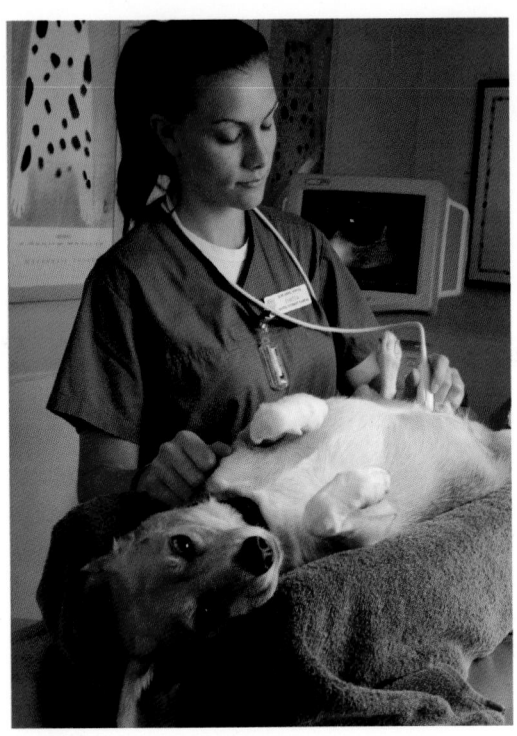

Veterinarian technician Christa Carlson examines a dog at Blum Animal Hospital in Chicago, Illinois.

techniques motivate people to follow advice. Trainers who want to work in the entertainment industry need to understand something about filmmaking and self-promotion.

In addition to on-the-job training, those interested in a sales career in pet products can turn to formal education. Junior college or college courses in accounting, business, and other relevant topics can lead to a store management position.

Most writing and editing jobs require a college degree in English, journalism, or some other liberal arts field, such as anthropology or history. Anthropology is a good foundation for studying and understanding the culture of dog ownership, which is a large part of writing for or editing a publication about dogs. Knowledge of history benefits all journalists and editors, because it allows them to place events they cover in context. And, of course, the study of English and journalism is the basis for learning how to write in a correct, clear, and entertaining manner—one that will hold readers' interest as well as inform them.

Sometimes formal education and on-the-job training go hand in hand. For instance, even though police work doesn't necessarily require formal education beyond the police academy, candidates with the best prospects are those who have studied criminal justice, psychology, or another related field in college. And people who want to be search-and-rescue handlers should have superb outdoor survival and navigation skills, usually acquired through personal experience.

Dog-related careers in the sciences require a different kind of hard work. Veterinarians and biologists must earn a four-year college degree,

Profiles of Master's Degree Programs

The Tufts University Center for Animals and Public Policy, established in 1983, offers a master of science in animals and public policy. According to the center, this program "explores historical, philosophical, scientific, cultural, legal and political underpinnings of contemporary human-animal relationships." The curriculum includes animals in society, human-animal studies, and public policy. With this degree, graduates may continue study in such fields as veterinary medicine or law or find work at nonprofit organizations, with corporations, or at government

agencies. Some graduates of the program become editors, writers, journalists, shelter administrators, or humane educators.

The University of Illinois (*above*) offers a master of science degree in biology with a specialization in applied animal behavior. The American Society for the Prevention of Cruelty to Animals (ASPCA) provides adjunct support. The in-residence, two-year interdisciplinary program is designed to provide graduate training for careers in such fields as applied animal behavior, companion-animal-behavior consulting, and training and behavior for shelter animals. Each student must complete a research project. Students applying to the program should be able to show evidence of animal-related experience, such as volunteering at an animal shelter, training animals, or exhibiting dogs or cats.

followed by three or more years of graduate study. Besides an understanding of anatomy and physiology, veterinarians need the fine motor skills to perform delicate surgery as well as the strength to perform difficult orthopedic surgeries on large dogs. Veterinarians who wish to specialize face additional years of study and testing before they can become accredited.

Amie Lamoreaux Hesbach, relaxing here with her dogs, worked as a licensed physical therapist before becoming a certified canine rehabilitation practitioner.

While veterinary technicians and technologists don't have the same lengthy course of study as veterinarians do, they must be graduates of two- or four-year programs in their fields. Because of advances in veterinary care that require prior training, strictly on-the-job training is a rarity.

Pet rehabilitation is another area that calls for extensive education. Pet rehab practitioners may start out by studying human physical therapy, which requires a bachelor's degree and a master's degree. Although any undergraduate major is acceptable, students in the initial stages of undergraduate preparation should consider a major in kinesiology or the biological sciences, which tend to be the most direct routes to a physical-therapy program. This path requires additional study to learn animal anatomy so that the rehabilitator can appropriately apply physical-therapy techniques. Other pet rehab practitioners are veterinarians who have gone on to study physical-therapy techniques so they can use them in their practices.

Professional Requirements and Licensing

Regardless of their paths of learning, people in the fields of grooming, training, and handling can improve their skills and build their businesses by meeting the requirements for membership in a professional organization, such as the National Dog Groomers Association, the Association of Pet Dog Trainers, or the Professional Handlers Association. Licensing is another factor to consider. Trainers and professional handlers can simply hang out a shingle and they're in business. Groomers, however, may be required to be licensed in the states where they work. They may also face restrictions on the services they're allowed to perform—such as cleaning teeth—unless they're working under the supervision of a veterinarian. Be aware of licensing and other professional requirements before you decide on your career path.

Experience Versus Education

Don't be discouraged if years of difficult study don't sound appealing. Not everyone is suited to that, and not every pet-related career requires a college degree. Sometimes experience does trump book learning. The success of dog trainer Cesar Millan is an example of what can happen if you have a knack for dealing with animals. You may find that apprenticing with a well-known trainer, groomer, or handler is considered just as valuable as a college degree, if not more so.

That said, it never hurts to have an education to fall back on, especially in a slow economy or in the event of an accident or illness that prevents you from continuing your chosen career. And in some instances, a college degree can give you an edge over people who have experience only. It can also help you develop better speaking and writing skills, which can be essential in communicating with clients and employees. It can give you a more in-depth background in your field as well. A dog trainer who has studied behavioral psychology is likely to have a better or more well-rounded understanding of why dogs behave in certain ways and how to motivate them.

Even better than a person who has either experience or formal education is one who has both. That's a combination that is hard to beat.

EDUCATION RESOURCES

- Blue Ridge Community College, Veterinary Technology, http://community.brcc.edu/vettech
- Bucknell University, Animal Behavior Program, www.bucknell.edu/AnimalBehavior.xml
- Canisius College, Animal Behavior, www.canisius.edu/biopsych/anbehav
- Purdue University, Center for the Human-Animal Bond, www.vet.purdue.edu/chab/edu.htm
- Tufts University, Center for Animals and Public Policy, www.tufts.edu/vet/capp
- University of Illinois at Urbana-Champaign, School of Integrative Biology, http://sib.illinois.edu
- University of New Hampshire, Thompson School of Applied Science, tsas.admit@unh.edu

CHAPTER 4

Getting the Job

Y ou've decided where your heart lies in the world of working with and for dogs. You've achieved the necessary education, and you're ready to go to work. Now you just need to find the perfect job for you. Bear in mind that in any job search, the two most important things you can do are individualize your communications, so you stand out from the pack, and build relationships with everyone you meet.

Your Job Search

Looking for a job has come a long way from running your finger down a newspaper column of classified ads, hoping that the right job will be there, waiting for you. Students have resources, such as internships and career placement offices; most major companies post job openings on their Web sites; professional associations and alumni groups are often sources of career opportunities; and of course, there's the Internet, with job-hunting sites such as Monster and professional networking sites such as LinkedIn. There are animal-specific job-hunting Web sites as well, such as AnimalJobHunter.com.

However you go about applying for jobs, do so in a way that sets you apart. Do not take that to mean that you should print your résumé on goldenrod paper or write follow-up letters on stationery with hippos dancing across the top. Those are the quickest ways to have your résumé

You can use the Internet to find information on companies and organizations in your field of interest and check out their job postings.

or cover letter thrown in the trash. You also want to avoid sending the same generic cover letter to every potential employer. Instead, tailor your introductory note to the specific job for which you're applying.

Let everyone who might help in your search know you're job hunting. You never know when someone will be able to give you a lead to that perfect position. In times of high unemployment, companies are overwhelmed with applicants. Instead of searching through hundreds or thousands of résumés, employers are more likely to rely on word of mouth and referrals. There's no reason why they shouldn't get referred to you. Use every resource available to make that happen.

Placement Offices, Job Fairs, and Associations

If you are in college or a trade school, start your job search in your school's career placement office. The counselors maintain job listings and can advise you on preparing a résumé and writing cover letters. Your school may also host job or career fairs that give students the opportunity to meet with many potential employers in one place. Graduates who are changing careers can contact their colleges' alumni associations for job leads.

Joining or contacting a professional association, such as the American Veterinary Medical Association, is another good way to find job opportunities in your field. Professional associations often have job listings on their Web sites that are accessible only to members. In fields such as advertising, marketing, or public relations, you are more likely to find a dog- or pet-related job through personal contacts than a professional association.

Networking

It's essential to develop networking skills and overcome the fear of approaching people you don't know well. Networking doesn't mean being pushy. It's a means of keeping in touch with people, sharing information, and simply reaching out. Networking is communicating with everyone you meet in your day-to-day life, from your dog's groomer to the people in your dog's play group to the other parents in your child's carpool. The people you know can introduce you to people they know or provide you with helpful information or leads, and you can do the same for them.

Informally, tell everyone you talk to that you're looking for a job and what kind of job you want. Once you have a few leads, begin by researching the companies of the people you'll be talking to. Check out their Web sites to learn as much as you can. Look at the job postings; there may be a specific position you will want to apply to. You need to sound like you've done your research before you call anyone, even someone you know.

Then start working the phone. Before you make that first call, though, write down key points you want to cover. Don't make it a word-for-word

Using Social Media

If you don't have any social media experience, get it! Many communications jobs require it these days, and most companies have a Twitter or Facebook account. There's a good chance that any job you get will involve managing or contributing to your company's presence on social media Web sites.

Sign up for Twitter and tweet at least once a day. Remember that unless you are some kind of guru in your field, you have to follow people to get followers. Volunteer to create a Facebook page for your local dog club or other organization, and create a LinkedIn page for yourself. Update them both regularly.

KEEP CURRENT

Keep up with news and trends in the pet industry, as this information can often provide leads to potential job opportunities. For instance, if you see that a company in which you're interested has been in the news for successfully launching a new product, send off a congratulatory note or e-mail to the hiring manager or to any contacts you have there and ask if they'll be hiring anyone for that division. You may well get a reply regarding upcoming job openings.

script; you'll end up sounding artificial. These notes keep the conversation relevant and concise. You don't want to waste anyone's time or have to make a second call because you left out an important detail.

If you're calling someone you don't know well or "a friend of a friend" whom you've never met, start by telling the person who you are and how or by whom you were referred, then explain that you are looking for a job in his or her field. Offer the most pertinent details about your education or experience. Mention that you've researched the company and are interested in the work it does. If there were no job openings on the Web site, say you didn't see any jobs posted but would appreciate being kept in mind if something comes up. You may also ask if there is anyone else in the field to whom he or she can refer you.

Your Résumé and Cover Letter

A résumé details your experience, skills, and education. In conjunction with the cover letter, your résumé is your first chance to make a good impression. You can find many books on the art of creating résumés and writing cover letters, but the following tips will get you started.

Résumé

Use a professional template when constructing your résumé. Write down your skills and experience. In addition to any jobs you've held, list activities that have given your valuable and relevant skills—training your dog, volunteering at an animal shelter, or participating in animal visitations at the local nursing home.

Tailor your résumé to the job. If you are applying for an event-planner position at a dog-related company, include your experience coordinating your breed club's annual show or professional organization's conference.

Write a succinct summary statement, focusing on what you want to achieve and showcasing your strengths. This is especially important if you are changing careers. Use it to show employers what you can offer.

Another tip if you're changing fields: include some details about previous companies you've worked for, not just their names. Employers in your new field may not be familiar with your previous employer. Telling them that it's a national business with 500 employees gives them context.

If you have experience in a particular field, include information about how your career progressed. If you held only one or two positions over a long period at a previous job, use promotions, awards, and other professional accomplishments to beef up your job description. Highlight any experience relevant to the job for which you're applying, even if it was twenty years ago. This is especially important if you're changing careers.

The editor of *Dog World* magazine, Jackie Brown (seen here with her Miniature Poodle, Jäger), advises job hunters to be "direct and honest" during an interview. That's good résumé-writing advice too!

Include a section outlining your experience with dogs. This can include membership in or offices held with breed clubs, professional associations, or dog-sport organizations; titles you've put on your dog; pet-related volunteer work, litters you've bred, or any other dog-related information.

Cover Letter

Even if you are submitting a résumé electronically, a cover letter is still essential. It's your introduction to the employer, and writing a standout cover

letter can give you a serious edge. Many people don't send one, so doing so puts you ahead. The other advantage of a cover letter is that you can tailor it to a particular job even more so than you can a résumé.

If possible, find out the name of the person who will be receiving your cover letter and résumé. It's always best if you can address it to an individual rather than the generic "Dear Sir or Madam," but that will do if you don't have a name. Don't use a breezy "Hey there!" or other informal greeting.

Explain why you are writing—in response to a job posting or because you were referred by someone, for instance. Follow by describing why you are a good candidate, with details to show you are familiar with the company and industry. Make the cover letter about how your skills can benefit the company, not about your goals.

The cover letter is a good place to highlight qualities or experiences that don't fit well in a résumé format, as well as specific achievements. Telling a story about your background, such as how you grew up in a family that was passionate about dogs and learned how to train and care for them at your mother's knee, can personalize your background.

Close your letter with a promise to follow up and thank the person for taking the time to consider your application, followed by "Sincerely" or "Cordially" and your name. If you're sending the letter by e-mail, your printed name is fine, but always sign a piece of correspondence sent by snail mail or fax. You can double your chances of an interview by following up an e-mail submission of your cover letter and résumé with a hard copy sent by regular mail. Include a handwritten note saying that it's a second submission and that you're very interested in the position.

Your Interview

Books have been written on mastering the interview process and making a good impression. The important points are summarized in the tips below.

Show up with time to spare. Being late can ruin your chances. Give yourself plenty of time in case you run into traffic or get lost.

Dress appropriately. It never hurts to be overdressed, but dressing too casually will work against you. Wear a business suit.

Don't tell stupid jokes. It's easy to offend someone when you aren't familiar with that person's sense of humor, and it makes you sound nervous.

Be polite to the receptionist. You may not realize it, but he or she is the first person interviewing you. In fact, be polite to everyone you meet.

State your credentials and experience simply. Elaborate on, don't just repeat, what is in your résumé. Use this information to lead into what you could do for the company and why you would be a good fit.

Explain how your education and dog experience relate to the company and the job.

Be prepared to answer certain questions. Many interviewees will ask how you dealt with a challenging work situation, what you consider your biggest failure, or what your greatest regret is. Make your answers real.

Be sure to answer all questions thoroughly. Answer without talking too much or too little. Be "direct and honest," says Jackie Brown, editor of *Dog World* magazine.

Read up on the company and the industry beforehand. "Establish that you did some research about the company and its needs," says Peter Kraatz, who often makes hiring decisions at EMC Corporation and frequently lectures to college students on interview techniques. "All good hiring managers want to see if people can put forward concrete ideas for getting things done, working on a problem, or making more money." And ask concrete questions about the position. It shows you are thinking about the realities of the job, Brown says.

Never bad-mouth your current employer, and never claim to be a victim. If asked why you left your previous job, talk about your desire for new opportunities and challenges and your interest in the company you are interviewing with.

GETTING THE JOB RESOURCES

- AnimalJobHunter.com, www.animaljobhunter.com
- *The Elements of Résumé Style: Essential Rules and Eye-Opening Advice for Writing Résumés and Cover Letters That Work,* by Scott Bennett. AMACOM, 2005.
- *Guerrilla Marketing for Job Hunters 2.0,* by Jay Conrad Levinson and David E. Perry. Wiley, 2009.
- *301 Smart Answers To Tough Interview Questions,* by Vicky Oliver. Sourcebooks Inc., 2005.
- *Riley Guide,* http://rileyguide.com
- Interview-preparation tips and company information, www.glassdoor.com
- Salary negotiation aid, www.payscale.com

Training and Behavior

Training and pet-behavior counseling rank among the most essential types of pet-related careers because they help ensure that dogs, cats, and other animals can stay with their families for life—not just until they get to be annoying. Understanding why animals do the things they do is the essence of ethology—the study of animal behavior—but pet behaviorists and trainers must also study and communicate with the human animal to succeed in this field. There are many different opportunities in the field of animal behavior and training, from consulting with pet owners and teaching obedience classes to training guide and service dogs.

CHAPTER 5

Dog Trainer

D
o you have a knack for getting dogs to do what you want them to do? Have you taught tricks to all of the neighborhood dogs? Do you enjoy trying to figure out why dogs do the things they do? If you like to teach and you love dogs, you might have a career as a dog trainer in your future.

For as long as people and dogs have been together, they have been learning from each other. After all, dogs teach us just as much as we teach them. But not everyone has a knack for communicating with or understanding dogs—that's where trainers come in. Their job isn't so much teaching dogs as it is teaching people how to work with their dogs.

What Trainers Do

Training dogs isn't a career for the person who wants the security, predictable hours, and benefits of a 9-to-5 job. Dog trainers often work nights and weekends, because that's when dog owners have time to attend classes. Unless a trainer has a steady job with, say, a service-dog organization, a police department, or a government agency, he or she must work hard to build and keep a steady clientele.

Dog training is not limited to teaching manners to companion dogs. Training is one of those careers that offers many different paths, depending on an individual's interests and abilities. In addition to showing owners

how to teach their dogs to sit, stay, and come, people with training skills may find careers teaching service dogs to help people with disabilities; teaching detection dogs to sniff out drugs, explosives, or evidence of arson; or working with search dogs as they learn to rescue people who are missing or trapped in the aftermath of a disaster, such as an earthquake, avalanche, or building collapse (see chapters 28 and 29 on working-dog handlers). A rare few train dogs to star on stage and screen or to perform amazing feats at theme parks or other performance venues.

For the most part, dog trainers are self-employed. Some work for dog-training businesses, teaching puppy kindergarten, basic obedience, therapy-dog skills, and dog sports such as agility and flyball. Others are employed by or contracted with veterinarians, animal shelters, pet-supply stores, or township recreation departments.

Who Trainers Are

What kind of people become trainers? What personality traits must they have? No matter what kind of training you do, an understanding of dogs is essential. Good trainers have insight into canine behavior and the ability to bring out the best in each dog they work with. A good trainer is patient. Training a dog means working with the dog and building or modifying behaviors in small steps over a period of days, weeks, months, and

Trainer Joel Silverman works with a dog rescued by the Mission Viejo Animal Services Center in California. Silverman wrote *Take 2: Training Solutions for Rescued Dogs* (Kennel Club Books, 2010).

sometimes even years. Training is much more complicated than "showing the dog who's boss."

Good people skills are important, too. A trainer must be able to work with, teach, and motivate people of all ages and skill levels. That entails good listening skills as well as the aforementioned patience. Other characteristics of good trainers are time-management skills and problem-solving abilities. When the usual methods just don't work with a particular dog (or person), a trainer must be able to come up with alternative ways of reaching the training goal.

Dog trainers should be physically fit. They spend a lot of time on their feet, walking around at classes, helping individual clients. Taking a dog through an agility course involves jogging or running. Teaching big dogs not to pull or jump up on people requires physical strength. That said, training is more about brain power than brute force, so being small is not a disadvantage.

A career as a dog trainer has many challenges. It's satisfying to help people live long, trouble-free lives with their dogs, but it can be frustrating not to be able to succeed in every case. "The worst is not being able to reach a dog owner and knowing that the dog will continue to suffer as a result," says Pennsylvania dog trainer and behavior consultant Susan Bulanda.

A Trainer's Day

Depending on the type of training being done, a trainer's day can range from routine to ever changing. For a companion-dog trainer such as Kim Toepfer of Fresno, California, no two days are alike.

"My days vary a great deal, which I enjoy," she says. "I have a few dogs that I work with while their owners are at work. I pick up the dog from the home and take him to a park or public place to work on behavior problems or just polish his training. I usually have a private client or two, and then teach a class in the evening. Lately, I have begun to do a lot more work online, developing Web sites for other trainers, plus a little bit of freelance writing. I try to fit that into my spare time."

Some trainers teach obedience classes at local veterinary clinics. That's how Toepfer got her start as a trainer. Other trainers offer pet manners or obedience classes through community colleges or community recreation programs, and house-call services have grown increasingly popular with dog owners who appreciate the quicker results achieved through intensive one-on-one training. Home visits allow a trainer to customize programs to the specific needs of an owner and his or her dog. Some dog-training businesses make sixty or more house calls per week.

Other trainers prepare dogs for work in movies, theater, or television, either on the side or as a full-time business. In Houston, Jim Burwell has trained dogs for local TV commercials, news shows, and theater productions. New York dog trainer William Berloni (*pictured on page 57 with canine performer PI*) specializes in theatrical animals. His canine students have appeared in Broadway shows, in ballets, in movies, and on TV.

Trainers who work with animal actors must be well versed in animal welfare requirements, public health regulations, and liability insurance, as well as experienced in obtaining permits and certifications. They must also know what filmmakers want. Generally, that means dogs with good looks, such as Golden Retrievers; dogs with loads of personality, such as Jack Russell Terriers; or scruffy mixed breeds with unusual coloring and attitude to spare.

DO YOU HAVE WHAT IT TAKES?

TRAINER

A dog trainer should have these characteristics:

- A knack for working with dogs
- Patience
- Good people skills
- Time-management skills
- Problem-solving ability
- Respect for clients, both canine and human
- A desire to improve the relationship between dog and person
- Physical fitness

Captain Haggerty:
The Trainer's Trainer

Arthur J. Haggerty, born in Manhattan on December 3, 1931, grew up around dogs and handled several breeds in dog shows at a young age. While serving in the U.S. Army in the 1950s, he became the commanding officer of the K9 Corps. In 1962, he founded Captain Haggerty's School for Dogs. The Captain (as he became known) proceeded to blaze a trail as a dog trainer with uncanny abilities. If dogs could do it, he prepared them for it. He worked with sentry dogs in Germany, Okinawa, and the Philippines; with police dogs in London, Hong Kong, Atlanta, and Washington, D.C.; with guide dogs in Germany, the Netherlands, and Belgium. He spent years working with avalanche dogs; sled dogs; messenger dogs; bird and varmint dogs; scout dogs; patrol dogs; and explosive- and narcotic-detector dogs.

The Captain also supplied dogs for the silver screen, the stage, and television. In the early 1970s he was called to supply dogs for the movie *Shamus*, starring Burt Reynolds. His distinctive look—tall, broad, and bald—appealed to the director, who hired him to play a "goon." Bitten by the acting bug, he would go on to appear in or handle dogs for more than 150 feature films and 450 television commercials. His dogs appeared in soap operas such as *As the World Turns* and *All My Children*, and he and his dogs were often guests on David Letterman's late-night talk show.

He also wrote. In 1977, with fellow New York dog trainer Carol Lea Benjamin, he wrote his first book, *Dog Tricks*, which became, and remains, a best-seller. Other books followed: *The American Breeds, How to Get Your Pet into Show Business, How to Teach Your Dog to Talk, The Zen Method of Dog Training*, and *Service Dogs*. Additionally, he wrote some 1,000 articles on dogs for various periodicals. He won many awards from the Dog Writers Association of America, and the Alliance of Purebred Dog Writers offers an annual Haggerty award for excellence in the field of dog writing.

Through training classes, seminars and workshops, books and articles, and television appearances, the Captain inspired thousands of dog lovers and helped many a professional trainer get a start. He also became a noted American Kennel Club judge. A true icon in the field of dog training, Arthur Haggerty died in July 2006, leaving his daughter, Babette, a well-respected and successful trainer in her own right, to carry on.

A dog can be beautiful and personable, but if he isn't well socialized, he won't perform reliably. He should be able to stay focused for long periods despite the distractions of strangers or unusual activity. Trainers who work in this field often find their canine stars in animal shelters. These animals are often too rambunctious and smart to fit well into homes, but those same characteristics can make them highly trainable.

In addition to working with paying clients, many trainers do volunteer work. Burwell is past president of the Lone Star Search and Rescue Dog Association, which trains dogs for tracking and air scenting and participates in searches for lost or missing people.

Education and Training

Anyone can print up some business cards and claim to be a dog trainer, but most respected trainers have some sort of relevant educational background or extensive personal experience before they start teaching. Dog trainers acquire their skills and knowledge in many different ways, from on-the-job training to formal education. Lots of dog trainers get started

Canine fitness trainer Gail Miller Bisher, owner of Super Fit Fido Club, puts a Dachshund through a workout course. Bisher helps couch-potato dogs and owners get into shape.

Service-Dog Trainers

Service dogs help people who have physical or emotional disabilities, enabling these people to get around and live more easily on their own. The dogs include guide dogs for people with visual impairments, assistance dogs for those with physical limitations, hearing dogs, and psychiatric service dogs.

A service-dog trainer must first teach skills to the dog and then teach owner and dog to work together. "A service-dog trainer needs to be patient and organized, with good communication skills and the ability to think creatively, critically, and objectively," says Nancy Fierer, director of Susquehanna Service Dogs in Harrisburg, Pennsylvania. "It really helps to be able to take information from one area of life or study and apply it to training. The person has to love people and animals and learning. Flexibility is also important. The trainer always needs to keep looking for better ways to train."

Before they can qualify to teach teams, service-dog trainers may need to complete a two- to three-year program that teaches them how to train the dogs and how to work with people of differing abilities. "Our training methods are very specific," Fierer says. "Most trainers will not be able to work in our program without extensive training. Good positive experience is important, too, either with dogs or people with disabilities."

The actual training of a service dog usually takes approximately six months after the dogs are returned as adults by their puppy raisers—the people who care for them, socialize them, and teach them basic manners until they are old enough to begin the training needed to become service dogs. Beyond actually teaching the dog, trainers are generally expected to care for the dog. Sometimes the dogs also live with their trainers (sometimes they live in a kennel situation). Filling out paperwork related to applications for service dogs is another facet of the job.

There are a limited number of openings for service-dog trainers at organizations. Some trainers volunteer with a service-dog organization before being accepted into the training program.

by training their own dogs for obedience trials or other dog sports and then move on to teaching other people's dogs. For the person who wants to make dog training a career, however, a more standardized educational route may be the way to go. Much more is known today about dog behavior than in the past, so an education in psychology and behavior is useful for dealing with and communicating concepts to dogs and their people.

Whether they have high-school diplomas or college degrees, dog trainers can achieve certification through organizations such as the Association of Pet Dog Trainers and the National Association of Dog Obedience Instructors. Accreditation isn't necessary, but it adds an element of credibility.

College

As a child, Kim Toepfer was attracted to animals of all kinds and read everything she could find about dogs and training. She developed "intelligence tests" for her pet dogs and participated in 4-H programs. When she began thinking about a career, she assumed she would become a veterinarian. In college, however, Toepfer discovered an interest in psychology and behavior that altered her career path.

"While there is no degree requirement for becoming a dog trainer, I think a good, solid education in science—biology and genetics—and psychology—abnormal behavior and ethology—is extremely valuable," she says.

Longtime dog trainer Susan Bulanda, who started learning about dogs and their training as soon as she could read and had an established clientele in her town by the time she entered high school, also found a psychology degree to be helpful in her career development. She earned a bachelor's degree in psychology, with courses in education, followed by a master's degree in education, with courses in behavioral science.

"When I started in the dog-training business, there were no schools, no Internet, and few opportunities to learn," she says. "By the time I graduated high school, I came to the conclusion that force was not the way to teach a dog, that education and psychology were the answer."

You won't find any degrees offered in dog training per se, but many colleges offer degrees in animal behavior. At Kutztown University in Pennsylvania, Bulanda has developed two popular and successful programs for people who want to enter dog-related fields, including training. Level I of Canine Training and Management is for students who want to become dog trainers. In addition to covering training methods and services, the program includes business-management practices and communication skills.

Training Herding Dogs

Susan Rhoades bought a 70-acre farm and stocked it with sheep to keep her dogs occupied, but the property and livestock ended up becoming her livelihood. She teaches herding-dog training and holds herding trials on the land, as well as judging American Kennel Club and American Herding Breed Association herding trials. She got her start after training with renowned trainer Wink Mason, who himself has a farm used for training stock dogs and raising sheep.

"I asked him to help me make a living at this and he taught me to train all breeds of dogs and understand how dogs think," Rhoades says. "I started giving lessons a few years after that, part-time, and it grew into a full-time business. It is really fun to see the reaction of the owner when the dog turns on to stock and does what he has been bred to do for ages. Sometimes the owners have tears in their eyes from seeing their dogs working."

"If you do not know how to manage a business, you could be the best trainer in the world and you would fail," Bulanda says. "And at some point, dog trainers must be able to promote themselves through written material such as brochures, pamphlets, and articles; they must give talks to interested groups; perhaps make a video; and most important of all, they must be able to teach and counsel their clients."

The Level II program focuses on research and behavior problems and is designed for people who want to become certified animal behavior consultants. Among other things, students learn about how to interview clients and gather facts about a behavior problem, the causes and treatments of behavior problems, and the way dogs learn. They also get a course in the behavior of cats and parrots so they can deal with interspecies issues.

Dog-Training School

Attending a dog-training school is an option for aspiring trainers. Such schools vary widely in the length of their programs and the training methods they teach. Some have actual campuses, while others have distance-learning programs.

Look for a thorough program that includes courses on the history of dog training, including a comparison of dog training with other animal-training methods; how animals learn; dog behavior, body language, and development; how to design classes and advise owners; and the basics of business management, such as marketing, accounting, customer relations, insurance requirements, and legal issues faced by small businesses.

Schools should offer programs that address shaping, targeting, clicker training, and other techniques; the science of learning; the use, advantages, and disadvantages of various types of equipment; and how to develop your classroom procedures. In addition to learning how to interpret dog behavior, students should also become adept at reading human body language and tailoring basic behaviors for the specific needs of each dog and owner.

At the San Francisco SPCA Academy for Dog Trainers, a full-time six-week course in science-based, positive-reinforcement methods results in a certificate in training and counseling. Students attend lectures, workshops, and seminars that cover animal-learning theory, dog behavior and development, obedience and clicker training, teaching classes, treating common behavior problems, critical thinking, and one-on-one counseling skills.

An online option is offered by the Karen Pryor Academy for Animal Training and Behavior. The six-month program combines distance learning with four two-day hands-on workshops. Between workshop sessions, students can get help by phone or e-mail from the workshop instructor or academy staff. While it's recommended that a student who aspires to enroll in this challenging program already have experience as a trainer, veterinary technician, or shelter employee, it's not required. The curriculum ranges from such topics as behavior chains and cuing to preparing business plans.

"A school or course should supply you with abundant knowledge in many different areas of becoming a trainer as well as behavior," says Pamela Dennison, a trainer in New Jersey. "There's a lot involved in being a good or great dog trainer, and the first thing to understand is that dog training is not really about dogs. It's about teaching people to communicate with dogs. Look for a school run by professionals who teach, compete with dogs, and write about and speak on dog training rather than one where all they do is charge a huge amount for a reading list."

In addition to lectures and reading assignments, a school should offer hands-on practice. Correspondence or video courses may teach you some of the basics, but there's nothing like real-life experience. The ideal school is one that provides a wide curriculum and plenty of opportunities to work

Ian Dunbar:
Patron Saint of Positive Training

Having founded the Association of Pet Dog Trainers in 1993, Ian Dunbar today is revered as the patron saint of positive training. As a dynamic lecturer and an innovative teacher, he has made a huge impact on the behavior and training community. In 1981 he developed the revolutionary Sirius Puppy Training technique, which advocated positive training methods to pet-dog owners. Dunbar focused his methods on training pet dogs and emphasized the use of food treats in training as well as the importance of puppy socialization. Dunbar received his veterinary degree from the Royal Veterinary College in London and his doctorate in animal behavior from the University of California in Berkeley. He hosted a popular television series in the United Kingdom called *Dogs with Dunbar*. Dunbar has written numerous books, including his *How to Teach a New Dog Old Tricks* and *The Good Little Dog Book*, as well as appeared on about a dozen Sirius Puppy Training videos. No other behaviorist-trainer today can lay claim to the lasting influence that Dunbar's dog-friendly positive methods have had on the international dog scene.

with a number of dogs. Such an opportunity might be spending time at a local animal shelter or rescue group, working with dogs who need house-training and manners to help them become more adoptable.

"Work with as many dogs as you can, especially those with problems," Toepfer says. "Volunteering at a shelter or rescue organization is an outstanding way to test your training skills and to make a significant difference for a dog who needs a home."

Before you send in your tuition check, ask school officials what type of training methods they advocate in their classes. You don't want to go to a "jerk 'em, choke 'em" school if your interests lie in clicker training and other positive-reinforcement techniques.

Certification

No one is required to obtain certification as a dog trainer, but having it can add to your credibility. Three organizations offer various levels of certification: the Association of Pet Dog Trainers (APDT), the International Association of Canine Professionals (IACP), and the National Association of Dog Obedience Instructors (NADOI).

To be eligible for the APDT's certification exam, trainers must show evidence of at least 300 hours of dog-training experience within the past five years. At least 75 percent of that time must be teaching experience. In other words, the trainers must have taught other people how to train dogs, not simply trained their own dogs. Other requirements are a high-school diploma or GED and written references from a veterinarian, a client, and another trainer.

The IACP is a professional organization not just for trainers but for anyone who works with dogs, including groomers, boarding kennel owners and employees, veterinarians and vet techs, pet-supply retailers, and writers. Trainers who have been professional members of the IACP for at least six months may take the certified dog trainer (CDT) exam. In addition to the multipart exam, applicants must provide case studies of dogs trained within the past year, as well as references from clients.

The NADOI offers two levels of certification to its members: provisional and endorsed. Applicants must meet minimum experience requirements for each category to qualify for the exam. Eligibility for provisional certification requires at least two years of experience in dog obedience training; experience as an instructor or assistant instructor is recommended. To qualify as an endorsed member, an applicant must have at least five years of experience in dog obedience training, with at least two of those years at the instructor level. They must have worked with a minimum of 100 dog-handler teams. Applicants for both levels must pass an extensive written test and may be interviewed or asked to provide a video of a class.

Apprenticeship

Studying under the guidance of an established trainer is a time-honored and still viable career path. That's the route that was pursued by freelance writer Susan McCullough, who specializes in dog-oriented topics. She was ready to try her hand at doing some of the things she had written about so frequently—like dog training. That led her to an apprenticeship with nationally known trainer Pat Miller.

Freelance writer Susan McCullough, seen here with her Golden Retriever, Allie, chose to apprentice with an experienced dog trainer to learn more about the profession.

"I began to investigate apprenticeship programs online and concluded that Pat Miller's program offered the best, most structured opportunity to gain such experience," she says. "Pat's program requires apprentices not only to assist with classes but also to assist with behavioral assessments of shelter dogs, sit in on one-on-one private sessions, train shelter dogs, and do a fair amount of reading. I also knew Pat already and was confident that I would learn a lot from her."

Working with a Mentor

Even if you don't apprentice with someone, finding a mentor can give your emerging training career a boost. A mentor can help when you need advice about dealing with clients or working with tricky dogs, or when you simply seek answers to business-related questions. A good mentor can be your best source of practical information. Look for someone who isn't devoted to a single method of training. The best teachers are those who recognize that there's more than one way to teach people and dogs and who are always seeking out new information and techniques.

Other mentors, in a sense, are the dogs. Whether you earn a college degree, attend a training school, or apprentice with an experienced trainer, you should seek out as many opportunities as possible to work with a variety of dog breeds and mixes. Just because you can train a Golden Retriever doesn't mean that you can train a Greyhound or a Jack Russell Terrier. All breeds, individuals within breeds, and mixed-breed dogs have their own quirks and will often require individualized techniques.

Personal Experience

Plenty of trainers have achieved successful careers without any type of formal education (think Cesar Millan). In those instances—and even with a college degree—gaining experience is essential.

"I was very involved with competitive obedience and flyball for many years before moving into providing training to others," Toepfer says. "I spent many years working in animal shelters as a volunteer trainer to improve the chances of a dog's being adopted. I learned a lot from those dogs!"

And no matter what your educational background or training philosophy, it's always valuable to spend time with other trainers. There's an old joke that the only thing two dog trainers can agree on is that a third trainer is wrong. Nonetheless, networking with other trainers and being open to learning from them is useful for aspiring dog trainers. Attending seminars held by dog-training or animal-behavior organizations is one way to learn the latest information about techniques and philosophies in the field.

Advanced Learning

Continuing education is important in every career, including dog training. Expect to devote at least a couple of weeks each year to attending conferences and seminars in this interesting field. You will always learn something that will help you with your clients, both canine and human.

"I read and 'talk dogs' with as many professionals as I can in as many fields of training as I can," Kim Toepfer says. "I am especially interested in finding unique solutions to problems, and I always find some gem in any conversation I have or book I read."

Barkworthy BITE

READ EVERYTHING

"Read everything you can, even if you think it's not your style. It is important to educate yourself on the full range of dog training before you develop a style. There are times when you will rely on some tidbit you picked up from an unlikely source."

—Kim Toepfer, dog trainer

Starting a Dog-Training Business

Starting and running a small business is challenging, even when it involves the pleasure of working with dogs. Like any small-business owner, a dog trainer must purchase or rent a work space; buy insurance; print business cards, stationery, and promotional materials; advertise his or her business; and pay for utilities and other bills. Here are some options and issues to consider before you jump in.

Trainers often work out of their own homes and visit private clients at their homes rather than renting or purchasing a facility. Trainers who teach classes or see clients on their own property must ensure that their insurance coverage is sufficient.

Trainers who want to offer classes must acquire space in which to hold them. Public parks usually require permits for events, such as classes, and may require proof of liability insurance. Trainers who work through community recreation departments, however, may have access to public parks or school parking lots, as well as coverage by city or county insurance. Some trainers rent space in buildings in industrial parks. These can be good choices because the buildings are large and it's easy to install rubber matting or other flooring that will make a comfortable and safe training surface.

Be prepared to spend time keeping records and paying bills. This drudge work is the bane of every small-business owner. If your business becomes successful enough, you can hire someone to take it off your hands, but until then, don't let it fall by the wayside. If you aren't organized, you'll lose business and incur late fees and penalties from vendors and the Internal Revenue Service.

Set specific work hours. It's all too easy for training to become a 24/7 job and take over your life. After all, who doesn't want to help people and dogs work better together? But if you don't set limits, you'll find yourself taking calls from clients every day, from early in the morning to late at night.

Employment Outlook

According to the U.S. Department of Labor's Bureau of Labor Statistics, employment of animal care and service workers—a group that includes dog trainers—is expected to grow by 21 percent through 2018. Every year, more and more people acquire dogs as companions. Those new pet owners will need the services of trainers. Even established dog owners continue to need the help of trainers as they become interested in new dog sports or acquire new puppies who need training.

More and more animal shelters are also hiring dog trainers. They recognize the need not only to prepare dogs for adoption but also to help new adopters deal with any behavior problems they may encounter. These "help desks" at shelters are often responsible for keeping animals in their homes instead of being cycled back to the shelters, so working at such a shelter can be rewarding for a trainer.

The income a dog trainer makes can range from a low of around $11 an hour to, well, the sky's the limit! Dog trainers may charge hourly rates for private lessons or fixed fees for group classes. Rates vary based on such factors as the area of the country, the trainer's level of experience, and the training venue. Private dog trainers in small towns or rural areas may make only $12 to $15 per hour, while private trainers who make house calls in cities on the East or West Coast may charge from $100 to $500

William Berloni works with one of the stars of his troop of theatrical canine actors, Chloe. Chloe took to the New York stage in the Palace Theater's production of *Legally Blonde*.

per hour. A group class at a dog-training facility may cost $150 for four one-hour sessions, while a private session at the same facility is $75 per hour simply because the trainer's attention is not divided. Trainers who run their own businesses must keep in mind that the recurrent costs of running a business can be high; facility rent, insurance, advertising, and other expenses will all take a bite out of a trainer's income.

"One also has to look at the economy," Dennison says. "I diversify as much as possible, writing books and articles, doing speaking engagements, producing DVDs, and selling select products."

And some clients are not above emotional blackmail. "There were many times people would threaten me with the well-being of their dogs if I would not help them for free or at little cost," Bulanda says. "People think that because you love dogs or cats, you are willing to work for nothing for the benefit of the pet. They often do not understand that it is your livelihood and that you make a living training dogs and cats. Everyone who wants to be a dog trainer should come to grips with this and decide how to handle it."

Dog training is not an easy way to make a living, to be sure, but for the right person, it can be extremely rewarding. "I could not be happier that my interests led me to become a trainer," says Toepfer. "I have the most amazing, dedicated dog owners as clients. They are beautiful people who truly love their pets. It is wonderful to be considered a partner in their dogs' well-being."

TRAINER RESOURCES

- Association of Pet Dog Trainers, www.apdt.com
- Certification Council for Professional Dog Trainers, www.ccpdt.org
- Hollywood Animals' Animal Actors Agency, www.animalactorsagency.com
- Indiana University, Center for the Integrative Study of Animal Behavior, www.indiana.edu/~animal
- Karen Pryor Academy for Animal Training and Behavior, www.karenpryoracademy.com
- Kutztown University, Canine Training and Management Program, Kutztown, Pennsylvania, www.kutztown.edu/academics/learning/canine_management.html
- Legacy Canine Behavior and Training, www.legacycanine.com
- National Association of Dog Obedience Instructors, www.nadoi.org
- Pat Miller, Peaceable Paws Dog and Puppy Training, Hagerstown, Maryland, apprentice and intern programs, www.peaceablepaws.com
- Pet Care Services Association, www.petcareservices.org
- San Francisco SPCA Academy for Dog Trainers, www.sfspca.org/programs-services/academy-dog-trainers
- Susan Rhoades, Keepstone Farm, www.keepstonefarm.com
- *So You Want to Be a Dog Trainer*, by Nicole Wilde, 2nd ed. Phantom Publishing, 2006.

CHAPTER 6

Applied Animal Behaviorist

When John C. Wright was a doctoral student in experimental psychology, he did his dissertation was on the development of social structure in German Shepherd puppies. Once people found out that he was doing research on how puppies bond with each other, they started asking him questions about their own dogs' behaviors—in other words, they wanted to know how to apply his knowledge to real-world problems. He started reading further on canine behavior and, inspired by leaders in the field, such as Peter Borchelt, Victoria Voith, and Katherine Houpt, he soon found that he, too, had become an applied animal behaviorist.

What Behaviorists Do

A behaviorist usually comes into the picture when no medical reason is found for a pet's aggression, fear, anxiety, obsession, or other abnormal behavior. Before deciding on a course of action, a behaviorist will typically take the following steps:

1 Assess a pet's living arrangements to see how the animal is interacting with family members and any other pets in the household;

2 Determine whether a pet is getting adequate exercise, nutrition, social interaction, and training; and

3 Determine whether a pet has an anxiety disorder.

Effie maintains a down position while Kathy Sdao desensitizes Nick to having his paws handled, in preparation for nail trims. Sdao is a certified applied animal behaviorist in Tacoma, Washington.

Once this information has been gathered, the behaviorist develops a program to help a pet deal with the circumstances that trigger the behavior. This can involve behavioral modification, environmental adjustments, or drug therapy. Only a veterinarian can prescribe medication, so an applied animal behaviorist who is not a veterinarian often works in partnership with one.

Behaviorists can work in many different settings. Clinical behaviorists who specialize in the behavior of companion animals work directly with clients, either in their own offices, in veterinary clinics, or at clients' homes. Like trainers, they may hold classes for pet owners, not only to assist with training but also to help prevent or solve behavior problems.

Sometimes they are employed by pet day-care programs or humane organizations. Behaviorists can become science writers, producing content for book and magazine publishers, Web sites, and broadcast programs.

Some behaviorists, such as John Wright, go into teaching and research at the university level in animal science, biology, psychology, wildlife biology, or zoology, or at veterinary or medical colleges.

It takes a certain kind of person to be a behaviorist, someone who turns to science when seeking answers to dog training and behavior problems. The principles of a behaviorist's approach include positive reinforcement and behavior change through rewards, prompts, and other methods, says Mary Burch, a certified applied animal behaviorist.

Brelands and Pryor: Clicker Icons

Graduate students of legendary behavioral scientist B. F. Skinner, Keller Breland and Marian Kruse (Breland) applied their professor's concepts of operant conditioning to the worlds of advertising and entertainment. In 1943, they opened Animal Behavior Enterprises to train a variety of animals using operant conditioning. They revolutionized the use of secondary reinforcers (clickers and whistles) to train dogs (as well as pigs, cats, ducks, and hamsters) for movies and television, decades prior to the positive-reinforcement training revolution. The Brelands also trained marine mammals for the U.S. Navy in the 1960s.

Behavior biologist and dolphin trainer Karen Pryor was using the Brelands' operant training methods at Sea Life Park in the mid-1960s. The clicker-training revolution that electrified the dog community in the 1990s was triggered by her 1984 publication *Don't Shoot the Dog* (Sunshine Books), which was excerpted in *Reader's Digest*. Through her book and her subsequent seminars around the country, she reached tens of millions of people. She also promoted her clicker-training methods on the Internet, still new to most people in the early 1990s. It helped deliver her gospel of positive training methods to all who cared to click on her Web site. Pryor also developed her own version of the clicker, which she called the I-clicker.

Who Behaviorists Are

Not surprisingly, the study of animal behavior attracts people whose breadth and depth of interests can be overwhelming. It's not easy for them to fit in everything they'd like to do.

"The most challenging thing is trying to have time to do everything I want," John Wright says. "I love the teaching, I love the research, I love the practice, I love my household of strange animals. Trying to find enough time to do justice to all of those endeavors is my biggest frustration."

In a post on her The Other End of the Leash blog, certified applied animal behaviorist Patricia McConnell lists the knowledge needed to work with canine behavioral problems. Ethology, the study of animal behavior, includes the influence of genetics on behavior, developmental influences, normal social structure of dogs, communicative signals, play behavior, and predatory behavior.

McConnell adds that a good dog behaviorist—in addition to having profound knowledge of the most common behavioral diagnoses, which behaviors are symptomatic of these problems, and the best ways to solve them—also has an in-depth understanding of which behavioral problems are often caused by or associated with medical problems; this includes a good working knowledge of canine structure and function, basic physiology, and which behavior problems necessitate a visit to the veterinarian.

A good behaviorist is also a good trainer, McConnell believes, with the ability to read a dog, know what the dog is or is not ready for, use movement and voice to influence a dog's behavior, and interpret a dog's visual signals.

Well-known trainer Victoria Stilwell, who also serves as a behavior adviser on rehabilitating rescue dogs, receives a warm welcome at APDT.

"No one should ever give clients instructions about what to teach their dog without being able to demonstrate how to do it successfully to the same dog, in the same context as the clients," she writes.

The ability to work with people is also an essential skill for a animal behaviorist. For instance, a good behaviorist must know how and when

Barkworthy INSIGHT

TRAINER VS. BEHAVIORIST

Sometimes the terms *trainer* and *behaviorist* are used interchangeably, and there are certainly times when their skills and knowledge overlap. In general, however, trainers teach manners, obedience, and other skills to animals who don't have any emotional problems, whereas behaviorists deal with pets who are aggressive, fearful, or have some other problem with a strong emotional component.

to interrupt the direction of a report from a client. Not all information is important to the assessment or treatment of an animal's behavior problem.

"A lot of people just want to talk forever about their animals, and you need to be able to direct or redirect some of the conversation," says Wright, who is now a certified applied animal behaviorist and a professor of psychology at Mercer University in Macon, Georgia.

McConnell notes that it's important to be able to help a client understand what can and can't be known about what is motivating a dog. This ability and the ability to teach clients how to interact with their pets require excellent verbal communication and teaching skills.

"Being a behavioral consultant means knowing how to successfully influence the behavior of two species, knowing how to present information in a way that clients can use and adopt," McConnell writes. "Consultants must have fantastic social skills with people and be able to create a welcome and supportive environment.

"Specialists who are great with dogs but not with people are not suited to do behavior consulting. There is no equivalent of surgery in behavioral treatment and rehab in which the specialist never has to interact with the 'patient.' You're either really, really good with people or you're in the wrong field."

DO YOU HAVE WHAT IT TAKES?

BEHAVIORIST

An applied animal behaviorist should have these characteristics:

- ○ An understanding of canine or feline ethology
- ○ An understanding of operant and classical conditioning, counterconditioning, and desensitization, and when and how to use each
- ○ The ability to read animal body language and other communicative signals
- ○ Experience working with pets who have behavioral problems
- ○ The willingness to refer pets to a veterinarian when necessary
- ○ Good people skills, including the ability to teach pet owners
- ○ Patience
- ○ Good listening skills

Education and Training

Even though anyone can claim to be a behaviorist, most people in the field have at least a master's degree and often a doctorate in animal behavior, psychology, or zoology, with an emphasis on animal behavior.

Portrait of a Behaviorist

John Wright's road to a career as an applied animal behaviorist began during his junior year in college when he enrolled in an experimental psychology course in animal learning. Wright (*pictured with Rosemary*) and his classmates did a study that ended up being published in a psychology journal—a real feat for undergraduates. He went on to graduate school, doing research in behavior genetics, and became interested in dogs and cats. A dissertation on puppy social behavior, followed by five years of research conducted with his students at Berea College, formed the basis for his entrée into the then-new field of applied animal behavior in 1979. As many friends and colleagues requested his help in resolving problem behaviors in their dogs and cats, Wright refocused his efforts to two new areas: dealing with solutions to pet behavior problems and identifying risk factors associated with dog and cat bites.

"I wanted to change my focus on animal behavior from basic research to applied research and practice. Could an experimental psychologist, formally educated and experienced in the science of animal behavior, apply that knowledge to help straighten out problem pets?"

The answer was yes. Wright has since then been involved in developing a behavioral test for assessing the likelihood that a dog will exhibit aggressive behavior and has conducted workshops on its use. He offers seminars on dog and cat behavior and has a successful house-call practice in the Atlanta area.

Some behaviorists are veterinarians with specialties in behavior. On top of an education, behaviorists ideally have experience working with the types of animals that they plan to treat.

That said, some people who call themselves behaviorists have no formal education and are competent and well suited to the work. Others may have strings of letters behind their names but still have no real skills at solving animal behavior problems.

While educational credentials are useful and, to an extent, expected of a behaviorist, a college degree is not absolutely necessary. Nonetheless, being able to look at an animal's behavior not only through the lens of your personal understanding but also with an understanding of the science of animal behavior will give you an advantage in assessing and solving behavior problems. A good behaviorist also has the ability to integrate animal behavior with principles of learning and brain–body mechanisms—essentially, what happens in the brain to set the behavior in motion. To help animals with emotional disorders, all of these areas must be understood and evaluated.

Behaviorists can gain professional certification in several ways. Veterinarians can specialize in behavior (see chapter 9). Non-veterinarians can seek certification in the field of applied animal behavior. Applied animal behaviorists are knowledgeable about the behavioral problems and training of companion animals and have demonstrated expertise in the principles of animal behavior, research methods, and application of animal behavior principles to behavior problems.

Certified applied animal behaviorist Mary Burch prepares for an author signing in New York to promote her book *Citizen Canine* (Kennel Club Books, 2010), an official AKC training publication.

Behavior Analyst to Animal Behaviorist

Mary Burch already had a PhD in psychology and was a board-certified behavior analyst for people when she decided to make a positive difference for dogs. While in New York City for a psychology conference, Burch wandered into the American Kennel Club unannounced and asked to speak to the person in charge of training. She met with Jim Dearinger, who was trying to start the Canine Good Citizen program." He said I was very smart, talented, and enthusiastic, and he asked me if I would go home and work to promote the program," Burch says.

Mary Burch with her dog, Ch. Noel's Wynn Wyn Situation, UD, OA, AXJ, CGC

"At the time, I thought I had been chosen because I was special. Only later did I find out that Jim was asking every single person he could find to help build the CGC program. As a community volunteer, I took CGC to 4-H groups. I wrote articles about the concept for dog magazines, and in 1991, I worked to get the first Canine Good Citizen resolution in the country passed by the Florida legislature."

Burch, also a certified applied animal behaviorist, is director of the AKC's Canine Good Citizen and S.T.A.R. Puppy programs. The programs teach good manners to dogs and responsible dog ownership. A favorite memory of hers is of the ninety-four-year-old woman who took the CGC test with her sixteen-year-old Dachshund. When they passed the test, there wasn't a dry eye in the house.

The Animal Behavior Society (ABS) offers two levels of certification as an animal behaviorist, depending on the candidate's education and experience. The first level, associate applied animal behaviorist, requires a master's degree in a biological or behavioral science with an emphasis on animal behavior; at least two years of professional experience, including independent studies, data analysis, and professional writing; and at least three written recommendations from ABS members.

In order to become a certified applied animal behaviorist, applicants must have a doctorate in a biological or behavioral science with an emphasis on animal behavior; have five years of professional experience; be able to demonstrate original contributions or interpretations of animal behavior information through published work; show significant work experience with a particular species as a researcher, research assistant, or intern; and have at least three written recommendations from ABS members. Once certified, the behaviorists must maintain and provide proof of liability insurance.

Employment Outlook

A number of different opportunities exist in the field of animal behavior, and it is an area that is growing quickly, Wright says. Flexible hours and the variety of work environments make it highly attractive. Even though the field is growing, there is stiff competition for jobs. Positions are available with government and private research facilities, with conservation groups and zoos, and at colleges and universities. Those who have a PhD will have the best opportunities. Self-employment as a counselor for pet owners is another option.

Income varies tremendously, depending on location and the demand for such services. For behaviorists working for someone else, salaries generally range from $35,000 to $90,000 per year. Behaviorists who are self-employed may earn more or less than this range, depending on their location, skills, and ability to promote their businesses.

BEHAVIORIST RESOURCES

- American Veterinary Society of Animal Behavior, www.avsabonline.org/avsabonline
- Animal Behavior Society, www.animalbehavior.org
- *Animal Behaviour* (journal), http://asab.nottingham.ac.uk/pubs/journal.php
- ASPCA Animal Behavior Center, www.aspca.org/about-us/aspca_animal_behavior_center
- Association of Animal Behavior Professionals, www.associationofanimalbehavior professionals.com
- Bucknell University, Animal Behavior Program, www.bucknell.edu/AnimalBehavior.xml
- Companion Animal Sciences Institute, www.casinstitute.com
- Emory University, Neuroscience and Animal Behavior, www.psychology.emory.edu/nab
- Indiana University, Center for the Integrative Study of Animal Behavior, www.indiana.edu/~animal
- International Association of Animal Behavior Consultants, www.iaabc.org
- *Journal of Comparative Psychology*, www.apa.org/pubs/journals/com/index.aspx
- Patricia McConnell, www.theotherendoftheleash.com
- University of North Texas, Department of Behavior Analysis, www.pacs.unt.edu/behavior-analysis

SECTION 3

Veterinary Medicine

Becoming a general practitioner in a private practice is not the only career path for veterinarians, although it's the first one most people think of. The field of veterinary medicine is highly diverse and offers many opportunities that aren't often considered. Veterinarians may find work with pet-food manufacturers, pharmaceutical companies, animal-welfare departments, federal and state agencies, the military, and colleges and universities. Some veterinarians choose to specialize in particular fields, such as dentistry or opthamology. Veterinary specialists offer a level of medical care that rivals anything available in top hospitals for people.

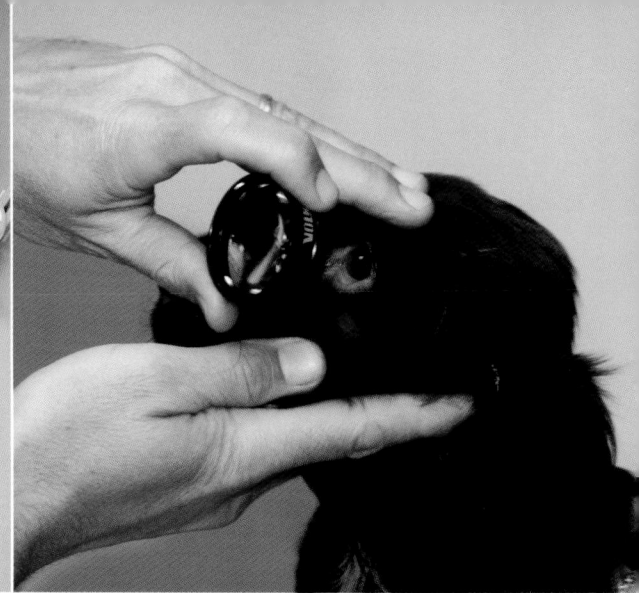
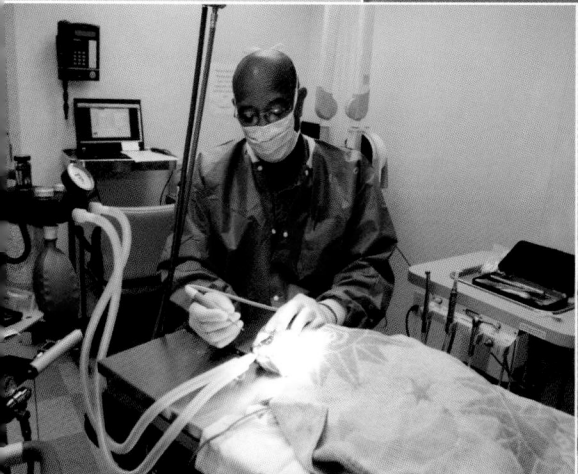

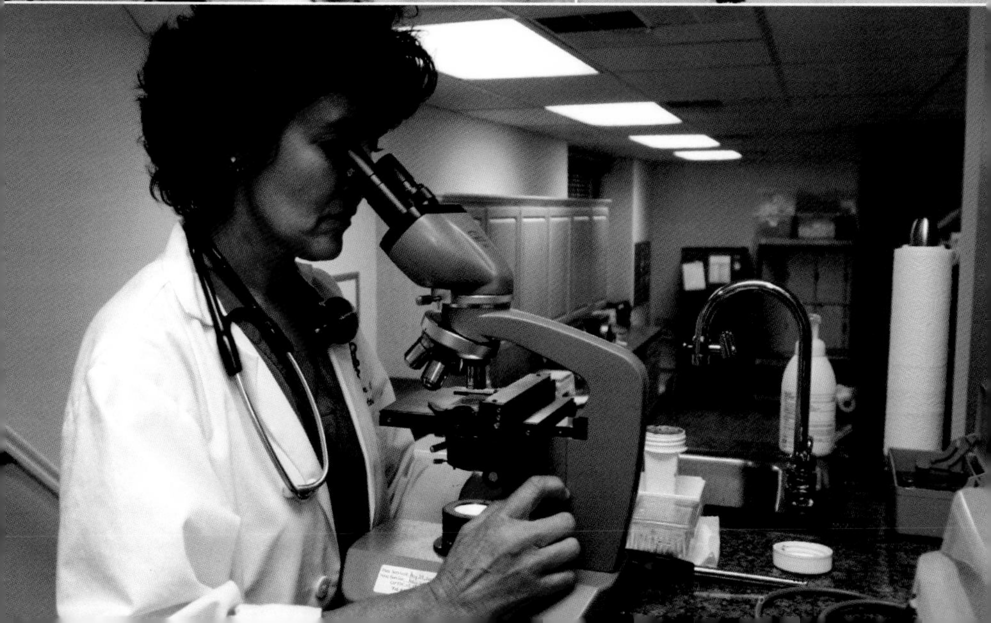

CHAPTER 7

Becoming a Veterinarian

Veterinary medicine is an appealing profession for anyone who has an interest in science and medicine and a desire to care for the health of dogs, cats, and other animals. When you also consider the expected employment growth rate of 33 percent between 2008 and 2018, it's no surprise that a career in veterinary medicine was named as one of the fifty best careers of 2010 by *U.S. News and World Report*. But becoming a veterinarian requires persistence and dedication, as well as years of hard work in veterinary school.

What Veterinarians Do

Veterinarians provide health care for animals of all types. The majority work in private practices, caring for small animals, such as dogs, cats, birds, and guinea pigs. Others work with large animals, such as horses and livestock, or care for animals in zoos. The medical equipment that is available to and used by veterinarians ranges from the basic stethoscope and standard surgical instruments to sophisticated radiographic and ultrasound equipment.

In a private practice, expect to work fifty or more hours each week. Veterinarians at emergency clinics work nights and weekends, and some private-practice veterinarians work at least one weekend day and are on call outside regular office hours.

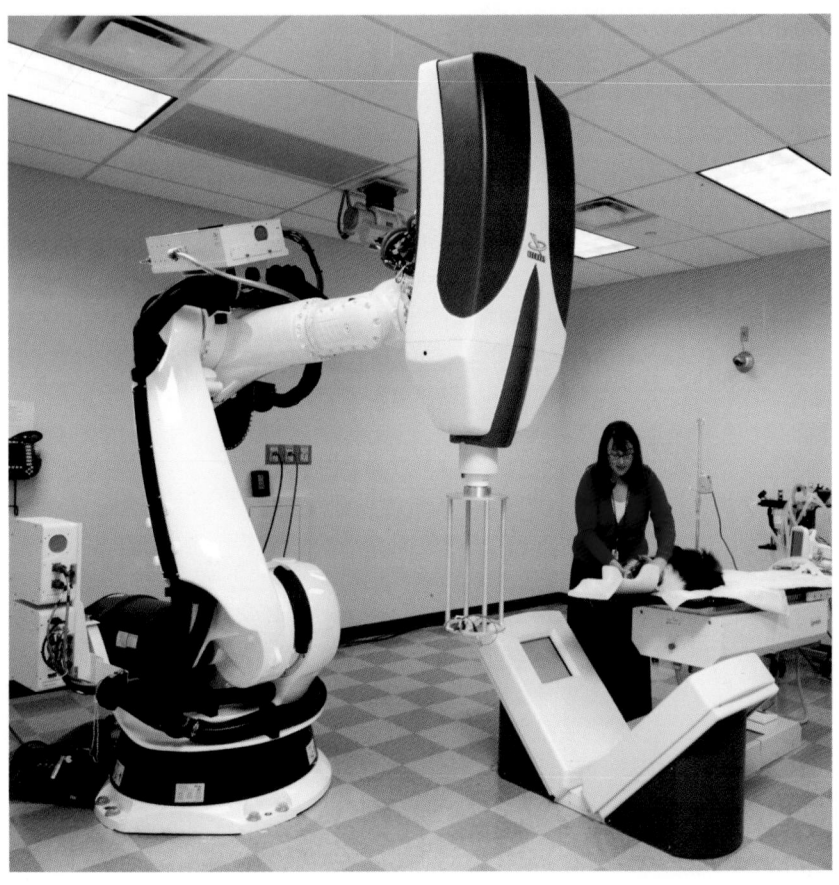

Sarah Charney, DVM, radiation oncology and oncology specialist, prepares a Shetland Sheepdog for the CyberKnife Robotic Radiosurgery treatment for tumors.

While it's satisfying to return sick or injured animals to health and help keep pets and working animals at the peak of wellness, the life of a veterinarian can be emotionally stressful. Veterinarians must deal with anxious owners, help people manage the costs of pet care, and euthanize animals that are very old or cannot be helped medically. The job can also be physically dangerous. Veterinarians are sometimes scratched, bitten, or otherwise injured by aggressive, frightened, or hurt animals, although advances in tranquilizers and technology make it easier to work with large or fractious animals. Despite these challenges, most people who become veterinarians find working with and caring for animals to be rewarding.

Maintaining a balance between their professional lives and their home lives is crucial for veterinarians and everyone else in the working world, says Sally Perea, DVM. "I think this is a personal choice, and I have made it a priority to have good balance in my life. It is easy for anybody in any career to make work their life. However, if you prioritize your life correctly, you should be able to create a good balance."

Who Veterinarians Are

In the age of globalization, veterinarians must have a wider knowledge of science, economics, politics, and societal trends, especially as these areas apply to public health issues. Veterinary schools and employers will be looking for people with good leadership skills and ethics, business and crisis management abilities, an awareness of how the law affects animals, and excellent written and verbal communication skills.

The science that veterinarians need to know encompasses ecosystems, comparative medicine, bioinformatics (the application of information technology to the field of molecular biology), genomics (the study of the genomes of organisms), and proteomics (the large-scale study of the structures and functions of proteins). They must also be able to coordinate and communicate information between scientists, policy makers, and the public.

As society's relationship with animals evolves, veterinarians will take the lead as spokespeople on animal issues, contributing to public-policy development and awareness of the correlation between the food system and human and animal health.

Camp Vet

The Arizona Animal Welfare League and SPCA has a summer program called Camp Vet for those age twelve to seventeen who are interested in veterinary careers. Among the activities included in the week-long program are watching spay/neuter surgeries, dissecting organs, studying anatomy, and learning pet first-aid techniques. It's not unusual for "campers" to return year after year.

A similar program takes place at the Cummings School of Veterinary Medicine at Tufts University, in North Grafton, Massachusetts. Open to adults and college, high-school, and middle-school students, the Adventures in Veterinary Medicine program allows attendees to hear lectures, participate in laboratory sessions, and get hands-on experience with animals.

VETERINARIAN

A veterinarian should have the following characteristics:

- ○ Adaptability
- ○ A love for and understanding of animals
- ○ An aptitude for the sciences, particularly biology
- ○ An inquiring mind
- ○ Compassion
- ○ Creative-thinking skills
- ○ Good decision-making and leadership skills
- ○ Good people skills for communicating with pet owners
- ○ Hand-eye coordination
- ○ Manual dexterity
- ○ Keen observation skills
- ○ Tolerance for a noisy work environment
- ○ Willingness and ability to help people deal with grief and loss

Education and Training

People who want to become veterinarians must earn a doctor of veterinary medicine (DVM) or veterinary medical doctor (VMD, which the University of Pennsylvania grants) degree from one of the twenty-eight accredited colleges of veterinary medicine. Competition for entry into any of these four-year programs is keen. There are sometimes four or five applicants for every opening at a veterinary school. Statistically, it's estimated that one in three applicants to veterinary schools nationwide is accepted. Expect the application process to take approximately six months.

Undergraduate School

Surprisingly, a bachelor's degree isn't necessarily a requirement, but depending on the school, applicants must have forty-five to ninety semester hours at the undergraduate level, and a bachelor's degree does increase the likelihood of acceptance by a veterinary school. Many undergraduates start applying during junior year and reapply the following year if necessary. Good grades and a strong foundation in science are advantageous. The higher your grade-point average, the better your chances, but relevant work experience also counts.

What's the best undergraduate degree for a pre-veterinary program? There aren't any specific requirements, but most pre-veterinary students focus on the sciences. Veterinary medical colleges typically require classes in organic and inorganic chemistry, physics, biochemistry, general biology, animal biology, animal nutrition, genetics, vertebrate embryology, cellular biology, microbiology, zoology, and systemic physiology. As for math, some programs require calculus, while others require only statistics, college algebra and trigonometry, or precalculus.

Most veterinary medical colleges look for well-rounded students who have taken core courses in English or literature, the social sciences, and the humanities. It's also a good idea to take classes in accounting, finance, and marketing. Veterinary practices are small businesses, and those business skills will help you succeed if you choose to set up your own practice. See the resources in the back of the book for a listing of colleges and universities with animal science or pre-veterinary programs.

Jill Richardson majored in chemistry during college and was admitted to veterinary school after her junior year. She obtained her bachelor's degree after entering vet school. "I transferred my credits from my first year in vet school back to obtain an animal science degree," she explains. She recommends that students "pick a degree that can be used for other careers. There's not much that you can really do with an animal science degree. With a degree in chemistry, I could have considered many other opportunities. You have to take a certain number of credits in various subjects, but you could have almost any major. I would recommend taking business classes and communication classes in addition."

Sally Perea, DVM, relaxes with Lupin, whom she saved from a shoe box left outside a dog grooming shop.

Sally Perea, who attended the University of

California at Davis, majored in animal science, with a minor in nutrition. She says that the major has its pros and cons. "At UC Davis, most of the animal science majors were pre-vet. I think that this major does help prepare and train you for the things that you need to know for veterinary school; however, it doesn't necessarily put you at an advantage over other applicants. The application committees like to see uniqueness in the applicants. However, there are specific courses that are required to apply to veterinary school, so it is a good idea to select a major that includes these needed courses."

Before you invest years of hard work and thousands of dollars in tuition and fees, make sure that you really want to be a veterinarian. Volunteering or otherwise getting experience in the field to truly find out if veterinary medicine is the right career for you is important. "I've heard many veterinarians say that being a veterinarian is the greatest profession in the world, but I don't necessarily think it is the greatest profession for everyone," Perea says. "You really need to get exposure and find out if it is for you."

If you decide that it is, start doing everything you can to prepare yourself. Because her father was a veterinarian, Perea had a head start in this area. In addition to helping out at her father's clinic, she started building her experience for admission to veterinary school while in college.

"At this stage, it is important for students to gain breadth of experience in both research and clinical settings," Perea says. "I volunteered at the UC Davis Veterinary Medical Teaching Hospital to gain more experience in a clinical setting. I also tried some new things, such as volunteering at a wildlife rehabilitation center over the summer. Finally, I got involved with a research project, which led me to run my own research project during my final year of undergrad. The tough thing at this stage is that pre-vet students have to distinguish themselves from other applicants. Grades and test scores are very important, but experience and well-roundedness are just as important. So you definitely have to start preparing early."

Veterinary School

Not every state has its own veterinary school to which you can apply as a resident. States without veterinary colleges generally have agreements with veterinary schools in neighboring states to accept a certain percentage of the other states' residents as students.

In addition to satisfying pre-veterinary course requirements, applicants must submit test scores from the Graduate Record Examination (GRE), the

Portrait of Two Veterinarians

Some people grow up knowing that they want to be veterinarians. Other people come to the profession later in life. Veterinarian Sally Perea (*pictured*) is one who was exposed to and became interested in a veterinary career at a very early age.

"My father is a veterinarian, so I grew up with a good exposure to the profession," Perea says. "I spent a lot of time in his clinic, helping out around the office and with the animals. My favorite thing was watching him do surgery and helping out with emergencies, such as emergency cesarean sections when they would need lots of hands with the new puppies.

"The thing that interested me the most about the profession was the investigative aspect of seeing a patient, running tests, and trying to determine a diagnosis and treatment plan. It seemed to me like a career that would never be boring and would always require learning about new developments and advancements."

Perea didn't rule out other career options, and she spent her high-school years ensuring that she would have as many opportunities as possible for college so that she would be able to choose any field of interest. To that end, she maintained good grades and acquired experience in sports, clubs, and student government.

Jill Richardson also wanted to be a veterinarian from the time she was very young. "I was always interested in animals more than dolls or toys," she says. "I think most veterinarians will say something similar to that."

Richardson began preparing for her career even before high school. Her first "job" in the field was as a volunteer at a veterinary clinic.

"I was thirteen. The veterinarian I worked for was a recent graduate, and working in his clinic gave me firsthand experience with this career. I would work all day on Saturdays, mainly cleaning up diarrhea and vomit, but I also had the opportunity to monitor surgery. The first time I watched a spay, I got very queasy and had to sit down for a few minutes to regain my composure. Fortunately, I got over it."

By the time she entered veterinary school, Richardson had worked part-time at several veterinary clinics. Her duties ranged from cleaning up to working behind the reception desk to assisting in surgery. Being able to list that kind of experience on a veterinary-school application is priceless.

Veterinary College Admission Test (VCAT), or the Medical College Admission Test (MCAT). The test you take depends on the preference of the colleges to which you are applying. Be prepared to provide letters of recommendation, including at least one from a veterinarian.

As discussed in the previous section, veterinary and animal experience will play a role in determining whether you're admitted to veterinary school. Formal experience, such as work with veterinarians or scientists in clinics, agribusiness, research, or some area of health science, is particularly advantageous.

Less formal experience, such as working with animals on a farm, in a stable, or at an animal shelter, is also helpful. Even if you don't work for them, get to know veterinarians in your community by talking to them about the profession. They are the ones who will be writing letters of recommendation for you.

Once you are in veterinary school, you can generally expect to spend the first two years in the classroom, studying physiology, anatomy, pathology, and more. Third-year students begin to gain experience in surgery and medicine. The fourth year is spent in rotations through the

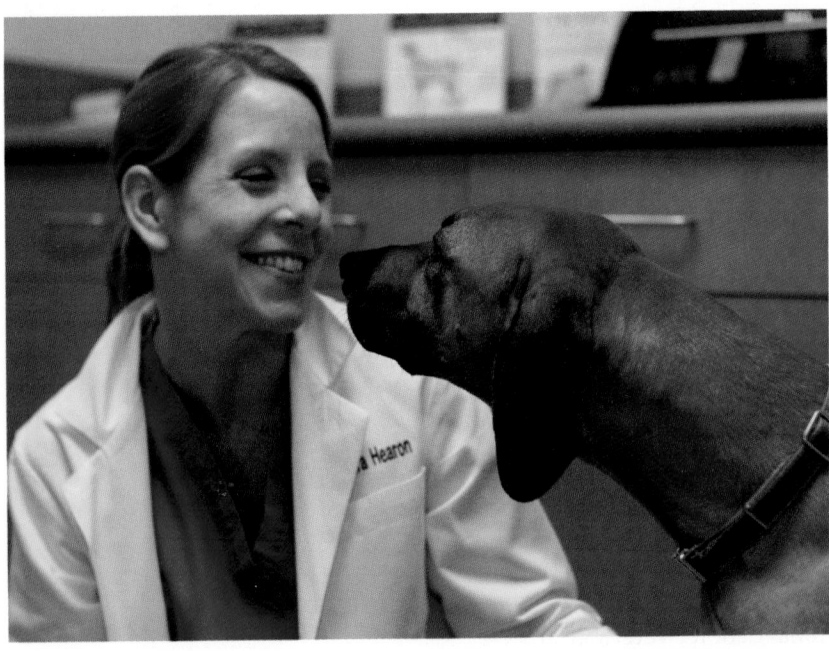

Surgery resident Kendra Hearon, VMD, takes a moment to get to know her Rhodesian Ridgeback patient.

Josephine Deubler, VMD: Veterinarian of Firsts

In 1938 M. Josephine Deubler became the first woman to graduate from the University of Pennsylvania School of Veterinary Medicine (UPSVM). She was also the first female to earn a graduate degree from the University of Pennsylvania, the first female member of the Pennsylvania Veterinary Medicine Association, and the first veterinarian to judge Best in Show at Westminster Kennel Club Dog Show. Deubler joined the faculty of the UPSVM in 1946 and remained there for half a century. In 1971 she instituted the University of Pennsylvania Annual Canine and Feline Symposium, the first veterinarian-breeder seminars in the country, which continue to educate dog fanciers in the United States. To honor Deubler's fifty years of service, the university named the Josephine Deubler Genetic Disease Testing Laboratory.

In the dog show world, Deubler (*above with show judge Samuel Draper*) was considered a "pillar in the sport," as described by former handler and judge Peter Green. She was a noted terrier breeder and a respected show judge, and in 1977 she became the show chairperson of the legendary Montgomery Kennel Club Dog Show, the world's most prestigious all-terrier event. She received the AKC's Lifetime Achievement Award in 2003, and the university established the Dr. Josephine Deubler Deans Scholarship to memorialize her contributions to animals. She died in 2009.

different specialties as well as in large- and small-animal clinics. Elective courses taken during the fourth year may be spent in veterinary practices, gaining real-world experience; in shelters; or in zoos. Over the entire four-year period, you can expect to spend approximately 4,000 hours in classrooms, labs, and clinics. That's approximately nine classes each quarter or semester.

Veterinary school is expensive. The costs for tuition, books, fees, and supplies can top $100,000 for the four-year period. The average educational debt for veterinarians was nearly $120,000 in 2010, according to the American Veterinary Medical Association. New graduates often face staggering student loan bills.

Barkworthy BITE

AN OPEN MIND

"Always keep an open mind to opportunities out there. A veterinarian's training is very broad. Veterinarians are very adaptable, ready learners, so the sky is the limit in terms of how we can apply our skills. Many of the skills we learn as veterinarians are translatable to other areas, things like the communications skills learned in talking to clients or the creativity required in working in a barn at three in the morning and maybe not having everything you would have if you were in a more-controlled environment. All of those skills are very easily applied to other areas that veterinarians can be very effective in."

—Katherine Feldman, DVM

Specialization

Only about 10 percent of veterinarians have met the requirements to become a specialist in a particular area. Beyond an undergraduate education and four years of veterinary school, board-certified veterinary specialists have an additional three to five years of advanced training in a particular area of veterinary medicine. Their knowledge and skills in a particular field have been evaluated and recognized by individual specialty organizations that have been accredited by the American Veterinary Medical Association (AVMA).

Veterinarians can choose to specialize in any of the following areas: anesthesiology, behavior, cardiology, dentistry, dermatology, emergency and critical care, epidemiology, internal medicine, microbiology (which encompasses bacteriology/mycology, immunology, and virology), neurology, nutrition, oncology, ophthalmology, pathology, pharmacology, radiology, surgery, theriogenology (reproduction), and toxicology—and that's not even a complete list. There are also specialties in avian, equine, and feline medicine; food-animal, dairy, and swine health management; laboratory animal medicine; and zoology. There is a shortage of specialists, especially in the teaching field, so just about any specialty is a good career opportunity.

Licensing and Continuing Education

Once they graduate, veterinarians must meet state licensing requirements. With some exceptions for veterinarians working for certain federal agencies or state governments, all states and the District of Columbia require that veterinarians be licensed before they can practice. Requirements to become licensed include successful completion of the DVM/VMD degree or equivalent education and a passing grade on a national board examination. A board exam consists of hundreds of questions and takes a full day to complete. Most states also require a passing grade on an exam that covers related laws and regulations of that state, and some test clinical competency as well. And just because you're licensed to practice in one state doesn't mean you're qualified to practice in another. Generally, you must first take and pass the new state's examination before being allowed to practice there.

Graduation and licensing aren't the end of education for veterinarians. There are frequent advances in veterinary medicine, and most states have continuing-education requirements for licensed veterinarians, which may involve attending classes or otherwise demonstrating knowledge of recent veterinary advances. For instance, state-licensed veterinarians in Oregon must earn at least thirty hours of continuing education every two years. Most veterinarians gain continuing-education credits when they attend seminars at local, regional, or national veterinary conferences. Veterinarians also spend a lot of time reading veterinary journals. In this career, the homework never ends.

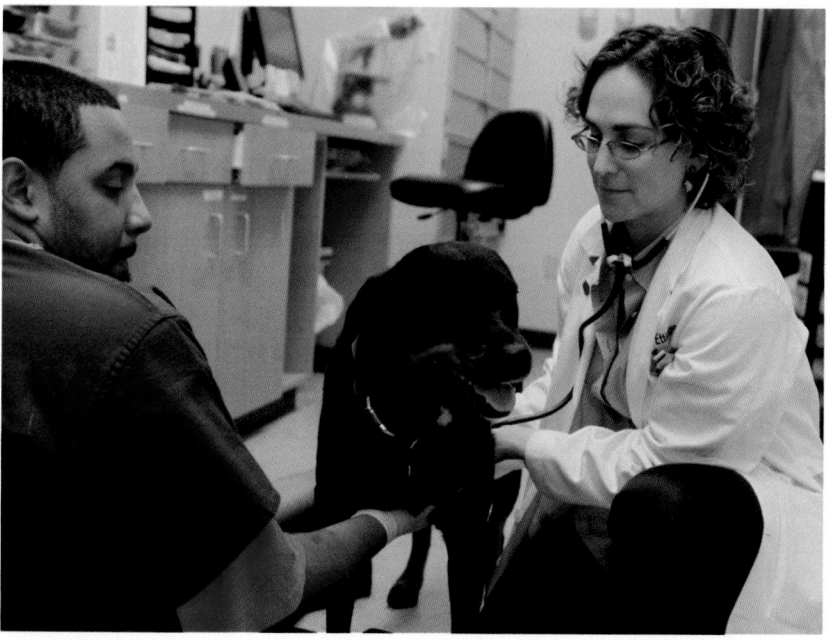

With the assistance of one of her vet techs, oncology specialist Susan Ettinger, DVM, examines a Rottweiler.

Employment Outlook

Some 59,700 veterinarians were employed in 2008. Most were of them self-employed or were salaried employees of a veterinary practice. Other employers of veterinarians include the U.S. government, chiefly the Departments of Agriculture, Health and Human Services, and Homeland Security; state and local governments; colleges of veterinary medicine; medical schools; research laboratories; animal-food companies; and pharmaceutical companies. A few veterinarians work full-time for zoos, but most zoo veterinarians are private practitioners providing part-time services.

Through 2018, veterinary medicine is expected to be one of the fastest growing professions, increasing much faster than the average rate for all occupations. Surveys and projections indicate a steady demand for veterinary medical services. Because there are only twenty-eight schools of veterinary medicine, there are a limited number of graduates each year. Those newly minted veterinarians can expect very good job opportunities, not only in private practice but also in animal welfare, in areas associated with biomedical and environmental quality, biosecurity, public health, regulatory medicine, and agricultural-animal health.

Quality of pet food and human health are also concerns that involve veterinarians, so jobs in those fields will likely increase as well. If you have an interest in working for the federal or state government, seek training in food safety, animal health and welfare, and public health and epidemiology. A currently inadequate supply of veterinarians in food-supply medicine (that is, dealing with animals used for food), biomedical research, public health, large-animal medicine, and companion-animal medicine means that good jobs will be available in those areas.

Veterinary medicine is a career in transition. Societal changes in demographics as well as approaches to politics, the environment, the economy, technology, and disease will all significantly affect the future of veterinary medicine and the education of veterinary students. Their concern for the health and well-being of animals, as well as their relationships with people, makes veterinarians critical to public health not only locally but also nationally and internationally. The convergence of animal health and public health in the area of zoonotic and newly emerging diseases is a critical link to societal well-being, according to a 2007 report in the *Journal of Veterinary Medical Education*, which states that research in veterinary science transcends species boundaries and is critical to the protection of public health. The need for good veterinarians has never been more important.

As in most professions, salaries depend on the chosen field, time since graduation, and geographic location. Small-animal veterinarians tend to make slightly more than large-animal veterinarians, and veterinarians on the East and West Coasts tend to make more than those in the South or Midwest. A veterinarian in Los Angeles might have a salary range of $66,000 to more than $94,000. Of course, living expenses in areas are also different, so such variations are not always as significant as they appear.

New graduates who enter private practice can expect an average starting salary of about $65,000 per year. For most veterinarians in the United States, that salary increases to more than $70,000 per year within a few years. Veterinary salaries range from $41,635 to more than $143,660. In 2009, the average annual salary for veterinarians in the federal government was approximately $93,500.

For veterinarians employed by a clinic or animal hospital, other factors to look at beyond salary are the length of the work week, the option for buy-in or corporation-share ownership, and the benefits package, which might include such things as a 401K match, health insurance with a health savings account, dental insurance, or a continuing-education stipend.

While compensation varies significantly, superior professional service usually is rewarded by an appropriate income. But the greatest reward for most veterinarians, is not measured in dollars. Says Perea, "The best thing about being a veterinarian is seeing the positive results you can have in individual pet's and people's lives. It is great to see a sick pet recover, and see how you are able to help out an important family member."

BECOMING A VETERINARIAN RESOURCES

- American Animal Hospital Association, http://aahanet.org/OtherSites/jobbank.aspx
- American Association of Housecall Veterinarians, www.homevets.org
- American Association of Wildlife Veterinarians, www.aawv.net/index.html
- American Veterinary Medical Association, www.avma.org
- Arizona Animal Welfare League and SPCA, Camp Vet, www.aawl.org/ed/ED_Camp_Vet_Summer.asp
- Association of American Veterinary Medical Colleges, www.aavmc.org
- Tufts Cummings School of Veterinary Medicine, Adventures in Veterinary Medicine program, www.tufts.edu/vet/avm/
- University of California, Davis, Koret Shelter Medicine Program, www.sheltermedicine.com
- University of Florida, Maddie's Shelter Medicine Program, www.ufsheltermedicine.com
- University of Florida, Veterinary Forensic Science Distance Education, www.forensicscience.ufl.edu

See appendix for a list of veterinary colleges.

CHAPTER 8

Private Practice and Other Choices

A newly licensed veterinarian usually begins his or her career in an established practice. Once new veterinarians gain some experience and save some money, they may choose to set up their own practices or purchase established ones.

Some veterinarians choose to work for practices owned by large corporations; that way, they can practice veterinary medicine without the headaches of management. Some of those practices are located in big-box pet-supply stores that offer veterinary services.

Corporate-owned practices can afford advanced equipment, nice facilities, and extensive advertising, but they often have strict guidelines on how a case should proceed. If you consider veterinary medicine an art as well as a science, you may find life in a corporate practice too restrictive.

Veterinarians can also look to careers in academia, government, and the military. All of these options offer interesting and sometimes lucrative opportunities for veterinarians to contribute to animal and human well-being. For someone with a yen for travel, this type of work can take you all over the world. Before you limit your choices, take a look at all of the options.

Private Practice

Private-practice veterinarians can no longer expect their patients to be only dogs or cats. These days, they can also expect to care for pet birds;

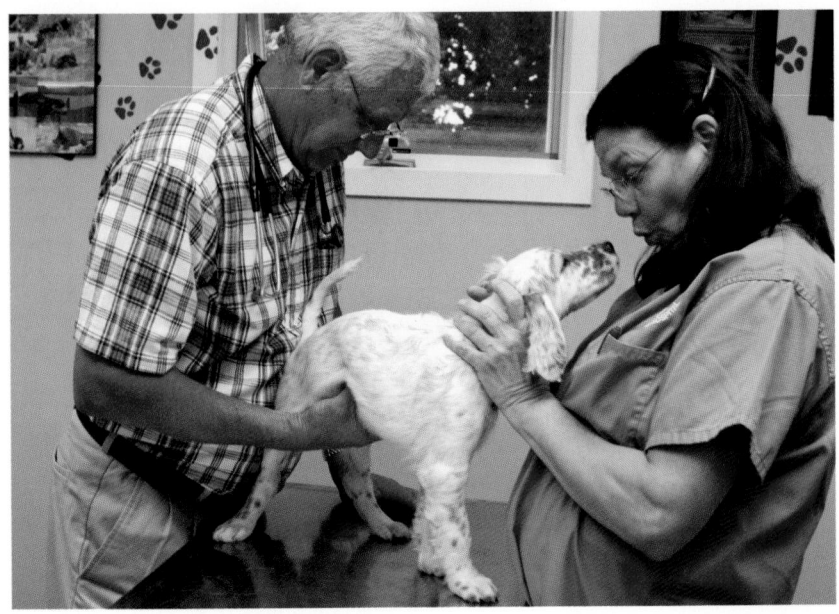

While a vet tech provides distraction, veterinarian John W. O'Neil examines a puppy at the Milford Animal Hospital, a private practice in Milford, Connecticut.

"pocket pets" such as hamsters, guinea pigs and gerbils; and aquarium fish. Rural veterinarians with a mixed or livestock practice may encounter not only dogs, cats, horses, cows, hogs, sheep, and goats but also llamas, ostriches, and catfish. Approximately 75 percent of veterinarians find their niche in some area of private practice, with the majority of them primarily treating small animals.

The advantages of owning a private practice include the ability to determine the type of practice you want to have—for instance, only dogs or cats, exotic animals, or large animals—and to set your own working hours. On the downside, it's expensive to set up or purchase a private practice because of the costs of equipment, office space, and staff salaries. Private-practice veterinarians must be involved with hiring employees, providing benefits, setting up retirement plans, and other management details. It also takes time and effort to build a steady clientele. For these reasons, owning a private practice calls for excellent business and communication skills.

Private practices also vary depending on location. Urban and suburban veterinarians usually practice in clinics or hospitals, although some may offer a house-call service. Rural veterinarians, especially those with large-animal

A Private Practice Veterinarian in Public Life

What Marty Becker loves about his job is that his days range from the miraculous to the mundane. "I love the sweet smell of puppy breath; I love a kinetic mass of kittens; I love the euphoria that comes from helping to extend an older pet's life."

When Becker isn't treating pets at North Idaho Animal Hospital in Sandpoint, Idaho, or at Lakewood Animal Hospital in Coeur d'Alene, Idaho, he's flying around the country to educate pet owners through TV, Web, and speaking engagements and conferences. He offers advice on ABC's *Good Morning America* and the syndicated *The Dr. Oz Show*, on which he appears regularly, and on his podcast for ABC News Now, *The Pet Doctor with Dr. Marty Becker*. He also works on books and articles with writing partner Gina Spadafori and is an adjunct professor at his alma mater, the Washington State University College of Veterinary Medicine, and at the colleges of veterinary medicine at Colorado State University and the University of Missouri.

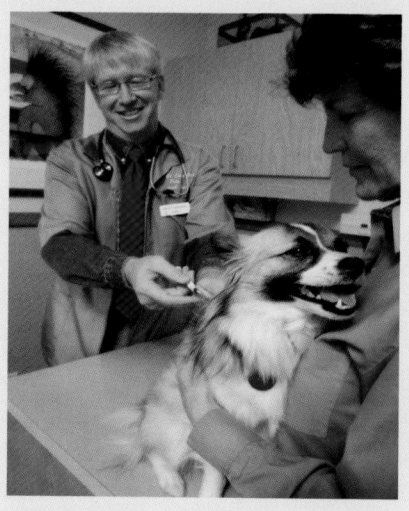

Nationally known veterinarian Marty Becker vaccinates a patient in his office in Coeur d'Alene, Idaho.

Yet his first love remains the challenge of divining a pet's problems through reading the animal's behavior, vocalizations, and body language. "It's incredibly rewarding to advocate for them, to crack the code of what's wrong, and then to work to prevent unnecessary pain, prevent problems where possible, and initiate a prognosis and a treatment plan."

Unlike medical doctors, who focus on a single species and sometimes on a single discipline, veterinarians must be knowledgeable about many different health problems in multiple species. Dr. Becker recently treated a 100-pound tortoise with stomatitis. "I hadn't seen a tortoise in twenty years," he says. "It's just crazy the amount of knowledge you have to have."

practices, are more likely to spend time driving to their far-flung clients, working out of fully equipped trucks or vans. They may be called out to farms or ranches at all hours of the day or night, in all types of weather.

For private-practice veterinarians, a typical day might involve meeting with clients and examining animals; administering vaccinations to puppies; advising owners about nutrition, behavior, and breeding; diagnosing illnesses; treating wounds; performing surgery; reading lab results and reporting on them to owners; and euthanizing animals that are terminally ill or very old with poor quality of life. They must also read veterinary journals to keep up with the latest news in veterinary medicine and attend conferences to earn continuing-education credits. Some veterinarians present educational programs to local groups of pet owners, donate time to low-cost spay/neuter groups, or become politically involved in issues facing animal owners.

Corporations

Large corporations in pharmaceutical and other industries employ many veterinarians. Opportunities include drug-development work and technical and regulatory positions. Veterinarian Jill Richardson works for a large animal-health company in the area of pharmacovigilance. She answers technical questions about the company's product line and reports information through regulatory affairs.

"It's a desk job, but I have to use my veterinary skills and the skills I learned in toxicology to be successful at it," she says. She didn't specialize in toxicology but has advanced training in the field. In a former job, she worked at a poison-control center for animals. The skills she learned there have helped her succeed in technical services and pharmacovigilance.

On a typical day in her current job, she comes in at 9 a.m. and logs in to the phone lines and takes calls and questions throughout the day.

"Sometimes I don't have the answer and have to do some investigation and call them back. I have to enter all the information into the software program. Once in a while, I have to travel for training or to visit a veterinary school or attend a veterinary conference. When I'm there, I represent the company and tell people about our products. Sometimes I do presentations about the products or the diseases they are used for."

Sally Perea, who also works for a corporation, says the ability to work as part of a team is an important skill to have. "Working with a large pet-food company, the most important thing that I have found is the importance of working as a team. I am able to offer my expertise in veterinary medicine and nutrition, but must also work with many other people that are knowledgeable in other areas, such as food science, production, and business management. Luckily, we have a great team and a good depth in expertise, so this has been more of an opportunity than a challenge."

Academia

For veterinarians with an interest in teaching, research, service, and administration, academia beckons. The field of education has many excellent career opportunities in veterinary schools, medical schools, and other colleges and universities. An academic career can permit a veterinarian to combine research, hands-on pet care, and teaching.

Depending on their positions, veterinarians on the faculty of a university may spend 80 percent of their time doing research, with the remaining time available for clinical practice and teaching, or 80 percent of their time in clinical practice and instruction, with the remainder devoted to research or administrative work.

Administrative Attributes

Large private practices are run by medical directors. Administrators, whether they are directors of large veterinary hospitals or deans of veterinary schools, must have demonstrated leadership ability, strong mentoring and team building skills, and excellent communication skills as well as business-management skills. Throughout your education and in practice, look for opportunities to build those skills if you want to take your career in an administrative direction.

At the administrative level, deans of veterinary schools oversee veterinarians, researchers, faculty members, staff, and students, a challenging task that brings many rewards. A dean spends his or her day attending meetings with associate deans and department chairs, managing programs, and communicating with the local government and other outside agencies. When a busy schedule permits, the dean may teach a class or two, affording him or her another way to stay in touch with students.

Another administrative position in academia is that of department chair. A department chair supervises all of the faculty members in his or her department, helps guide their careers, and is responsible for teaching and research programs. As with any management position, the skills needed include conflict resolution and the ability to handle personnel issues.

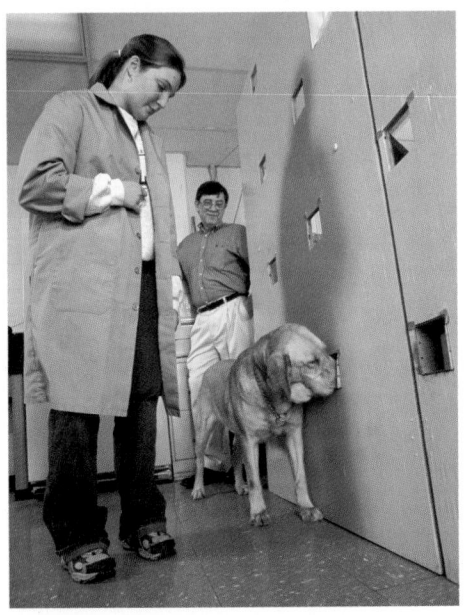

Under the direction of associate professor Larry Myers, Auburn University veterinary student Erica Blackman trains a Labrador Retriever to sniff water samples for compounds that produce off-flavors in catfish.

Federal, State, and Local Agencies

Many federal agencies, such as the Food and Drug Administration (FDA) and the U.S. Department of Agriculture (USDA), hire veterinarians for jobs in public health and research, animal welfare and safety, disease control, epidemiology, and more. Some veterinarians are commissioned officers in the U.S. Public Health Service (USPHS) or various branches of the U.S. Armed Forces. The USDA employs more veterinarians than any other single agency. Most of these jobs focus on the prevention and control of infectious and parasitic diseases and food-safety inspections; tasks include writing and enforcing regulations and advising academia, industry, and professional groups on the effectiveness of food-safety controls. The USPHS employs veterinarians in the development and administration of programs concerned with the control of animal diseases transmissible to humans.

In all of these positions, veterinarians are more likely to work with people and paperwork than pets. For veterinarians who are OK with that, government service is a growth field. There's a critical need for the services of veterinarians. A 2009 report from the Government Accountability Office says there's a dangerous shortage of veterinarians to fill essential positions in the federal government, a problem that could seriously affect animal and public health.

State governments employ state veterinarians to enforce laws and regulations to protect animal health, as well as to advise the state on animal diseases that may affect human health. State veterinarians also investigate

John M. Olin: Hip (and Elbow) Dogman

"Well-known inventor, industrialist, philanthropist, conservationist, and sportsman" is how the Orthopedic Foundation for Animals (OFA) describes its founder John M. Olin. Olin's legacy lives on at such universities as Harvard, Yale, Georgetown, Stanford, Columbia, and Washington University, whose libraries, programs, or fellowships bear his name. Beyond his business and philanthropy, Olin was a dog man and participated with his Labrador Retrievers in field trials. His most famous Lab was King Buck, the National Championship Stakes winner in 1952 and 1953, whose likeness was immortalized by the U.S. Post Office on a postage stamp. After a number of his dogs were struck with the debilitating disease known as hip dysplasia, Olin set out to rectify the situation and formed the OFA in 1966. Today the OFA maintains databases for purebred dogs for hip dysplasia as well as for at least twenty other diseases. The organization also offers DNA testing for other diseases and databases for cats. Olin's intentions in creating the OFA are reflected in the organization's mission statement: "To improve the health and well being of companion animals through a reduction in the incidence of genetic disease."

In Korea, at a mobile veterinary treatment facility, two veterinarians, Lt. Park Sung-gu and Maj. Michelle Franklin, help load an injured working dog for transport to a recovery area.

outbreaks of such diseases. (See chapter 10.) Municipal governments also hire veterinarians for their public health departments. Their duties involve the sanitary control of meat and milk production and investigation of food-poisoning epidemics. State veterinarians are also involved in the protection of the public—humans and animals—in the event of a natural disaster or a terror attack. Jacob Casper, DVM, is past coordinator of disaster services for the Maryland Department of Agriculture and past cochair of the Maryland Animal Disaster Planning Advisory Committee. These positions called for him to resolve any agricultural or animal-related problems that developed during disasters. The preparation exercises he took part in involved nuclear power plants, winter storms, hurricanes, and terrorism.

Military

Military veterinarians may receive post-DVM training in such areas as public health, pathology, pharmacology, physiology, toxicology, food technology, and laboratory-animal medicine. They help improve animal-care systems in underdeveloped and war-torn countries. Like other government veterinarians, they are more likely to work with policy than pets.

Colonel Donald L. Noah, DVM, who has a specialty in veterinary preventive medicine, is a foreign-animal-disease diagnostician and an international expert on protecting animals and people against biological terrorism. In his job as acting deputy assistant secretary of defense for force health protection and readiness, he directs the development and implementation of policies and programs regarding deployment medicine, health protection, national disaster support, and medical readiness for 2.3 million service members. He frequently speaks on protection against biological terrorism to audiences of veterinarians, students, businesspeople, and government and military officials, stressing the role that veterinarians play in protecting the food supply and public health.

Some military veterinary jobs do involve direct contact with dogs and other animals. The U.S. Army Veterinary Service (AVS) offers career opportunities in public health and food safety and clinical practice. Members of the AVS help care for military working dogs, working animals for various Department of Homeland Security organizations, ceremonial horses, and pets owned by service members.

U.S. Air Force veterinarians serve as public health officers in the Biomedical Science Corps. Their job involves surveillance of disease trends, food-safety practices, and facility sanitation. At air force bases around the world, they manage programs to control occupational illness, food-borne disease, and communicable disease.

Zoos and Beyond

For veterinarians with an interest in wildlife, there are many exciting opportunities. Those who choose to work with wildlife close to home may find careers in zoos, aquariums, and animal parks. Some wildlife veterinarians work at universities or government agencies or for nongovernmental organizations. Others are employed by corporations. A wildlife veterinarian may be employed by the Centers for Disease Control as an international epidemiologist or by a university to study the effects of climate and other environmental changes on wildlife health. Those seeking wider adventure may find themselves performing fieldwork around the world.

PRACTICE CHOICES RESOURCES

- American Animal Hospital Association, www.healthypet.com
- American Veterinary Medical Association, www.avma.org
- Centers for Disease Control, www.cdc.gov/about/opportunities/careers/veterianarian.htm

- U.S. Army Veterinary Service, www.veterinaryservice.army.mil
- U.S. Department of Agriculture, www.aphis.usda.gov/animal_health
- U.S. Public Health Service Commission Corps, www.usphs.gov

CHAPTER 9

Practice Specialties

A veterinarian may choose to be a general practitioner or become a specialist in a certain field, such cardiology, neurology, dermatology, nutrition, or rehabilitation. Of course, general-practice veterinarians do plenty of work in specialist areas. But for uncommon or serious problems—for example, congestive heart failure or skin cancers—a veterinary specialist is needed. Some veterinary careers involve working primarily in large specialty hospitals, university teaching hospitals, or veterinary emergency hospitals. These specialties include anesthesiology and emergency and critical care. Most specialties require additional years of education and training. This chapter discusses a few of the areas in which a veterinarian could specialize. There are many more.

Anesthesiology

Managing pain in companion animals will be one of the defining issues in veterinary medicine in coming decades. Increased demand by owners for pet pain relief has led anesthesiologists to do a better job of recognizing and treating pain in animals, something that in the past was not of great concern. There's much more awareness that animals benefit from pain relief and that different species react differently to individual drugs. Advances in veterinary anesthesiology have led to more, safer, and better uses of pain medications in dogs, cats, and other animals.

Like most specialties, anesthesiology requires a veterinary medical degree, at least one year of postgraduate practice, a three-year residency, and completion of difficult written and oral exams. Specialists have a broad understanding of veterinary anesthesiology and pain management, and they understand the changes in physiology caused by diseases or organ-system abnormalities as well as their effects on anesthetic management and life support. They are prepared to offer cardiopulmonary resuscitation and have the technical skills to provide specialized support and management of critically ill or injured animals in special-care units. Those technical skills include performing tracheotomies; catheterizing arteries and veins; monitoring the depth of anesthesia, local and regional blocks; and administering constant-rate infusions.

While the role of the anesthesiologist doesn't involve "curing" animals, it does allow a veterinarian to contribute materially to an animal's well-being. "Anesthesiology requires

Anesthesiologist Alicia Karas stands in the induction room, where small animals are anesthesized prior to treatment.

intensive understanding of drug pharmacology and cardiology (the way drugs affect the heart), as well as multitasking," says Alicia Karas, assistant professor of anesthesia at Cummings School of Veterinary Medicine at Tufts University. "The day can range from relatively boring (everything goes OK and the patients are healthy) to nerve-wracking (very sick patients or challenging surgery). At any moment, I have a number of patients under anesthesia, individually cared for by vet students, technicians, or residents."

Anesthesiology is a flexible career, offering different opportunities. Anesthesiology specialists are trained in the capture, physical restraint, and chemical immobilization of various species, including captive and free-ranging animals, so their abilities are useful in zoos, wildlife parks, and wilderness areas. "As a specialist, you can take care of any or all species,"

Karas says. "You can become a zoo-animal or wildlife specialist and be sought after across the world or limit your practice to anesthetizing fancy horses at equine practices. You can be a scientist who studies improved methods of anesthesia or pain management or work in laboratory animal medicine."

Behavior

Some veterinarians treat behavior problems in animals. Such problems can include aggression toward people or other animals; noise phobias, such as fear of thunderstorms or fireworks; and compulsive disorders, such as constant chewing, licking, or tail chasing.

Veterinary behaviorists are experts in domestic- and wild-animal behavior, and they use that knowledge of behavior, combined with learning theory, behavior modification techniques, and sometimes medication to develop treatment plans for companion animals with issues that make them difficult to live with. Veterinary behaviorists are also able to diagnose medical problems that can affect a pet's behavior.

A veterinary behaviorist evaluates an animal's living arrangements, including the people and any other animals with whom the pet lives. He or she looks at how all family members—human and animal—interact with each other, determines whether the pet has any anxiety disorders that may be contributing to the behavior problem, and assesses whether a pet's needs are being met in terms of exercise, nutrition, training, and social interaction. The behaviorist then prepares a plan to help the owners deal with the behavior. It might include changes in the animal's environment and behavior-modification exercises to help the animal learn new ways to cope with situations that trigger the undesirable behavior. If medication is needed, a veterinary behaviorist can prescribe it.

Aspiring veterinary behaviorists must complete an internship and residency at a university with an approved program or at another facility with an approved mentor. The program involves seeing, under supervision, a certain number of cases, writing a scientific paper based on original research and publishing it in a peer-reviewed journal, writing three peer-reviewed case reports, and completing a comprehensive two-day exam.

Terry Curtis, DVM, is a clinical behaviorist in the department of small-animal clinical sciences at the University of Florida. She decided to specialize in behavior after spending time working in a practice devoted to cat care. Many of her clients had cats with behavior problems, and Curtis was often frustrated when she tried to help them because she didn't feel as if she knew enough. But she enjoyed the one-on-one interaction with clients that is such a large part of dealing with behavior problems, and she decided to pursue a residency in the subject at the University of Georgia. The three-year program not only allowed her to complete the requirements to become a veterinary behaviorist but also gave her a master's degree in psychology.

The main challenge in Curtis's work is letting people know that help is available for pets with behavior problems. To that end, she frequently does continuing-education programs for veterinarians and speaks directly to the public, as well as working with clients. She's also concerned about making sure that people get accurate information.

Says Curtis, "One of the more frustrating things is the presence of incorrect and often very dangerous information out there on TV and the Internet. People need to be careful and choose a person with qualifications, not just 'flash.'"

A specialty in veterinary behavior is one with many opportunities in the future. Because people are more likely to view pets as part of the family, they are less likely to consider them disposable and more willing to seek treatment for problems such as behavior issues. There are fewer than fifty board-certified veterinary behaviorists in the United States.

Cardiology

Specialists in this branch of medicine treat animals with diseases of the heart and lungs, such as congestive heart failure, hypertension, dilated and hypertrophic cardiomyopathy, and valvular disorders, as well as lung diseases. After completing advanced training, including training in diagnostic imaging techniques such as echocardiography and angiography, they are certified by the American College of Veterinary Internal Medicine.

Cardiology specialist Sarah Miller was influenced in her career choice not only by her father—a medical cardiologist—but also by the cardiologists she met at Ohio State University, where she attended veterinary school. Before choosing veterinary cardiology over human cardiology, she shadowed several doctors and veterinarians. "All the doctors were jaded, but every veterinarian I shadowed was excited about the work," she says.

Complementary Medicine (Holistic Medicine)

Complementary medicine is the use of nontraditional therapies, such as acupuncture, botanical medicine, chiropractic, and homeopathy. In the past decade, because of client interest and their own experiences, more veterinarians have chosen to integrate these techniques into their practices.

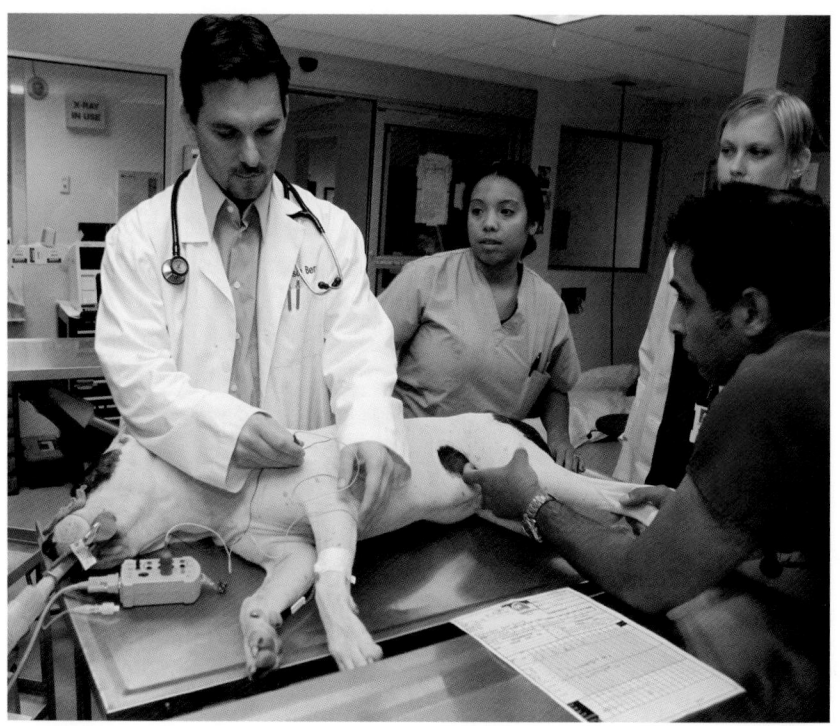

Jason Berg, DVM, internal medicine and neurology specialist, performs tests on a patient under anesthesia.

Texas veterinarian Shawn Messonnier first became interested in complementary medicine, sometimes called holistic medicine, because he saw so many pets with skin diseases, especially allergies. Traditional approaches using corticosteroids and antihistamines provided no more than temporary relief.

"As a result, pets were always in the office for more medication. This approach doesn't benefit the patient, and pet owners and I were increasingly frustrated at the lack of successful therapies," Messonnier says.

He began investigating holistic approaches to skin problems and was excited by the results. Applying the therapies to other health problems yielded good results as well. Now he uses complementary therapies along with more traditional veterinary medicine.

"In my practice, the best results I get for cancer combine them," Messonnier says. "Many of these alternative therapies help chemotherapy and radiation work better. They help minimize side effects from conventional therapies."

Complementary Therapies

Acupuncture is the stimulation of certain points, known as meridians, in the body. It works by stimulating nerve fibers and, in general, the entire nervous system, normalizing nerve function. What acupuncture does, in effect, is assist the body in restoring normal firing patterns in the nerves. This stimulation, which can be done with needles, lasers, water, or pressure, has been shown to help relieve the pain of arthritis, hip dysplasia, and other conditions and to help with some neurological problems. Acupuncture has been well researched in many species, and the neurophysiologic changes it causes are thoroughly documented. It is also one of the safest therapies. Veterinary acupuncturists are certified by the International Veterinary Acupuncture Society, which offers extensive coursework.

Botanical medicine is the use of Chinese or Western herbal remedies to treat illness. Two useful herbs are milk thistle, used to treat liver disease, and hawthorn, used in conjunction with heart-disease medications. Because cats and dogs metabolize chemicals differently than humans do, and because metabolism can vary greatly from one animal to the next, learning about the safe use of herbs can take a lifetime.

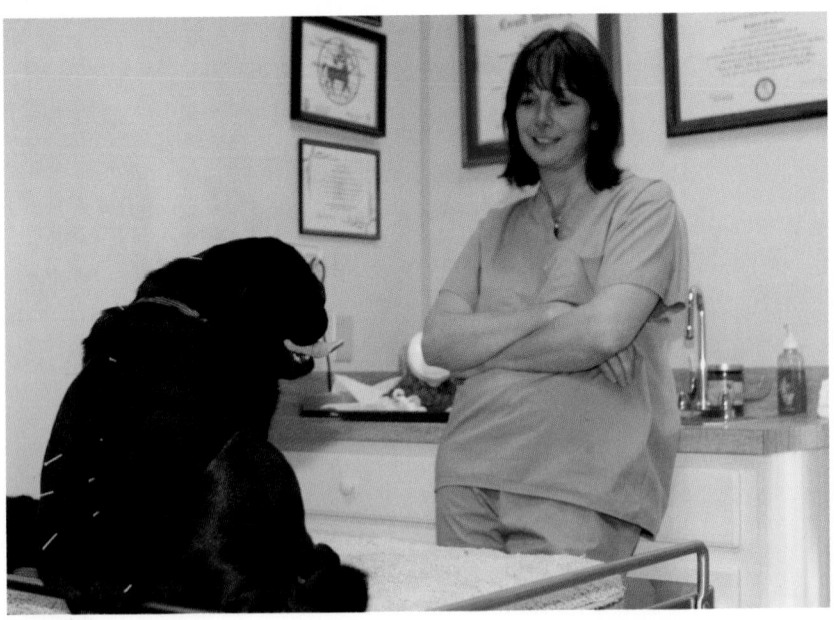

Certified veterinary acupuncturist Donna Raditic waits while the treatment takes effect. Raditic also has a degree in animal nutrition and training in veterinary chiropractic care and herbeology.

Chiropractic is the treatment of functional or structural changes in the spine, bones, joints, and muscles that affect the body's biomechanical or neurophysiological workings, possibly causing problems with organ function or general health. Chiropractors treat these malfunctions with *adjustments*, described as specific, quick, controlled thrusts meant to correct the condition. Chiropractic is not necessarily a fix in and of itself. A veterinary chiropractor (that is, a veterinarian who has chiropractic training) must also be able to discern and treat the underlying cause, or the condition will recur.

Chiropractic treatment for animals is taught at several U.S. schools and veterinary colleges. One is Options for Animals in Wellsville, Kansas, founded by Sharon Willoughby, a veterinarian and a chiropractor. Veterinary chiropractors are certified by the American Veterinary Chiropractic Association and the International Veterinary Chiropractic Association.

Homeopathy is the treatment of health problems by administering diluted substances that, if given at full strength to a healthy animal, would produce clinical signs of illness similar to the signs exhibited by a sick animal.

Dentistry

Veterinary dentists perform deep cleaning below the gum line, complicated tooth extractions using specialized equipment, root canals, and orthodontic work such as crowns, which can be important for working animals injured in the line of duty. They may also work with oncologists, internists, and anesthesiologists to diagnose and treat dental disease related to other health problems, such as cancer or lung, heart, and kidney disease.

Board certification in dentistry requires graduation from an accredited veterinary college, a year of internship or other veterinary-practice experience, a two- to three-year residency under the supervision of a dental specialist, a credentials review, and a board examination.

For example, if a dog is vomiting, a homeopathic veterinarian would prescribe a substance that, if used at full strength, would cause vomiting; the prescribed homeopathic drug is a highly diluted form of that substance.

Education and Training

There are well-established ways of using such remedies. To learn how to use the remedies effectively, a veterinarian should receive extensive training. The Animal Natural Health Center offers such training. The 130-hour classroom course, which leads to certification by the Academy of Veterinary Homeopathy, is taught by Richard H. Pitcairn, DVM, PhD, a driving force behind holistic and homeopathic medicine in the United States. Veterinary organizations have formed to standardize training and certification, establish professional standards, and offer ongoing education.

Dermatology

The American College of Veterinary Dermatology certifies veterinarians who have expertise and specialized training in the diagnosis and treatment of animals with benign and malignant disorders of the skin, mouth, hair, ears, nails, and hooves; allergic disorders; infectious (bacterial, fungal, or viral) and noninfectious skin diseases; parasitic skin diseases; hair loss; autoimmune skin diseases; and skin diseases caused by hormonal disorders. They learn to recognize the ways that systemic diseases—including internal malignancies—are expressed on the skin. For instance, the patterns formed by skin lesions and sores can help dermatologists determine the best diagnostic procedures.

Dermatologists identify and treat skin cancer, cysts and other skin tumors, and chronic ear infections and other inflammatory conditions. In fact, chronic ear disorders are one of the most common problems that veterinary dermatologists see.

Another part of a dermatologist's job is to interpret complicated test results. Specific environmental allergens can be pinpointed with an intradermal allergy test, and certain blood tests can document relative levels of allergy-related antibodies in the blood.

"Regardless of the test, interpretation is critical," says Lowell Ackerman, who is dermatology course director for Cummings School of Veterinary Medicine at Tufts University. "It is not as simple as just sending a blood sample to a laboratory and getting a diagnostic result back."

Beyond allergy tests, veterinary dermatologists perform many specialized diagnostic procedures: microscopic examination of skin-biopsy specimens, cytological smears, potassium-hydroxide preparations, video otoscopy (use of a camera to see inside ear canals), fungal cultures, and

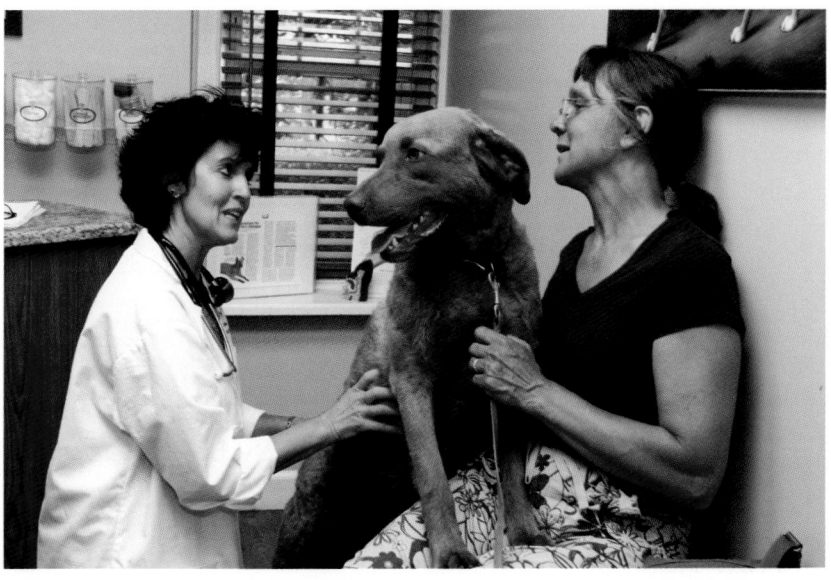

Board-certified veterinary dermatologist Karen Helton-Rhodes consults with her patient's owner. She wrote *The 5-Minute Veterinary Consult Clinical Companion: Small Animal Dermatology* (Wiley-Blackwell, 2002).

other microbiologic examinations of skin scrapings and secretions. Once a dermatologist has determined a problem's source, he or she may treat the animal with externally applied, injected, or internal medications or certain dermatologic surgical procedures such as cryosurgery (the use of freezing surgical units), laser surgery, nail surgery, biopsies, and excisional surgery (removal of lumps or bumps that are at or near the surface of the skin).

There are few veterinary dermatologists in North America. They represent only about one-quarter of 1 percent of the total veterinary population. They work closely with primary-care veterinarians on a referral basis to treat pets with a variety of skin diseases.

Emergency and Critical Care

Working nights and weekends, emergency and critical-care specialists treat animals with severe injuries and sudden or life-threatening diseases. Among the animals needing their help are trauma patients, such as dogs or cats hit by cars; pets having trouble breathing; pets in shock or in need of a blood transfusion; and animals suffering seizures that are not responsive to medication. The specialists use the same high-tech equipment as that found in a top emergency room or intensive-care unit at a human hospital, allowing them to provide close monitoring and life-support measures.

During their three years of intensive training in emergency medicine, surgery, and critical care, emergency and critical-care specialists learn the latest techniques for diagnosing and treating diseases during emergency situations. Whether they work at a busy full-service twenty-four-hour emergency center in a large city such as Los Angeles, or at a vet school's small-animal hospital in a university town, they can expect to work long or odd hours. But the rewards include a constant stream of interesting and challenging cases and access to a full range of diagnostic and surgical equipment that they can wield to save lives.

Neurology

A neurologist diagnoses and treats diseases of the nervous system, which encompasses the brain, spinal cord, and muscles and includes such problems as epilepsy, slipped disks, spinal and head injuries, meningitis, and brain tumors. Veterinary neurological knowledge and equipment are highly advanced, as are treatment options. Many neurological disorders are treatable with medication or surgery. For instance, tumors of the meninges—the outer covering of the brain and spinal cord—can be removed surgically, and the patient can go on to live for many more years.

Neurologists must have superb observation skills combined with knowledge of animal movements, reflexes, behaviors and responses. When they conduct a neurological examination, they must be able to interpret subtle actions to identify the location of the problem. They also use advanced diagnostic-imaging techniques, such as computed tomography (CT) scans, magnetic resonance imaging (MRI), spinal-fluid collection, and electric nerve-impulse tests.

Neurologists see specialized cases on a regular basis, so they have a greater knowledge of nervous-system problems than do general practitioners, who rarely see such cases. Neurologists also collaborate with other veterinary specialists. For example, an orthopedist or surgeon may

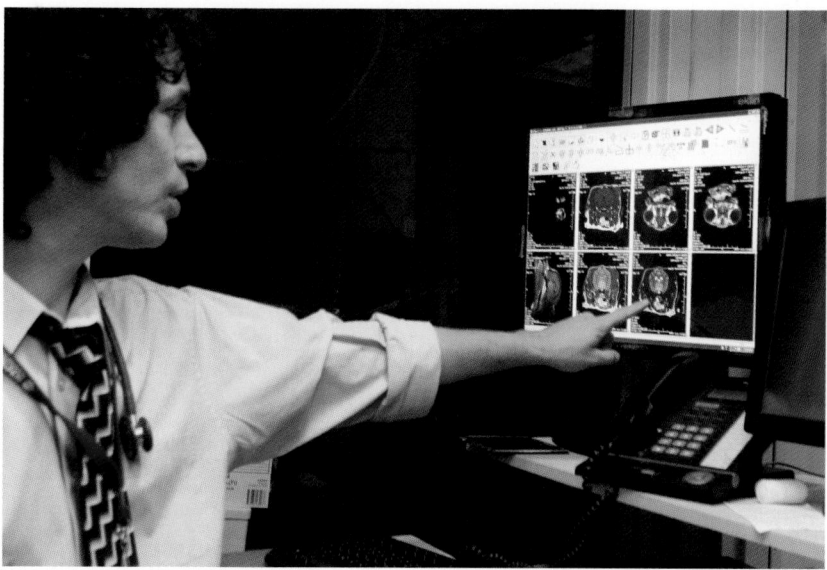

Board-certified veterinary neurologist Richard J. Joseph reviews a patient's X-rays. Joseph is also a veterinary acupuncturist.

consult a neurologist about a dog with a vertebral fracture who needs a postsurgical rehabilitation plan, or a neurologist may advise a dentist or ophthalmologist about problems of the face and eyes. Some neurological problems are related to systemic illnesses, so neurologists may work with cardiologists or internists to prepare effective treatment plans.

Board-certified neurologists have an additional three years of residency training in veterinary neurology and neurosurgery. Although they are trained in neurosurgery, some limit their practice to the medical aspects of neurology and work with surgeons on cases requiring a scalpel.

Nutrition

Veterinary nutritionists are experts in all aspects of the nutritional needs of animals, from the practical—how to feed them—to the medical—the diagnosis, treatment, and management of nutritionally related diseases. To become certified in nutrition, a veterinarian must complete a residency program, publish a nutrition research paper in a peer-reviewed journal, submit three case reports for evaluation by a credentials committee, and pass a two-day written exam.

Sally Perea became interested in nutrition during her undergraduate schooling, majoring in animal science with a minor in nutrition. During veterinary school, she also completed a master's degree in nutrition.

It was during her residency that she encountered one of her more memorable patients, a male Dalmatian with a history of urate bladder stones. "I formulated a therapeutic home-cooked diet for this dog to help prevent the recurrence of these stones. The diet was successful, and the dog was able to be weaned off his medication. I've been able to follow up with this patient in recent months and am glad to report that he has continued to be stone-free on his home-cooked diet."

After her residency, Perea took a job with a veterinary-nutrition consulting firm, where she advised pet-food manufacturers as well as veterinarians in practice. She also held a part-time position at the nutrition support service offered by the UC Davis Veterinary Medical Teaching Hospital.

Perea currently holds a position as senior nutritionist for a pet-food company, where she's involved in new research and development. A typical day is spent reviewing scientific literature, creating educational and training materials, designing research projects, working on formulations, and juggling various long-term ongoing projects.

Juliette de Bairacli Levy: Grandmother of Herbal Medicine

Regarded as the "grandmother of herbal medicine," Juliette de Bairacli Levy was the inspiration for the herbal movement, a pioneer of holistic veterinary medicine, as well as a breeder and an author of groundbreaking books. Born in Manchester, England, in 1912, to a wealthy family, Levy attended veterinary school for two years but left before graduating to pursue alternative healing techniques she learned from gypsies, peasants, and nomadic people in Europe, Africa, and America.

In the 1930s she developed Natural Rearing Products, a line of herbal supplements for animals that were the only such products available for a half century. Her Afghan Hounds (Turkuman prefix) were well known in England and America, and her most famous dog, Ch. Turkuman Nissim's Laurel, won the Hound Group at Westminster in 1950, handled by the famous Sunny Shay.

In 1952 Levy published the *Complete Herbal Handbook for Farm and Stable*, the first herbal veterinary book; her book *The Complete Herbal Book for the Dog and Cat* followed three years later. A documentary film of Levy's life, *Juliette of the Herbs*, directed and narrated by Tish Streeten, took seven years to film and was released in 1998 when Levy was eighty-six. Levy died in 2009, at the age of ninety-seven, her longevity a testimony to the healthy lifestyle she advocated.

Ophthalmology

Twombly, a Bulldog, suffered from keratoconjunctivitis sicca, more commonly known as dry eye. Most dogs with dry eye must take medication daily for the rest of their lives to keep the condition under control, but Twombly was lucky. His owner took him to see veterinary ophthalmologist Jennifer Welser. She surgically redirected salivary ducts from Twombly mouth cavity into his eyes, solving the problem.

Veterinary ophthalmology is a growing field. Pets can develop a variety of eye problems, including some of the same ones that affect people. The approximately 300 board-certified veterinary ophthalmologists in the United States are trained to diagnose eye disease and injury using specialized diagnostic equipment that isn't usually available at a general practitioner's clinic. With the advanced equipment available to them, veterinary ophthalmologists can offer such treatments as retinal reattachment surgery or the use of lasers to lower the intraocular pressure of dogs with glaucoma. In practices with large numbers of patients, the ophthalmologists have the opportunity to conduct clinical research studies.

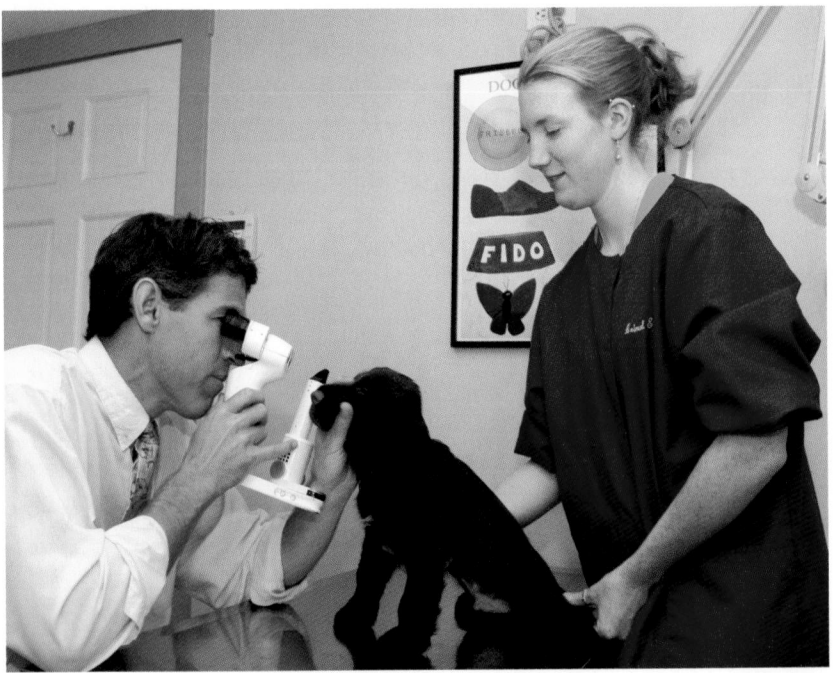

Veterinary ophthalmologist Charles Stuhr exams the eyes of this Field Spaniel puppy for disease. Stuhr heads up the Animal Eye Clinic in Wilton, Connecticut.

Ophthalmologists also work with other veterinary specialists, such as cardiologists, internists, neurologists, and oncologists, because eye diseases can be linked to other problems in the body, including diabetes and hypertension. For instance, dogs and cats with hypertension—high blood pressure—can suffer retinal hemorrhage and detachment, so an ophthalmologist and cardiologist may work together to come up with the best treatment plan.

Ophthalmologists must meet the following criteria: a veterinary degree, a one-year internship, a two- to three-year residency in ophthalmology at a veterinary teaching hospital, a credentials package that includes published work and case reports, and successful completion of a four-day written, practical, and surgical exam.

Radiology

Radiologists use radiographs (X-rays), CT scans, ultrasound, nuclear imaging, and MRIs to help diagnose medical conditions. They are often consulted for second opinions because of their depth of knowledge. It's not unusual for them to see thirty to forty radiographic cases each day, whereas a general-practice veterinarian might see only four or five such cases a day.

Radiology is a subtle and complex art. It requires the ability to reconstruct three-dimensional animals from flat images, a skill that combines knowledge of anatomy, physiology, and the physics of radiological imaging. A radiologist correlates medical-image findings with other examinations and tests, recommends further examinations or treatments, and consults with the referring veterinarian. Radiologists often work at "referral-only" animal hospitals, meaning that they only see patients that are sent to them by primary-care veterinarians. Some offer mobile services, driving specially equipped vans to practices that lack specialized equipment and performing MRIs and other imaging services.

Board certification in radiology requires graduation from an accredited veterinary college, three to four years of residency training under the tutelage of at least two board-certified specialists, and acceptable performance on board examinations. Radiologists can become certified in diagnostic imaging or in radiation oncology, also known as radiation therapy. Highly sophisticated radiation oncology procedures are used to treat cancer. Some radiologists earn certification in both areas.

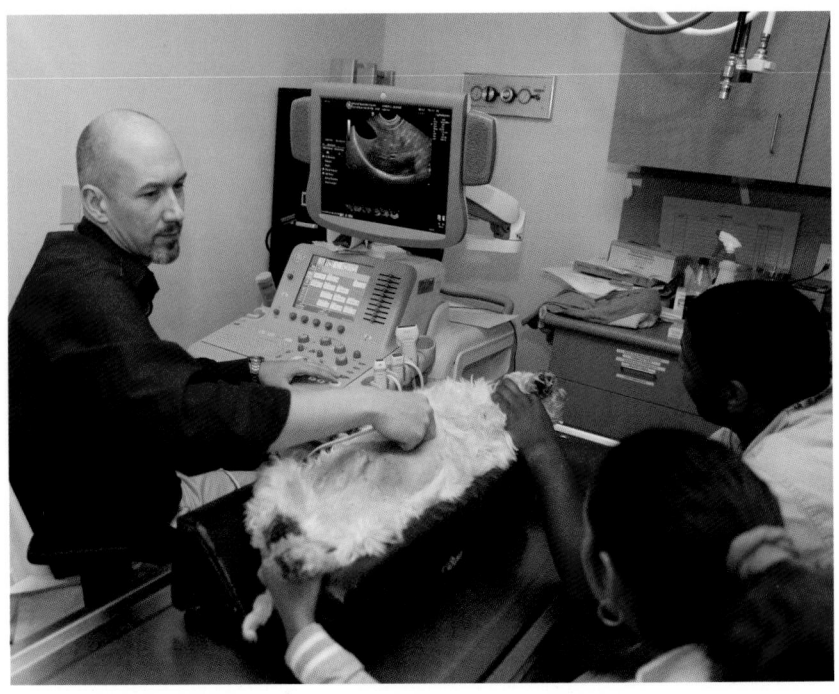

Kerry Heuter, a specialist in veterinary internal medicine, performs an ultrasound.

Rehabilitation

Mikey was hit by a car, fracturing his upper front leg. Mocha had severe degenerative joint disease that affected his elbows, hips, knees, and back. Doc had a painful ruptured disk, causing him to lose the use of his hind legs and control of his bladder and bowels. With the help of underwater treadmills, electrical stimulation, range-of-motion exercises, massage, and other equipment and techniques derived from human physical therapy, Mikey and Mocha are now active dogs with full use of their limbs. Doc can walk and no longer suffers from incontinence.

If Mikey, Mocha, and Doc had been people, physical therapy would have been an expected part of their treatment, but as dogs, they were fortunate to benefit from veterinary rehabilitation, a relatively new and rapidly developing field. According to the American Animal Hospital Association, physical rehabilitation is emerging as a helpful tool for animals recovering from surgery for orthopedic or neurological problems, those having incurred injuries to joints or soft tissue, or those suffering from the chronic pain. It's also popular for conditioning athletic or working dogs.

What Pet Rehab Veterinarians Do

Rehab can help pets recover more quickly from injury, increase mobility and flexibility, improve endurance and agility, and reduce pain and the need for medication. Before surgery, rehab can help pets lose weight, reduce pain, and gain muscle, all of which can either eliminate the need for surgery or improve its chances for success. After surgery, weeks of cage rest have been replaced by rehab techniques, with cold therapy to reduce inflammation, range-of-motion exercises, and massage.

At VetHab, his clinic in Raleigh, North Carolina, the late John Sherman, DVM—who treated Mikey, Mocha, and Doc—often saw pets with ruptured anterior cruciate ligaments or developmental diseases such as hip and elbow dysplasia as well as top field-trial dogs whose owners wanted conditioning programs to help prevent injury and older pets whose joints had stiffened with age. Sherman attributed the growing popularity of rehab to two main factors: the place pets occupy in the American family and the popularity of dog sports. "A lot more people do things with pets these days," he noted. "If you look at the list of sports or activities you can do with your dog, it's a lot longer than you would think. People want their dogs to be as good as they can be and be safe."

And because pets are living longer, more of them face health issues that affect mobility, such as osteoarthritis. Helping older pets maintain quality of life and mobility is becoming a new area of medicine.

Rehab can also help pets that need to lose weight. Abby's stomach dragged on the ground when she walked. The corgi weighed 48 pounds, about twice as much as the breed's recommended weight. Abby's owner had physical disabilities of her own and couldn't give the dog the exercise she needed. "This poor little puppy's stomach had sores on it from dragging on the ground," says veterinarian Pam Nichols of K-9 Rehab Center in West Bountiful, Utah. "She couldn't even walk from our exam room to our scale without stopping and sitting and huffing and puffing."

After six weeks of workouts on the underwater treadmill, Abby could do three sessions of forty-five minutes each and had lost fifteen pounds. "She still comes in a couple of times a week, and it's so exciting to see so huge a change for this little dog," Nichols says. "The mom's goal was just for her to be able to climb stairs, and now she runs and jumps and plays."

A veterinary rehab therapist starts treatment by taking the patient's medical history. An exam of the dog involves testing and measuring strength, range of motion, balance and coordination, posture, muscle performance, respiration, and motor function. The therapist designs a treatment or conditioning plan based on the results of the history and exam.

Treatment may include exercises to improve flexibility and range of motion or to increase balance, coordination, strength, and stamina. Massage, ultrasound, lasers, underwater treadmills, electrical stimulation, hot packs, and cold packs are also part of a pet rehab therapist's toolkit.

Who Pet Rehab Therapists Are

Many veterinarians who have studied rehabilitation techniques became interested in pet rehab when one of their own animals or a client's dog needed help recovering from an injury or surgery, or after they themselves suffered injuries and required physical therapy. In Portland, Oregon, veterinarian Bianca Shaw began investigating rehabilitation after a truck hit her six-month-old puppy. "He had a lot of broken bones, and I wanted to give him the best quality of life," Shaw says. "In my search to find that, I was able to learn a lot about what we don't provide as veterinarians and understand what it's like to be the owner, going through an injury with a pet."

Marta Sanchez, DVM, from Miami, Florida, integrated acupuncture into her practice in an attempt to help pets with conditions such as chronic pain and paralysis. She realized that she still needed to learn ways to help manage or reverse conditions such as muscle atrophy and gait defects. She decided to earn certification in canine rehabilitation and has found it a rewarding addition to her practice.

When veterinarian Laurie McCauley fell down the stairs and needed physical therapy, she realized that the techniques could help dogs, too, especially police dogs and other athletic dogs, whether injured on the job or in competition, or just in need of some conditioning. She studied with a physical therapist and is now widely known for working not only with top agility dogs but also with dogs who have neurological diseases such as intervertebral disc disease, spondylosis, and fibrocartilaginous embolism.

Ava Frick was practicing veterinary medicine before rehab techniques were available for pets. She learned on her own, studying chiropractic for animals and attending physical-therapy conferences. Her other interests were helpful as well. "My years of personal weight training, dog showing, and horseback riding have been a great asset in my ability to design or customize programs for animals," she says.

Canine sports medicine consultant Chris Zink, DVM, PhD, examines a German Shorthaired Pointer. Zink evaluates canine structure and locomotion and designs individualized rehabilitation and conditioning programs for canine athletes.

Education and Training

Veterinarians can become certified in canine rehabilitation through the programs at the University of Tennessee and the Canine Rehabilitation Institute. At this time, the University of Tennessee is the only university offering credentialing in pet rehabilitation techniques.

In both of these programs, typical requirements for certification include classes in anatomy and regulatory and ethical issues; response of tissue to disuse or immobilization; common orthopedic and neurologic conditions; use of physical agents, such as heat, cold, lasers, ultrasound, and electrical stimulation; evaluation techniques; therapeutic exercises and other rehabilitation techniques; range of motion; sports medicine; therapies for arthritis; and pain management. Clinical experience, case studies, and written and practical exams are also part of an education in pet rehabilitation.

Surgery

Veterinary surgeons who are board certified may specialize in a particular species, such as dogs or horses, or in a certain type of surgery, such as orthopedic, oncologic, or neurologic. Some even narrow their focus to specific procedures, such as organ transplantation.

No matter what their specialties, they do more than surgery; they are responsible for the animal's assessment and care before, during, and after surgery. That includes pain management and rehabilitation, using specialized equipment, massage, stretching, and exercise. They work with other specialists who may be involved in the animal's care, such as anesthesiologists, cardiologists, internists, or radiologists. Many veterinary surgeons help keep general practitioners up to date on the latest in surgical techniques or teach veterinary students and residents.

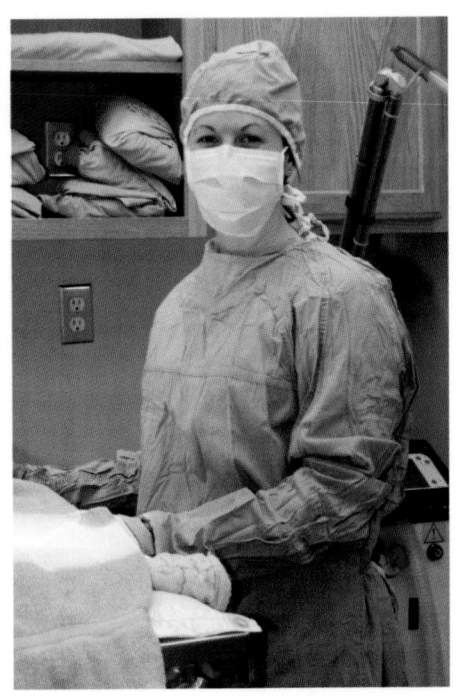

Veterinary surgeon Kimberly Bolduc also practices veterinary orthopedic manipulation.

To achieve this level of skill, board-certified surgeons complete four additional years of specialized training in the form of a one-year internship and a three-year residency. They must meet specific training and caseload requirements, perform research, and have their research published. It's a highly competitive specialty, and there are only a certain number of residencies available each year. Many interns find that they can't be accepted into a residency unless they are already published, so students who want to pursue this path must be aggressive in their preparation.

Surgery is hard work, requiring some physical strength and manual dexterity, but developing surgical skills is not unusually difficult. Most people develop serviceable surgical skills during the course of a three-year residency and a few years' experience afterward. Controlling stress can be a challenge, though, both in and out of the operating room. A surgeon must be able to stay calm in difficult situations. A surgeon must also keep up with surgical advances, which is time consuming. The rate at which new information becomes available is fast and getting faster.

Once they've completed their training, veterinary surgeons have several career options. They may own or be employed by specialty practices, accepting cases on a referral basis from primary-care practitioners. Other surgeons teach, conduct research, work in teaching hospitals, or are employed by companies in positions that involve them in pure surgical research and the development of new products and treatments.

Some surgeons even specialize within their own specialty. For instance, John Berg, chair of the Department of Clinical Sciences at Cummings School of Veterinary Medicine at Tufts University, specializes in soft-tissue surgery in small animals, such as dogs and cats. In other words, he does surgery on every part of the body except the bones and joints. A large part of his work involves removing cancerous tumors.

Transfusion Medicine

Pebbles went into shock after delivering a litter of five puppies. Her owner, Amy Lane of Berkeley Springs, West Virginia, rushed the three-year-old Goldendoodle and her pups to the local veterinary emergency hospital, where Pebbles was stabilized but still losing ground because her blood wasn't clotting. Lane was advised to transfer Pebbles to a larger emergency hospital. There, she barely hung on for several days, and veterinarians expressed doubt that she would survive. On the sixth day, Pebbles was given a blood transfusion, with blood donated by a pit bull belonging to one of the veterinary technicians. "That turned her around," Lane says. "Two days later, she came home."

Blood transfusions for animals have been available for approximately thirty years, but these days there is more availability than ever, according to Elizabeth Rozanski, DVM, assistant professor of clinical sciences at Cummings School of Veterinary Medicine at Tufts University and member of the emergency and critical care team at the school's Foster Hospital for Small Animals. Transfusions save the lives of dogs such as Pebbles, serving as a bridge to life until they can get better on their own.

That's where animal blood banks come into the picture. It's expensive for veterinarians to maintain donor animals—dogs and cats that live at the clinic and donate blood as needed—or to find and screen volunteer donors. Sometimes there aren't enough donors to meet the demand. Commercial animal blood banks evolved to fill the need.

Berg went into surgery wanting to do research, but over the span of his career in the academic world, he has come to enjoy teaching as much or even more. He also appreciates the variety inherent in an academic career.

"There are opportunities to teach and to do research in private practice, but generally not to the extent that they can be done in academia," Berg says. "A common reason that people like academia is that when you do clinics and take care of pets, you're taking care of an individual pet. When you teach students to take care of pets, you're indirectly helping a larger number of pets, and when you do research you're potentially helping all pets."

Although surgeons can make more money in private practice than academia, that may shift as more people enter the specialty. "I think practices are filling up and getting more competitive, and I'm sure with time it may be that practice salaries fall or at least stop increasing as fast, " Berg says.

Theriogenology

The term *theriogenology* was created by combining the Greek words *therio* (beast), *gen/genesis* (offspring, sex), and *ology* (study of). Thus theriogenology is the study of reproduction in animals, including the physiology (processes or functions) and diseases of male and female reproductive systems and the practice of veterinary obstetrics, gynecology, and semenology.

Board certification in theriogenology can be achieved in one of two ways. The first is graduation from an accredited veterinary college, plus one year of clinical practice and at least two years in an established, supervised training program that includes experience in teaching, research, and/or practice of theriogenology under the supervision of a boarded theriogenologist.

Then there's the learn-by-experience route. A candidate with a veterinary degree but no formal theriogenology training may take the board-certification exam if he or she has at least six years of practice experience with a primary emphasis in theriogenology. He or she must also complete a two-year preapproved study and mentorship program with a diplomate of the American College of Theriogenologists or the European College of Animal Reproduction, or a fellow of the Australian College of Veterinary Scientists (Animal Reproduction).

Reproductive specialists assist breeders whose animals are having difficulty conceiving or maintaining a pregnancy. They perform a fertility exam and prepare a plan for treating the problem. They also play a role in maximizing an animal's reproductive potential through such techniques as artificial insemination or freezing semen for later use. Artificial insemination in dogs, for instance, means that a female can be bred with a suitable male in another part of the country without ever leaving her hometown, eliminating the stress and expense of flying her across the country to be mated. Theriogenologists may be employed by private specialty practices or universities, where they also teach.

"The miracle of fertilization and development of a microscopic embryo into a fetus and on into a living, breathing creature never ceases to amaze me, even though I have watched it occur thousands of times," says theriogenologist Cheryl Lopate of Reproductive Revolutions in Newberg, Oregon. "I chose to specialize in reproduction because it is a creative field of medicine, requiring the application of knowledge of all species when problems with infertility arise in order to solve them. There is nothing more satisfying than being able to help breeders produce quality athletes, working animals, and companions from the starting point of an ideal to fruition of a living creature. The joy of watching young animals be delivered and starting out in the world is always thrilling. I would recommend this career path to anyone."

PRACTICE SPECIALTY RESOURCES

- Academy of Veterinary Homeopathy, www.theavh.org
- American Academy of Pain Management, www.aapainmanage.org
- American Academy of Veterinary Acupuncture, www.aava.org
- American Association of Rehabilitation Veterinarians, www.rehabvets.org
- American College of Theriogenologists, www.theriogenology.org
- American College of Veterinary Anesthesiologists, www.acva.org
- American College of Veterinary Behaviorists, www.veterinarybehaviorists.org
- American College of Veterinary Dermatology, www.acvd.org
- American College of Veterinary Emergency and Critical Care, www.acvecc.org
- American College of Veterinary Internal Medicine, www.acvim.org
- American College of Veterinary Nutritionists, www.acvn.org
- American College of Veterinary Ophthalmology, www.acvo.org
- American College of Veterinary Radiology, www.acvr.org
- American College of Veterinary Surgeons, www.acvs.org
- American Holistic Veterinary Medical Association, www.ahvma.org
- American Veterinary Chiropractic Association, www.animalchiropractic.org
- American Veterinary Dental College, www.avdc.org
- Canine Rehabilitation Institute, www.caninerehabinstitute.com
- International Veterinary Acupuncture Society, www.ivas.org
- *Journal of Veterinary Internal Medicine*, www.wiley.com
- *Manual of Canine and Feline Cardiology*, by Larry P. Tilley, Francis W. K. Smith Jr., Mark Oyama, and Meg M. Sleeper. Saunders, 2007.
- *A Practical Guide to Canine and Feline Neurology*, edited by Curtis W. Dewey. 2nd ed. Wiley-Blackwell, 2008.
- Society for Theriogenology, www.therio.org

CHAPTER 10

Public Welfare and Policy Specialties

All veterinarians are concerned at some level with the welfare of all animals. Some veterinarians, however, choose to focus on developing ways to prevent disease and set policy to ensure a better life for dogs and other animals. Among these are preventive medicine specialists, public health specialists, and shelter veterinarians.

The specialty of veterinary preventive medicine focuses on improving animal and human health in a number of ways beyond traditional health care. Public health specialists are closely allied with preventive medicine specialists. Their field, also known as epidemiology, is the study of health and disease in populations of animals. The knowledge gained by studying populations is important in preventing the spread of disease and illness. Veterinarians with an interest in shelter medicine are concerned with the welfare of animals in shelters.

Preventive Medicine

Specialists in this field are involved in the surveillance, recognition, prevention, control, and management of disease in all types of animals. They work to prevent and control zoonotic diseases and food-borne illnesses; reduce bites, injuries, and other environmental and occupational human health hazards related to animals; maintain the safety and wholesomeness of foods; promote humane animal care; and encourage the use of

APHIS veterinarian John Duncan performs a test for scrapie susceptibility as students, including Future Farmers of America members (in blue shirts), watch.

animal-facilitated therapy. That's quite a range of goals and responsibilities. To achieve certification in this field, veterinarians must have six years of experience in one or more areas of preventive medicine or four years of experience plus a certificate from a formal residency program or a master's in preventive medicine, public health, or another relevant medical science. Veterinarians with a doctoral degree in preventive medicine or public health plus a year of experience may also qualify.

Diplomates of the American College of Veterinary Preventive Medicine can be found working for public agencies, private industry, institutions, and the military. They are involved in regulatory and diagnostic medicine, public health, epidemiology, research, teaching, herd-health management, population medicine, and other related activities.

Barkworthy BITE

THE LUCKY ONES

"I know that the animal who ends up in my shelter is the lucky one. It's the ones who don't end up in the shelter that you have to worry about. Once they're in our hands, we're rehabilitating them, we're rehoming them, we're loving them, and we're taking care of them."—Martha Smith, shelter veterinarian

Portrait of a Public Health Veterinarian

Maryland public health veterinarian Katherine Feldman took a roundabout path to her career in public health, first earning an undergraduate degree in computer science. When that didn't prove to be satisfying, she decided to take her interests in science and animals and attend veterinary school. She followed that with a master of public health degree in epidemiology. Her degrees, combined with her computer science, proved ideal for public health work.

"My role as state public health veterinarian is to look after the health of Maryland citizens wherever animals might be involved in disease risks or transmission," Feldman says. "Issues that are common for me to deal with are things like exposure or potential exposure to rabies or other zoonotic disease issues."

Public Health

Veterinarians in this field play a role in defining what's normal for different species and breeds, identifying risk factors for certain diseases, analyzing test results, and more. For instance, when a new diagnostic test is introduced, general-practice veterinarians record the test results and how their patients progress afterward. Clinical epidemiologists then analyze that information to determine the accuracy of the test. They may collect and analyze data on healthy animal populations and study patterns of disease cases. Veterinary epidemiologists also play a role in human public health, especially when it comes to *zoonoses*, or zoonotic diseases—diseases that can be transmitted between animals and people through direct contact or consumption of certain animal products.

You'll find veterinary epidemiologists working with doctors in government, public health, and environmental health. They are concerned with such issues as food-borne diseases and food safety, investigation of disease outbreaks, and prevention and management of such zoonotic diseases as bovine spongiform encephalopathy (mad cow disease), West Nile virus, SARS (severe acute respiratory syndrome), and avian influenza (bird flu). They help to develop drugs that benefit both animals and people. This is another career that is well suited to people with analytical minds who enjoy solving puzzles and are good at making connections.

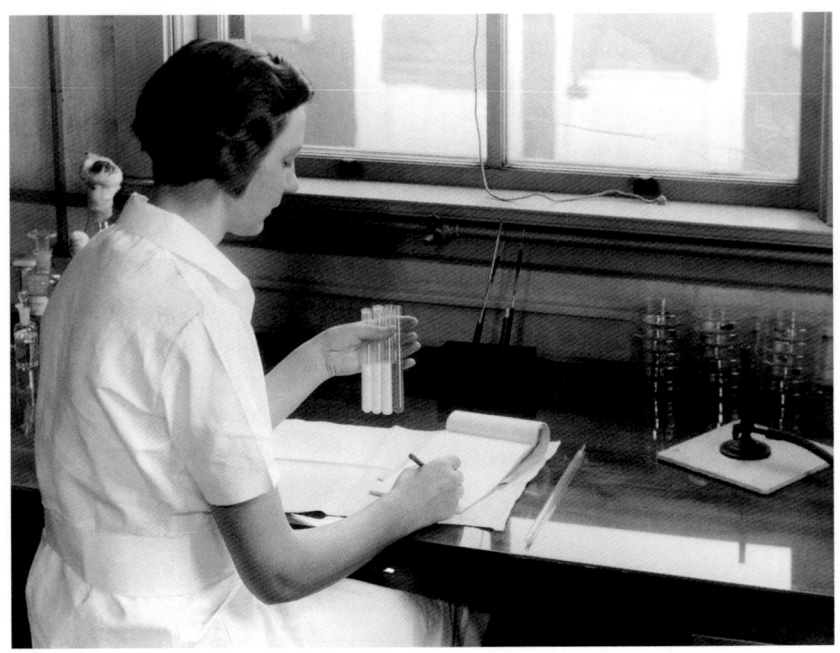

At the University of Minnesota Veterinary School, in October 1934, a laboratory scientist conducts a pH test on bovine milk samples, extracted to study an outbreak of mastitis.

There's no such thing as a typical day in public health work, which makes it all the more attractive to Katherine Feldman, public health veterinarian for the state of Maryland. In the course of her work, she takes questions from the public about disease concerns, works with Maryland's twenty-four local health departments, writes policy on such things as rabies prevention and control, and gives presentations. For instance, she recently spoke to summer-camp directors about ways to help prevent campers from developing Lyme disease or being exposed to rabies.

The job isn't necessarily one that Feldman can leave at the office at the end of the day. She carries a pager and is available 24/7, primarily for rabies issues. She may also put in overtime when preparing presentations or working on other demanding issues, but it's a career that's perfect for her skills and interests, and she wouldn't have it any other way.

Shelter Medicine

Veterinarians who work in animal shelters treat homeless animals that are sick or injured. Their care gives these animals a second chance at a new home. Veterinarians with an interest in shelter medicine have the goal of improving the quality of life for animals in shelters through better preventive medicine and management of disease. They provide hands-on help to shelter animals by developing cleaning and disinfection programs and helping to control outbreaks of infectious diseases such as parvovirus and distemper. Shelter medicine specialists may also be involved in research with the intent of improving the welfare of shelter animals as well as assisting with cruelty investigations or setting up community-wide spay/neuter clinics for dogs and cats or trap/neuter/return programs for feral cats. Shelter veterinarians help design shelters that will decrease the stress of the animals in residence, and of course, they evaluate and determine the medical needs of the animals in the shelter's care.

Shelter medicine is an emerging specialty. The Koret Shelter Medicine Program at the University of California at Davis was the first program for shelter medicine in the nation. It not only trains veterinary students and residents who want to make a career in this field but also provides outreach and consultation services to shelters nationwide, which often have critical animal-health and management issues. In a single year, program staff may respond to more than 500 requests for consultation; there is a definite need for veterinarians trained in the field of shelter medicine.

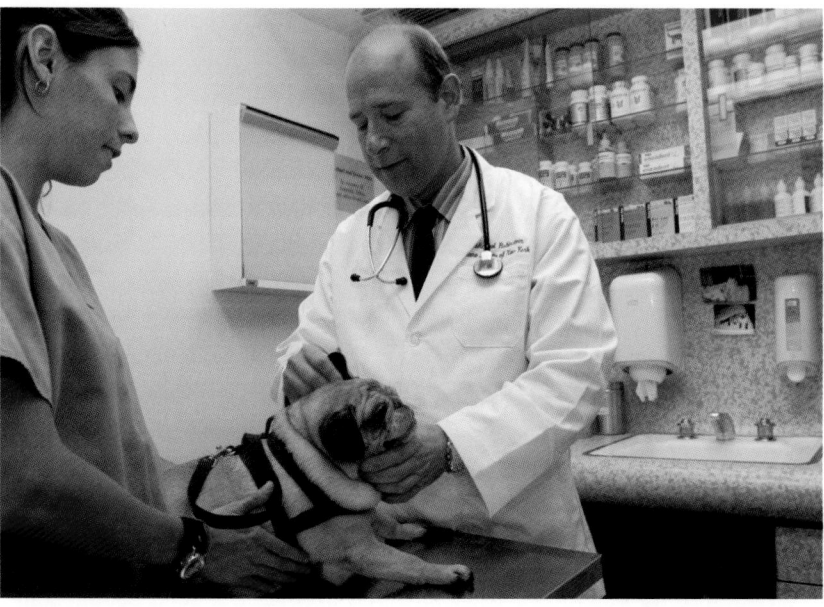

Michael Rubinstein, DVM, examines a homeless pug at the Humane Society of New York. Rubinstein is the clinic's director.

Portrait of a Shelter Veterinarian

Martha Smith, graduate of the Cummings School of Veterinary Medicine at Tufts University, is director of veterinary services at Boston's Animal Rescue League. She became a shelter veterinarian before there were any specialized training programs or the notion that a shelter veterinarian might need particular skills. During a two-week rotation at the shelter attached to Angell Animal Medical Center, she learned how to approach small animals with abandonment issues and how to evaluate them for placeability and adoptability.

"It was supposed to be an easy two weeks where you just take a break from the intensive work that you do as an intern and just vaccinate and examine animals, but during those two weeks I think I learned more in many ways than I think I had from the rest of my internship," she says.

After graduation, Smith went into private practice but didn't enjoy the environment. Work at Angell's emergency room was a better fit, but still not quite right. In her spare time, she volunteered at the shelter. When an opportunity to become the shelter veterinarian came along, Smith took it, thinking that she would eventually move on to something else. Three months later, she realized she had found her veterinary home.

"In some ways, it's a very pure form of veterinary medicine. It's more of an intuitive practice because we've got fewer tools and resources, and you're working directly with the animal," Smith says. "You're still consulting with the shelter manager and the staff, but basically you're looking at this animal as a relationship between the two of you."

The University of Florida also has a shelter medicine program. It offers shelter assessment services; trains veterinarians on the issues of homeless animals, sheltering systems, and shelter medicine; and works to develop new ways to solve existing and emerging problems faced by animal shelters. Now, twenty-four veterinary schools have or are developing shelter medicine programs, including those at Auburn, Colorado State, Cornell, Purdue, Tufts, and the University of Wisconsin.

In addition to veterinary skills, shelter veterinarians need people skills. They often walk a fine line in dealing with the emotions and hot-button issues surrounding shelter animals and the management of shelters, calling for high-level diplomatic skills as they interact with board members, staff members, volunteers, members of the community, and local officials.

Shelter veterinarian Martha Smith majored in international relations as an undergraduate. "I was going to be a diplomat, and I am one," she says. Another skill that comes in handy is the ability to shift focus quickly from meeting the specific needs of an individual animal to meeting those of the entire shelter population. That's especially true with the increasing societal pressure for shelters to become "no-kill."

"As society has higher and higher expectations that we aren't going to throw animals away," Smith says, "these animals are going to need to be rehabilitated and rehomed. And the population problem is still pressing. We have to work hard to get that under control as well."

There is no typical day for a shelter veterinarian. It might include performing spays and neuters, examining animals brought to the shelter, treating cats or dogs with health problems, counseling adopters, deciding how best to care for an injured animal, or performing administrative tasks. In shelters with law-enforcement departments, a shelter veterinarian may be called to testify in abuse cases; this requires the veterinarian to pay special attention to such cases, as he or she may be cross-examined about them in court at a later time. A perk is that the job tends to be Monday-through-Friday, 9-to-5, a rarity in the field of veterinary medicine.

Shelter medicine calls for a strong foundation in veterinary skills. Shelter veterinarians often work on their own, without access to much high-tech equipment. They must be able to quickly gauge what they're seeing and how to respond to it. Smith recommends going through a good internship training program, followed by a shelter internship training program. Then be prepared for low pay, but lots of emotional rewards.

PUBLIC WELFARE AND POLICY RESOURCES

- American Association of Public Health Veterinarians, www.aaphv.org
- American College of Veterinary Preventive Medicine, www.acvpm.org
- ASPCA Professional, Shelter Veterinary Medicine, www.aspcapro.org/shelter-medicine.php
- Association of Shelter Veterinarians, www.sheltervet.org
- Cornell University, College of Veterinary Medicine, Maddie's Shelter Medicine Program, www.sheltermedicine.cornell.edu
- Food Safety and Inspection Service, USDA, Public Health Veterinarians, www.fsis.usda.gov/careers/Veterinary_Medical_Officer_Positions/index.asp
- *Preventive Veterinary Medicine*, www.elsevier.com/wps/find/H05.cws_home/journals
- University of Tennessee Veterinary Public Health Concentration, www.vet.utk.edu/vph/

CHAPTER 11

Research Specialties

Not every veterinarian helps animals by caring for them in a practice. Research veterinarians devote their careers to determining causes of and ways to prevent and control animal diseases. Their areas of study range from behavior to cardiology to neurology and everything in between.

Researchers work at universities, for private organizations, and in corporate settings. Not only do research veterinarians have the satisfaction of contributing to animal health but in many cases their work also benefits people. For instance, a vaccine to treat canine melanoma was developed in a cooperative venture that brought together the Animal Medical Center (AMC) in New York, Memorial Sloan-Kettering Cancer Center (MSKCC), and Merial, a company that produces drugs for animals. A similar vaccine for people is in the works. Now AMC and MSKCC are working to create a lymphoma vaccine for dogs and people.

The discovery of a DNA mutation that is a major risk factor for degenerative myelopathy (DM), a debilitating spinal-cord disease in dogs, was the result of a collaborative research effort involving scientists at the University of Missouri and the Broad Institute of MIT and Harvard. Two of those scientists were veterinarians: molecular biologist Gary Johnson, DVM, PhD, and veterinary neurologist and neurosurgeon Joan Coates, DVM, DACVIM. Coates's contribution included using magnetic resonance imaging and

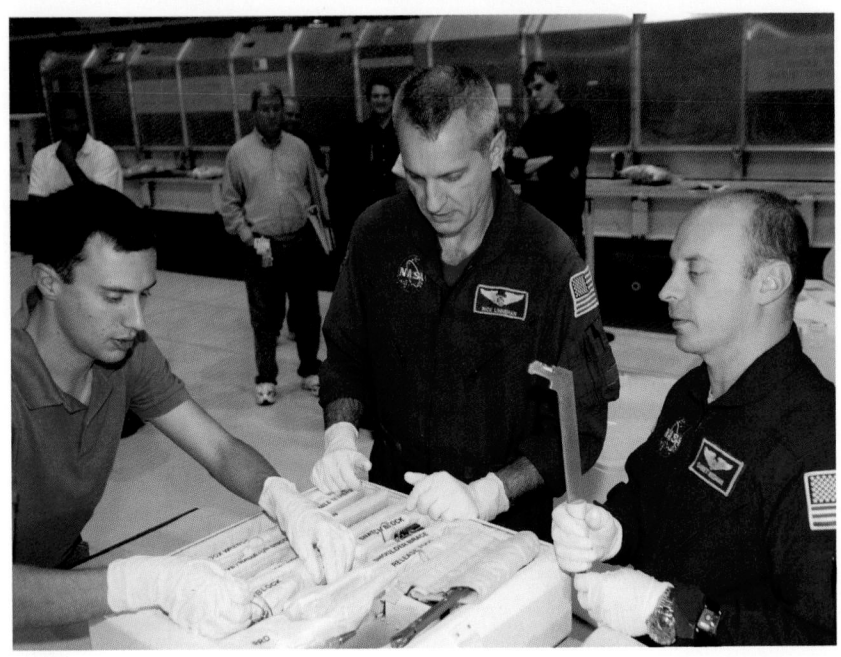

NASA mission specialists Richard Linnehan (*center*), DVM, and Garrett Resiman (*right*) practice with tools that will be used on their mission.

other techniques to determine which dogs had DM and which did not, an exacting and difficult task. As a result of the research, a genetic test was developed to identify dogs that are clear of the mutation, those that are carriers, and those at high risk of developing the disease. The researchers hope eventually to discover other genes that play a role in the development of the disease. Their findings could help breeders control the condition as well as contribute to new or better therapies for DM.

There has even been a veterinarian in space. Richard Linnehan, DVM, was commissioned a captain in the U.S. Army Veterinary Corps and then trained as an astronaut with NASA. He has since been on three missions in space, including one in which he helped to upgrade the systems of the Hubble Space Telescope. Linnehan predicts that one day, veterinarians will become planetary exobiologists, traveling to other planets and discovering new life.

Clinical Pharmacology

Veterinary clinical pharmacologists are specialists with advanced knowledge of the complexities that surround drug therapy in pets, livestock, and other animals. In addition to a veterinary degree, they may have a doctorate in veterinary pharmacology.

Clinical pharmacology affects the day-to-day lives of dogs and cats, even if pharmacologists don't work with the animals in a practice setting. For instance, some dog breeds may react adversely to certain drugs, while others aren't sensitive to them at all. Certain drugs are effective in dogs but not cats, or they may be effective in cats if used in a different way than they are in dogs.

The three-year residency required to become a clinical pharmacologist involves the study of the different types of drugs used in veterinary treatments, the mechanisms and other features of various diseases, and how drugs are used to mediate the progress of diseases. In other words, pharmacologists learn such things as how drugs work; the different effects of drugs on various species and individuals; how to recognize adverse drug effects; how factors such as disease, age, and pregnancy can influence a drug's effects; reasons a drug might fail; and how to diagnose and treat various complex therapeutic problems. Treatments include management of pain or inflammation, management of infections in major organ systems, management of medical emergencies that might call for use of multiple drugs, and management of drug reactions that might be caused by anesthetics or allergies. A resident must also develop a related research project and take part in clinical teaching rounds.

By the time the residency is completed, the clinical pharmacologist is able to interpret experimental and statistical data from drug studies, use statistical methods to evaluate studies on drugs in animals, calculate drug doses and modify them as needed, and understand the process of drug development and approval as well as the legal and regulatory considerations that apply to off-label drug use, drug compounding, and prescription writing. All of this prepares him or her for a number of career options: veterinary pharmacologists may find work in drug development, patient care, or teaching. Sometimes their careers lead them to positions in which they can influence public health or environmental safety.

Forensic Veterinary Medicine

Crime-scene investigation has gone to the dogs. The University of Florida and the American Society for the Prevention of Cruelty to Animals have formed the first veterinary forensic sciences program for teaching, research, and application of forensic science in the investigation and prosecution of crimes against animals. Such crimes include neglect, abandonment, animal hoarding, and blood sports, such as dog fighting.

Investigation of animal-cruelty cases is an emerging field. Forensic veterinarians will not only help prosecute people who harm animals but also play a role in uncovering instances where animal abusers are targeting people. Their efforts may help build a database for the national tracking of animal-cruelty cases.

Veterinarians who enter this field should have an interest in microscopy, genetics, and serology. They will study forensic entomology, buried-remains mapping and excavation, blood-stain-pattern analysis, bite-mark analysis, and animal crime-scene processing, which includes evidence collection and preservation. Part of their job will involve categorizing skin, hair, and blood samples. They will also learn what to look for to establish cause and manner of death, how to prove that a crime was committed, and how to present evidence in court.

"The standards of investigations and of the science used in documenting what has happened to animals are much, much higher than even five years ago," says Randall Lockwood, PhD, ASPCA senior vice president for anti-cruelty field services.

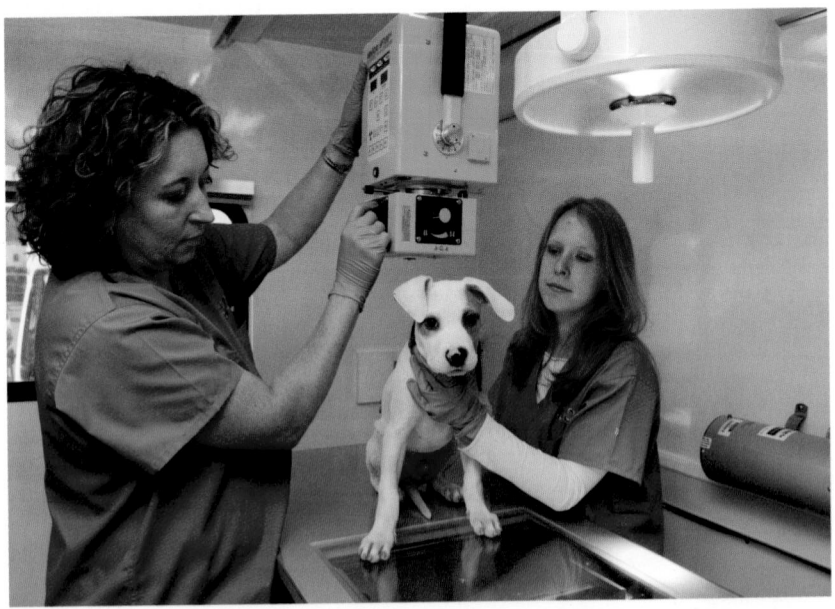

Melinda Merck, ASPCA forensic veterinarian, and veterinary technician Felicia Earley get ready to X-ray a dog, looking for signs of trauma.

Barkworthy BITE

CRUELTY INVESTIGATIONS

"Veterinarians are frequently asked to participate in cruelty investigations, yet we don't receive special training on that in veterinary school. There is a substantial unmet need for that training to be provided to veterinarians."—Julie Levy, DVM, PhD, director of Maddie's Shelter Medicine Program at the University of Florida

That's good news for animals. There is no national tracking of animal-cruelty cases, but each year the ASPCA investigates more than 5,000 such cases. The new program will allow for better collection of data on animal-related crimes. In turn, veterinarians will be better able to contribute to the prosecution of these cases.

Lab-Animal Veterinarian

If you love animals, you might wonder how a career as a lab-animal veterinarian could be satisfying. But the job of a veterinarian in a research facility is to be the advocate for experimental animals, whether mice or dogs or primates.

Lab-animal veterinarians manage facilities and ensure the enforcement of regulations concerning the welfare and use of research animals. Their daily responsibilities may include reviewing experiment protocols, verifying that procedures are carried out correctly, and ensuring that appropriate pain-management techniques are in use. When lab-animal veterinarians can make animals more comfortable, they improve both the animals' lives and the results of the research.

Laboratory veterinarians also regulate the numbers of animals used in experiments. No one wants too many animals used. Finally, they work with medical doctors and other researchers to compare human health and animal health. This leads to a better understanding of disease processes and the development of more effective medications, surgical procedures, and other treatments. Veterinarians employed by government agencies, laboratories, colleges, and commercial firms often have responsibility for large health programs and may manage many people, so communication and management skills are essential for this work.

Specialists in this field are in short supply and can command high salaries. Veterinarians trained in laboratory-animal medicine can earn starting salaries of as much as $100,000, depending on location.

Microbiology

Veterinary microbiologists are more likely to spend hands-on time with a microscope than with a mammal. Microbiologists are immune-system experts, knowledgeable about illnesses caused by bacteria, viruses, and other microorganisms. They are often employed by universities as researchers and professors; by drug companies, where they may be involved in development or testing of vaccines, antibiotics, or other pharmaceutical products; or by local, state, or federal agencies or the military, where they play a role in the prevention of, response to, and recovery from infectious diseases that threaten food security or public health. For instance, microbiologists may find jobs with the Centers for Disease Control, National Institutes of Health, or the World Health Organization. In these jobs, they may help trace outbreaks and develop emergency protocols.

Pathology

If you enjoy solving puzzles, and won't quit until you know the answer to something, veterinary pathology may be the career track for you. Veterinary pathologists study how diseases develop and progress. They teach and do research at universities or work in private or state diagnostic laboratories, for government agencies, or for pharmaceutical companies, where they are involved in basic research and testing of new drugs. Successful pathologists question everything in their search for answers—answers that may well save both animal and human lives.

There are two different types of veterinary pathologist: anatomic and clinical. Anatomic pathologists perform necropsies and histopathology on biopsy specimens. Clinical pathologists analyze blood and other body fluids and assess samples that have been aspirated or smeared. In other words, they are looking at cytological specimens, usually of individual cells.

A veterinary pathologist's job may involve diagnosing disease in pets or livestock; examining a biopsy sample for evidence of a tumor; ensuring the safety of food, drugs, or biological products, such as vaccines; helping prevent or manage disease outbreaks; protecting animal and human health by researching the ways that diseases develop; contributing to the protection of threatened and endangered species by investigating suspicious causes of death; and of course, teaching the next generation of veterinarians.

Salaries can range from $30,000 to more than $200,000, depending on years of experience, geographic location, and type of industry or agency.

This is a field with a broad range of possibilities. Veterinary pathologists with the National Fish and Wildlife Forensic Laboratory, for instance, can expect to work outdoors as well as in laboratories. They assist detectives who are investigating poaching or other violations-of-wildlife crimes. They use or develop microscopic, analytical, instrumental, computer, and electronic methods and procedures to determine the cause and manner of death to animals and may testify in court as expert witnesses. In a job like this, the salary for a senior-level position ranges from $65,000 to $78,000.

At a university, on the other hand, veterinary pathologists are more likely to spend the day performing necropsies on small animals to determine the cause of death, as well as teaching classes. They may also work with researchers to test the safety and quality of new drugs; find sources of infectious disease in food animals, birds, or aquatic mammals; or investigate global outbreaks of infectious disease. Sometimes they work with outside facilities such as the Centers for Disease Control or zoos and aquariums.

A board-certified veterinary pathologist has earned a degree in veterinary medicine and has at least three years of post-veterinary school training. It's not unusual for a pathologist to obtain a doctorate in toxicology, molecular biology, or another scientific field, which can take five to seven years. The board exam is difficult, too. The majority of people who take it fail. It usually requires at least one year of almost constant focused study to pass, which can be hard on job and family commitments.

Several personal characteristics distinguish the good pathologist. One is a desire to understand disease processes that is stronger than the satisfaction that comes from treating an individual patient. Pathologists must also have strong analytical skills.

"Much of what we do involves recognizing the visual patterns of disease, so the ability to quickly analyze visual patterns is important," says veterinary pathologist Betsy Uhl. "Pathologists also need to sort out what happened to the animal from the clues left in the tissues, so the analytical skills of a good detective are also critical."

Becoming a pathologist has advantages and disadvantages. The main disadvantage to specializing in veterinary pathology is the time it takes to complete the training—a total of seven to ten years, including veterinary school, depending on how the program is set up. That's a long time to be in training. Another disadvantage is that there are more jobs than pathologists. That's

Portrait of a Veterinary Pathologist

Betsy Uhl didn't start veterinary school thinking that she would go into pathology, but once there, several factors influenced her decision to become a pathologist.

"I am visual and like anatomy, as the structure of tissues and organs is really amazing," Uhl says. "I like that as a pathologist I study disease in all species, from millipedes to elephants, and all organ systems. But the main reason I went into pathology was the desire to truly understand disease; in other words, how and why animals get sick."

Uhl says that some pathologists come to the field for another reason. Colleagues who had been in practice before turning to pathology were fatigued by the emotional effects of having to euthanize animals. They chose instead to devote their time to studying disease so they could help prevent it.

Uhl is an academic anatomic pathologist. A typical day involves lecturing to sophomore veterinary students or residents and graduate students; going to the laboratory to review results, help perform assays and plan the next experiments; and attending a committee meeting or seminar. That's in the morning.

"In the afternoon, if I am on service, I work on the necropsy floor with the senior veterinary students and residents and review histopathology slides from biopsy or necropsy cases with a resident," she says. "If I am not on service or teaching, I am finalizing case reports, working in the laboratory, working on a paper or grant, or preparing for my next lecture."

great if you're looking for a job, but not so good if you already have one. That's because you have to do a lot more work to take up the slack because either there is no one to hire or the person hired has little experience.

Depending on years of experience, location, and whether a pathologist is employed in academia, in industry, in government, or privately, salaries range from $30,000 to $280,000. Another advantage is that pathologists do not need to take 2 a.m. emergency calls.

"A bigger reward is that you develop both a broad and deep understanding of disease," Uhl says. "Many, if not most, of the major medical breakthroughs in understanding of disease came as a result of studying the diseased tissue. And veterinary pathology is arguably the most comparative specialty in medicine. Our knowledge of disease in a variety of species puts us in a unique position to make really important contributions. A veterinary pathologist [Tracey McNamara] at the Bronx Zoo was instrumental in recognizing the outbreak of West Nile virus in New York City [in 1999]. The MDs thought they were dealing with St. Louis virus encephalitis, based on antibody tests. She questioned the diagnosis because she had birds dying of viral encephalitis and knew that birds are not killed by the St. Louis virus. It was her persistence that led to the discovery that West Nile virus was the cause of the outbreak in both people and birds."

Toxicology

A toxicologist's job is to ensure animal, human, and environmental safety. The purview of veterinary toxicology ranges from biotoxins (natural chemicals produced by plants, animals, bacteria, fungi, and phytoplankton) to the toxic effects of pharmaceuticals, feed additives, radiation, and environmental agents on pets, livestock, wildlife, and humans. To determine the potential risk of a substance, a toxicologist requires expertise in chemistry, physics, immunology, pathology, physiology, molecular biology, developmental biology, public health, epidemiology, and risk assessment.

Veterinary pathologist Tracey McNamara was instrumental in recognizing the outbreak of the West Nile virus in New York City in 1999.

A toxicologist's job goes beyond safety assessments. Toxicology research provides insights into physiological functions, resulting in a better understanding of disease processes as well as the development of therapeutic strategies. A few of the questions toxicologists try to answer are how toxic substances affect various cells and organs, how veterinarians can treat animals that become ill after exposure to toxic agents, how industrial chemists can design safe pesticides and drugs, and why some animals experience adverse reactions to certain drugs.

Veterinarians trained in toxicology can choose from a number of career paths in animal, human, or environmental health fields. They do safety testing, risk assessment, and regulation for pharmaceutical companies or government agencies such as the Food and Drug Administration. At universities, companies, and institutes, they do research that contributes to understanding the pathophysiology, diagnosis, and treatment of chemically induced diseases in animals and people. Clinical and forensic toxicologists determine the causes and characteristics of accidental and malicious poisoning, and they work to protect animal and human food supplies from contamination. They work at veterinary colleges, in diagnostic laboratories, at poison-control centers, and in public-health departments.

Veterinary toxicologists play a role in the health of the environment and wildlife, using their knowledge to recognize chemically induced damage to ecosystems and to improve the management of such ecosystems. Toxicologists even go global, assessing the effects of chemicals on threatened or endangered animal species around the world and training veterinarians in less developed countries in toxicology.

The University of Illinois Veterinary Toxicology Residency Program is an example of the course work, research, and rotations encountered by toxicologists in training. Students spend time in the university's Veterinary Diagnostic Laboratory (VDL) and poisonous plant garden, and at the ASPCA Animal Poison Control Center (APCC).

The VDL has a caseload of more than 15,000 toxicology examinations per year. Residents become involved in toxicological analytical testing and interpretation, participate in diagnostic rounds with fourth-year veterinary students, and take part in field investigations. They learn about determining the appropriate analyses to run, sampling techniques and submissions, analytical methodology, and interpretation of test results.

At the ASPCA Animal Poison Control Center, which provides twenty-four-hours-a-day, seven-days-a-week telephone assistance to veterinarians and animal owners on more than 100,000 cases a year, residents gain experience in rapidly using scientific and medical information to identify relationships between illness and exposure to toxic substances. Residents acquire extensive training in clinical toxicology by managing cases over the phone and participating in APCC case rounds.

The poisonous plant garden is where residents, veterinary students, and practitioners can come to learn how to identify plants poisonous to livestock, companion animals, and human beings at all stages of growth and maturation over the growing season.

Board certification in toxicology requires graduation from an accredited veterinary college, four years of residency training, with at least two years under the supervision of a boarded toxicologist, completion of an advanced degree, publication of two peer-reviewed papers or completion of two funded research projects, and passing scores on the exam. There are two alternative routes to certification, requiring varying amounts of experience along with publication of peer-reviewed papers or completion of funded research projects in the field of toxicology.

John Tegzes, VMD, planned to be a surgeon when he was in veterinary school, but a lecture by a forensic toxicologist set his feet on a new path. He went into private practice after graduation but remained interested in the field. After practicing for five years, he did a residency in veterinary toxicology.

"I love it because it's comparative," he says. "We have to know a lot about all different species. It's not enough to know just about dogs and cats; we have to know how cows, horses, goats, sheep, chickens, people, rodents all react to different poisonings. And it's one of those areas where it's an emergency kind of thing. I like dealing with the acuteness of it. In these days of worry about pesticides in our environment and bioterrorism, it's actually a really important field for people to go into."

RESEARCH RESOURCES

- American Board of Veterinary Toxicology, www.abvt.org
- American College of Laboratory Animal Medicine, www.aclam.org
- American College of Veterinary Clinical Pharmacology, www.acvcp.org
- American College of Veterinary Microbiologists, www.acvm.us
- American College of Veterinary Pathologists, www.acvp.org
- American Society for Veterinary Clinical Pathology, www.asvcp.org

Canine Well-Being

For the person who has a scientific bent, an interest in pet health, and a desire to care for and work with animals, a career as a veterinary technologist or technician can have many rewards, but it's not the only option for people who want to work with animals to promote physical health and well-being. Other careers in this field include pet rehabilitation therapist, animal massage practitioner, dietary consultant, groomer, and even pet flight attendant. A person in any of these fields has the opportunity to affect pets for the better, helping to improve their mobility, nutrition, and appearance.

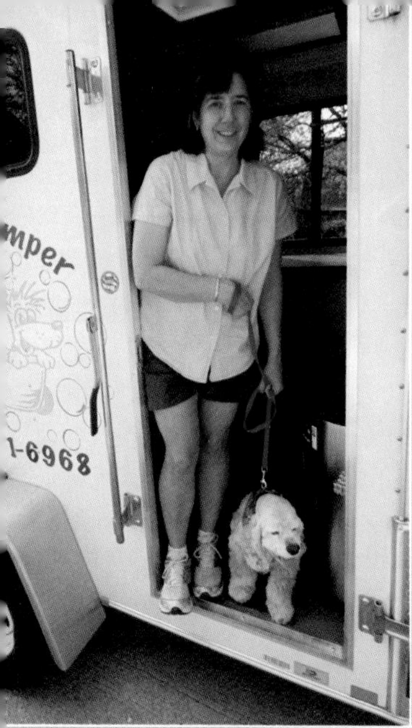

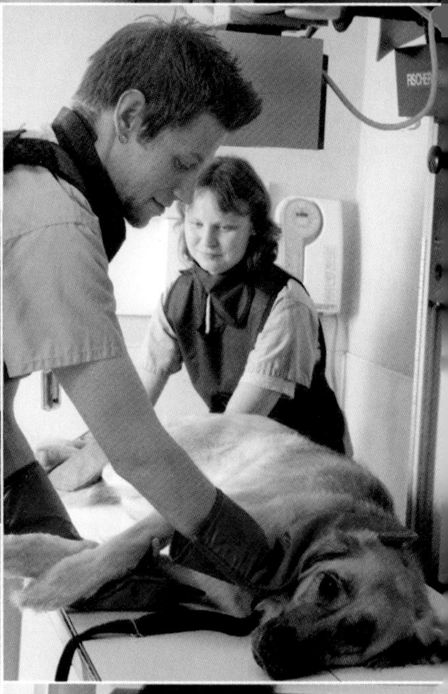

CHAPTER 12

Veterinary Techs and Rehabilitation Therapists

Veterinary technologists and technicians (vet techs, for short) usually work under the supervision of veterinarians, performing a wide range of tasks. For someone who loves animals, a career as a vet tech is satisfying and offers opportunities to specialize in certain fields, such as behavior or dentistry. Another specialized field a vet tech can enter is pet rehabilitation therapy; this field requires extensive education. Pet rehabilitation therapy is also open to people trained as physical therapists or physical-therapist assistants for humans.

Technologists and Technicians

When Julie K. Shaw was in second grade, she told her teacher that she wanted to be an animal nurse. The teacher responded, "You mean a veterinarian." "No," Shaw said, "an animal nurse. I just want to take care of them." She went on to become a veterinary technologist, a career that has only had a formal educational option since the 1970s. Most people picture vet techs working in private practices, but there are plenty of other places they can work; some have even started their own private endeavors.

What Vet Techs Do

The tasks performed by vet techs in private practice include taking case histories and doing preliminary examinations that consist of taking the pet's

temperature, listening to his heart, and recording his weight. Vet techs take blood and urine samples, prepare tissue samples, and perform tests such as urinalyses and blood counts. The techs also assist with teeth-cleaning procedures, and they help ready animals, instruments, and equipment for surgery. With experience, their duties may involve training new technicians, technologists, or other clinic personnel and discussing a pet's care or condition with the owner. Vet techs often deal with aggressive or frightened animals, running the risk of being bitten or scratched. Vet techs may also spend part of their work day cleaning cages or mopping up after animals who had accidents in the lobby.

A typical work week consists of forty hours, but certain jobs may call for fifty hours or more. It's not unusual for vet techs to work evenings, holidays, and weekends. At facilities with twenty-four-hour services, some vet techs need to work night shifts. And it's not necessarily a job you can leave behind when you go home.

Veterinary technologists and technicians may also find jobs at animal shelters or in animal- or human-health research facilities. Some vet techs work at diagnostic laboratories; drug- or food-manufacturing companies; boarding kennels; grooming salons; zoos; and local, state, and federal agencies. Duties in those jobs may include administering vaccinations, giving

What's in a Name?

There's a difference between a veterinary technician and a veterinary technologist. A technician has an associate degree in applied science in veterinary technology. A technologist has a bachelor of science degree in veterinary technology. Technicians and technologists may have overlapping skills, however, and may perform some of the same tasks.

Veterinary assistants act as aides to veterinarians or vet techs. They do routine tasks, such as setting up certain types of equipment or cleaning the surgical suite, scheduling appointments, and checking patients in. They may also clean kennels or do other janitorial work. Veterinary assistants usually learn on the job and are not required to pass any kind of credentialing exam. They usually have a high-school diploma or may have taken a certificate program online or through a local college.

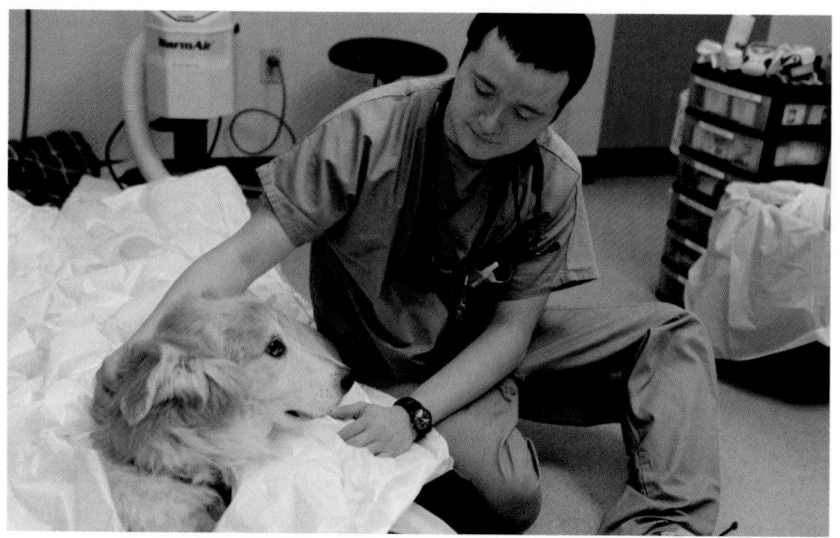

Surgery technician Eric Zamora checks on a patient. A surgery technician's duties include preparing animals for procedures, providing assistance during surgeries, and maintaining the surgical suites and supplies.

medications, and recording information about an animal's vital signs, diet, and weight. They may be required to euthanize animals who are ill, injured, or unwanted, and they may encounter people who neglect or abuse their animals. Those aspects of the job can be emotionally stressful, and they require someone who can remain calm and professional when dealing with uninformed or abusive pet owners.

Job opportunities are also found in wildlife medicine, genetic research, pharmaceutical sales, and the military. Wildlife techs may work at universities, zoos, or private organizations. In the field of genetic research, vet tech Mike Bannasch assisted in the development of genetic markers for use in evolution studies of male dogs.

Some veterinary technologists are certified to specialize in a particular area of care, such as anesthesia, behavior, dental care, or oncology. The responsibilities of a veterinary oncology tech, for example, include client relations and education, administration of oral and injectable medications, preparation and administration of IV solutions as directed by a veterinarian, IV catheter placement, taking digital X-rays, general patient care, lab work, and administration of chemotherapy and radiation treatments.

Julie Shaw is now a veterinary behavior technologist. Vet techs who specialize in this field work to improve the relationship between pets and their people, to promote animal welfare, and to decrease the euthanasia of healthy animals because of behavior problems.

Shaw works at the Animal Behavior Clinic at Purdue University's School of Veterinary Medicine in West Lafayette, Indiana. On a typical day, she assists with behavior consultations; determines an animal's trainability, anxiety, and aggression levels; and teaches clients how to apply the recommended behavior modification techniques.

"We can't diagnose, but we assist with the treatment plan and problem prevention," she says. "The best thing about

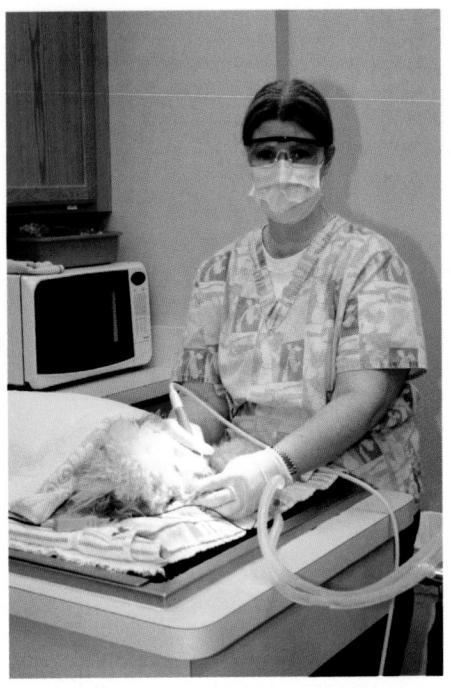

Vet tech Karen Reames cleans the teeth of a sedated patient. Reames specializes in dentistry.

being a behavior tech is improving the communication between owners and pets." When she's not working with clients, Shaw travels frequently, delivering lectures on behavior to veterinary professionals.

Registered veterinary technician Linda M. Campbell is the director of behavior and training at the Humane Society of Missouri (HSM) in St. Louis. She began her career at HSM in 1976 with a job assisting technicians there. In 1988, when she was offered the chance to attend school to become a vet tech, she took it. No day is typical in her current position, she says.

"Sometimes I work with the animal shelter and veterinarians to identify shelter animals with behavior issues that require modification; other

Barkworthy BITE

ALWAYS ON MY MIND

"It's more than a career; it is part of who I am. I'm always watching animals and reading their body language, whether I'm working or not. I'm never 'off' the job; veterinary medicine is always on my mind."—Julie K. Shaw, veterinary technologist days I may assist out in the field during a disaster and rescue or work with animals brought to our facility as a result of rescues and disasters. I provide public pet-training classes, work with veterinarians in our clinic to assist clients with problem animals, help educate staff and volunteers on animal behavior and handling, and manage a community-wide behavior helpline. I love the variety of experiences."

At the University of California at Davis, registered veterinary technologist Mike Bannasch is program coordinator for the Koret Shelter Medicine Program. Working with the veterinary team, he investigates infectious-disease problems in shelters, identifies trends at shelters, and establishes goals to improve the health and well-being of animals in shelters.

The work that Bannasch does requires medical, technical, and presentation skills. He collects biologic samples, performs cell cultures and biochemical analysis of bacterial samples, and takes case histories on animals with health problems common to animals in shelters, such as upper-respiratory infections and infectious diarrhea, which he then presents to clinicians and faculty members for their input. He developed and maintains the shelter medicine information Web site (www.sheltermedicine.com/about/welcome.php) and presents lectures around the country on topics ranging from infectious-disease control to changes and advances in the veterinary technician's role in pet-population control.

Bannasch, who holds a BS in biology, says, "I get to work with an unbelievable team of deeply dedicated and highly skilled professionals in an emerging field whose main objective is to improve the health and welfare of homeless animals. It's highly challenging and equally rewarding."

Who Vet Techs Are

One of the most important skills you will need as a vet tech is the ability to communicate with people about their pets' medical or behavioral needs. "It's one thing to understand the big theories or scientific details about a disease and talk about the disease as a professional," Amanda Eick-Miller says. "It's a completely different world when you have to talk to the client who is crying and upset because her husband told her to euthanize the dog for chewing up the couch. You also have to learn how to keep your personal convictions or crusades out of your work. There are things I may not feel are ethical, such as use of shock collars or prong collars, but it doesn't give me the right to inflict those views upon others. I had to learn how to take those situations that made me personally uncomfortable and use my education and training to teach the client and allow them to make the decision or come to a point where they asked me what I would do. The ability to relate to humans is what will ultimately help or hurt your patient."

The ability to communicate with people is also essential for your own growth in your career, especially if you choose to go into business for yourself. You'll need to build relationships with people you do business with, such as the veterinarians who refer business to you, the behaviorists and trainers to whom you refer clients, and of course the clients themselves, who rely on you to help them understand their pets' behavior and medical needs. A vet tech must also be able to gain an animal's trust while ensuring that no one gets injured.

Education and Training

If you think this is the career for you, take as many math and science courses as possible, starting in high school. For many animal lovers, those classes can be the most challenging aspect of becoming a vet tech, but they can't be bypassed. Coursework in a degree program also emphasizes the practical skills necessary in a clinical or laboratory setting. Experience counts, too. Volunteering at humane societies and fostering pets is a wonderful way to gain experience and help animals.

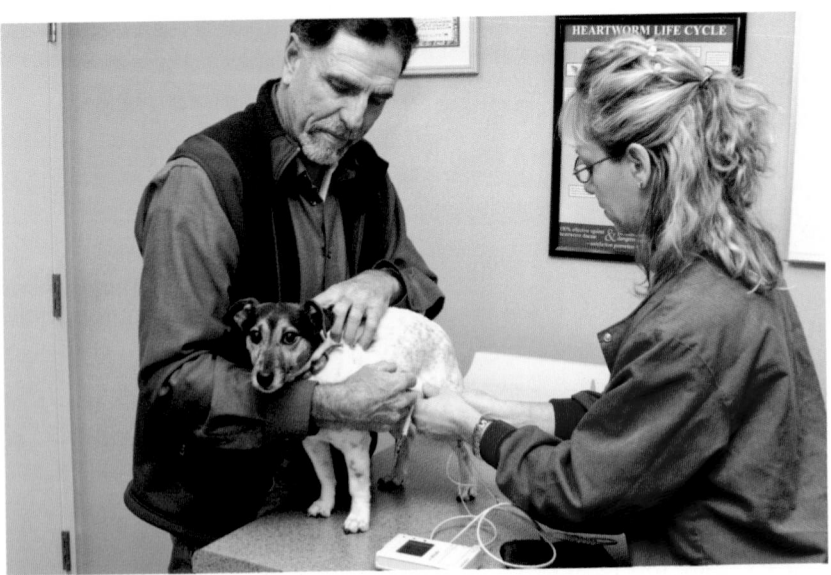

A veterinary tech does an EKG reading of Molly's heart during a visit to the local veterinarian.

Practical Experience

For some vet tech students, home life was a good preparation for this type of work. Eick-Miller grew up on a farm in rural Ohio, with dogs, rabbits, hogs, horses, sheep, cats, and ducks. In high school, she worked for a woman who bred Golden Retrievers, a job that involved exercising and grooming the dogs and helping socialize puppies.

Randi Golub, a certified vet tech in Eugene, Oregon, is the proprietor of Cat Nurse On Call. Working through referrals from veterinarians, she does in-home nursing care for terminally ill, geriatric, and diabetic dogs and cats. Golub's early preparation for her career included a seasonal job at the Philadelphia Zoo when she was in high school. "I did animal care in the Children's Zoo with exotic and domestic animals," she says. "I also did educational shows for zoo visitors and in schools. It was a great job with a lot of responsibilities. It taught me how to be comfortable working with lots of different kinds of animals as well as people, and it gave me experience in handling, restraining, performing simple medical treatments on, feeding, and cleaning up after animals."

Observing and reading about animals and their behavior are two more ways to gain knowledge. Keep a diary or blog of your observations about your own pets and other animals you encounter, including wildlife. If you want to figure out why animals do what they do, try to think like them and use your intuition, Golub advises.

There are many avenues that can lead toward a career as a vet tech, and there are numerous opportunities to grow and develop in the direction you desire. "Don't allow yourself to give up," Campbell says. "Anything worth accomplishing takes hard work."

DO YOU HAVE WHAT IT TAKES?

VET TECHNOLOGISTS AND TECHNICIANS

Vet technologists and vet technicians should have the following characteristics:

- ○ A calm demeanor, especially in stressful situations
- ○ Attention to detail
- ○ Excellent communication skills with both people and animals
- ○ Compassion
- ○ Flexibility
- ○ Good listening skills
- ○ Good organizational skills
- ○ Patience
- ○ Physical strength to lift, hold, and restrain animals
- ○ A sense of humor
- ○ The ability to be a team player

Pet Airways Flight Attendant

A new option for vet techs who want to take to the skies is a job as a flight attendant for Pet Airways, which transports only pets, not people. For ground-crew and flight-attendant positions, the company likes to hire people trained in pet first-aid or with a background in dog training or behavior. The ideal candidate has a background as a veterinary technician, says Arden Moore, who has completed the airline's flight-attendant training. Besides a love of dogs and cats and a yen to travel, attendants need people skills, time-management abilities, knowledge of positive-reinforcement training techniques, and the ability to give medication. Because they have access to the tarmac, they must pass a security background check as well. Pet Airways cofounder Alysa Binder says the job requires an outgoing personality, a sense of responsibility, a willingness to work irregular hours, the ability to lift fifty or more pounds, and a can-do attitude.

Pet Airways founders Alysa Binder (*left*) and Dan Wiesel (*right*) and newly minted flight attendant Arden Moore.

Ground-crew members call pet owners ahead of time to ensure that they bring up-to-date health certificates and other required items, and they check pets in as they arrive at the Pet Airways lounge. As they do so, they make sure none of the "pawsengers" looks sick. Assertiveness and tactfulness are necessary to tell an owner that a pet who is sneezing or has runny eyes can't fly that day. Pets are checked in during a two- to three-hour window, so early arrivals must be walked or cared for as needed until boarded. In the air, flight attendants check on pets every fifteen minutes to make sure they are calm and comfortable.

Many of Pet Airways' flight attendants are vet techs or have worked at shelters or dog day-care centers. Some are flight attendants who like animals and made the switch to this pets-only airline. Says Moore, "This is a job for a person who brings together the skills of health care, training, and hospitality and is interested in being in a new field."

College

The profession of veterinary technology is young. It received a jump-start at the State University of New York at Delhi in 1961, when a program was developed to provide trained team members for local veterinary clinics, Eick-Miller says. Currently, the American Veterinary Medical Association (AVMA) accredits more than 100 U.S. veterinary technology programs.

Aspiring veterinary technicians must complete an associate degree program, while veterinary technologists need a bachelor's degree. Degrees can be obtained at community colleges and vocational schools with accredited veterinary technology programs as well as by distance learning. Some colleges and universities, such as Purdue, offer a bachelor's degree in veterinary technology or an associate's in laboratory-animal science.

At Purdue University, which has the only veterinary technology program taught within a school of veterinary medicine, students get real-life clinical training at the Purdue Veterinary Teaching Hospital. Students in the AVMA-accredited program, which offers training for technicians and technologists, learn such skills as how to use stomach tubes; perform skin scrapings; prepare, give, and dispense vaccines and medications; monitor vital signs; run electrocardiograms; perform needle biopsies; identify external parasites; perform first aid for emergencies; apply and remove bandages; organize surgical instruments; prepare pets for ultrasound; place IV catheters; monitor animals under anesthesia; order and store equipment and supplies; sterilize instruments; calculate dosage levels; counsel clients on the use and administration of medications; and more.

Students in the veterinary technology program also learn leadership and problem-solving skills that help prepare them for work as supervisors. They may become clinic staff supervisors, hospital managers, or instructors in veterinary technician programs or veterinary school hospitals.

Credentialing Exam and Continuing Education

Earning a two- or four-year degree is only the first step in working as a vet tech. Vet techs must then pass a credentialing exam to prove their competency. A graduate of an AVMA-accredited vet tech program may take the credentialing exam in any state. Those who pass assume the title certified, licensed, or registered veterinary technologist/technician. They must also earn continuing-education credits throughout their careers.

Vet techs who wish to work in a laboratory should seek certification from the American Association for Laboratory Animal Science (AALAS), a professional association. The program focuses on animal husbandry, facility management, and animal health and welfare. The AALAS certifies vet techs at three different levels. Techs must pass a multiple-choice exam for each level as well as meet education and work-experience requirements. Whether you specialize or not, continuing education is essential. Technology and medical and behavioral knowledge change rapidly.

Specialty Programs

The degree offers other career opportunities as well, such as becoming a specialty-practice technologist with expertise in such fields as dermatology, surgery, internal medicine, emergency care, or behavior. Achieving recognition as a vet tech specialist requires additional study and experience. For instance, veterinary technician specialists in dentistry must have graduated from an AVMA-recognized technician program and have at least 6,000 hours (three years) of experience as a credentialed technician within the state in which they are employed, with approximately 3,000 of those hours having been spent in dentistry.

Applicants accepted into the credentialing program must keep a certain number of case logs in different areas of dentistry, write five case reports worthy of publication in a peer-reviewed periodical, and take forty-one hours of continuing education in various aspects of dentistry. This program takes about two years to complete. A three-part qualifying exam is the final hurdle, but to maintain the credential, vet techs must take continuing-education courses and labs throughout their careers. Vet techs who want to specialize in anesthesia, behavior, emergency and critical care, or internal medicine must meet similar requirements in those fields.

 **Barkworthy ADVICE**

WORK-LIFE BALANCE

With any job that involves caring for others, it's often difficult to leave work behind at the end of the day. To remain fresh, it's important to set aside time for yourself, your family, and your own pets. "When I was in practice, I was constantly bringing home projects and journals and staying late to help with emergencies. I felt guilty asking for a day off or to leave early to meet family commitments because I knew how much I was needed and we were always short on help," says vet tech Amanda Eick-Miller. "You have to be able to tell your employer no. I think a lot of technicians are afraid to do this because they don't want to lose the opportunities for overtime or advancement."

Practice Management

Some veterinary technicians become practice managers. They handle the business side of running a veterinary clinic, such as bookkeeping, payroll, ordering supplies, customer service, and staffing. A good practice manager can get the most out of a clinic's income through careful monitoring and management of the clinic's invoices, inventory, and workflow.

Other practice manager duties include checking the appointment schedule, resolving client complaints or billing issues, facilitating promotions, reviewing and renewing advertisements, meeting with pharmaceutical and equipment representatives to learn about new products, and ensuring compliance with OSHA and AAHA regulations and standards. A practice manager may also be in charge of maintaining a clinic's Web site or Facebook page.

Often, practice managers, such as Judy Colan of Foster, Rhode Island, learn on the job. Colan began as a vet tech. Her only formal education as a practice manager involved going back to school to study bookkeeping and computer techniques. "Most people don't start out in a management position; they start out as a tech or receptionist," she says.

There is, however, a certification program for veterinary-practice managers through the Veterinary Hospital Managers Association. Applicants must document their educational background, practice experience, leadership experience, and any achievements. Minimum requirements in each of these areas must be met before applicants qualify to take the written exam, which covers management knowledge in such areas as human resources, law and ethics, marketing, finance, and practice organization. The exam may have as many as 200 multiple-choice and true-false questions and must be completed within three and a half hours. Once achieved, certification must be maintained through continuing-education classes and work experience.

Experienced certified practice managers or credentialed veterinary technicians can become practice consultants for the American Animal Hospital Association. Practice consultants perform on-site evaluations for accreditation and help clinics improve patient care and client service. The job requires excellent communication and computer skills as well as a willingness to travel frequently.

Employment Outlook

Employment in this field is expected to grow by 36 percent through the year 2018, much faster than the average for all occupations. The job of veterinary technician ranks fifth among the fastest growing professions. Employment is expected to remain stable, even during times of economic recession. No matter what the state of the economy, people do their best to take care of their animals, and that means jobs for vet techs. Vet techs who specialize in fields such as dentistry or surgery may do especially well.

While vet tech jobs are relatively available in most areas, competition exists in zoos, primarily because there are a lot fewer zoos than veterinary practices and the people who land zoo jobs tend to stay.

The annual mean, or average, salary for a vet tech is $29,850. Vet techs who work for state governments may earn salaries ranging from $28,000 to $52,000. Experienced vet tech instructors at junior colleges can make $55,000 to $79,000. Employers may also offer paid vacation, sick leave, retirement plans, health insurance, and other benefits, such reimbursement for uniforms. Income varies according to education level, experience, and responsibilities; the geographic location; and the type of practice or facility. Certified or licensed vet techs will probably earn more than will assistants without such credentials.

Whatever the salary, being a vet tech is generally a rewarding career. Vet techs help return pets to good health, inform pet owners about health care, and help solve medical and behavior problems.

"The best thing for me is seeing clients 'get it' for the first time when you are working with them to correct a problem behavior," Eick-Miller says. "When they tell me how they implemented what I taught them in order to solve a different problem, I know they have gained a new understanding of how to communicate with their pet in a positive manner."

Campbell appreciates being able to salvage a relationship between pet and owner or rehabilitating an animal that might not have been adoptable. For Golub, it's having the ability to provide care and comfort to animals.

What else is there to know about being a vet tech?

"You'll never be able to wear black during the day again," Golub says.

Pet Rehabilitation Therapist

Like pet rehabilitation veterinarians, pet rehabilitation therapists (who are not vets) must receive specialized training in rehab techniques for animals. If they have been trained in human physical therapy, they must learn animal anatomy. They use their knowledge of rehabilitation techniques and animal anatomy to help their patients recover from injuries, trauma, other physical ailments, and surgery.

Portrait of a Vet Tech

Vet tech Amanda Eick-Miller (*pictured with Sally*) took a roundabout route to her career. She was a history major in college and worked in veterinary practices to pay her tuition. During her senior year, she was hired by a veterinary clinic where she was able to see different ways of treating medical cases, talk to the veterinarian about surgery, and become more involved in treatment and nursing care. The veterinarian suggested that she look into a career as a vet tech.

"I really enjoyed the idea of all of the different things I would learn and the ability to work anywhere in the United States once I had my VT degree," Eick-Miller says. "There wasn't a huge job market for historians. I started my first VT class one week before graduation."

Now she's a registered veterinary technician and certified dog trainer in business for herself as the owner of Pawsitively Pets in Wooster, Ohio. On a typical day, she travels to clients' homes in the morning to work with them and their pets. Afternoons and evenings are spent meeting new clients. One to two days a week are devoted to management and business details such as ordering supplies, billing, marketing, and record-keeping. Phone calls to clients or referring veterinarians take up one to two hours each day. She teaches one or two nights a week for a local vet tech program, speaks at national veterinary conferences, and contributes articles on animal behavior and training to veterinary journals.

Currently, she's investigating programs that would allow her to earn a master's degree or PhD in animal behavior. In the meantime, she attends hands-on seminars on animal learning and training as well as veterinary behavior seminars at national meetings, and reads textbooks, animal-training books, and scientific journals on animal learning and behavioral research. "I spend a lot of time reading, researching, and implementing techniques with my own animals and my clients' animals."

What Pet Rehab Therapists Do

The task of a pet rehab therapist is to help animals regain lost physical functions and improve mobility. They help relieve the pain of arthritis, hip dysplasia, and other ailments or injuries and assist animals recovering from surgery. They help healthy, athletic animals maintain overall fitness and health and reduce their risk of injury through conditioning plans. Their patients include dogs hit by cars, police or other working dogs with

Pet Ambulance Service

When Darcy, a tricolor Cavalier King Charles Spaniel, was taken to the emergency room because she was having difficulty breathing, she was able to spend the night there, but the next morning she had to be transferred to another veterinary hospital with twenty-four-hour facilities. To arrive there safely, though, she needed to be transported in an oxygen cage. A pet ambulance was the answer.

Ambulances aren't just for people anymore. The vehicles are the same as those used for people, just modified with cages and oxygen masks made for pets. They are equipped with such features as climate control, technology for fluid and airway control, kennels to hold the patients, padding, stretchers, and ramps. Some have a crash cart for cardiac treatment or are stocked with medications and fluids to treat animals in immediate need of care. All they lack are sirens.

A driver for Animal Ambulance of Southern California is ready to roll.

Pet ambulances are staffed by emergency medical technicians or veterinary technicians who have specialized training in moving and restraining injured animals and providing emergency care at the scene and en route. Some companies will send a veterinarian to accompany the pet in the event of a severe injury or illness that requires specialized assistance.

Some pet ambulance companies also have an air ambulance or offer services beyond transporting sick or injured animals. They can serve as nonemergency pet taxis, delivering pets to or from the veterinary hospital, boarding kennel, groomer, or airport if their owners are unable to do so; bring a veterinarian to euthanize an animal in the home; and remove a pet's body for burial or cremation. Other companies offer services such as picking up animals from a home after a disaster if the owners aren't present. They are generally available twenty-four hours a day.

Costs to consider in starting this type of business are the purchase or lease and modification of vehicles, office rent, insurance, employee salaries and benefits, and advertising. Expect to invest as much as $80,000 to get started.

injuries sustained in their line of work, dogs with disabling conditions such as intervertebral disc disease, dogs with neurological conditions such as spinal stenosis, and even severely overweight pets.

After taking a medical history, a pet rehab therapist examines the dog to determine the level of his strength, range of motion, balance and coordination, posture, muscle performance, respiration, and motor function. Once this is done, the therapist can design an appropriate treatment plan.

A rehabilitation session may include exercises to improve flexibility, increase range of motion, or restore balance, coordination, and strength. Tools a pet rehab therapist may use include massage, ultrasound, lasers, underwater treadmills, electrical stimulation, and hot or cold packs.

Who Pet Rehab Therapists Are

Pet rehab therapists—the terms *physical therapy* and *physical therapist* are protected and may be used only by licensed physical therapists who work on people—come to their work in many ways. Some are veterinarians who have studied rehabilitation techniques, but becoming a pet rehab therapist doesn't require a veterinary degree. Physical therapists may become certified canine rehabilitation therapists or certified canine rehabilitation practitioners, and veterinary technicians and physical therapy assistants can earn the designation of certified canine rehabilitation assistant. Sometimes veterinarians and physical therapists pool skills.

Amy Kramer of Santa Monica, California, holds a doctorate in physical therapy and became certified as a canine rehabilitation therapist after studying at the Canine Rehabilitation Institute, which has campuses in Florida and Colorado. She became interested in pet rehab when her Rottweiler, Lucy, required knee surgery.

Education and Training

At this time, the University of Tennessee is the only university offering training in pet rehab techniques. Training is also available at the Canine Rehabilitation Institute in Florida. Certification in canine rehabilitation is open to veterinarians, physical therapists, veterinary technicians, and physical therapy assistants.

Typical requirements for certification include classes in anatomy, regulatory, and ethical issues; response of tissue to disuse or immobilization; common orthopedic and neurologic conditions of dogs; use of physical agents such as heat, cold, lasers, ultrasound, and electrical stimulation;

Pet rehabilitation practitioner Amy Kramer demonstrates stretches to help improve a dog's range of motion.

evaluation techniques; therapeutic exercises and other rehabilitation techniques; range of motion; sports medicine; therapies for arthritis; and pain management. Clinical experience, case studies, and written and practical exams are also part of an education in pet rehabilitation. Course requirements may differ depending on whether the student's background is in veterinary medicine or physical therapy.

Some practitioners specialize in areas such as sports medicine or treatment of neurological diseases, but most work wherever needed.

Becoming a Physical Therapist

One road to becoming a pet rehab therapist is to first become a licensed physical therapist. Being a licensed physical therapist requires an understanding of physical and neurological conditions that can affect movement, function, and health. Would-be physical therapy students at the undergraduate level should take courses in biology, chemistry, physics, and mathematics.

In addition to a bachelor's degree, a physical therapist must complete graduate-level work in biomechanics, neuroanatomy, signs of disease, and other science courses to earn a master's degree from an accredited physical therapy program. Beyond classroom work, physical therapy programs include laboratory work and supervised clinical experience. Most such programs take two years to complete. Some physical therapists obtain a doctorate in physical therapy, which calls for another three years of study. To practice, they must pass a national exam and meet the licensing requirements of the state in which they practice.

Amie Lamoreaux Hesbach of Port Republic, Maryland, has a master's degree in physical therapy and became certified as a canine rehabilitation practitioner through the University of Tennessee's program. "In 2000, I was recruited by a pair of boarded veterinary surgeons to further develop their small-animal physical rehabilitation program," she says. "Thinking it might be rewarding to dabble in this new field, I have found it to be overwhelmingly positive as a career path."

In part, that is because veterinarians and clients have been receptive to the benefits of rehabilitation therapy. The field of canine rehabilitation has evolved in only a short time. At first, dogs were referred mainly for postsurgical treatment.

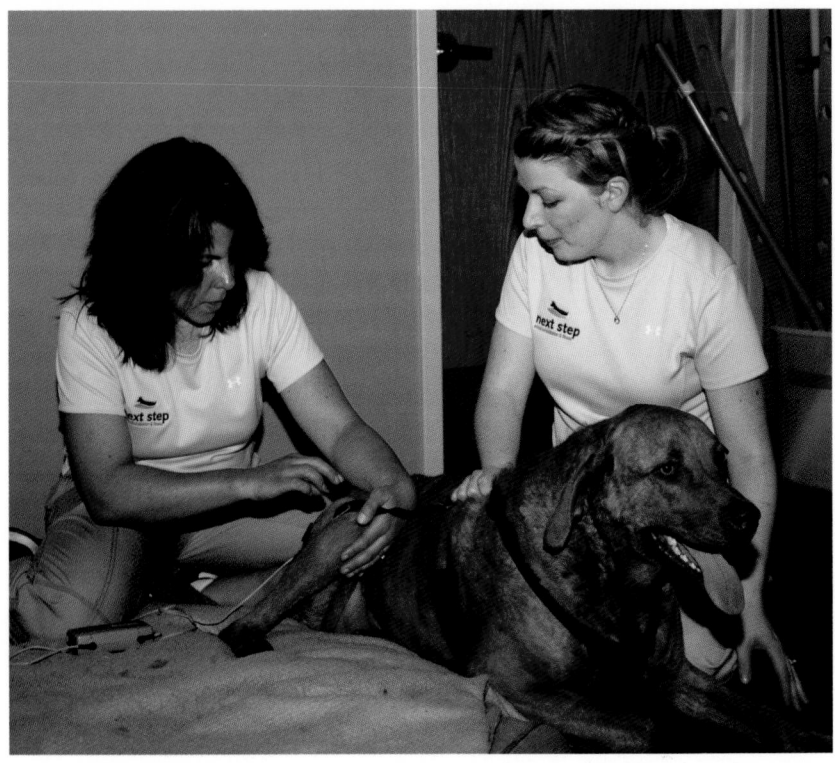

Canine rehabilitation therapist Amie Lamoreaux Hesbach and her colleague help a client. She is the owner of For Paws Rehabilitation in Huntingtown, Maryland.

"We now see canine patients prior to surgery and when surgery is not indicated," Hesbach says. "Tendonitis, muscle strains, peripheral nerve injuries, hip dysplasia, arthritis, obesity, and other degenerative, traumatic, or developmental disorders are commonly seen in the canine rehabilitation center."

Becoming a Therapy Assistant

Another pathway to pet rehab is to become a physical therapy assistant. Physical therapy assistants generally must complete a two-year associate degree in an accredited physical therapy assistant program. Like physical therapists, they must study the sciences: anatomy, physiology, biology, chemistry, and psychology. Physical therapy assistants are often certified in first-aid techniques, including cardiopulmonary resuscitation (CPR), and programs also include supervised clinical experience. Some states require assistants to meet certain licensing requirements.

Employment Outlook

Because the field of pet rehabilitation is so new, it's difficult to say what the outlook for employment will be. But pet care, especially in health, is important to most dog owners. Employment opportunities for veterinarians, veterinary technicians, physical therapists, and physical therapy assistants are projected to increase much faster than average, so it's safe to say that anyone with these skills can do well over the next decade.

The income range for physical therapists is $45,000 to $95,000; for physical therapy assistants, it is $26,000 to $57,000. The potential salary for a pet rehab practitioner is likely to fall somewhere in one of these ranges, depending on educational background, years of experience, and geographic location.

Fees for pet rehab work vary depending on the type of therapy and the location of the therapist; fees are generally higher in large metropolitan areas. A pet rehab practitioner may charge $115 to $200 or more for an initial one- to two-hour evaluation that includes a thorough history, physical exam, neurological exam, gait analysis, and treatment plan.

A day of treatment may cost $50 to $130, based on the complexity of treatment, the problem's severity, the technology required, and the size of the dog. A therapeutic ultrasound session may be billed at $40, while a session on an underwater treadmill may be charged at $50 to $80. Some practitioners lease equipment to pet owners for home use. For an average recovery period, fees can range from $500 to $1,500.

VET TECH AND PET REHAB RESOURCES

For a listing of AVMA-accredited veterinary technology programs, contact the American Veterinary Medical Association, www.avma.org.

- Academy of Internal Medicine for Veterinary Technicians, www.aimvt.com
- Academy of Veterinary Behavior Technicians, www.avbt.net
- Academy of Veterinary Dental Technicians, www.avdt.us
- Academy of Veterinary Emergency and Critical Care Technicians, www.avecct.org
- American Physical Therapy Association, Orthopaedic Section, Animal Rehabilitation Special Interest Group, www.orthopt.org/sig_apt.php

- Canine Rehabilitation Institute, www.caninerehabinstitute.com
- First Priority Emergency Vehicles, www.emergencyvehiclecenter.com
- National Association of Veterinary Technicians in America, www.navta.net
- Society of Veterinary Behavior Technicians, www.svbt.org
- UC-Davis Koret Shelter Medicine Program, www.sheltermedicine.com
- University of Tennessee Certificate Program in Canine Rehabilitation, www.utc.edu/Faculty/David-Levine/Veterinary.htm
- Veterinary Hospital Managers Association Inc., www.vhma.org

---

CHAPTER 13

Massage Therapist, Dietary Consultant, and Dog Groomer

Massage feels as good to pets as it does to people. It relieves pain and stiffness, helps improve healing time for soft-tissue injuries, increases flexibility, enhances muscle tone and range of motion, relaxes pets who are stressed, and helps keep working and athletic dogs sound. Conditioning is just as important for dogs that herd sheep and cattle or compete in agility, disc, or flyball events as it is for human athletes.

Nutrition is an essential component of a dog's good health. Not only does the right diet benefit canine skin and coat, but it can also be part of treating certain health problems, including allergies, cancer, and diabetes. Pet-nutrition consultants help pet owners and veterinarians ensure that a dog's diet is appropriate for his age, health status, or even breed.

Modern-day pet groomers brush, bathe, and scissor all breeds of dogs—and cats—and can be found working in corporate pet-supply stores, veterinary clinics, kennels, private salons, and mobile grooming vans. Pet groomers turn muddy, smelly dogs into neat, sweet-smelling companions welcome in their families' homes.

Pet Massage Therapist

Rubi Sullivan was attending a massage-therapy convention with a friend when she saw someone demonstrating massage techniques on a dog.

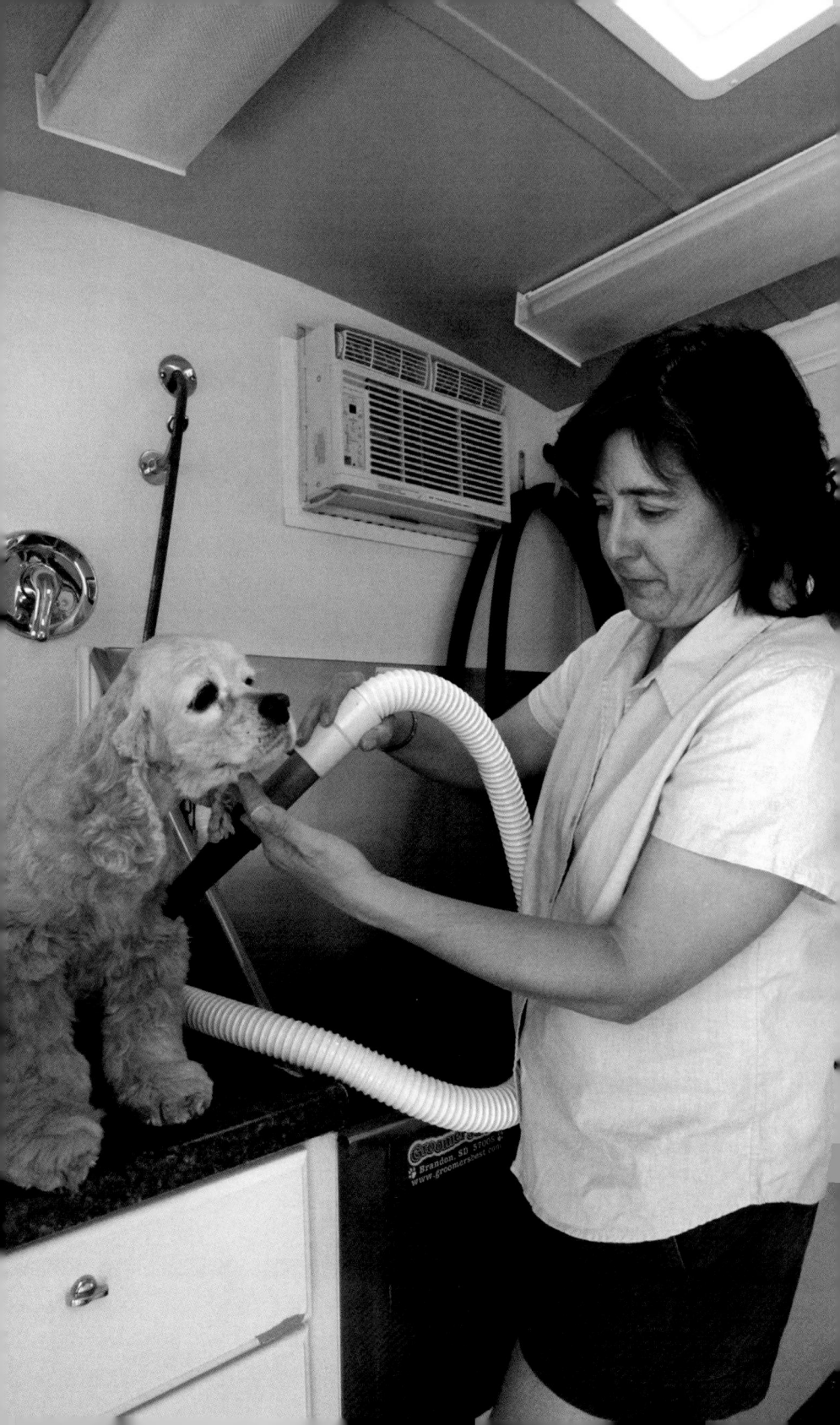

Sullivan's elderly dog, Bob, was suffering aches and pains, so she bought the DVD the demonstrator was selling, watched it several times at home, and practiced on Bob. "Bob loved it!" Sullivan says. "It was nice to see how it made him feel better."

As a result, Sullivan decided to study small-animal massage therapy at the Northwest School of Animal Massage in Fall City, Washington. After practicing for a year and a half, she earned further certification in rehabilitation massage therapy. Sullivan's clients have included a thirteen-year-old dog with severe arthritis who began to walk more smoothly and with less pain after beginning his massage sessions and a dog recovering from back surgery who had suffered nerve damage and needed to use a canine wheelchair, which required Sullivan to figure out new massage strokes to use on him because he was using different muscles with the wheelchair.

A dog relaxes under the skillful ministrations of pet massage therapist Rubi Sullivan.

What Pet Massage Therapists Do

Pet massage practitioners may be self-employed or on staff at a veterinary hospital, pet rehabilitation clinic, grooming salon, dog day-care center, boarding kennel, or other facility. One of the benefits of being self-employed as a pet massage therapist is the low cost of overhead. While a massage therapist for people may need to rent office space, purchase massage tables and other equipment, and pay for lighting and soft music, a pet massage therapist only needs transportation to go to clients. Some cities, counties, or states may also require the purchase of a business license.

Every practitioner's experience will be different, but for Sullivan, a typical day involves seeing two to six clients. She travels to homes, offices, veterinary hospitals, and other facilities to do her work. Preparation involves

Portrait of a Pet Massage Therapist

When Rubi Sullivan started her work as a pet massage therapist, she thought her clients would be animals with injuries or age-related aches and pains. That is certainly the case, but she has also found herself doing hospice work, massaging animals who are in the last stage of life. It is emotionally challenging but also rewarding.

"When I started, I figured most of the work I would be doing would be helping an animal rehabilitate and get better, but sometimes it's about being there for that geriatric or sick pet during those last hours," Sullivan says. "I feel so honored when a client asks me to be part of that transition—something I hadn't thought of before I started my career."

Pet massage wasn't really a career option when Sullivan was in high school or college, but when she did take it up, her background gave her useful experience. Her family had many pets during her childhood, and in high school she worked as a veterinary technician, assisting the veterinarian with many lab and patient procedures, including surgeries. She graduated from Oregon State University with a bachelor's degree in education and taught school for a couple of years. Eventually, she became interested in studying massage therapy and, from there, pet massage therapy.

After becoming a pet massage therapist, Sullivan found all of her background experience to be helpful. Her teaching experience comes to the fore when she does public presentations, and it has benefited her in her employment as an assistant instructor at the Northwest School of Animal Massage. Her work takes her to veterinary hospitals, dog day-care centers, and other local animal businesses.

At the end of the day, Sullivan is sometimes sore from doing too many massages or sad because a client has died, but she says the positives outweigh the negatives. She is excited every time she sees a big breakthrough in a pet's response to massage, whether it's seeing an animal finally relax during a session or working with a pet for a while and seeing a real difference in attitude and physical ability.

The best thing about practicing pet massage, she says, is getting to spend quality time with animals and help them feel better. "Not many people can say they get to make life better for animals for a living."

keeping a file for each animal she sees and reviewing her notes on the pet from past visits before starting the new session.

"Clients receive different massage work based on their specific needs," Sullivan says. "Updates from the parents are always good to get before seeing the animal again. Occasionally, there is an emergency e-mail or phone call when a client isn't feeling good or just needs a little extra that day."

Sullivan stays in communication not only with a pet's people but also with the animal's veterinarian, day-care staff, physical therapist, dog walker, or other caretakers.

"Working with each animal's specific community is great to do," Sullivan says. "You get a well-rounded perspective on what everyone is seeing. A community effort is best for the animal, so keeping in touch with everyone is a weekly duty."

Not all of Sullivan's time is spent working with paying clients. As her schedule allows, she volunteers her skills at local shelters and rescue groups, providing massages to stressed shelter dogs.

Who Pet Massage Therapists Are

To be successful in pet massage, you need some knowledge of breeds and their temperaments, as well as be physically in shape. Patience is essential. When an animal is uncertain or in pain, going slow can help him relax enough to benefit from the massage. Being able to read animals' body language is also important.

A pet massage therapist's work involves much more than just laying hands on animals. There's also billing, setting up your weekly calendar, and marketing your business to veterinarians, other pet-business owners, and pet owners themselves. Finally, Sullivan notes that pet massage is difficult and rewarding on both an emotional and a physical level.

Education and Training

Several schools offer courses in animal massage. No previous experience

DO YOU HAVE WHAT IT TAKES?

MASSAGE THERAPIST

A pet massage therapist should have the following characteristics:

- People skills
- An interest in animals, pet wellness, and anatomy
- Familiarity with animal behavior and body language
- Physical strength
- Patience

is necessary, but of course you should be comfortable handling dogs, cats, and other animals. Some people enter the field by taking classes in pet massage after becoming certified in massage therapy for people.

Courses that may be included in a pet massage program are massage techniques, canine and feline anatomy and biomechanics, rehabilitation techniques, massage for canine athletes such as agility dogs or sled dogs, first aid, business ethics, and business development.

Credentialing for pet massage is in its infancy. Schools offer certifications to students who have completed their course requirements, but there is no recognized national certification. Pet massage schools can be accredited by the National Certification Board of Therapeutic Massage and Bodywork, which is recognized by the Association of Bodywork and Massage Professionals and the American Massage Therapy Association.

While there are no federal requirements to become a pet massage therapist, individual states may require that pet massage therapists work under veterinary supervision or obtain a human massage license in addition to training for animal massage. Check with your state board of veterinary medicine, state board of massage, or department of health for current requirements.

Employment Outlook

Pet massage is a relatively new field, but it appears to be gaining in popularity. Pet owners may seek it out for aging or injured animals, or it may be recommended by a veterinarian as part of a rehabilitation program.

Depending on where they are located and their level of experience, pet massage practitioners charge $50 to $120 per hour, according to the

Northwest School of Animal Massage. There may be additional fees for specialized treatments or travel expenses. The length of a pet massage may vary based on the size of the animal, the type of injury, and the animal's comfort level and attention span.

Pet Dietary Consultant

Monica Segal became interested in nutrition when her dog Zoey had a gastrointestinal problem not treatable with medication or commercial diets. She began reading about canine nutrition, focusing on material written by veterinary nutritionists, and followed up her reading with courses at the University of Guelph in Ontario, Canada. Today she is certified in animal health care through the University of Guelph, with studies in animal nutrition, physiology, diseases, parasites, and pet care, and she has written two books on canine nutrition.

Certified pet massage therapist Theresa Randolph relaxes a canine client. Randolph, who is also certified in energy healing and Reiki, owns Gentle Sensations in Clemens, Michigan.

"I was fortunate enough to have an extremely knowledgeable veterinary nutritionist take me under her wing, and I learned much from her," Segal says. "This translated to a better-rounded education because it was a combination of study and practical experience."

At first, Segal used her knowledge only with her own dogs, and then someone in a puppy class asked for her advice. Now she has an Internet consulting business with clients who are referred to her by their veterinarians or who hear about her from other clients.

There were challenges in setting up her business, two of them being cash flow and finding a market. At the time, people were skeptical not only of Internet businesses but also of home-prepared diets for dogs. But Segal persevered and gradually built up a clientele. She gained exposure by writing magazine articles and by appearing on local radio and television shows.

Gaining confidence in herself proved to be challenging as well. Segal says she had to let go of previously formed ideas about nutrition and understand the reactions of the individual dogs she was dealing with rather than relying only on what she had read in books.

What Pet Dietary Consultants Do

Susan Lauten has a master's degree in animal nutrition and a PhD in biomedical sciences from Auburn University. She teaches nutrition at the University of Tennessee College of Veterinary Medicine and has a business as a pet-nutrition consultant, working with pet owners, veterinarians, and veterinary specialists. Lauten not only makes nutrition recommendations for dogs and cats but also formulates custom diets for working dogs or canine athletes, pets with health problems, and those pets whose owners simply want to provide them with the most appropriate diet for their breed or lifestyle. She also gives advice on choosing commercial diets or adding supplements to a pet's diet.

"What makes me a good nutritionist is that I am dedicated to dogs and cats, respect the human animal bond, and love working with and meeting new people," Lauten says. "I'm a geek about numbers and details, being a former CPA, so this suits me perfectly, and I'm extraordinarily passionate about my work. This is truly my place in the world."

Ideally, a pet-nutrition consultant meets personally with clients, allowing the consultant to see the animals and better gauge their conditions before making recommendations. Frequently, however, consultants do their work by phone or e-mail. Analyzing homemade diets for pet owners is easily done this way.

Nutrition consultants may also educate clients or the veterinary community by holding workshops and writing articles. Lauten has contributed to articles that have appeared in peer-reviewed publications such as the *Journal of the American Animal Hospital Association* and the *American Journal of Veterinary Research*.

For Segal, a typical day involves replying to client e-mails, commenting on or otherwise dealing with dietary changes the client has made, answering calls or e-mails from veterinarians, and beginning work on new client files. She must also meet deadlines for books, booklets, and articles.

"My days are extremely full and challenging. I often struggle to prioritize the priorities. For example, if four clients have dogs with cancer and three have dogs with serious diseases, all of them are priorities, but there are only twenty-four hours in a day."

Education and Training

It's best to have an advanced degree in animal nutrition or a degree in animal science with an emphasis in nutrition. Some universities offer certificate programs in animal nutrition. North Carolina State University's certificate program comprises four courses, which can be completed on

Career Rewards

The best thing about her career is when a dog who was desperately ill becomes well or at least surpasses expectations, says pet nutrition consultant Monica Segal. Often, her clients are dogs with serious health problems. One client in particular stands out—a thirteen-year-old Boxer who is cancer-free despite the prevalence of the disease in that breed. Her owner, Segal says, believes in taking a proactive approach to nutrition rather than waiting until there's a problem.

"This dog's age is wonderful for a Boxer to begin with, but what makes this more interesting is that this dog's sire, dam, and two siblings died of cancer many years ago. The dog owner started feeding a homemade diet when her girl was one year old and comes back to me yearly for dietary changes as needed to support the dog's age, weight, and so on. I can't claim that diet alone has spared this dog from cancer, but obviously the owner and I are proud of the results because the dog is full of energy and looks wonderful. This client stands out and has my utmost respect because she's never taken a 'wait and see' approach to her dog's care."

campus in Raleigh, via distance education, or in combination. If possible, apprentice with a veterinary nutritionist who can guide your studies.

Employment Outlook

There is no established income level for canine dietary consultants, most of whom are self-employed. Owning your own business can be financially challenging because there is no guarantee of a set income from month to month or year to year. Other opportunities for people with a background in this field include sales or marketing positions with pet-food companies. Nutritionists with advanced degrees, such as Lauten, may be employed by veterinary schools to teach students, consult with veterinarians in private practice, and provide continuing education for veterinarians.

Dog Groomer

A career transforming dirty mutts into Parisian Poodle lookalikes is a popular choice among dog enthusiasts—for good reason. There are a lot of dogs in the United States that need grooming, and there are a lot of owners willing to pay for it. In 2009, American owners spent $45.5 billion on pets, with $3.36 billion going toward grooming and boarding services. That's a big chunk of change.

What Pet Groomers Do

If you are interested in becoming a pet groomer, you must know that a groomer's primary goal is a neat, clean pet. To achieve that goal, the groomer bathes the pet; brushes, combs, trims, and styles the coat; cuts the toenails; cleans the ears; and sometimes expresses the anal glands or brushes the teeth. Depending on the environment in which a groomer works, there can be many other duties, such as answering the telephone,

Portrait of a Mobile Groomer

When veteran competitive groomer Teri DiMarino sold her grooming salon in south Florida after twenty-seven years and moved to Southern California to start a mobile grooming business, she enjoyed a "Zen-type experience." There were no sick employees, no barrage of telephone calls, no worries that had been regular parts of her fifty-dogs-a-day business. In the quiet solitude of her State of the Arf grooming van, she gained a new perspective. "Mobile grooming helped me rediscover my craft," she says.

Mobile grooming, in which the groomer drives a specially equipped vehicle to the client's home and grooms the pet in the vehicle, is an important niche within the grooming industry. Owners who do not wish to leave their pets at a salon for hours, as well as owners of elderly or young pets, often choose mobile grooming.

DiMarino, who retired from competitive grooming in 1993 and closed her mobile business in 2007 to open a small private salon in her home, appreciates that mobile grooming gave her a renewed sense of control over her time and money. Mobile groomers can set their own schedules because they are not tied to traditional business hours associated with a brick-and-mortar salon, and prices for mobile grooming are higher than salon prices because of the element of convenience. DiMarino usually worked three days a week, from 7:30 a.m. to 5:30 p.m., scheduling appointments about every two hours in a particular locale.

Mobile grooming allows for a more personal interaction with customers, says DiMarino, because groomers work at their clients' homes. For DiMarino, it was not unusual to hear a tap on the grooming van's door and be offered fresh-baked cookies or hear about an ill family member. Mobile groomers can also accommodate customers who wish to watch their pets being groomed.

The most expensive investment for a mobile groomer is the customized van, which can cost up to $85,000. DiMarino considers buying a well-equipped van, in spite of its high cost, a good investment. She suggests that mobile groomers think of their vans as a "location on wheels"—once the van is paid off, the groomer owns it, and there are no future worries about leases or monthly payments.

While there are numerous upsides to a mobile grooming business, DiMarino says that it may not be the best choice for a fresh-out-of-school groomer. Beginners are wise to work with other experienced groomers, suggests DiMarino, to improve and perfect handling, styling, and customer skills.

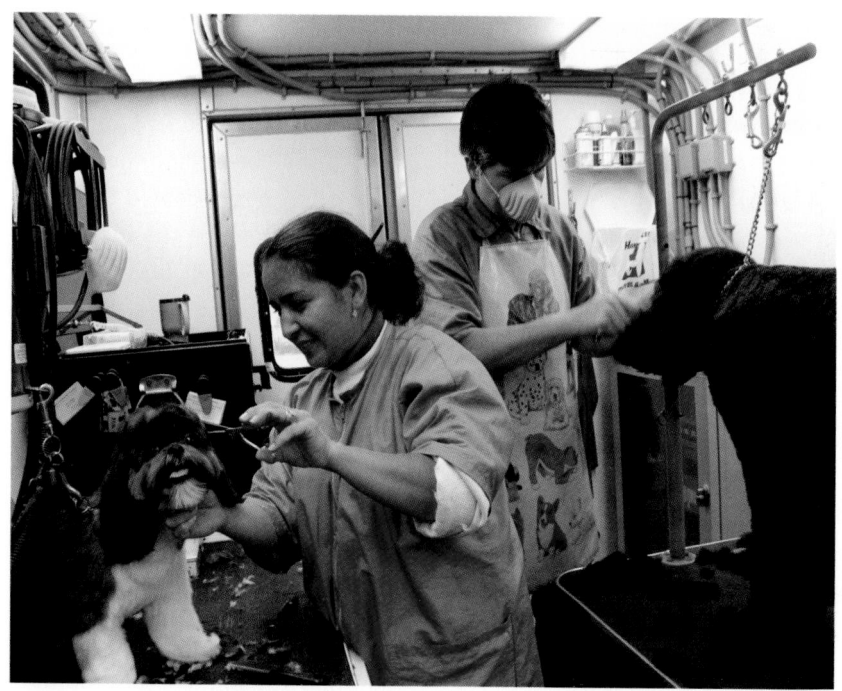

Two groomers of Rosa's Mobile Pet Grooming, in Kensington, Maryland, spruce up clients. Mobile groomers offer owners full service as well as convenience.

responding to e-mail, scheduling appointments, keeping records, handling payments, driving, talking with clients, showing or suggesting products, cleaning cages and grooming equipment, cleaning up feces and urine, sweeping and vacuuming hair, mixing shampoo, ordering supplies, and doing laundry. Groomers can work a varied schedule depending on their employers. It is not unusual to work part time.

The average groomer who owns his or her own business begins the day before the business opens and clients arrive. He or she prepares for the day by setting up equipment, checking supplies, folding towels, mixing shampoo, and checking phone and e-mail messages. Preparation is important, because once the business opens and clients arrive, the groomer is *very* busy with numerous tasks at once, including answering the telephone, discussing grooming options with clients, placing dogs (and cats) securely in cages, and usually, cleaning up a mess from an excited dog.

Once the mad rush is over, the groomer begins working on clients. A groomer's day is a race against the clock. The goal is to have all clients

DOG GROOMER

A dog groomer should have the following characteristics:

- ○ Artistic vision
- ○ Sense of proportion and balance
- ○ Willingness to work hard
- ○ Understanding of canine and feline behavior
- ○ Confidence in handling animals
- ○ Calm demeanor
- ○ Patience
- ○ Physical strength
- ○ Enthusiasm for turning dirty pets into clean, beautiful pets

finished on time, so which dogs are groomed in what order depends on when the pet is scheduled for pickup, as well as the breed and the services requested. A heavy-coated Samoyed, for example, may be the first dog in the tub even though he goes home last to ensure drying time.

The groomer first prepares each pet for bathing. This varies according to breed, but usually includes a thorough brushing, toenail trim, ear cleaning, and rough trimming if the owner requests a haircut. Bathing, drying, and combing out are next, followed by a second "finish" trim. A final touch of coat polish, bows, and often cologne complete the grooming session. The groomer doesn't always groom each pet in order, from start to finish, but may prepare, bathe, and dry a few dogs, then prepare two more dogs for bathing, finish another dog's trim, dry another, prep another, and so on.

It is not an exaggeration to say that on an average workday, a groomer is in constant motion—moving from grooming table to tub to drying table to grooming table—lifting, bending, walking, and moving to meet deadlines. There is usually no time for formal breaks or extended lunch periods. Groomers take breaks when they can. By late afternoon, the groomer is very busy again. In addition to grooming unfinished dogs, he or she is waiting for customers and answering calls regarding whether a pet is ready.

The groomer's day doesn't end when clients go home. There's cleanup, including vacuuming hair, sanitizing and putting away tools, wiping out cages, mopping the floor, laundering towels, and emptying trash. There is also record-keeping (maintaining a file on each dog that details the services performed at each visit), checking supplies, and reviewing appointments for the next day. The entire process starts all over again in the morning, unless the groomer enjoys a well-deserved day off.

Who Pet Groomers Are

What type of person is best suited to a career as a pet groomer? First, anyone considering grooming as a career must like and not be afraid of animals, particularly dogs and cats. A potential groomer must also understand—or be willing to learn about—canine (and feline) behavior. Handling dogs all day successfully requires great finesse, a calm demeanor, and patience.

Enthusiasm is essential for a grooming career, too. You have to want to groom dogs to work so hard and get so dirty for clients who sometimes try to bite you. Some of the work is unpleasant, while the general work environment is noisy and can be difficult. Grooming is best suited to those with an eager, positive attitude toward the profession and a willingness to work hard.

Groomer Lorie Thomas works on a canine client in a PetSmart grooming salon.

There is no question that groomers must have the physical stamina to do the job. Grooming is physically demanding, and it gets harder, not easier, with age. Potential groomers should be able-bodied, healthy, able to stand all day, and capable of lifting at least 40 pounds. Groomers often lift, hold, or restrain pets, risking bites or scratches. The work can include repeated bending or lifting heavy dogs in and out of the tub or onto a table. To make things easier, some groomers limit their clientele to small dogs. Grooming isn't all hard labor. It is also quite artistic. Turning a shaggy, dirty coat into an expertly sculpted style requires artistic vision and a skilled sense of proportion and balance. Potential groomers should have artistic aptitude and an interest in style.

Education and Training

There are several ways you can learn how to groom pets: grooming school, apprenticeship, and online/correspondence courses. Do your homework before choosing. The skills and credentials of the instructors are the most important considerations. Your training is only as good as your teacher.

Grooming-school programs—which provide students with hands-on, supervised training in the grooming of all breeds of dogs and cats—vary, and training courses can range from six to eighteen weeks in length. Some benefits of such a program are supervised, individual instruction on all breeds and coat types; exposure to current grooming equipment and trends; and training/experience in safe animal-handling practices. Good schools often offer financial aid, dormitories, and job placement. Some drawbacks are that tuition can be expensive ($6,000 to $10,000), and schools may not be located in the student's area. Though attending a school is the most expensive way to learn grooming, many industry

John Nash:
Founder of the Nash Academy

Dog groomers today regard John Nash, the founder of the Nash Academy, as the inventor of dog-grooming training. He set out to revolutionize the grooming industry, bringing his unique vision and innovation to the industry by standardizing the training of professional dog groomers. The Nash Academy was established in New Jersey in 1979 and then opened in Lexington, Kentucky, in 1988. Nash established highly successful and prestigious foreign-exchange-student programs with Japan and  Germany. Wife Vivian Nash served as the president of the Nash Academy. She was the International Dog Groomer of the Year in 1986 and has won the highest awards at Intergroom.

In 1998 John and Vivian cofounded the International Judges Association of Dog Grooming Competitions to standardize the judging of grooming shows around the world. In 2008 Nash launched the company's first online encyclopedia, www.CanineReference.com, followed in 2009 by www.GroomersReference.com, an international lexicon of grooming terminology. On January 1, 2009, he opened Nash Europe. On December 17, 2009, Nash lost his three-year battle with cancer.

These Poodles are competing at the Andis Poodle Tournament, one of the contests at Groom Expo, the largest grooming tradeshow in the world. It's held annually in Hershey, Pennsylvania.

professionals believe that, assuming the school is reputable and has skilled instructors, this is the best way to get an education in grooming.

Groomers can learn the trade as an informal apprentice or employee of a skilled groomer, a corporate-owned grooming salon, or a professional dog handler. The benefits of apprenticeship include supervised individual instruction, no tuition, and if an employee, getting paid to learn. On the downside, it can be difficult to find a willing mentor, it takes longer to learn this way, and you may have limited exposure to breeds depending on the variety of your mentor's clientele.

One of the latest trends in grooming education is courses offered online. Training is also available by mail with videos and written material. This method offers convenient, flexible study at home and can be combined with hands-on grooming-school classes. It's less expensive than attending grooming school. But there is no personal supervision or instruction, and you don't have access to professional equipment or a workplace. Students must locate dogs to groom and establish their own grooming setup.

Currently, there are no formal licensing requirements in the United States for pet groomers. However, many groomers are *certified*, which means that they have had their skills and knowledge tested by a certifying organization; they also compete for titles in grooming competitions. Groomers are certified by three primary organizations: the National Dog Groomers Association (national certified master groomer), the International Professional Groomers (certified master groomer), and the International Society of Canine Cosmetologists (ISCC certified). Certification is not required, nor does it guarantee employment, but it does reflect the groomer's serious commitment to training and education. Many grooming professionals recommend certification as a way to create and uphold professionalism, safety, and quality in the grooming industry.

Employment Outlook

Pet grooming is a career with some flexibility, and there are several options available. Groomers may work as employees for any business that offers grooming, including a large corporate business, mom-and-pop salon, mobile grooming business, veterinary clinic, do-it-yourself dog wash, dog day care, or boarding kennel. Groomers may also own and operate their own grooming business by purchasing an existing grooming business or starting from scratch. Some groomers operate their businesses from home if the location meets municipal business zoning regulations.

Getting a job as a pet groomer is no different than getting a job in any other industry. That means checking newspaper ads, online job boards (the Pet Groomer.com job board is very active), visiting groomer chat rooms, making phone calls, visiting businesses at which you'd like to work, and attending grooming trade shows.

Emily Meadows bathes a client before a grooming session. Sometimes groomers begin their careers as bathers, working as assistants to experienced groomers. Bathers are typically paid hourly.

Income varies for pet groomers, and depends upon area (grooming prices are higher in metropolitan areas, for instance), skills and experience, and how fast the groomer works. The professional groomer in a salon usually works on commission, often receiving 50 to 60 percent of each pet he or she grooms. The more pets groomed each day, the more money the groomer makes. Typically, a novice will complete two to three pets per day, while a pro may groom ten. The grooming business can also be seasonal. Holidays are usually busy, as well as spring and summer. Because of so many variables, and a changing flow of customers, income ranges from $15,000 to $60,000 a year. Small businesses do not usually offer benefits such as health insurance, savings plans, or paid vacations; corporate grooming positions do offer such benefits, though the pay is usually lower.

MASSAGE, NUTRITION, AND GROOMING RESOURCES

- Cal Poly San Luis Obispo, Animal Science Department, www.animalscience.calpoly.edu/areas_of_study/nutrition/index.asp
- *Canine Massage: A Complete Reference Manual*, 2nd ed., by Jean-Pierre Hourdebaigt. Direct Book Service, 2003.
- Catherine Lane, http://thepossiblecanine.com
- Colorado State University, Department of Animal Sciences, www.ansci.colostate.edu
- *Dog Massage: A Whiskers-to-Tail Guide to Your Dog's Ultimate Petting Experience*, by Maryjean Ballner. St. Martin's Griffin, 2001.
- Groomer to Groomer, www.groomertogroomer.com
- International Association of Animal Massage and Bodywork, www.iaamb.org/member-schools.php
- International Association of Animal Massage Therapists, www.iaamt.com
- International Professional Groomers, www.ipgcmg.org
- International Society of Canine Cosmetologists, www.petstylist.com/ISCC/ISCCMain.htm
- Iowa State University, Department of Animal Science, www.ans.iastate.edu
- Monica Segal, Pet Dietary Consultant, www.monicasegal.com
- National Board of Certification for Animal Acupressure and Massage, www.nbcaam.org
- National Dog Groomers Association of America, www.nationaldoggroomers.com
- North Carolina State University, certificate in animal nutrition, www.ncsu.edu/nds/certificates/undergrad/animalnutrition.html
- Northwest School of Animal Massage, www.nwsam.com/index.html
- Pet Care Services Association, www.petcareservices.org
- Pet Groomer.com, www.petgroomer.com
- Pet Massage Training and Research Institute, www.petmassage.com
- Pet Nutrition Consulting, www.petnutritionconsulting.com
- Tallgrass Animal Acupuncture Institute, www.animalacupressure.com
- Tellington TTouch Training, www.ttouch.com
- *The Healing Touch for Dogs: The Proven Massage Program for Dogs*, rev. ed., by Michael W. Fox. Newmarket Press, 2004.
- The Lang Institute for Canine Massage, www.dogmassage.com
- University of Alberta, Companion Animal Nutrition, www.ales.ualberta.ca/afns
- University of California, Davis, Postgraduate Certificate in Animal Science, http://animalscience.ucdavis.edu/students/graduates/certificate
- University of Wisconsin, Madison, *Animal Sciences Graduate Degrees Emphasizing Nutrition*, www.ansci.wisc.edu/students/areas/nutrition.pdf

Canine Science

If you love the quest for knowledge in and of itself, a career in scientific research is one to consider. The work can take you from the laboratory to the field to the classroom, and its reward is greater understanding of animal health and behavior, plus the spread of that knowledge to others.

Such a career requires a heavy investment of time in obtaining advanced degrees. Researchers usually find work at colleges or universities or in private industry, but depending on the type of work they do, some create their own unique jobs.

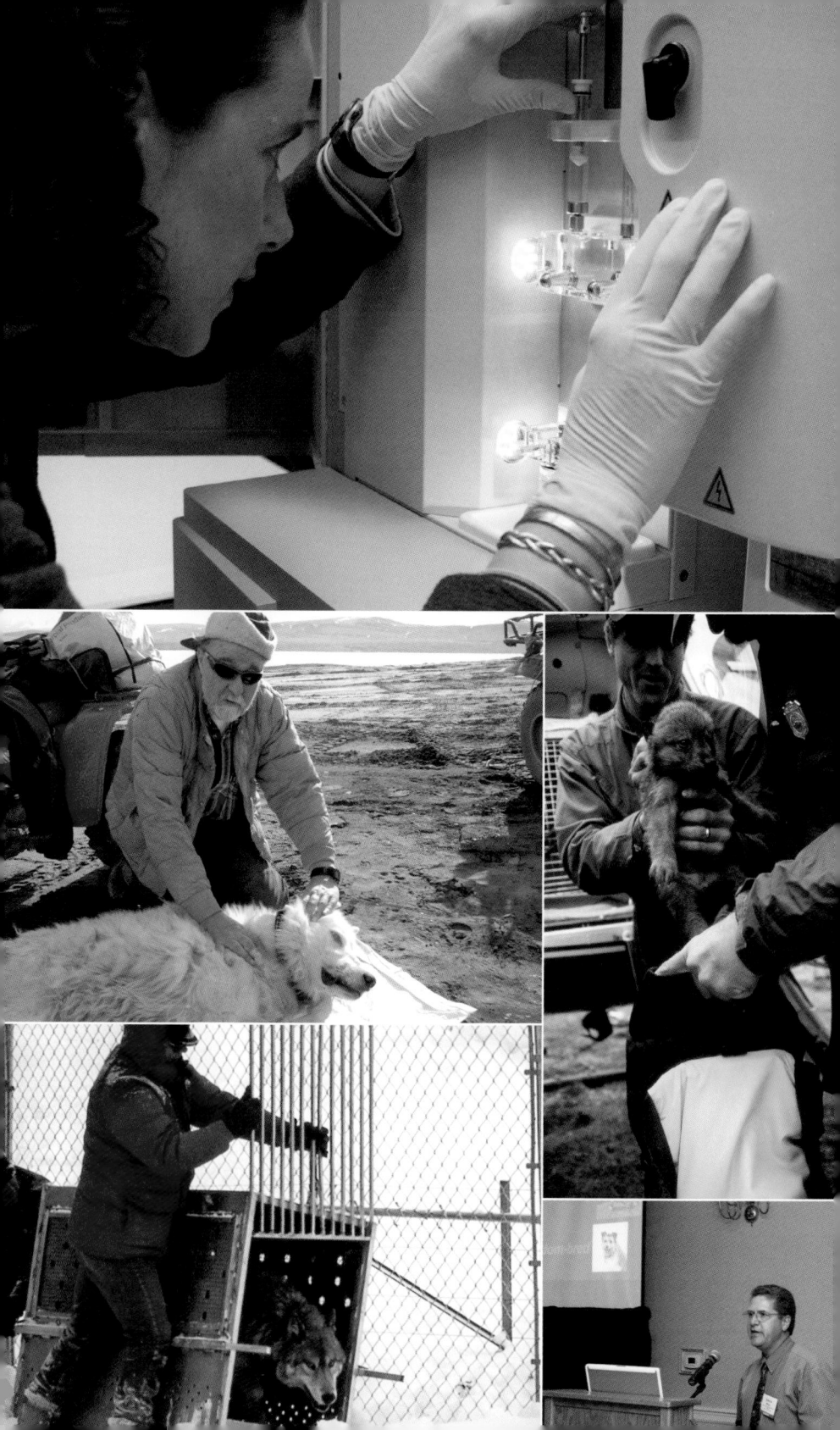

CHAPTER 14

Canine Genome Researcher

Canine genome research is a fascinating and productive area for scientists. As a species, dogs are unique, being the oldest domesticated mammal and the one with the richest assortment of breeds, sizes, shapes, coat colors, and behaviors. Unfortunately, dogs also suffer from a huge variety of genetic diseases, many of them similar to diseases in people. In studying diseases, researchers find that canine subjects have an advantage over human subjects because dogs are classified into hundreds of different breeds. That gives scientists more power to understand the mutated genes that contribute to disease; they can see how some genes stay normal in certain breeds while others mutate in certain breeds. Scientists can compare the dog genes to the same human genes.

By comparing the canine and human genomes (*genome* is all the genetic material in an organism), researchers can better understand the structure and function of human genes and develop new disease-fighting strategies in both species. In addition, comparative genomics provides a powerful new tool for studying evolutionary changes among organisms, helping identify the genes that are conserved among species along with the genes that give each organism its unique characteristics.

Research is done by veterinary specialists or evolutionary or molecular biologists. Their research may be basic, as in the search for new knowledge, or applied, with the goal of solving a particular problem. Research

involving the canine genome is being conducted at universities and at government and private laboratories around the world. The advances being made benefit the health of dogs and people as well as help people to better understand canine behavior and how to treat problems. For instance, genetic studies have shown that there are certain breed dispositions for abnormal behaviors, such as noise phobias and compulsive licking.

What Canine Genome Researchers Do

Scientists working on genome projects isolate genes and determine their functions, with the goal of understanding how certain genes work within an entire organism. They discover genes associated with specific diseases and inherited health risks. Their work leads to the development of new drugs, treatments, and diagnostic tests.

Nathan Sutter (*pictured on page 197*), PhD, is assistant professor of medical genetics at Cornell University College of Veterinary Medicine. His work regularly brings him into contact with dogs of many breeds, at Cornell's animal hospital and at events such as conformation shows, obedience trials, and hunt tests. "All of the work we do relies on collecting DNA from blood samples

Jerold S. Bell, associate professor and director of the Clinical Veterinary Genetics Course, Tufts Cummings School of Veterinary Medicine, speaks at a genetics conference.

from privately owned dogs in New York and all across the country," he says. "When dogs go for a regular vet visit, the owner brings along special vials that the veterinary technician draws the blood into. The owner then mails us the blood, a signed consent form, a copy of the dog's pedigree, and other information relevant to our research studies. We simply could not do our research without hundreds of contributions of time and effort from dog owners across the country."

It's not all fun and centrifuges, though. When they are not in the laboratory, research scientists spend a lot of time in their offices, writing grant proposals to obtain funding for their projects, writing up the results of their work, and reading journals to keep up with the latest research discoveries. They typically work forty-hour weeks, without a lot of overtime.

While earning his PhD in evolutionary biology, Robert K. Wayne found himself drawn to the study of dogs because of their diversity. For his dissertation, he studied development in four dramatically different dog breeds: the Lhasa Apso, the Cocker Spaniel, the Labrador Retriever, and the Great Dane. He wanted to discover how these breeds diverged from being fairly similar puppies to being very different adults. "Dogs seem unique in the range of conformations and morphologies they go through from puppyhood to adulthood," he says.

Later in his career, Wayne and his research team used a technique called mitochondrial sequencing to create a molecular clock that would span the millennia back to the time when dogs became domesticated. Using mitochondrial DNA of sixty-seven breeds and five cross-breeds representing a total of 140 dogs, plus DNA from 162 wolves, twelve jackals, and five coyotes, Wayne's team arrived at results that clearly support wolf ancestry for dogs. The wolf and dog sequences diverged only 1.5 percent on average, bringing welcome confirmation of what many canine ethologists had already suspected.

At the University of Pennsylvania School of Veterinary Medicine, professor of medical genetics and ophthalmology Gustavo Aguirre and his colleague Gregory M. Acland, professor of medical genetics at Cornell University's Baker Institute for Animal Health, as well as other researchers in their laboratories, are engaged in multiple research projects relating to the inheritance of retinal degeneration in dogs, humans, and other mammals. Their research includes efforts to identify the genes and locate the mutations associated with several separately inherited forms of progressive retinal atrophy in dogs. They collaborated with Elaine Ostrander in the construction of a linkage map of the canine genome, which is useful for genetic studies in both dogs and humans. They were the first to use gene therapy to restore the vision of blind dogs, and their work has led to the development of several DNA tests for inherited diseases.

Jerold S. Bell is a clinical associate professor and director of the Clinical Veterinary Genetics Course for the Cummings School of Veterinary Medicine at Tufts University. He studied genetics at Michigan State University and the University of Missouri and earned a DVM from Cornell University. A popular lecturer for breeders and clubs, he has published many articles on breeding and genetics in the *AKC Gazette*. He is the project administrator of genetic disease control programs for national parent clubs, and practices small animal medicine at Freshwater Veterinary Hospital in Enfield, Connecticut. He and his wife breed Gordon Setters.

Genetic tests allow breeders to identify carriers of certain diseases, breed away from defective genes, and ensure that they do not reintroduce defective genes. New research may lead to new forms of treatment for genetic diseases. Once genomic information is available for the molecular basis of a particular cancer, for instance, researchers may be able to target the specific pathways involved in the disease by stimulating receptors in a gene with specific drugs or chemicals, or to insert a normal gene into the DNA of cells to compensate for a nonfunctioning or defective gene.

Who Canine Genome Researchers Are

Elaine Ostrander received her PhD in 1987 from Oregon Health Sciences University; from there she went to the University of California at Berkeley to begin the Canine Genome Project. She wrote the first paper for the project in 1992, published in *Proceedings of the National Academy of Sciences*; in it she described a new method to isolate genetic markers. In 1993 she became a professor at the clinical research and human biology divisions at the Fred Hutchinson Cancer Research Center in Seattle, Washington, where she and her team made the first meiotic linkage map of the dog, based in part from DNA samples generated from the team at Cornell.

Ostrander's lab has published more than 250 papers covering a wide variety of topics, including finding genes for canine epilepsy, kidney cancer, vision disorders, body size, and leg width and leg length. She collaborates extensively, working with colleagues all over the world. The most rewarding part of her job, she says, is the interactions with dog owners and breeders who provide the DNA samples her lab uses. "Talking with the dog owners reminds me how precious each canine life is, and how important these animals are to the families that love and care for them."

Ostrander is currently a senior investigator and chief of the cancer genetics branch of the National Human Genome Research Institute (NHGRI) in Bethesda, Maryland. She continues to coordinate the Dog Genome Project, the highly respected group of American and European

Elaine Ostrander, PhD, headed up the Canine Genome Project at the University of California, Berkeley. She is now chief of the cancer genetics branch at the NHGRI.

researchers whose work in genome sequencing identifies variants that are important in disease susceptibility in dogs and humans. Her comparative genetics laboratory is working on mapping the genes responsible for susceptibility to cancer, the number-one killer of dogs.

Ostrander describes her present work as focused on two things. "First we are mapping genes that increase a dog's susceptibility to getting cancer," she says. "Dogs die of cancer at the same rate that humans do and get many of the same types. Our goal is to find the genes that make some breeds more likely to get some kinds of cancer than others. That information can then be used to help both dogs and humans as our expectation is the same genes are involved in canine and human cancer. We are also interested in the genetics of growth regulation and, toward that end, we are mapping genes associated with aspects of body size, such as leg length, skull shape, overall size of the skeleton, etc. That allows us to better understand how dogs develop and what the genes are that control the extraordinary difference in body size and shape we see between the very smallest dogs . . . and the very largest."

Kerstin Lindblad-Toh: Gene Mapper

Kerstin Lindblad-Toh earned her PhD from the Karolinska Institute in Sweden in 1998. She is the codirector of the Genome Sequencing and Analysis Program at the Broad Institute in Cambridge, Massachusetts. She is the leader of the Mammalian Genome Initiative and as such has been at the forefront of research into the genome sequencing and analysis of canines as well as other animals. Her research abroad was made possible by a Svenska Institutet scholarship. Lindblad-Toh remains enthusiastic about her research: "The domestic dog encompasses hundreds of genetically isolated breeds,  many of which show an increased risk for certain diseases. With the availability of the canine genome sequence, understanding of the canine genome structure, and availability of disease gene mapping tools, we are now in a unique position to map canine disease genes to inform human biology and medicine."

As Ostrander's words and endeavors clearly illustrate, good research scientists are driven to find answers. Says Sutter, "Many days, you will work hard all day in the lab, put your samples into a machine, and then go home while the machine collects data. A good scientist is eager to get up in the morning and get back to the lab to see what the data's result was. Ultimately, science is the art of asking questions and then being curious enough to figure out how to answer them."

A careful nature is another important scientific trait. Researchers must perform the right sequence of steps in just the right way, or the experiment won't work. Samples must be handled properly so they don't become contaminated or mixed up with other samples. Being careful also entails properly interpreting the results of data to come up with the next experiment. Most importantly, a scientist must be honest. Says Sutter, "When I find out something new in the laboratory, . . . [it] is my responsibility to correctly communicate what I have learned to other people so they can think about it, poke at it, and repeat it for themselves."

Education and Training

Expect to earn a bachelor's degree in biology, evolutionary biology, or genetics. You'll need to take courses in biology, chemistry, mathematics, physics, and computer science. Computer courses are necessary for modeling and simulating biological processes, operating certain types of laboratory equipment, and performing bioinformatics research—decoding the biological information contained within genes and genomes.

Sutter emphasizes the importance of verbal and written communication skills for anyone who is interested in a research career. Scientists communicate by giving presentations or displaying posters at scientific meetings.

Dr. Donald F. Patterson:
Momentous Mentor and Geneticist

Born in Venezuela in 1931, Donald F. Patterson graduated from Oklahoma State University in 1954. He taught at Oklahoma State prior to being appointed chief of the first Section of Medical Genetics at the University of Pennsylvania School of Veterinary Medicine in 1970. He became a pioneer in the field; he set out to study how understanding human diseases could enlighten veterinarians about animal disease. He was the first to standardize canine chromosomes and to detect and identify chromosome defects in dogs. With his team at the Section of Medical Genetics, he conducted the first systemic study of inherited metabolic defects and developed the first tests for carrier detection and disease diagnosis in dogs. In 1994 Patterson founded the Center for Comparative Medical Genetics at the University of Pennsylvania. His most lasting contribution to the field, representing over twenty years of research, is the Canine Genetic Disease Information System, a 2001 CD ROM covering the 300 then-known genetic diseases in nearly 200 breeds of dogs, which accompanied his book *Genetic Disease of Dogs*. His extensive project was largely funded by the American Kennel Club, which honored him with its Career Achievement Award in Canine Research. A mentor to countless research veterinarians, Patterson is a member of the emeritus faculty at the University of Pennsylvania, which honored him in 2007 (*above*).

They write articles for scholarly magazines, book chapters and reviews, and grant applications. They also talk to each other. A lot. "Sometimes we imagine the super-smart scientist all alone in his laboratory with bubbling beakers all around him but no other people nearby," Sutter says. "In reality, scientific research is intensely social and requires effective communication and teamwork at every stage in one's career and in one's research projects."

Once you have earned a bachelor's degree, you will need to earn a veterinary medicine degree, a PhD, or both if you want to go into genomic research. That means five or more years of full-time study. Once you obtain your advanced degree, you may spend time in a postdoctoral position for specialized research experience or the opportunity to publish research findings. Without published research, you'll find it difficult to obtain a permanent position as a faculty member at a college or a university, where much of the specialized research is done.

But don't despair if you have only a bachelor of science degree in biology. That and a few years of experience can qualify you for such positions as a genome-sequencing project manager, responsible for managing all aspects of sequencing projects, such as shipping and receipt of samples, reporting on project status, preparing materials for meetings, and ensuring that projects are completed on time and within budget.

Employment Outlook

Canine genome researchers are employed by the National Institutes of Health, scientific research and testing laboratories, and colleges and universities. Employment of biological scientists in general is expected to increase much faster than the average for all occupations, by 21 percent through 2018. It's suggested that they are less likely to lose their jobs during economic downturns because they are often employed on long-term research projects, but a recession can affect how much money is spent on new research or whether existing projects are renewed or extended.

Salaries in this field vary widely depending on the researcher's level of education and experience, whether the job is with a government agency or private industry, the type of job, and where the job is located. Salaries start at approximately $33,000. Geneticists employed by the federal government can expect to earn an average salary of $99,000. Average annual salaries for all biological scientists range from $48,900 to $79,490.

GENOME RESEARCH RESOURCES

- AKC Canine Health Foundation, www.akcchf.org
- Animal Health Trust Dog Genetic Research, www.aht.org.uk/genetics.html
- Breen Lab at North Carolina State University, www.breenlab.org
- Broad Institute Dog Genome Project, www.broadinstitute.org/mammals/dog
- Ensembl Genome Browser, Wellcome Trust Sanger Institute, www.ensembl.org
- GenBank at NIH's National Center for Biotechnology Information, www.ncbi.nlm.nih.gov/genome/guide/dog
- Morris Animal Foundation, www.morrisanimalfoundation.org
- NHGRI Dog Genome Project, www.research.nhgri.nih.gov/dog_genome
- University of California, Davis, Veterinary Genetics Laboratory, www.vgl.ucdavis.edu/cghg
- University of California, Santa Cruz, Genome Browser, www.genome.ucsc.edu

CHAPTER 15

Wildlife Biologist

C ountless wildlife and marine biologists probably date the genesis of their careers to a childhood spent watching *Daktari, Wild Kingdom*, and Jacques Cousteau specials on television. That was certainly the case with Bill Given, a wildlife biologist in Colorado whose career has taken him from bald eagle surveys to the study of his favorite predators: lions and African wild dogs.

You might not have thought of wildlife biology as a dog- (or cat-) related career, but studying wolves, coyotes, African wild dogs, lions, tigers, and other canid and felid wildlife is only a step beyond studying their domesticated relatives. Wild dogs exhibit many of the same behaviors we see in our canine companions, and with the exception of size, the little lion lounging in your den isn't all that different from her fiercer cousins. The knowledge gained from studying the behavior, health, and habitat of wild animals can contribute to the well-being and knowledge of domestic dogs and cats.

What Wildlife Biologists Do

Biology is the study of life, including origin, behavior, diseases, and reproduction. A wildlife biologist's tasks may involve collecting and analyzing biological data to determine the environmental effects of the uses of land and water areas; performing research to gain a better understanding of animals, their life processes, and their relationship to the environment; or

On Ellesmere Island, Canada, U.S. Geological Survey biologist Dave Mech takes notes on two Arctic wolves. Because the wolves there don't fear humans, Mech has been able to study them at close range, something he has been doing for more than twenty years.

conducting field surveys to establish population counts for animals that may be threatened or endangered. With advances in the knowledge of genetics and organic molecules, biologists can isolate genes and determine their functions, leading to better information on specific diseases and inherited health risks, especially as they affect wildlife populations with small gene pools. Some biologists may consult on humane ways to deal with wildlife in cities or neighborhoods.

A wildlife biologist's day can vary greatly, depending on the type of work done and with what species. Conducting surveys calls for long days of ten to twelve hours or more in the field. Certain protocols must be followed, which may mean spending mornings and evenings actually conducting the survey, while the middle of the day may be devoted to mapping, collecting information on vegetation, and laying out additional survey transects for the future. Time of year is also a factor.

"Because work is often concentrated during a certain time of year, it is critical to accomplish as much as you can during that period," Given says. "Once the field season ends, there is usually a combination of report writing and searching for funds for the next year's projects."

Portrait of a Cheetah Biologist

Laurie Marker is a cheetah biologist. She has a PhD from Oxford University, and the dissertation she wrote there on cheetah biology is regarded as the most complete source of information about this member of the cat family. She is also the founder and executive director of the Cheetah Conservation Fund (CCF, www.cheetah.org), in Namibia, which seeks to protect the cheetah. (*Pictured: Marker with Chewbaaka, an orphan she hand-reared from three weeks of age, who became the CCF's first cheetah ambassador.*)

Marker also breeds dogs—Anatolian Shepherds, to be exact—as part of the CCF's efforts to ensure the cheetah's future. The large flock-guarding dogs from Turkey's Anatolia region help African shepherds and goatherds protect their flocks from predation by cheetahs, in turn helping the cheetahs to survive by preventing them from being killed by farmers, who often view them as vermin. Since 1994 Marker has distributed more than 280 Anatolian puppies to farmers, ranchers, and villagers in Namibia to help protect the slender, fragile cats. Farmers who have the dogs report fewer losses to cheetah predation. The decrease in livestock losses is reported to be 80 percent.

In recognition of her work, Marker was nominated to receive the 2010 Indianapolis Prize, awarded by the Indianapolis Zoo. The prize is "the world's leading award given to an individual animal conservationist who has made significant achievements in advancing sustainability of an animal species or group of species." Marker was one of the six finalists. The executive director of the Dallas Zoo called her "a shining example of how science, nature, and human needs can be met for the long-term benefit of all." She is also an example of how wildlife biologists can work with domestic and wild species to make a difference.

Biologist Adam Boyko and his team are sampling village dogs from seven distinct regions of Africa, comparing the genetic signatures of these dogs to those of Pharaoh Hounds, Rhodesian Ridgebacks, and other breeds thought to be native to Africa, as well as to Puerto Rican street dogs and mixed breeds from the United States. Their work provides insight into the origins of some breeds and how domestication has affected the level of diversity in dogs. They hope to develop a better understanding of how the domestication process affects genetic diversity and learn more about migration patterns and population history by comparing the

Wildlife biologist Bill Given, seen here with captive African wild dogs, developed a process for decreasing livestock losses to wild dogs and other predators in Botswana.

gene markers found in purebred dogs to those in the geographically isolated village-dog populations. Using genetics to trace the movements of dog populations across continents will likely provide insights into the migrations of people during the same period.

Who Wildlife Biologists Are

Self-motivation is an essential quality for a wildlife biologist. Factors such as weather and the unpredictability of animals mean that things often do not go as planned.

"It takes dedication and motivation to keep going at times," Given says. "It's also important to be resilient. Things like the death of a study animal can be discouraging as well as completely set your research back."

On the other hand, Given's office is the natural world. It's the rare penthouse corner office that can top that working environment.

"I have a job that I am passionate about—that I believe is important—and I am privileged to observe many extraordinary species going about their lives," he says. "A most satisfying experience came when my thirteen-year-old daughter and I went to Rocky Mountain National Park to celebrate Father's Day and we were watching a coyote. When it moved off, I was able to anticipate where it would go, and we got out ahead of it. When the coyote came into view, I howled at him, and then in our clear sight he howled back to me, going on and on with a sensational song. I am sure it is a moment my daughter will never forget and will be a symbol for all of the natural world that I have tried to share with her."

Perhaps the best part of being a wildlife biologist is the opportunity for discovery. It is not every career that allows a person to become "the first" to do or see something. "There are so many stories that encompass different chapters of my career. Some of my favorites are when I am able to find a rare species or observe rare behavior," Given says. "I was the first person to document the flammulated owl in the state of South Dakota. The sense of discovery and accomplishment when I discovered a new species for the state was tremendous, and something I will always cherish. I also had the great fortune to be in Botswana at a time when an African wild dog pack had two litters that were four months apart, almost unheard of, and then the pack displayed a range of behaviors that had never before been documented, which resulted in my first published popular article in *Africa Geographic*."

DO YOU HAVE WHAT IT TAKES?

WILDLIFE BIOLOGIST

A wildlife biologist should have the following characteristics:

- ○ Ability to work independently or as part of a team
- ○ Ability to communicate clearly and concisely, both orally and in writing, for presentations, studies, and grants
- ○ Attention to detail for taking notes or measurements, doing counts, and mapping areas
- ○ Physical stamina for field research
- ○ Outdoor skills and interests such as off-road driving, hiking, and camping
- ○ Patience and self-discipline for conducting long and detailed research projects

Education and Training

Most colleges and universities offer bachelor's degrees in biological science, and many of them offer advanced degrees. A number of universities, including state universities, offer excellent wildlife biology programs. They include the University of Alaska at Fairbanks, Humboldt State University and UC Davis in California, Colorado State University, the University of Delaware, Emporia State University in Kansas, Murray State University in Kentucky, the University of New Hampshire, Oregon State University, Penn State University, South Dakota State University, the University of Tennessee and Tennessee Tech, Southwest Texas State University and Texas A&M University, Virginia Tech, and West Virginia University.

Even if you don't get a degree in wildlife biology, it's not impossible to transition into the field. Given took honors biology in high school but found it so difficult that he avoided the sciences, waiting until his senior year in college to take the two classes required for graduation. It wasn't until he started a career in an unrelated field that he rediscovered his love for wildlife. He took the first step toward a career with wildlife when he signed on as a volunteer for the U.S. Fish and Wildlife Service. He then earned a master's degree in interdisciplinary science studies from Johns Hopkins University.

Wildlife biologist Doug Smith (*center*) and colleagues draw blood from a wolf to test for diseases and administer vaccines to her before releasing her in Yellowstone National Park.

Barkworthy BITE

Undergraduate School

Majors in wildlife biology usually find themselves studying chemistry, math, physics, engineering, and computer science, as well as biology. Computer courses teach them how to model and simulate biological processes, operate certain types of equipment, and perform research in bioinformatics. They may take courses in environmental studies and political science, because legislation and regulations will be a big part of their working lives.

Wildlife-specific courses emphasize ecology, populations, habitat, techniques, and policy, all of which are essential in successfully managing wildlife. Some classes involve conducting wildlife-habitat field studies using telemetry or habitat-assessment techniques, or participating in research programs in conservation biology or endangered species.

If you're a science geek, you may be relieved that courses in writing and literature don't appear to be part of a biology curriculum, but don't think you will escape so easily. Usually at least one writing course is required, and if you're smart, you'll take more. Wildlife biologists spend a lot of time writing reports and grant requests. Those who are especially skilled in putting words to paper may supplement their income or even make a living by writing articles for publication in such magazines as *Outside*, *National Geographic*, and *Smithsonian*. Biologists who blog can promote their research and gain support for it from the public. The ability to write clearly and concisely can only add to the success of your career. Photography and videography are other creative skills that can be useful to a budding biologist.

There are some jobs in wildlife conservation for graduates with bachelor's degrees, in particular with state and federal agencies responsible for managing wild-animal populations, but often these are technician-level jobs that may be short-term or seasonal rather than career positions. Teaching high-school biology or going on to veterinary school are options, as is wildland recreation, which involves planning, development, interpretation, and management of private and public lands for recreational purposes.

Graduate School and Postdoctoral Work

Graduate degree work is more specialized and requires original research. Graduate study programs are usually tailored to individual students, with the goal of developing specializations such as habitat use and analysis, population dynamics, natural history, or behavior, in combination with advanced management skills and research capability.

Advanced degree programs typically include classroom work and fieldwork, laboratory research, and a thesis or dissertation. The projects required to complete master's and doctorate programs provide valuable experience that can help meet job requirements. A master's degree is required for most wildlife-management or research positions, and many research or development positions require a PhD in biology.

If you plan to do research or teach at the university level, expect to spend time doing postdoctoral work in the laboratory of a senior researcher to gain specialized research experience. Postdoctoral positions may offer the opportunity to publish research findings. A solid record of published research is essential in obtaining a permanent position involving basic research, especially if you're interested in a permanent college or university faculty position. The competition for independent research positions in universities and for college and university faculty is a prime example of "nature, red in tooth and claw."

Field Experience

Not all of a wildlife biologist's knowledge is gained in the classroom. Many people are fascinated by the natural world from an early age—roaming the woods and collecting box turtles, lying on their stomachs and watching ants gather food, practicing bird calls, and scooping up tadpoles in a jar, hoping to see how they develop. Those early years of exploration and inspiration are as much a part of a wildlife biologist's education as any book learning.

More formal field experience can be had through volunteer work and field courses in high school, college, and graduate school. Given's volunteer jobs included working at a wildlife rehabilitation facility, where he received hands-on and up-close experience with injured wild animals, and conducting bald-eagle surveys for the U.S. Fish and Wildlife Service. In graduate school, field study opportunities included learning radiotelemetry with tiger salamanders and various wildlife-survey techniques.

Visits to zoos and museums also help lay a foundation for a career in wildlife biology, especially for city kids or those whose families aren't

Portrait of a Wildlife Biologist

Bill Given recalls a seventh-grade trip to Yellowstone and Grand Teton National Parks: "To see such splendor and huge animals like moose and bison in person forever changed my soul and probably planted the first seeds of working in the wild. My parents forced us to keep a daily journal, and looking at mine today reveals the discovery of a wildlife biologist: it was basically a list of all the species seen with the quantities recorded and occasionally some anecdotal observations."

Given has been a program manager for a nonprofit conservation organization and a consultant, specializing in threatened and endangered species. The consultant job was more financially stable and gave him more time in the field with less administrative work. Then he took an African safari, and it led to a new twist in his career. Using his knowledge of wildlife, he began leading safaris.

As a result, he was asked to consult on a situation involving the conflict between predators and livestock owners. "I had often dreamed of doing conservation research with large predators," he says. "By being more involved in Africa, it helps advance my pursuit of my lion and African wild dog research that I hope will be the pinnacle of my wildlife biologist career."

"It would have been unlikely for me to ever win a full-time job working with big predators, but I was willing to invest my own time to match a small grant to do a small research project that I created," Given says. "Followed by my unorthodox Africa efforts, I now find myself as a research associate of the Denver Zoo and working on a fascinating African lion project."

He has since scaled back his North American wildlife consulting and started offering full safari planning services.

outdoorsy. So does reading the literature of wildlife adventure, research, and lore: *Swamp Screamer* (University Press of Florida, 1998), Charles Fergus's story of the Florida panther; *The Company of Wolves* (Vintage, 1996) by Peter Steinhart; *Tigers in the Snow* (North Point Press, 2001) by Peter Matthiessen; and *Cry of the Kalahari* (Mariner Books, 1992) by Mark and Delia Owens.

In the end, however, you may have to make your own opportunities. Be creative and be willing to be a bit of an entrepreneur.

Employment Outlook

A career in wildlife biology can take you from Africa to the Amazon to Antarctica, conducting research or managing wild game, natural resources, scenic reserves, or recreational areas. If your interest in wildlife is more intellectual than practical, your career path may lead to teaching at the high-school or college level or to laboratory research. Wildlife biologists work for natural-resource management agencies at local, state, and national levels, investigating problems in agriculture, forestry, land conservation, parasitology, and public health. They are also hired by consulting firms, nonprofit conservation organizations, private businesses, landscape architects, and land-use planners. Opportunities are available for ecologically trained curators and guides in museums and at nature camps, zoos, nature reserves, and state and national parks. Want to combine your love of math and wildlife? Some wildlife biologists specialize in systems analysis, setting up mathematical models of the life systems of particular species of animals and, with the aid of computers, predict or control populations.

"The most difficult part is getting started," Given says. "The profession has ample short-term seasonal jobs, but finding solid year-round

In Namibia, Laurie Marker enjoys the evening with Anatolian Shepherd Koya and Chewbaaka, both raised by her. A job at Oregon's Wildlife Safari at age twenty led her to her life's work.

employment at the entry level is hard to do. Many starting in the profession are hired into three- to six-month field technician jobs because the majority of wildlife biology work takes place during certain seasons, depending on the species. Once the seasonal job ends, the biologist often either has to move to a different location that has different seasonal opportunities or perhaps during the winter will work in an unrelated field until the next field season comes around again. I have met many different people working in diverse non-science-related jobs who tell me they had undergrad wildlife biology degrees but changed fields due to not being able to get full-time employment."

Once a wildlife biologist is gainfully employed, the hunt begins to find funding for the kind of work he or she wants to do. Funds are most often available for game species, which raise revenue because they are hunted and hunters must buy licenses, and species listed by the federal government under the Endangered Species Act. To work on anything else typically requires winning grant money for research, and only about 25 percent of grant proposals are approved for long-term research projects. The constant pursuit for funding and the political issues that may accompany it can be the most difficult aspects of working as a wildlife biologist.

You aren't likely to make big bucks in this field. The median annual salary of zoologists and wildlife biologists was $55,290 in 2008. The middle 50 percent earned between $43,060 and $70,500. The lowest 10 percent earned less than $33,550, and the highest 10 percent earned more than $90,850. Depending on your outlook, the other advantages of the job may or may not compensate for the moderate income.

"It is hard to get started and make it in this field, but the payoff of having an exciting and rewarding job that holds your interest and that you are passionate about is worth all of the persistence and struggles," Given says.

WILDLIFE RESOURCES

- Botswana Predator Conservation Trust, www.bpctrust.org
- Cheetah Conservation Fund, www.cheetah.org
- Defenders of Wildlife, www.defenders.org
- International Union for the Conservation of Nature, www.iucn.org
- National Science Foundation, www.nsf.gov
- The Wildlife Society, www.wildlife.org
- Village Dog Genetic Diversity Project, http://villagedogs.canmap.org
- Wildlife biology colleges, http://education-portal.com/wildlife_biology_colleges.html

SECTION 6

Visual, Written, and Spoken Arts

D r. Doolittle talked to the animals, but people in creative careers talk to—or otherwise communicate with—people about animals. They are in the field of communications: art and photography, writing and editing, public relations and communications, and broadcast formats such as radio and televsion. Creativity is an essential element of these jobs as is facility with the written and spoken word. Knowledge of dogs and other animals establishes credibility, but it can be learned on the job. Potential employers for salaried positions and freelance jobs include book and magazine publishers, pet-product manufacturers, humane organizations, online media outlets, and professional veterinary associations.

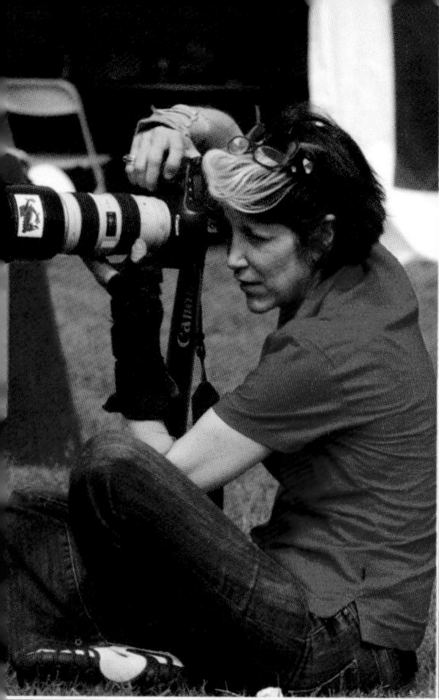

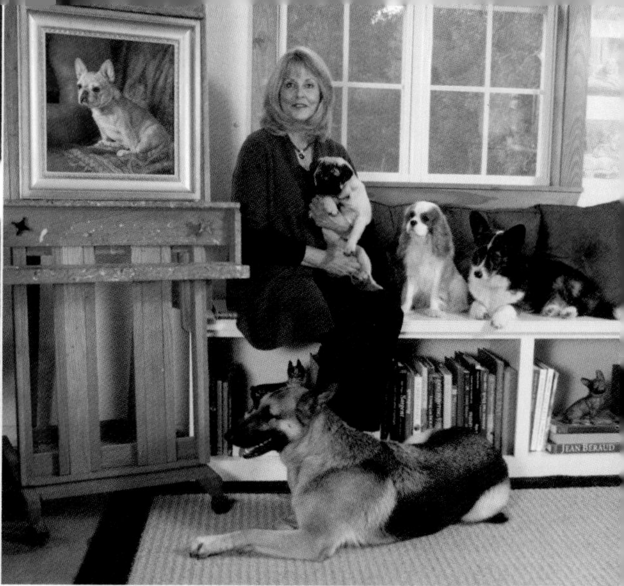
JEAN BERAUD

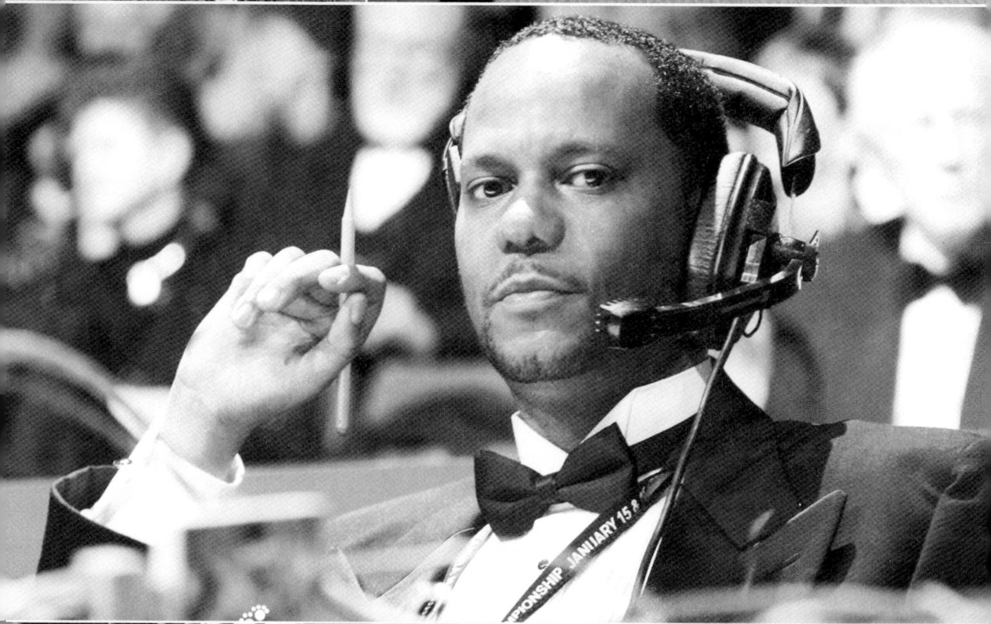
JANUARY 15 &

A DIVISION OF
CATFANCY
WOOF!

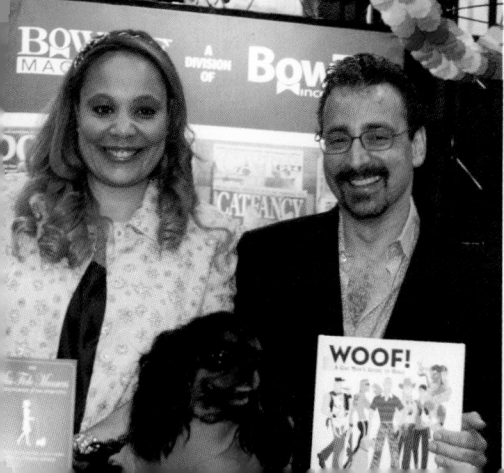

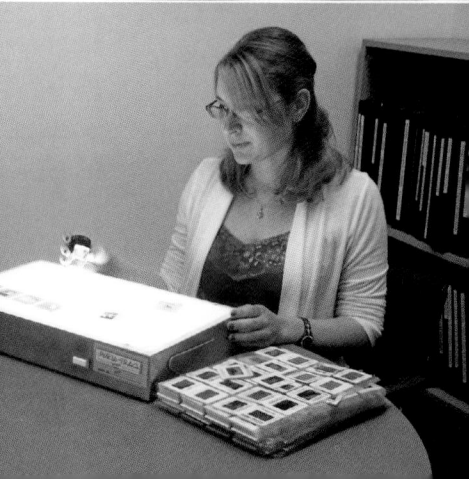

CHAPTER 16

Artist and Other Art-Related Careers

Art at its most basic tells us what animals look like, but it also expresses emotion and depicts cultural moments in time. People have been drawing pictures of dogs for at least 15,000 years. We see them depicted in cave art, participating in hunts. During the Renaissance, dogs frequently made appearances in paintings as symbols of fidelity. In the Victorian era, many artists immortalized well-known hunting dogs as well as ladies' canine companions. Today, cards, calendars, and books with pictures of dogs are big sellers. And these days, commissioning a portrait of a beloved pet is making a comeback. All of that means work for dog-loving artists. Becoming an artist, especially one specializing in dogs and other animals, is a career fraught with uncertainty, but for the person who succeeds, it can be incredibly satisfying.

Types of Artists

People come to art in many different ways. They can be self-taught or study art in college. Although artistic talent is something a person is born with, classes enhance and polish that ability. Not every artist is a painter or a sculptor. Some people use their artistic skills to become art directors at dog magazines such as *The Bark*, *Dog Fancy*, and *Dog World*, where they are responsible for creating a distinctive appearance for the publication through page design and layout, type selection, and art and photo choices.

Whether oil on canvas or ink on paper, as here, the animal portraits created by Bruce Padgett are captivating, revealing great attention to detail and use of light and shadow.

Fine Artist

The work of fine artists appears in museums, art galleries, corporate collections, and private homes. Fine artists who paint dogs usually work on commission; this means that the clients approach the artists with assignments for paintings or sculptures. Artists also sell their work themselves or through art galleries or dealers. It's rare for artists, particularly dog artists, to be able to support themselves solely through sales of their works, but it's not unheard of. Many fine artists, however, have at least one other job to support their art careers. They may work in museums or art galleries, planning and setting up art exhibits; teach art classes or conduct workshops in schools or in their own studios; or hold full-time or part-time jobs unrelated to the art field and pursue fine art as a second career.

Art Director and Graphic Artist

Art directors and graphic artists develop design concepts for advertising magazines, newspapers, books, and other printed or digital media. Their job is to present the information in an eye-catching and organized way. An art director works with photographers, illustrators, and editors to choose the images and artwork that will illustrate a given piece, and supervises the design and production of the publication.

Besides artistic ability, art directors must have computer skills, knowledge of current graphic-design and publishing software, and leadership skills, because they may manage or supervise the workflow of other employees. Ideally, the art director at a dog magazine will have a good knowledge of dog breeds or at least the willingness to do a little research. He or she needs to be able to choose images that show not only the correct breed for an article or book but also a good example of that particular breed. Each dog breed has a specific look defined by what's known as a breed standard—a written description of the breed—and an art director who works for a dog magazine should take the time to become familiar with the various breeds and what good-quality dogs look like.

Art directors usually begin as entry-level artists in advertising or publishing firms. Some art schools offer coursework in art direction.

Cartoonist

Two of the most famous cartoon strips in the world—*Peanuts* and *Garfield*—feature pets, but cartoonists who have successful pet strips are few and far between. That small group of animal cartoonists includes *MUTTS* creator Patrick McDonnell and Darby Conley, who draws *Get Fuzzy*.

McDonnell always loved cartoons and can't remember a time when he didn't draw. He attended the School of Visual Arts in New York and majored in illustration. He started out as a freelance illustrator, and in 1994—twenty years after beginning college—he created *MUTTS*, based on his dog, Earl. Like most creative people, McDonnell draws on his own experiences in creating the strip, saying that strips featuring Earl and Ozzie (Earl's owner) together are often autobiographical. Good cartoonists also draw on broad cultural knowledge, both literary and

DO YOU HAVE WHAT IT TAKES?

ARTIST

An artist should have the following characteristics:

- ○ Artistic talent
- ○ Ability to work alone for long hours
- ○ Self-discipline
- ○ Ambition
- ○ Ability to accept rejection
- ○ Ability to market his or her work

Doghouse Architect

Barbara Beck's Rhodesian Ridgeback, Chopper, had two favorite personal retreats: his crate and a closet. Beck hated the look of the crate and preferred to have Chop near her, so she decided to draw on her architectural training and build him something nice that she would enjoy looking at as well.

"I designed Chop a Prairie-style doghouse [*pictured*], based on designs by Frank Lloyd Wright, and my friends suggested I start selling it," she says. "I realized that not all people like modern architecture, so the second design, based on the buildings of Andrea Palladio, was born, followed by a third design in the vein of Antonio Gaudi."

People who purchase the homes from Beck's business Artful Dogs consider them functional art. Dogs just view them as home, using them primarily as a sleeping space. All of the houses are painted a deep blue inside, which Beck says is a soothing color for dogs and gives the house a denlike feel. The houses are built to specific dimensions so the dog's own crate can fit inside. The houses are also appealing to dogs in other ways.

"The houses are fairly enclosed so there is a feeling of protection, but the animal can see out through the windows and watch whatever the family is doing," Beck says. "Chopper used to love to do that. He reminded me of a child building a cushion fort on a sofa and peering out."

Beck has carried over her love of dogs into her designs for people. Homes built for dog owners may include practical features such as built-in food-and-supply storage lockers or a private entry for dogs so they can get out to a contained yard area. "One client had a separate dog entry with a dogwash system and drain, holding kennel, and a washer and dryer."

While Beck works mainly as an architect on a human scale, she says that she prefers pet architecture. "Dogs are so much less demanding."

An architect's education, from one of 117 programs accredited by the National Architectural Accrediting Board, takes a minimum of five years to complete, culminating in a bachelor's degree in architecture. Most states require architects to complete a three-year internship before sitting for a licensing exam.

At a book signing, Jason O'Malley (*right*) holds a copy of *WOOF: A Gay Man's Guide to Dogs*, which he illustrated for author Andrew DePrisco (*left*).

cases. Needless to say, they must have a detailed knowledge of anatomy and surgical and medical procedures as well as artistic ability. Illustrators who can draw dogs and other animals will definitely find work, but it is unlikely that they can support themselves creating only dog-related images.

Jeweler

The beautiful jewelry you see at dog shows in the image of different breeds is created by artists in precious metals and gemstones: jewelers. Jewelers combine sculpting and fine art to create beautiful rings, necklaces, bracelets, brooches, and earrings using gold or other precious metals, jewels and semiprecious stones, and materials such as resin and wood. Following their own designs or those by other designers or customers, they use tools such as lasers, welding equipment, computer-aided design software, and manufacturing techniques to shape metal or carve wax to make models for casting the metal. Individual parts then are soldered together, and jewelers may mount gems on or engrave designs into the pieces.

Jewelers can learn on the job, at vocational or technical school, or at art or design school. The work requires dexterity, hand-eye coordination,

Sculptor and painter Georjean Busha Hetzwig is an award-winning artist. She does a thorough study of her subject before beginning a piece.

patience, concentration, and artistic ability, as well as an eye for current fashion and, of course, canine form and personality.

Sculptor

Sculptors design three-dimensional pieces of art either by molding and joining materials such as clay, glass, wire, plastic, fabric, or metal or by cutting and carving forms from plaster, wood, or stone. Some sculptors combine various materials to create mixed-media figures. Sculptors whose subject is the dog often sell their works at dog shows or through art galleries.

Becoming a Portrait Artist

Being a portrait artist who specializes in painting dogs can be a rewarding (though not always monetarily) career. Here are three artists who decided on this career and an inside look at their working days.

Paths to Portraiture

Terry Albert did her first pet portrait when she was in college. The portrait was of her grandfather's Shih Tzu, Mac, and was a present for her grandfather.

As a child, she loved drawing animals, but she never dreamed she could make it a career. Commercial art, however, seemed like an achievable goal. She took art classes in high school and majored in art in college. After graduating, she took some commercial design classes at Otis Art Institute and attended workshops with other artists. Albert eventually became a commercial artist, doing product illustrations and ad layouts for retailers. It wasn't until later in her career that she began to focus on portraits of dogs and other animals, after a friend asked her to paint a picture of her dog. Albert also creates notecards, prints, tiles, and other objects that display her work. She has a contemporary style that appeals to modern pet owners. Her work can be found in many homes and has been exhibited at the American Kennel Club (AKC) Museum of the Dog in St. Louis.

Christine Merrill started drawing animals when she was two years old and painted her first dog portrait when she was only five. She studied art at Baltimore's Schuler School of Fine Art and has been painting portraits of dogs and horses ever since. She works in oils, and her paintings hang in many private homes and public collections, including at the American Kennel Club in New York and at the AKC Museum of the Dog. She has also done illustrations for three children's books by author Jean George.

Constance Payne grew up with dogs, exhibiting them in conformation and competing with them in field trials, as well as painting them. She honed her artistic talent at the University of Wisconsin, where she earned a bachelor of fine art, a master of art, and a master of fine art. In addition to oils, she works in pencil, charcoal, pastel, and bronze. In her quest to capture an animal's form and movement, she has studied anatomy through the use of articulated skeletons and observation of surgeries at Cornell University's College of Veterinary Medicine. Payne's artistic muse is nineteenth-century French artist Rosa Bonheur. To gain a better understanding of Bonheur's style, Payne studied her technique intensively, even researching the chemical composition of nineteenth-century French oil paints. Payne's work hangs in the Castellani Art Museum at Niagara University, at the AKC, and in private collections.

The Portrait Artist's Day

Dog portrait artists spend long hours studying their subjects. Artists such as Merrill and Payne travel—at the owner's expense—to meet the dogs and see them in their home settings. The artists watch their canine subjects play, study them in repose, take photos of them, make sketches of their expressions, note their favorite toys, and even go hiking with them. Getting to know the dog is essential to capturing his essence.

Not every artist is able to meet his or her subjects in person. Instead, the artist works from photos provided by the owner. The artist may also interview the owner about the dog's personality and habits or ask the owner to write a description of the dog.

Albert spends her days taking photos of her subjects, working on the computer to plan painting layouts, and then painting the portraits, in whatever time she has free from her other job of pet sitting. She also spends time working on her Web site and blog and communicating with clients.

Her best advice for would-be dog artists? "Go to school. Learn everything you can. Paint from life, not just photos. Practice, practice, practice. And realize that not every piece will be a masterpiece."

The Challenges of Being an Artist

Many artists work in fine- or commercial-art studios located in office buildings, warehouses, or lofts. Others work in private studios in their homes.

The most successful and sought-after living dog painter in the United States, Christine Merrill is seen in her studio with Rudy, who also appears in the painting beside them.

Some fine artists share studio space, where they also may exhibit their work. Working in an art studio may sound glamorous, and the surroundings are usually well lit and well ventilated, but there is a down side. Artists may be exposed to fumes from glue, paint, ink, and other materials as well as splattered paint, spilled fluids, and dust or other residue from filings. Artists who sit at drafting tables or who use computers for extended periods may experience back pain, eye strain, or fatigue.

Artists employed by publishing companies, advertising agencies, and design firms work a standard workweek. During busy periods, they may work overtime to meet deadlines. Self-employed artists can set their own hours, but they spend much time and effort marketing their artwork to potential customers and building their reputations. That means having their own Web sites, seeking gallery representation, and exhibiting at shows. Spending time and money to have work framed is also necessary.

One of the challenges of being a dog artist is the nature of the buyer and the diversity of the species. Pet-portrait artist Terry Albert says that with cats and horses, people will usually buy any painting they like, but a dog painting must look like a particular dog or breed. And with hundreds of dog breeds, it's difficult for an artist to have studied them all.

"You can be sure that whatever breed someone wants is the one breed you haven't done yet," Albert says.

Education and Training

No matter how talented, all artists can benefit from training in their field. Formal training is not required, but it is difficult to become skilled enough to make a living without some training. Many colleges and universities offer programs leading to a bachelor's or master's degree in fine arts. In addition to art history and studio art, students are required to take core subjects such as English, social science, and natural science, which help to inform an artist's work. Formal educational programs in art also provide training in computer techniques. Computers are used widely in the visual arts, and knowledge and training in computer graphics and other visual-display software are critical elements of many jobs in art-related fields.

Independent schools of art and design also offer postsecondary studio training in craft, fine, and multimedia arts. Typically, these programs focus more intensively on studio work than do the academic programs in university settings, and they can be good choices if you have your heart set on an in-depth art education. Albert, for instance, says her college had a limited art program, and she regrets not attending an art school, where she could have received more training in painting techniques. The National Association of Schools of Art and Design accredits about 250 postsecondary institutions with programs in art and design; most award a degree in art.

Other Art-Related Careers

You don't have to be an artist yourself to be involved in the art world. A few individuals with an interest in art have chosen to become gallery owners or museum curators. Art galleries that specialize in animal works are few and far between, but they do exist and are successful in their unusual niche. Although many museums contain works featuring dogs, only one specializes in dog art: the American Kennel Club Museum of the Dog.

Gallery Owner

After William Secord earned his art history degree from Carleton University, Ottawa, in 1975, he enrolled in graduate school at New York University. He anticipated that his studies in arts administration and art education

Edwin Landseer: Artist to Royalty

Sir Edwin Henry Landseer was born in 1802 and became the most famous animal painter of all time. As a child, Landseer displayed a natural talent for sketching and drawing and received encouragement from well-known artist Benjamin Robert Haydon. At the precocious age of twelve, Landseer had his first exhibit at the Royal Academy. Landseer's association with the Royal Academy lasted his whole life, as he was named an Associate and an Academician before he was thirty years old. Knighted in 1850, he was one of Queen Victoria's favorite artists, and the value and demand for his art continued to rise. Landseer was extremely fond of the Newfoundland breed, in particular the black and white variety, and he painted it frequently—so much so that the black and white Newfoundlands are now known as "Landseers" in Europe. Landseer's most famous portraits of a black and white Newfoundland are *Distinguished Member of the Humane Society*, circa 1838, *Princess Mary and Nelson*, circa 1839, and *Saved*, circa 1856. Ironically, it's neither paintings nor dogs that are the basis for Landseer's most enduring claim to fame: it's the four lions at the feet of Lord Nelson's Column in Trafalgar Square in London.

would eventually take him back to Canada, where he planned to work in a museum. However, in 1980, he needed a job and took one as director of special projects, writing catalogs and organizing exhibits at New York's American Folk Art Museum. During the year he spent there, Secord heard that the American Kennel Club was opening the Dog Museum of America and needed a director. The opportunity was too good to pass up, so Secord applied and got the position based on his academic credentials. "I was interested in dogs, but not at a serious level," says Secord. "My background was in museum work, and I learned about purebred dogs as I went along." He had been director for five years when the AKC decided to move the museum to St. Louis, Missouri. Secord decided to stay in New York.

That decision changed the direction of his life. Instead of looking for another museum job, Secord chose to strike out on his own by starting a gallery. Working out of his apartment, he bought one nineteenth-century painting on installment over a five-month period, then slowly built up his inventory, buying and selling dog-related works of art and acting as an agent for collectors. In 1989, he signed a lease for what would become a unique gallery, one that would specialize in dog art of the nineteenth century—the golden era of sporting-dog and other canine art—as well as display dog art by contemporary artists. The gallery opened in 1990.

Running a Gallery

Today, the gallery is flourishing, and Secord is considered a noted authority on nineteenth-century dog art. From a tiny second-floor showroom on East Seventy-Sixth Street in Manhattan, Secord displays beautiful paintings of dogs of many breeds, filling all of the wall space from ceiling to floor. He and a small staff put on exhibitions, send out press releases, take part in art and antique shows in other cities, display a selection of works at the annual Westminster Kennel Club dog show, and keep their Web site up to date.

William Secord is seen here with some of the unique works of art that he exhibits in his popular stand at the Westminster Kennel Club (*pictured*) and his main gallery, which is located on the Upper West Side in New York City.

"The gallery here does everything that a big gallery does, but in a small, specialized way," Secord says. "I've done antique shows in Palm Beach; I do one in Thomasville, Georgia. I've done them in other places, as well, and [displayed art] at Westminster, which I consider the equivalent of having an antique show. I have a gallery director; I have an assistant sales person; I have my own assistant, who helps me with writing and research and whatever needs to be done. In a small organization like this, everybody is very flexible. Right now, my sales assistant is cleaning out the humidifiers that we have to have to keep the air humidified in the dry heat of a New York City building. He packs paintings. So we do everything.

"There's a lot involved in a gallery that most people don't think about, like payroll and insurance and fine art insurance, and restoration-conservation, in addition to buying inventory. We deal with nineteenth-century paintings, but also with living artists. There are a whole set of things you have to do with a living artist [that] you [don't need to worry about] with nineteenth-century pictures."

Inventory comes from all over the world. Secord used to make frequent trips to London and Paris, but now he is able to rely on trade publications, connections in the art world, estate sales, and the ubiquitous Internet.

"I think that if I were to start a gallery today, in this specialized market, I would have a really tough time finding the inventory, so I think timing is really important," he says. "A friend of mine in England started a small gallery, and she has a few nineteenth-century things, but really what she's dealing with is contemporary, because that's what's available. The dog paintings are so breed-specific that it requires specialized knowledge of the history of the breed but also how popular the breeds are and what kind of people have those breeds to determine whether you even buy a painting or not. I sold a painting, a $36,000 painting, to a client years ago because it looked like her Gordon Setter, but it was a nineteenth-century painting. Pointer people want the dogs on point with the tail as close as possible to 12:00. In other words, the way the dog points, not just the breed, not just what the dog's doing, but the way it's doing it can make the difference between a sale or not."

In addition to running a gallery, Secord writes. He has written four books on nineteenth-century European dog art and is working on a fifth, which focuses on the work of Christine Merrill, one of the living artists represented by his gallery. "It's called *The American Dog at Home: The Dog Portraits of Christine Merrill.* I'm interviewing thirty-five of her clients all around the country, from people who rescue dogs to big show dog people," he says.

Being Successful

Secord attributes his success to an ability to see the viewpoints of his clients, to visualize what they might want from a dog painting. That's an important skill any time you're selling something.

"You want to create an environment in which buying is made easy," he says. "It should be fun to buy dog paintings. I think that's a skill that you really need if you're going to sell anything, but especially dog paintings. Everybody needs tissue or paper towels or whatever in their house, but as much as I like to think they do, not everybody thinks they need a dog painting. So I ask myself, 'If I were buying this painting, what would

I want? If I collected King Charles Spaniel paintings, what kind of painting would I want? What price range? What would I want to hear from a gallery?' I put myself in the position of the collector, and I think that's a skill that not everyone has."

Museum Curator/Director

The job of a museum curator is to acquire, maintain, and exhibit art, artifacts, literature, and other objects at research, breed and sport, and art museums. Through their work, curators inform the public and aid researchers seeking information about an artist, breed, or sport. Dog-loving curators can work for specialty museums, such as the AKC Museum of the Dog in St. Louis or the National Sporting Art Museum in Middleburg, Virginia. Museum directors often host special events, such as dog-club meetings, galas to honor canine celebrities and notable figures in the dog world (such as Uno, the 2008 Westminster-winning Beagle, and his traveling companion David Frei), or demonstrations by such talented dogs as the Dalmatian Formation Drill Team of St. Louis. The job calls for a love of art,

Barbara Jedda McNab is the director of the American Kennel Club Museum of the Dog in St. Louis, Missouri.

Portrait of a Gallery Owner

Jaynie Milligan Spector (*pictured with Lucy*), of Dog and Horse Fine Art and Portraiture in Charleston, South Carolina, opened her gallery after years of working in other areas of the art world. Spector began her career in the 1970s after she graduated from the University of North Carolina with a liberal arts degree and completed an intensive art program at Sotheby's Auction House in London. "I studied with art scholar Donald Kuspit, who is one of America's most distinguished art critics," she says. "Mr. Kuspit inspired my interest in contemporary art."

Her early jobs included working at Christie's Contemporary Art Department, an art gallery in New York City's SoHo neighborhood; and as an account executive in the business department for *Art and Antiques* magazine. One day, she chanced upon a gallery in Manhattan that specialized in dog art and the idea enchanted her.

"The idea of top-quality contemporary artists painting dogs started to come together in my mind," she says. But it wasn't until thirteen years later that she held her first exhibit of dog art, "A Celebration of Dogs," at the Ryland Inn in Somerset County, New Jersey.

"I was helping a friend decorate her living room and came across her father-in-law's painting of a Golden Retriever and remembered my dream about a gallery of dog paintings. For over a year, I worked on getting my stable of canine artists together." It was a success, and Spector followed it with a move to Charleston, where she opened her dream gallery.

The gallery represents contemporary and traditional American and British artists who specialize in works featuring dogs and horses. Part of the gallery's success can be attributed to its location in Charleston, which has a thriving art community and is a destination for people who collect art and antiques. With her faithful sidekick Lucy, an English Cocker Spaniel, Spector welcomes visitors from all over the world to the gallery.

---

a desire to preserve the past, the ability to evaluate potential additions to the collection, excellent communication and computer skills, great people skills, and knowledge of the dog world for fund-raising purposes.

A curator or director of a specialty museum generally must have an advanced degree in art history or museum studies. The current director of the AKC Museum of the Dog, Barbara Jedda McNab, holds a degree in studio art and art history from Washington University (St. Louis) School of Fine Arts and began her art career as museum assistant in the Department of Prints, Drawings, and Photographs at the St. Louis Museum of Art. McNab had been unfamiliar with the Museum of the Dog until an acquaintance took her on a visit. She was charmed. A couple of years later, she was asked to help curate an exhibit at the museum called St. Louis Collects, which involved borrowing dog art from private collectors in the city and pulling together a show. Later, when the directorship became available, the museum offered McNab the position.

"Life takes you, I think, down certain paths that are meant to be," McNab says. "Art has always been my passion, and I love dogs. The marriage between the two couldn't have been more ideal."

Employment Outlook

Despite the hard work required and difficulty making a living, art—even dog art—has a reputation as a glamorous field. What that means is that it's hard to find a job, salaried or freelance, and there's usually someone snapping at your heels for the work you do find. Be prepared to always be searching for your next job or client. The number of talented artists out there far exceeds the amount of work available, especially in the niche of dog-related art. Dog-loving art directors, for instance, will find only a handful of opportunities at pet publications or with ad agencies that have pet-business clients and may have to satisfy their interest in dogs in some other way.

Despite all that, Albert loves her career. The best moment, she says, is when someone tears up after seeing a pet's painting. "I know I've done something special for them. I have a real emotional connection to the animals I paint."

Most artists, approximately 63 percent, are self-employed. They freelance for advertising agencies, design firms, or publishers; offer specialized design services; or work for other businesses on a contract basis, meaning that they are not employees and do not receive benefits.

The Bureau of Labor Statistics predicts that employment of artists will grow about as fast as average for all occupations through 2018. That's for artists in general, though, not artists who specialize in canine art and illustrations. Only a very few of those canine artists are likely to find full-time work that will allow them to support themselves or a family. Even harder to find are positions with dog-related museums and galleries. Jobs for museum curators in general are expected to increase by 20 percent through 2018, but there is little opportunity for dog-related jobs in this field. The same is true for positions at dog-related art galleries.

Albert says bringing in enough income is the most challenging aspect of life as an artist. Her artwork alone does not support her, so she supplements her income with other careers related to her interests, including pet sitting and Web site design.

Earnings for self-employed artists vary widely. The amount of income they bring in depends on how much work they are able to do in a given period and how much they can charge for their work. Art is subjective, and for most people, works of art are luxury items. What one person can or will pay for a painting of his or her dog may be very different from what someone else will. Some well-established artists earn more than salaried artists, while others find it difficult or impossible to rely solely on income earned from selling art.

Art directors are most likely to be salaried employees. Their earnings may range from $35,000 to more than $120,000. Expect salaries at pet publications to fall toward the lower end of the scale, while those at ad agencies will be at the mid-range or higher, depending on your level of experience and the size of the agency.

The earnings of fine artists and craftspeople have a much lower range, from less than $15,000 for the lowest 10 percent to more than $68,000 for the highest 10 percent. Artists who paint portraits of dogs may charge rates that range from $300 for a head study to $18,000 or more for a large oil painting with multiple figures and a detailed background.

Annual wages for museum curators range from $26,850 to $83,290.

ARTIST RESOURCES

- American Association of Museums, www.aam-us.org
- American Institute of Architects, www.aia.org
- American Institute of Graphic Arts, www.aiga.org
- American Kennel Club Museum of the Dog, www.museumofthedog.org
- American Society of Interior Designers, www.asid.org
- Animal Arts, www.animalarts.biz
- ARQ Architects, www.arqarchitects.com
- *Artist's and Graphic Designer's Market.* Writers Digest Books, current ed., www.artists-market.com
- Dog and Horse Fine Art and Portraiture, www.dogartdealer.com
- Iditarod Trail Sled Dog Museum, www.iditarod.com
- Jewelers of America, www.jewelers.org
- Manufacturing Jewelers and Suppliers of America, www.mjsa.org
- The Museum of Hounds and Hunting, www.mhhna.org
- National Association of Schools of Art and Design, http://nasad.arts-accredit.org
- National Bird Dog Museum, www.artmuseumtouring.com/Bird_dog.html
- National Council of Architectural Registration Boards, www.ncarb.org
- William Secord Gallery, www.dogpainting.com

CHAPTER 17

Photographer

Many people dream of becoming professional photographers, and not surprisingly, competition for the work is keen. Few salaried jobs are available in the field, however. More than half of all photographers are self-employed, a much higher proportion than for most occupations. If you want to specialize in pet photography, you will find even greater competition, because few paying outlets exist for that type of work. About half a dozen monthly and bimonthly magazines purchase photographs of dogs for their pages. Some photographers specialize in taking photos at dog shows, and others concentrate on pet portraits and ancillary products such as note cards and calendars.

Photographers specializing in images of animals never know from week to week what types of dogs they'll be working with. In front of their camera lenses may be a group of Rottweilers, the Breed or Group winner at a dog show, a pampered Cavalier King Charles Spaniel, an energetic Jack Russell Terrier, a pair of Siamese cats, a trick mule, a prize-winning cow or pig, or even a pet rat or a hermit crab. Their work is used in advertising and print publications and hangs in homes and in private and public collections.

What Photographers Do

Photographers produce images that present a picture, tell a story, or record an event. A skilled pet photographer uses technical expertise, creativity,

A collection of transparencies, with a loop for magnifying them, awaits the photographer's consideration. Photographers use a light box and loop to view images in this form.

and equipment to enhance the animal's appearance with natural or artificial light, photograph the animal from interesting angles, or draw attention to a particular aspect of the animal.

There's a lot more to the business of photography than just taking the pictures. A photographer who wants to be successful must arrange for advertising, schedule appointments, set and adjust equipment, purchase supplies, keep records, bill customers, pay bills, and hire, train, and manage any employees. In their spare time, photographers may be processing images, designing albums, or mounting and framing finished photographs.

For animal photographer Jean Fogle, every day is different. It's one of the things she loves about her work. "Typically, I am editing images, setting up shoots, and working on articles," she says. "If I get bored or frustrated with one chore, I can switch and work on a completely different form of work. I often have three or four projects going on at once."

Who Photographers Are

Even though their subjects are animals, pet photographers must have good people skills. When they are not taking photos of dogs, cats, and other animals, they are dealing with pet owners, graphic designers, editors and art directors at publishing companies, and creative directors at advertising agencies.

Animal photographers should be prepared to crawl around on the floor, wipe slobber and drool off camera lenses, make funny noises to attract the animals' attention, and clean up after the animals, and be ready to laugh when shoots go wrong.

"One day I was shooting five Rottweilers running in the snow, crouched down to capture the action," Fogle says. "My husband, Terry, came out to watch. After the Rotties left, Terry casually mentioned that I might want to wash my jacket. Apparently, one the Rotties had slipped up behind me and used me as a fire hydrant."

Fields of Specialization

Within the field of animal photography, there are several specialization areas. Among them are portrait photography and dog show photography.

Portrait Photography

Portrait photographers take pictures of pets for posterity. They may work in their own studios or travel around the country, working on location. Pet portrait photographer Jim Dratfield, for instance, is based in New York City. When he's not photographing pets locally and in surrounding areas such as New Jersey, Westchester, Long Island, and Connecticut, he is traveling to other places in the country as well as to Europe. In addition to pet portraits, he creates custom photo albums of animals, custom notecards, and jewelry featuring the animals' portraits. Some photographers, such as William Wegman, famous for his photographs of his Weimaraners, are considered to be fine art photographers. Their work is often exhibited at galleries and museums.

In addition to talent, pet portrait photographers need patience and an understanding of animal and human psychology. They travel with toys and treats to attract their subjects' attention and elicit those endearing expressions or perfect poses, and they are willing to sing or dance, wave feathers, or click their shutters repeatedly for as long as it takes to get the

Rudolph W. Tauskey: Celebrated Photographer

Born in Vienna in 1888 and educated in Budapest, Tauskey immigrated to Canada in 1905. At the age of twenty-three, he apprenticed with a horse photographer in New York City. He returned to photography after serving in World War I. Tauskey was introduced to the world of dogs by wealthy horseman Charles Chauncey Stillman, the owner of Kenridge Irish Setters. Tauskey began photo-

graphing dogs at the finest kennels on the East Coast, including Mrs. Dodge's Giralda Farms, Louis Murr's Romanoff, Hayes Blake Hoyt's Blakeen, and Herman Mellenthin's My Own. In 1924, the American Kennel Club hired him as a staff photographer, though he continued to shoot portraits privately. Private commissions from the crème de la crème of the dog world kept Tauskey in business, and he formed close friendships with the dog world elite. He created his signature stark black-and-white portraits of the most famous dogs of the day, including Westminster Best in Show winners and all of the nation's top show dogs. While Tauskey

was old-fashioned in his insistence upon using the same ten-pound army Graflex camera for his whole career—which lasted seven decades—he was ahead of his time with his ability to retouch negatives to improve a dog's appearance. (This was decades prior to the invention of Photoshop.) He studied breed standards with great care and had an eye for a dog that any breeder would envy. Kerrin Winter-Churchill, photographer and student of Tauskey, believes that Tauskey's efforts were so seriously regarded that "[h]is images became the yardstick by which all breeders' efforts were measured." He was dedicated to the craft of dog photography, which he virtually invented. He was a demanding perfectionist and became the icon of future generations of dog photographers. He died in 1979—at the age of eighty-seven.

best shots. Props, themed backdrops, and costumes often appeal to owners, and making the experience fun for pets and their people helps lead to repeat business and referrals.

Pet portrait work can be done at the client's home, at the photographer's home or studio, or at pet-supply stores or other businesses. Ways to increase profits include setting a collage of photos to music, as well as offering products onto which a pet's photo can be transferred, such as mugs and T-shirts.

Dog Show Photography

Some photographers specialize in photographing the winners at dog shows. They take photos of the winners of each class, plus Best of Opposite Sex, the other dogs that place or earn Awards of Merit in a class, Group winners, and of course, Best in Show. Owners and handlers buy the photos for their records and for use in advertising their dogs' show records.

A dog show photographer may prepare albums with photos of the winners of Best in Show, Group First, High in Trial in obedience, and Best Junior Handler for the show chairman and club secretary of an all-breed show. For a specialty show, an album may include photographs of the winner of each class.

A dog show photographer needs to have a professional photographic background for indoor shows and a sign board with the club logo displayed for use in each photo. The photographer needs good record-keeping skills and should be prepared to accept payment in the form of a check or by credit card in addition to cash. Dog show photographers must work quickly and skillfully to get the best shot of each dog and keep the process moving.

Gay Glazbrook began her career as a professional photographer and graphic designer in 1988. She currently raises Giant Schnauzers on a small farm in Arlington, Texas.

Freelancing

Freelance photographers work for themselves. They carry out assignments for dog-related publications, license the use of their photos through stock photo agencies, or market their work directly to the public. Like other photographers, a freelance photographer spends much of his or her time, when not actually taking photos, editing images, selling his or her work, and looking for more work.

"An editor likes to see published images, but if you haven't been published, that is impossible," Jean Fogle says. "Make sure you have a good portfolio, and look into some form of online presence so editors can view your work."

Freelance pet photographers have a flexible schedule, and they get to work with animals. What could be better? Not much, but there are some drawbacks. For one thing, income is sporadic and uncertain if a freelancer isn't working consistently. Without regular paychecks, freelancers must be good at managing money. The lack of a regular income and the constant search for more work are stressful.

Freelance photographers will need to work when their clients are available, which can mean evenings and definitely will mean weekends, as most dog shows take place over weekends.

Photographers click away trying to get the best shot of Westminster's 2006 BIS winner, the colored Bull Terrier Ch. Rocky Top's Sundance Kid ("Rufus"), with handler Kathy Kirk.

Digital Photography

The advent of digital photography meant that photographers such as Jean Fogle and Mary Bloom had to learn a whole new set of skills, which has advantages and disadvantages. It means that a photographer spends quite a bit of time sitting in front of a computer. Digital photography is costly, says Mary Bloom. "You need a powerful, fully loaded computer with the software necessary for editing and other equipment needed for organizing photos and for data storage."

Yet working digitally also allows photographers to send images anywhere in the world at a moment's notice and to display electronic portfolios on their Web pages. Digital photography also offers the chance to experiment.

"The worst part of the job is the financial insecurity and working every day of the week," photographer Mary Bloom says. "If I'm not shooting, I'm editing. It never ends. The best thing is meeting lots of dogs and the people who love them. Having something in common with dog people helps create friendships that are valuable to me. I live and work alone most of the time, but I'm certainly not a loner, so my dog friends and clients bring balance to my life."

Because freelance and pet portrait photographers are generally self-employed, they must purchase their own equipment. It can cost thousands of dollars to acquire and maintain cameras and accessories. Photographers need lenses, filters, tripods, flash attachments, and specially constructed lighting equipment to achieve the quality and effects they want.

Most photographers these days use digital cameras instead of traditional film, although some use both. Digital images are edited on computers, so good photographers must be knowledgeable about processing or editing software, which allows them to crop or modify images, enhance them through color correction, create larger images, or produce special effects. They also need high-quality printers to bring their final images alive.

Unless they have their own darkrooms, photographers who shoot with film bear the expense of sending their film to laboratories for processing and printing. A fully equipped darkroom for a photographer who prefers to develop his or her own pictures requires developing and printing equipment and chemicals along with, of course, the technical skills to produce the desired effects.

Portrait of Two Photographers

Jean Fogle (*left with Molly*) decided to pursue photography full time twelve years ago, not long after her husband brought home a Jack Russell Terrier puppy. "I found Molly enchanting and started photographing her and all of her new doggy friends," she says.

Even before Molly's arrival, Fogle had been interested in photography. She honed her skills on her sons and then began to sell gardening images to national gardening magazines. "I enjoyed putting photo essays together and found it was a nice niche," she says. "Selling both words and images together made it easier for editors."

When she switched to dog photography, she was fortunate to have some photos accepted by *Dog Fancy* magazine, published by BowTie Publications. From there, she began doing work for other magazines and for books. Fogle has published two books of her own: *Salty Dogs* (Howell Book House, 2007) and *Tricks for Treats* (BowTie Press, 2010).

When Mary Bloom (*right with Fiona*) was a child, her mother bred Poodles and Dalmatians. Mary would pore over the dog magazines in the house, admiring the photos. Bloom began taking photos of animals when she became a volunteer at the ASPCA in New York City. She wasn't trained as a photographer, but her job involved taking photos of animals available for adoption and documenting their stories for the ASPCA's publications. That led to an opportunity to go to northern Canada to photograph the harp seal hunt. "It was that experience that changed my life," Bloom says. "I realized I could make a contribution to the lives of animals and their needs if I became a photographer."

The photos Bloom took of the seal hunt were the first ones she sold. Afterward, she found that if she could illustrate an interesting story with good photos, she could find a market for her work. Now she works primarily for magazine and book publishers.

Success for Bloom means doing something meaningful that has importance to the people she works for, whether they are magazine editors or dog owners. "It's rich and rewarding work," she says. "I feel like I'm preserving history by creating photos of dogs. An example is photos I did for an AKC children's book fifteen years ago. Recently, a woman came up to me at a dog show and remembered that I was the person who took pictures of her white Bull Terrier for the book. She said that the dog had just passed on, which was hard for her, but thanks to the photos in the book, her dog has gained a place in history, which made her proud. That meant so much to me."

Education and Training

A pet photographer can gain his or her expertise by pursuing a college degree, by attending training programs and workshops, or through that old standby—experience. It is one of the few fields in which a degree is not required, although it certainly doesn't hurt.

Formal Education

There are colleges and art schools that offer degrees in photography, and photography courses are offered at community colleges, vocational schools, and trade and technical schools. Courses you may study include composition, photography techniques, darkroom skills, digital printing, and the use of Adobe Photoshop or other retouching software.

An aspiring photographer needs to learn technical skills. A photographer is more likely to succeed if he or she develops a distinctive look or style, one that sets him or her apart from the competition. Developing that style can begin with the study of design and composition in school. Learning doesn't stop with graduation. For successful photographers, the study of all aspects of the field is a lifelong process.

Another key factor in a photographer's success is knowledge of the subject matter, whether dogs, cats, horses, or wildlife. Studying movement, anatomy, behavior, and breed standards should be part of every animal photographer's education. Again, you can begin your education in these areas in school, by taking anatomy and biology courses, but you will want to continue to learn throughout your career.

If you aim to be a self-employed photographer, you also should take business courses, such as accounting and marketing, which will help you run a portrait studio, commercial photography business, or other freelance business. Negotiation skills are useful, too. You should know how to prepare a

Barkworthy BITE

READ THE BOOK
"No matter what kind of camera you have, get it out, read the book, and experiment. Too many people never read the instruction manual and never learn about the functions of the camera. There are some great online courses to help advance your camera skills, and taking a class forces you to learn how to operate your camera, how to visualize better photos, and how to get the kind of pictures you want to capture."—Jean Fogle, photographer

business plan, submit bids, write contracts, keep financial records, get permission to shoot on locations that normally are not open to the public, obtain releases to use photographs of people, license and price your photographs, and secure copyright protection for your work.

Other Learning Avenues

Not everyone learns technical skills at school. Some beginners apprentice with experienced photographers, helping with equipment and setting up shots. Other ways

Nancy Spelke of Custom Dog Designs continues to be one of the most admired and sought-after photographers on the dog show circuit.

to learn or improve photography skills are to subscribe to photography newsletters and magazines, join camera clubs, or find part- or full-time work in camera stores or photo studios.

While a photography degree would be helpful, Fogle says, she believes experience is one of the best teachers. So is something as simple as reading the camera's manual and then experimenting with the camera.

"Join camera clubs and let others critique your photos. Spend time analyzing photos that you like," says Fogle. "I recently expanded into studio lighting and find that I am always looking at ads that catch my eye to see how they achieved the lighting."

Employment Outlook

Anyone can hang out a shingle as a freelance photographer, but the competition is keen for both salaried jobs and freelance work. Expect to market yourself and compete in an already full environment. Animal photographers who are most likely to get and keep freelance or salaried work are those with special skills in handling animals, excellent contacts among pet owners or exhibitors, photography- and imaging-related computer skills, and the ability to quickly learn new technologies and techniques.

People's love for their pets appears to be unceasing, so there is likely to be a steady or increasing demand for pet portrait photographers. More online versions of newspapers, magazines, and journals translate into more opportunities for photographers to place their work, but how well these particular outlets will pay is yet to be seen. In times of recession, print media can suffer.

Employment of all photographers is predicted to grow 12 percent through 2018, which is about as fast as average for all occupations. It doesn't help those seeking work that photography is a favorite hobby of many individuals. Widespread availability of digital cameras and editing software means that more people may be creating their own photos of beloved pets and less likely to hire professionals.

Start by freelancing on the side. Unless you have a steady client list and are confident in your ability to continue to find work, don't quit your day job just yet. Becoming a photographer is a big commitment, and it involves much more than taking pretty pictures. But for someone who loves animals and photography, the appeal of this career can be overwhelming.

"Make sure you are doing it for reasons other than earning a good living, and be prepared to constantly educate yourself not only in the business world but in the technology world as well," Bloom says. "It's a lot harder than it seems but well worth the rewards. If I earn enough to pay the bills, which is hard at times, I'm satisfied that I'm taking care of my responsibilities and doing a service."

Depending on skill level, business savvy, and marketing ability, a dog photographer's income can range from very low to very high. A rare few photographers may earn high incomes, but their success often comes at a cost of long work days and frequent travel.

PHOTOGRAPHY RESOURCES

- Art and Photography Schools, www.art-photography-schools.com
- Cowbelly Pet Photography, www.cowbellyblog.com
- *How to Photograph Dogs: A Comprehensive Guide*, by Kerrin Winter and Dale Churchill. Howell Books, 1998.
- *Photographer's Market.* Writers Digest Books, www.photographersmarket.com
- Professional Photographers of America, www.ppa.com
- *Professional Photographer Magazine*, www.ppm.com
- *Professional Techniques for Pet and Animal Photography*, by Debra H. Muska. Amherst Media Inc., 2003.

CHAPTER 18

Writer, Editor, and Publisher

Print and digital publications about dogs and other pets have grown steadily since 1990. Publishers of books, magazines, newsletters, newspapers, journals, trade publications, and Web sites produce content about dogs, and they all need writers and editors to create and edit the content. Journalists and authors who specialize in pet writing bring to life the information people need to care for their animals and the stories that inspire their readers to help animals through adoption, training, proper care, or bringing about changes in animal health and welfare. Editors who work for pet publications must plan issues, stay aware of trends in the animal world, and shine up a writer's work until it shines on the page. The green-eyeshaded editor of yesteryear has morphed into an individual who not only works in print but also can develop content using a variety of multimedia formats for readers, listeners, or viewers.

Writers

You may picture a pet writer sitting at the computer, briskly typing away, a dog at his or her feet or a cat curled on top of the monitor. But before the words and sentences come into being, writers must gather information through interviews with experts, Internet and library research, and personal observations. Not until they have satisfied their curiosity on

Writer and top Poodle breeder Karen LeFrak shows off two of her labors of love: the children's book she wrote, *Jake the Philharmonic Dog*, and her Poodle.

a subject—or feel that they know enough to satisfy the curiosity of their editors and readers—do they begin to write, fashioning facts, statistics, anecdotes, and quotes into articles, blog posts, or books that will inform and/or entertain readers in an organized, interesting way. Strong research and the use of appropriate sources form the body of the work; creative use of language is the fabric that clothes it; and correct grammar, spelling, and punctuation are the accessories that pull it all together.

The words don't always flow at the writer's command. There's a lot of sitting and thinking and staring out the window before the writer's work is done to his or her satisfaction. It takes self-discipline and perseverance to sit alone in front of a computer and complete the work by the given deadline. Later, with help from editors, writers may revise or rewrite sections, searching for the best organization or the right phrasing.

Most writers—70 percent in 2008—work freelance, meaning that they are self-employed, selling their ability to craft words into prose and

Portrait of a Teenage Writer

For a talented writer, age is no barrier. Kate Eldredge (*pictured with her dogs: Flash, a Pembroke Welsh Corgi, and Tia, an Australian Shepherd*) pitched her first book when she was thirteen and got a contract for it a year later. It all began when she accompanied her mother, veterinarian Deb Eldredge, to the 2004 Cat Writers' Association conference.

"The original reason I attended the conference was because my mom was having back trouble and she needed me to carry her bags around. On the plane we started brainstorming, because I might as well have something to pitch if I was going to be there, and realized what a good idea it was," Eldredge says. "I pitched it at the meeting, and a year later was contacted by Wiley, which wanted to go through with it."

Her book, *Head of the Class: A Teen Dog Expert Teaches You to Raise and Train the Perfect Pal*, was published by Howell Book House in 2006, when she was fifteen years old. By age nineteen, Eldredge had coauthored two more books, written a rally column for the *United States Australian Shepherd Association Journal*, and was majoring in English at Cornell University.

poetry to book and magazine publishers, news organizations, or corporate or nonprofit clients. They either propose their own story ideas to editors or are assigned articles. A single pet writer's work in the space of a month can include blog posts, magazine or newsletter articles, weekly or monthly columns for print or online publications, book or product reviews, one or more book chapters, or even a complete book.

Who Pet Writers Are

All Marion Lane ever wanted to do was something involved with animals and writing. A liberal arts degree in literature in hand, she headed off to the Big Apple to offer her talents to New York City's million-and-one publishers. Eventually, she landed a job at the American Kennel Club, which hired her to work in the obedience department as administrative assistant to the director.

"As I learned more about obedience, I began to offer to write about different aspects of the sport for the AKC's magazine, the *Gazette*," she says. "The magazine tried to provide regular coverage of obedience, but no one

Award-winning writer Mordecai Siegal displays the caricature of him that appeared in the *Wall Street Journal*.

on staff knew anything about it, so the editor was thrilled to have my offerings, especially free of charge. After a year or two of this arrangement, she invited me to join the *Gazette* staff. At that time, the editors were writing half of every issue, so I sort of became a pet writer and pet editor at the same time."

Alaskan Malamute breeder Charlene LaBelle of Saratoga, California, came to writing through her love of dogs and backpacking. Although she wrote about hiking with her Malamutes for her local breed club newsletter, she hadn't thought of taking her writing any further than that. Then, one day, she was climbing Mount Whitney with three dogs, and several people she encountered on the trail asked her if there was a book on packing with dogs.

Finally, she replied, "There isn't one. I haven't written it yet." That evening, she used the back of her food planner for the chapter list. The result was *A Guide to Backpacking with Your Dog* (Alpine Publications, 2004), followed by *MUSH! A Beginners Manual of Sled Dog Training* (Barkleigh Publications, 2007), now in its fourth edition.

Veterinarian Shawn Messonnier got into writing because he wanted to educate pet owners and fellow veterinarians about the benefits of using natural therapies. Today, his writing includes newspaper and pet magazine columns, a blog, and books, the latest of which is *Unexpected Miracles—Hope and Holistic Healing for Pets* (Forge Books, 2009).

Newspaper columnists Gina Spadafori, Maryanne Dell, and Ranny Green jumped into pet writing from their perches as reporters or editors at their respective newspapers. Spadafori began her column in 1984 at the *Sacramento Bee*; it was later syndicated by McClatchy in 1987 and then Universal Press in 1998. Spadafori still writes the column today, along with a blog, online articles, pieces for *Parade* magazine, and a number of award-winning, top-selling books, coauthored with her writing partner, Marty Becker, DVM.

Mordecai Siegal never set out to become one of the best-selling pet authors in history. Instead he wanted to be a "Novelist," as in the type who would write the "Great American Novel." Before a badly trained Husky puppy derailed Siegal's grand plan, he even had a short stint on the New York stage, once as an off-Broadway actor and once on Broadway with Bea Arthur and Ed Asner in a musical. The Siberian Husky's name was Pete, and it was this puppy who led Siegal to dog trainer Matthew Margolis, who soon thereafter became Siegal's coauthor for a dog book. Siegal thought *Good Dog, Bad Dog* was mostly a whimsical project that he agreed to do while trying to sell his "important literature." Released in 1973, *Good Dog, Bad Dog* (Henry Holt) swiftly became a best seller, and the entire pet-publishing world came sniffing at Siegal's reluctant paws.

No fewer than two dozen books on dogs and cats followed, along with monthly pet columns in major national periodicals such as *House Beautiful*, *Good Housekeeping*, and *Women's World*

DO YOU HAVE WHAT IT TAKES?

WRITER

A good dog writer should have the following characteristics:

- ○ Imagination
- ○ Curiosity
- ○ Creativity
- ○ A broad range of knowledge
- ○ Organization
- ○ Research skills
- ○ Clarity of expression
- ○ Patience and perseverance
- ○ Ability to concentrate and work under pressure
- ○ Ability to meet deadlines
- ○ Self-discipline
- ○ Command of the English language
- ○ Ability to handle rejection

as well as forty-three dog club publications. Siegal went on to win countless awards from the Dog Writers Association of America (DWAA), an organization that honored him with its Distinguished Service Award twice and then with a lifetime achievement award, inducting him into the Hall of Fame in 2007. He served as president of DWAA from 1994 to 2000. Siegal's dedication to the organization remained strong until his death in 2010.

Many other pet writers get their start writing articles and columns for nonprofit organizations, breed club publications, or Web sites and then move on to larger or more widely disseminated publications.

The Challenges of a Freelance Writer

Most freelance writers work from home. Laptop computers and advances in electronic communication make it easy for writers to do their work wherever they may be: a veterinary meeting, a pet-product trade show, the annual Westminster Kennel Club dog show, or at home in their pajamas.

The pleasure of being a freelance writer is the ability to set your own hours, but you'll probably find that you write best if you work established hours or follow a routine, which will help prevent you from wasting too much time surfing the Web or chatting online with your fellow dog-writer friends. And don't think that being a dog writer means you get to sleep in late. You might be on the phone at 6 a.m. because that's the only time your East Coast source can talk to you. Even if you try to keep regular hours, there are times you will find yourself working nights or weekends to meet a deadline or to revise an assignment to your editor's satisfaction.

Juggling multiple projects while always seeking out new assignments is a standard part of the job. Many writers suffer from insomnia, anxiety, neck and back pain, and carpal tunnel syndrome, all due to the emotional and physical stresses associated with their work. Still, most wouldn't have it any other way.

Then there is the uncertainty about the future of traditional publishing, which is being challenged by digital media. How it will evolve and survive remains to be seen. That is why it is more important than ever for a free-lance writer to stay up with the most current technologies and develop a personal online presence.

Blogs present constantly updated news and commentary on every subject conceivable, including dogs, and they are changing the face of journalism. A blog, short for weblog, can be personal or part of a mainstream form of media. It gives every writer a voice and connects him or her to readers around the world. Whatever their interest in dogs and writing, writers are finding that it's imperative to have blogs or Web sites that showcase who they are and what kind of writing they do. Blogging on a regular basis hones

Walter R. Fletcher: A Writing Celebrity in the Sport

Walter R. Fletcher wrote about dog shows in *The New York Times* and other metropolitan newspapers across the United States for more than sixty years. His weekly column in the *Times* covered dog activities such as shows and obedience and field trials, as well as the personalities involved in the sport. Born in New York in 1906, Fletcher attended City College and worked as a campus correspondent for the *Times* and the *New York Post*. Full-time employment at the *Times* began in 1927, and Fletcher worked as a sportswriter, copy editor, photo editor, and makeup editor. After retiring in 1976, Fletcher continued to cover dog shows for the *Times* and for *Dog World* magazine from 1977–1995. He was the only staff writer for the *Times* who was regarded as knowledgeable in the world of purebred dogs, and his obituary in that newspaper referred to him as "something of a celebrity in the sport."

Fletcher covered dog shows from coast to coast and in fourteen foreign countries, but his favorite show was the Westminster Kennel Club Show in Madison Square Garden, which he reported on more than forty times. Roger Caras, former ASPCA president and long-time Westminster announcer, referred to Fletcher as "the Walter Lippmann of the hydrant set." Fletcher shunned technology and never used a computer, writing his stories on a beat-up portable typewriter. Walter Fletcher's book-writing accomplishments include *Dogs of the World* and *My Times with Dogs*.

writing skills and sharpens your point of view, and blogging is one more skill that will make you more marketable as a writer.

Education and Training

Writers, whether they attend college or not, should always be learning, studying animal-related subjects on their own, and acquiring practical experience with animals, if they want to write about pets.

A college degree in English, journalism, or communications is the most common foundation for a career as a writer, but any background is acceptable for someone who can demonstrate good writing skills. People who write about pets or wildlife may have degrees in fields as diverse as anthropology, biology, history, and psychology. There are no courses in pet writing per se, but if you want to focus on the science or the culture of dogs, you may want to consider getting a master's degree in a specialized form of journalism, such as science writing or cultural criticism. A number of universities have graduate programs in these areas.

What's more important than a degree is a love for and understanding of your subject, because passion is what makes writing stand out. If you want to write about dogs, other pets, or wildlife, start building a broad and deep knowledge of your subject by reading everything you can find on it: fiction, nonfiction, essays, articles, and books about training,

John Keys: The World's First Dog Author

John Keys (name later Latinized to Johannes Caius) died in 1573 and still qualifies as an icon of the dog world. Keys was an English doctor who is credited with writing the first known dog book, *Of Englishe Dogges*, possibly the most frequently quoted dog book in history. The book, first published in Latin as *De Canibus Britannicis* in 1570, attempted to name and classify dog breeds. In his day, Keys was the physician to Edward VI, Queen Mary, and Queen Elizabeth I and possibly the inspiration for Shakespeare's Doctor Caius character in *The Merry Wives of Windsor*. Caius College in Cambridge is named after this famous figure in British history.

Other early icons for dog writers include J. H. Walsh (aka Stonehenge), Vero Shaw, and Hugh Dalziels in the nineteenth century and Robert Leighton, Walter Hutchinson, and Edward Ash in the early twentieth century.

behavior, the different breeds, humor, and art, to name just a few subjects.

Experience with dogs, even if they are your own pets, will inform your writing and help you come up with good story ideas. More in-depth involvement, such as participating in a dog sport or conformation showing, can only be a plus.

Employment Outlook

Many publishers are downsizing, and competition is keen for all writing jobs. The BLS predicts that employment for writers will grow by only 8 percent through

Marion Lane, seen here with Natasha, knows the challenges of editing as well as writing and has worked in magazines and books.

2018, about as fast as the average for all occupations. Publishers, businesses, and organizations will seek writers with Web, multimedia, and social media experience.

Staff writers in any field may earn from $28,000 to more than $100,000 for those with talent and experience, but it is unlikely that they will be hired to write solely about pets. Freelance writers earn income from their articles and books, written for multiple publishers and other clients. They are paid per assignment, often by the word. They work as long as it takes to complete the assignment and meet the deadline; therefore, a faster work pace equals a higher hourly paycheck when you break it all down. A writer's income usually varies from year to year, sometimes as little as $10,000 and in extremely rare cases as much as $100,000 or more. Keep in mind, too, that freelancers generally must provide for their own health insurance and retirement plan.

A writer's goal is to earn enough to make a living, however meager, but other payoffs are often more treasured. "It has been a thrill to have my magazines and books nominated for awards, and sometimes to win," Lane says, "but the most personally gratifying aspect of my job is hearing from readers who have been moved, amused, or impacted by something that I've written."

Editors

The verb *edit* has a variety of meanings. An editor is one who supervises or directs the preparation of a publication; collects, prepares, and arranges material for publication; and revises or corrects that material. Editors fall into several categories, including newspapers, magazines, books, and newsletters. The editors may work for general-interest publishers, publishers specializing in material about animals, or animal-related organizations such as the American Society for the Prevention of Cruelty to Animals. The biggest categories are magazine and book editors.

DO YOU HAVE WHAT IT TAKES?

EDITOR

A dog editor should have the following characteristics:

- O Excellent writing ability
- O Excellent organizational skills
- O Ability to express ideas clearly
- O Computer and other technical skills
- O Creativity
- O Curiosity
- O A nose for news
- O Knowledge of or interest in dogs
- O Self-motivation
- O Good judgment
- O Ability to work under pressure and meet deadlines
- O Tact

Magazine Editor

A magazine editor's first job is to plan the content of a publication so it will appeal to the targeted reader. Dog owners come in many different forms and have many different interests, so there are numerous publications about dogs, each with a different focus. A magazine may be aimed at people who have purebred dogs, people who compete with their dogs in canine sports, people who are interested in canine health, people who rescue dogs, people who breed dogs, people who train dogs, people who have a specific breed, people interested in all-natural pet care—well, you get the picture.

To fill a magazine's pages, editors assign articles to staff writers or freelance writers. Editors read queries and manuscripts from freelance writers and review the writers' work to decide what is most likely to appeal to their readers. Editors read

Portrait of a Magazine Editor

A typical day for Nicole Sipe (*pictured with Winston*), managing editor of the Popular Dogs Series at BowTie Publications, begins with responding to reader e-mails. They may want to know where to find a good breeder, why their dogs are behaving a certain way, or when the magazine plans to feature their breeds. When Sipe can't answer a question, she refers readers to an expert.

She then spends half an hour or so cruising the Internet, catching up on dog news. It's essential for editors to stay informed about dog-related news and other stories. Sipe's day varies depending on the stage of the magazine cycle. Mid-production, she gives stories a second read, on paper, and marks them up with any corrections. She uses proofreading marks to indicate changes, additions, or deletions. From start to finish, she and the rest of the editorial team do four edits on every article.

Photo selection is another important part of an editor's job and calls for discrimination as well as an eye for a great shot. Sipe tries to find photos of dogs who look happy, although that can be difficult sometimes—for example, breeds such as Bulldogs just look grumpy. When possible, she looks for photos of dogs with a sparkle in the eye and an engaging expression. She also takes the nature of the article into account. Her first instinct for an article on breed rescue is to select photos of sad-looking dogs, but then she reconsiders. Who wants to see pages full of unhappy dogs? Instead, she tries to find photos of dogs who look as if they've found a "forever home."

Choosing photos for an article can take from twenty minutes to two hours. Afterward, Sipe sends slides to the imaging department to be scanned and electronically formats digital photos before sending them to imaging. Then she might attend a team meeting to discuss the planning of a new title or to come up with cover blurbs for an upcoming magazine. All of these tasks make for a full and fulfilling day for a dog lover.

and rewrite, as needed, the work of writers, and editors may also do some writing themselves, from the editor's note to an article or story. The responsibilities of magazine editors vary by employer and the type and level of their editorial position.

Editor and managing editor: Executive and managing editors generally hire other editors and sometimes art directors, plan budgets, set contract requirements for freelance writers, and plan and oversee the content of each issue. They attend veterinary and other pet-related trade shows and conferences to keep up with the latest news and knowledge about health, training, nutrition, products, grooming trends, odor control, and more. In small organizations, the editor may do everything—including manage the production of the publication—or may share responsibility with a small staff.

Marion Lane recently retired as special projects editor for the American Society for the Prevention of Cruelty to Animals and was previously the features editor for the American Kennel Club's monthly magazine, the AKC *Gazette.* Both jobs have many facets, ranging from planning all issues for the upcoming year to reading every word of every issue before it goes to the printer. The editor decides the length of each article, who will write it, and how much to pay for it. The editor also works with the publication's art director to discuss ideas on how to illustrate each article or column, and meets with the production staff to determine the order in which features will appear and where advertisements will be placed.

Associate editor: An associate editor's duties include doing read-throughs and edits on articles, making corrections on paper or electronically, contacting authors with follow-up questions, assigning articles to writers, sending out photo guidelines, writing captions, sorting and choosing photos and returning them to photographers after use, updating the magazines' Web sites, handling readers' calls and mail, and attending various dog-related events throughout the year.

"This job requires making a lot of judgment calls regarding editing articles and choosing photos, so it helps to have an independent nature and to be able to trust yourself," says Nicole Sipe, who began her career at BowTie Publications as an associate editor. "On the flip side, you really need to be able to work with others and accept other people's ideas, some of which you may not agree with. Being an associate editor means being flexible, open to ideas, and willing to share ideas."

Copy editor: Copy editors review articles and other content for errors in grammar, punctuation, and spelling and check the copy for readability and agreement with editorial style; that is, they ensure that the articles have the look, tone, and voice that set the magazine apart from its competitors. Copy editors may change words or rearrange sentences or paragraphs to improve the article's flow or accuracy. Often, their job involves verifying

Portrait of an AKC Editor

When Mara Bovsun (*pictured with Lisa and Maggie*) was a child, she desperately wanted a dog but wasn't allowed to have one. As an adult with an undergraduate degree in liberal arts and a master's degree in journalism from New York University, she set aside the idea of a dog as "kid stuff" and devoted herself to working twelve-hour days as an editor and freelance writer, specializing in scientific and medical topics. Then Megan entered her life.

The old yellow Labrador Retriever had belonged to Bovsun's father-in-law. After his death, no one else in the family was able to give the dog a home. Bovsun and her husband, Michael, had misgivings. They lived in a studio apartment in New York City and had busy careers. But sending Megan to a shelter didn't seem right. The decision to take her in changed Bovsun's life. "Slowly but surely, I began spending less time with my work and more time with Megan," Bovsun says. Megan was old, though, and within a few months she was diagnosed with osteosarcoma: bone cancer. Treatment gained her another seven months of life, but it was clear that she would die soon.

"After having no dog all my life, I now couldn't live without one," Bovsun says. She turned to Petfinder.com and found another yellow Lab. A call to the shelter elicited the information that unless Bovsun could take her right away, the dog would be euthanized. Bovsun agreed to adopt her sight unseen. "She was wild. She was a nine-month-old Lab who'd had no training and I was a total novice. She was dog-aggressive. I wasn't prepared for this dog, but instead of giving up on her, I decided I was going to bring her into line. I went through a crash course in dog training." In addition to Maggie the Lab, who now has a Canine Good Citizen title and is a therapy dog, Bovsun lives with Lisa the Leonberger, another adopted dog with issues who has since made good in the agility ring.

Through a series of events—losing her job, sending a letter to the editor of *Your Dog*, a newsletter for dog owners, and her reluctant attendance at a holiday party for science writers—Bovsun began writing about dogs. When her editor at the *AKC Gazette* resigned to move to Arizona, she suggested that Bovsun apply for her job. Bovsun has been features editor at the *AKC Gazette* since October 2005. Acquiring and editing articles for the publication requires a talent for communication, making complex concepts understandable to readers as well as getting the best out of writers. "When I work with a writer, I'm very specific in what I want and the effect I want the story to have," she says.

facts, dates, and statistics, either by contacting the author or doing their own research. At some magazines, this work is among the tasks of feature editors or associate editors. Due to budget reductions, copy editors are quickly becoming an endangered species, which is a pity because their work is what gives a book or magazine polish.

Assistant editor and editorial assistant: Assistant editors and editorial assistants are entry-level employees. They may read and evaluate manuscripts submitted by freelance writers; proofread articles; prepare the calendar, news, and new-product sections; and answer phone calls and e-mails. They also perform administrative tasks, such as filing photos, returning photos, and maintaining author files.

Book Editor

Turning a manuscript into a book is a lengthy process, one that usually takes at least a year from the time a manuscript has been accepted for publication to the day it arrives on the shelves of a book or pet store. Several different kinds of editors are involved in the process, beginning with the acquisitions editor, whose job it is to find manuscripts for the publishing company.

Acquisitions editor: Acquisitions editors review proposals for books and decide whether to buy the publication rights from the author. When book manuscripts arrive, they review and edit them to ensure that they meet

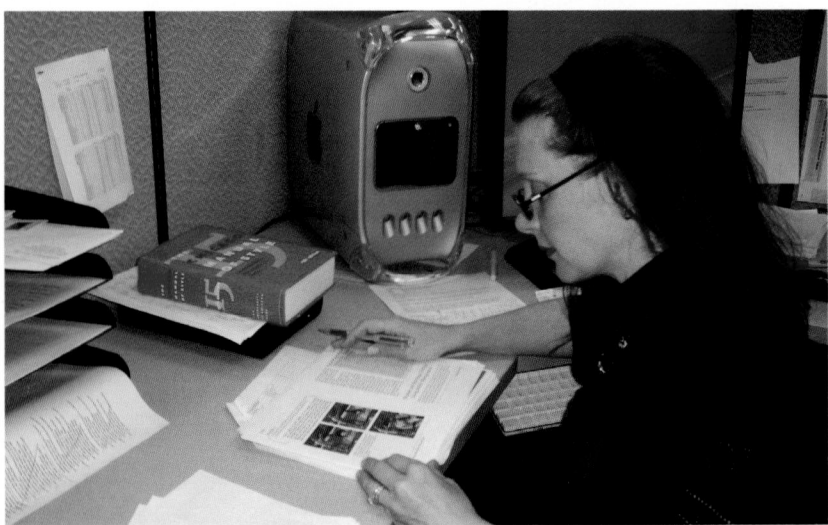

Senior editor Amy Deputato makes corrections on the layouts of a book. Her cubicle contains the tools of the editor's trade: computer, reference books, and editing pens.

the requirements of the author's contract; if a manuscript does not meet the requirements, the editor may return it to the author with suggestions on how to rewrite the manuscript. Once a manuscript has been accepted, the acquisitions editor sends it on to a lead or project editor, who will oversee the process of turning the manuscript into a published book.

Substantive editor: The substantive edit is the organizational edit of the book; you might call it the "big picture" edit. The substantive editor—usually a senior- or associate-level editor who shepherds the book through all editorial phases—reads through a manuscript to evaluate the content and its presentation. Is the information appropriate and comprehensive enough for the intended readers of the book? Is the material presented in a logical order? Are the main statements well supported? The editor works closely with the author during the substantive edit, and this is the time for the editor to suggest reorganizing text as needed and to point out "holes" in the manuscript where information needs to be further developed or added.

Copy editor: You could call the copyedit the "little picture" edit—though there's nothing small about the copy editor's job. The copy editor makes sure that everything is grammatically correct and that all words and names are spelled correctly. He or she also checks that all descriptions and details are consistent throughout the manuscript, and that all aspects of house style and the book's individual style sheet are followed. The copy editor also makes sure that transitions from one idea to another are in place, and that the information in the book is clearly presented. Some copy editors think of themselves as the "consumer advocates" of publishing. If they don't understand something that the author is saying, then the reader probably won't either. So it's up to the copy editor to "protect" the reader by pointing out any flaws and making sure that they are fixed before publication. That way, the reader will get the most information and enjoyment out of the book.

Work Environment

Count on spending your day in a cubicle if you work in the editorial offices of a pet publisher. Your work space will have a desk with a computer and telephone, shelving for past issues of your magazine or printed editions of your books, and a collection of reference books that will make up your library, a style manual, and of course, a good dictionary. Outside your cubicle will likely be tables topped with printers, fax machines, and large-screen computers where you can review stories or chapters after they have been designed and put into layouts by the art director. Your work environment will be generally quiet, except for the sound of ringing phones, whirring printers, and clacking keyboards. If you are the editor-in-chief, you may have a private office where you can hold meetings, make phone calls, and prepare your budget or editorial calendar.

Who Editors Are

Editors must demonstrate good judgment and a strong sense of ethics in deciding what material to publish. They also need tact and the ability to guide and encourage others in their work. Managing people can be difficult, and it's not always easy to review staff, talk to employees and contributors about their weaknesses, and be a disciplinarian.

Don't think that being an editor means you don't have to do math. Magazine editors must have a certain balance of editorial content and advertising, which requires a knowledge of percentages, and must fit ads of different sizes on pages, which calls for a certain skill with fractions. Book editors need math skills to determine what a book's approximate page count will be, based on the manuscript's word count and the number of images to be used. Another part of an editor's job is to prepare and live by a budget.

Lane says that editors must be able to work as part of a team—a team in which some members may know more than others do about some aspects of the job—and must be organized and detail oriented. She also describes one of the most difficult aspects of the job: "Having the strength of character to say 'no' a lot and to send material back to the authors for rewrites when necessary."

The best part of the job is the creativity involved, both on the part of the editor and the contributors or authors with whom the editor works. Lane enjoys the challenge of planning issues, getting wonderful story ideas from freelancers, and reaping the emotional rewards brought by publishing stories and columns that will help animals receive better care or promote groups and organizations involved in animal care and welfare. It's also satisfying to do the nuts-and-bolts work of editing: improving the clarity and organization of text and working with page layouts using desktop publishing software.

Education and Training

Most publishers look for a degree in communications, English, or journalism. Some will hire people with other liberal arts degrees, such as anthropology, history, or psychology. Lane majored in English and general literature and has a bachelor of arts degree from a four-year liberal arts college, plus a certificate from a two-year continuing-education course in magazine publishing from an accredited university. A good editor in the pet field will have three types of knowledge: language, pet, and computer.

Language Knowledge

There's a reason publishers look for language degrees. An editor must have more than just grammar, punctuation, and spelling skills. He or she must also have a firm grasp of the intricacies of the English language.

"You need to know how to come up with clever, engaging headlines and blurbs and know when a sentence or paragraph just doesn't sound right, along with the ability to tweak it without taking away from the author's voice. You also need to be able to disseminate complicated information and make it understandable to the public," Sipe says. "I always think to myself, 'Is this something my mom would understand?' If it isn't, I'll try to reword it."

Kennel Club Books associate editor Jennifer Calvert uses a light box and loop to review images submitted for publication in a book she is editing.

Pet Knowledge

Depending on the position, knowledge of dogs or other animals may be acquired or required. Most people who come to work on a pet publication have at least had pets, but they may not have the in-depth knowledge that comes with training, showing, or breeding animals. Some magazines and books are geared toward a highly knowledgeable audience and would prefer to hire someone with a strong background in the subject matter, but others are more open to hiring people who can learn on the job.

"If a magazine is about animals, some of the staff or most of them should have animal-related experience, ideally with the specific animal the magazine covers," Lane says. "As long as some of the editors have this experience, it's possible for others with good technical skills, whether in writing or editing or designing or acquiring photos, to do a fine job even though they don't have animal-related experience. All things being equal, though, it's always advantageous to be knowledgeable in a magazine's subject area. It would take an exceptional person to move into the top editorial position on an animal magazine without a background in animals, but it can be done. In my own case, the situation was reversed: I was quite knowledgeable about the subject matter but completely green at working on a magazine."

Of course, a love of dogs is important for a pet editor. An editor who is interested in dogs is better able to come up with or recognize topics that will interest readers. Sometimes a love of dogs develops once an editor has gotten the job. When she started working at BowTie, Sipe was afraid of dogs.

"I had this idea that all dogs could sense my fear and that they all were planning on attacking me," she says. "After reading about dog nature and learning what makes dogs tick, I realized my fear was irrational. Now I love dogs, and it's a pleasure to look at dog photos all day, read about dogs, and interact with dog lovers. Sometimes I can't believe they pay me to do this."

Computer Knowledge

Finally, in most communications jobs these days, including editing, a thorough knowledge of programs such as Microsoft Word is essential. Although some parts of the editing process are still done on paper, the majority of the work is done on screen, using functions such as track changes, which show what has been deleted, replaced, reformatted, and moved. A background in Web design or computer graphics, while not usually essential for an editor, is considered a plus, as many editors do some basic work with a book's or magazine's layout.

Portrait of a Book Editor

Taking a book from idea to manuscript to publication requires a whole team of editors. Amy Deputato at Kennel Club Books is one of them. Editing books about dogs is not much different than editing other types of books, she says, but it does require some specialized knowledge that can be learned on the job." You learn quickly about dogs and the world of dogs, the show world, the competitive world, about ownership and care and the different breeds. There's a lingo that goes along with dog showing and breeding and dog sports that it's helpful to be familiar with."

Deputato became a dog book editor after graduating from college with a degree in English and education. Realizing that teaching was not for her, she sought a different way to use her degree. A classified ad for a dog book editor sparked her interest. She applied for and got the job.

"It was an entry-level job with entry-level pay, but it was a good start in the business because the publishing company did everything in-house from accepting manuscripts to binding books, so it was a well-rounded education in editing work and the publishing business."

The shepherding of a book through the publishing process takes as long as a year. Authors are sometimes surprised by the lengthy process, Deputato says.

As lead editor on a book, Deputato does a substantive edit, reading the entire manuscript, deciding the best way to structure it, and consulting the author about ways to make it better. Then another editor copyedits the manuscript, ensuring that it conforms to publishing house style, checking for consistency, and pointing out factual errors or redundant language.

After the book is laid out, it is proofread and then checked by the author. The editors work with the author to incorporate changes and with the art directors and art department to implement any design changes. Deputato's advice for would-be dog book editors? "It's not necessary to have knowledge of dogs, but it's helpful if people have a passion for or at least an interest in the subject matter."

It also helps to have a facility with social media outlets and the ability to use communications equipment such as netbooks and smart phones to stay in touch with staff and sources, read and send e-mail, and review and transmit copy, whether from home, from the office, or while traveling. Successful editors, particularly full-time Web editors, will be familiar with electronic publishing, graphics and video production, and computer software so they can combine online text with graphics, audio, video, and animation.

Employment

One of the many good aspects about being hired for an editorial position on a pet-related publication is that even entry-level employees can usually begin editing material very soon. Publishers and organizations that produce pet-related content often have small staffs, and everyone needs to jump in to get the job done. A self-starter can go far in a short period of time. The corollary is that editors face keen competition for jobs. In this field, knowledge of the subject matter can be the secret to success.

Employment of editors is expected to grow about as fast as the average for all occupations through 2016; that is, approximately 10 percent. Much of that demand will be created by Web-based publications and others writing for interactive media. Many print magazines for pet owners have Internet-only content available on their Web sites. Pet-related companies need technical writers to describe their products and how they work.

Median annual wages for salaried editors were $49,990 in May 2008. The middle 50 percent earned between $36,690 and $69,140. The lowest 10 percent earned less than $28,090, and the highest 10 percent earned more than $95,490. Median annual wages of editors working specifically for newspaper, periodical, book, and directory publishers were $49,280.

"Don't go into magazine editing to make a lot of money, because being an editor will never pay as well as being the person on the magazine staff who sells advertising or works in the business office," Lane says. "Just know that you can make a decent living if you work really hard. Being the lucky person who gets to work with words and ideas is a large part of what you will get out of this career."

Portrait of a Publisher

Ericka Basile (*pictured with Coco Chanel and Bella*) loves animals. She lives with four dogs and twenty-two other pets, loves going to pet boutiques in search of the latest unique dog item, and does volunteer work and fund-raising for local shelters. She knew there were many businesses and activities that would be of interest to fellow dog owners, but it wasn't always easy to find them. So the decision to start a pet publication for her community of Naples, Florida, was a natural one. "I heard rumors of a dog beach but could not locate it online. I also heard there was a dog bakery somewhere. I decided there should be a magazine where people in Naples could go to read all about dogs and their lifestyle in our area."

The result was a quarterly publication, *Naples Dog Magazine*, launched in 2006. Out of curiosity, Basile sent a copy of the inaugural issue to Samir Husni, director of the Magazine Innovation Center at the University of Mississippi's School of Journalism (and known in the publishing world as "Mr. Magazine") to see what he thought of it. Husni named it one of the "top 30 new launches" in 2006, out of approximately 900 new magazine launches that year.

At first, Basile did everything herself, from selling ads to writing articles to overseeing design. After publishing the third issue, she realized it was time to take the next step. She hired an editor, a copy editor, writers, sales representatives, and a bookkeeper. Doing so allowed her to focus on community involvement. "I attended every dog event, dog wash, and gala to dig into needs and unique 'finds' in Naples," she says. "By the second year I was doing an *About Town* TV segment on our local cable TV station, which further expanded *Naples Dog Magazine*'s contribution in our area by reaching 350,000 people."

But it wasn't until the magazine began performing makeovers on shelter dogs that Basile recognized the real power of the media. "Every dog who had a makeover in my magazine was adopted within a week of the photo shoot," she says.

Even popular magazines with good management can fail when the economic environment isn't supportive. *Naples Dog Magazine* ceased publication in 2009.

Publisher

A publisher usually runs the business side of a publication, although he or she may also be involved in deciding the editorial vision of a magazine or the books to be published. This job involves advertising sales, circulation, promotion, and strategic planning. The publisher is concerned with printing, paper, and other manufacturing costs. The publisher's focus is the bottom line—ensuring that a magazine, newspaper, or book earns a profit.

What Publishers Do

Publishers are responsible for a publication's daily operations and the overall acquisition, launch, or development of an industry-specific or themed publication. They read publishing trade journals, attend conferences and trade shows, and may develop ancillary products or events that share the same market focus as the publication. Successful publishers recognize the need to create Web and print strategies that combine editorial coverage with an event, contest, or other offers to woo both readers and advertisers.

Some magazine publishers, known as group publishers, oversee more than one publication. One of the jobs of a group publisher is to sell advertisers on the marketing opportunities presented by the group of magazines.

In the dog world, publishers make it easier for people to learn about dogs and find breeders or rescue groups, allow advertisers to better target their products, and level the playing field for exhibitors. For instance, the advent of *Kennel Review* magazine allowed people who showed dogs to promote them through advertising, even if they couldn't afford a full-time handler or travel to shows across the country.

Rick Beauchamp is an distinguished author as well as a publisher.

Education and Training

Publishers come from all types of backgrounds. Some have a liberal arts degree in a subject such as history or English, while others may have an MBA. Some journalism schools offer courses or certificates in publishing, and New York University offers a master of science degree in publishing that includes courses in traditional and digital media, management and leadership, marketing and branding, and financial analysis. It's not unusual, though, for a publisher to start in advertising sales or on the editorial side and learn on the job.

Employment Outlook

Publishing is an entrepreneurial business, and because of that there are no statistics on the potential for jobs. Publishers create their own products in the form of magazines, newspapers, books, and Web sites, and success depends on the ability to predict what people will be interested in reading as well as on the state of the economy. Low ad sales, for instance, can kill a magazine or a newspaper.

With the advent of digital formats and e-readers, plus the new ease of self-publishing, the field of publishing is in a state of flux. Periodicals, in particular, face the challenges of a society that wants its information immediately and in an easily digestible format, says Richard Beauchamp, former publisher of *Kennel Review* magazine. The Internet won't entirely replace printed dog publications, Beauchamp believes, at least not any time soon, but he says the publishing business will have to offer something unique to succeed.

WRITING, EDITING, AND PUBLISHING RESOURCES

- Alliance of Purebred Dog Writers, www.purebreddogwriters.com
- American Copy Editors Society, www.copydesk.org
- Cat Writers' Association Inc., www.catwriters.org
- City College of New York, publishing certificate program, www.ccny.cuny.edu
- Columbia Journalism School, www.journalism.columbia.edu
- *Copyediting: Because Language Matters*, newsletter, www.copyediting.com
- Dog Writers Association of America, www.dwaa.org
- Emerson College, Master of Arts, Publishing and Writing, www.emerson.edu
- *Folio Magazine*, www.foliomag.com
- Iowa Writers' Workshop, www.uiowa.edu/~iww
- Johns Hopkins Master of Arts in Science Writing, http://writingseminars.jhu.edu
- JournalismJobs.com, http://journalismjobs.com
- Media Bistro courses and resources for media professionals, www.mediabistro.com
- National Association of Science Writers, www.nasw.org
- New York University, graduate publishing program, www.scps.nyu.edu
- Portland State University, book publishing program, www.publishing.pdx.edu/pubindex.html
- Publishing Central, www.publishingcentral.com
- Stanford Publishing Courses, http://publishingcourses.standford.edu
- *Writer's Market*, Robert Lee Brewer. Writers Digest Books, current ed., www.writersmarket.com.
- Yale Publishing Course, http://publishing-course.yale.edu

CHAPTER 19

Communications and PR Professionals and Broadcast Hosts

Those with a talent for communications and a love of animals can consider several career possibilities. Some options are communications, public relations, and media relations professionals and broadcast hosts. Pet-related businesses and organizations also seek the skills of a director of communications and public and media relations professionals who specialize in the pet field. These professionals use their knowledge of communication media to maintain the support of consumers, stockholders, or the public.

Back in the day, having a syndicated radio show was the dream of every silver-tongued pet expert. Some may have had local shows, but only a talented few ever achieved that pinnacle of having a broadcast that reached a nationwide audience. Well, podcasting—a method of online audio distribution—has changed all that. It has evolved from an audio blogging experiment to a mainstream way to allow pet experts to deliver their messages without a station, a syndication deal, or a satellite radio, or to expand their existing radio, TV, cable, or satellite audiences.

Communications Director

The job of the communications director is to describe and promote a business or organization and its products or message. This is a management position that can involve a wide variety of tasks, such as developing

promotional campaigns, conducting market or public-opinion research, and counseling executives on effective communication and use of social media, as well as managing staff, budgeting, and interacting with vendors. Development or fund-raising experience may also be necessary.

A communications director must have excellent writing and creative skills because a large part of the job is spent writing or overseeing the writing of everything from press releases and annual reports to articles and speeches. Communications directors frequently interact with the press, from issuing media credentials for events to being interviewed about an organization and its mission. Here is a look at some specific communications positions.

AKC Director of Communications

As director of communications at the American Kennel Club, Lisa Peterson is responsible for the organization's corporate communications and communications to the thousands of AKC-affiliated clubs. She oversees the club communications and public education department programs, such as Responsible Dog Ownership Days, Public Education Coordinators, and Canine Ambassadors. Peterson also assists with creative development of PR campaigns, press releases, and press conferences. She helps maintain the press center on www.AKC.org and manages the press room for AKC's premier dog show, the AKC/Eukanuba National Championship. In addition, Peterson serves as the department's resident purebred dog expert and AKC spokesperson for media interviews. She has

Lisa Peterson, AKC director of communications, speaks at a conference.

appeared on the *Today Show*, *Good Morning America*, the *CBS Evening News*, *Martha Stewart Living*, *The O'Reilly Factor*, and *Fox and Friends*, and other programs to promote AKC's mission of responsible dog ownership, to educate the public about the predictability of purebred dogs, to outline AKC's position on legislative issues, and to announce new initiatives such as the AKC Canine Partners program and events such as Meet the Breeds.

AKC Communications/PR Department

The Communications/PR Department of AKC oversees the release of information about the organization and responsible dog ownership to the public and the fancy. Staffers work with the media to secure favorable coverage of AKC as well as cultivating company spokespersons and pitching ideas for stories. Positions include director of communications, director of public relations, and supporting PR and communications coordinators. The director of public relations directs and implements all media outreach, develops creative strategies, and effectively implements programs that favorably highlight AKC products, services, and positions on issues as well as builds positive media relationships. This position is also responsible for managing PR campaigns, creating press materials, developing advertising and public service messages, and implementing strategies and tactics that promote them. A degree in communications, public relations, or journalism is most helpful as well as excellent writing skills, creativity, attention to detail, and enjoying a fast-paced, ever-changing work environment.

AKC Publications Department

AKC publications staff include positions such as senior editor, features editor, and graphic designer. These staffers edit, write, and design two award-winning magazines: *AKC Gazette* and *AKC Family Dog*. They also create the AKC Annual Report, *AKC New Puppy Handbook*, and program guides for AKC events such as the AKC/Eukanuba National Championship and Meet the Breeds. A degree in journalism, English, art, or graphic design is essential.

WKC Director of Communications

A background in dogs never hurts when you're looking for this type of position in the pet world, and sometimes it can take you places you never expected to go. That's what happened with David Frei, director of communications for the Westminster Kennel Club (WKC); president and CEO of the Angel on a Leash Foundation, a nonprofit charity that promotes the benefits of therapy dogs in health care facilities nationwide; and television cohost of the *Westminster Dog Show* on USA Network and the *National Dog Show* on NBC.

Frei didn't grow up with dogs. In fact, he didn't get his first dog until he was in college, after moving into a house off campus. He and his girlfriend at the time decided to purchase an Afghan Hound puppy. That single decision, made some forty years ago, set him on an unexpected and exhilarating career path.

The son of a football coach at the University of Oregon, Frei studied a little journalism and a little animal science and at one point contemplated going to veterinary school, but he says his educational background ended up having nothing to do with his eventual career.

David Frei, WKC director of communications, and Uno, the 2008 WKC Best in Show winner, make an appearance on *The Martha Stewart Show.*

"I started doing some things with Afghans. I went into the army and came to Walter Reed, where I met Wally Pede, who was a great Afghan Hound person, and he helped me get a little more involved in showing dogs."

In the meantime, Frei was employed in various sports-related jobs. He started as a sportswriter and then worked in public relations for the Denver Broncos, the San Francisco 49ers, and ABC Sports.

Frei's first wife also showed Afghans. Together, they showed and finished a number of dogs and bred and showed the one-time top-winning Afghan Hound bitch in the history of the breed, Ch. Who's Zoomin Who.

"Running around the country showing her in 1989 led me to some people who thought I could do television," he says. "I came back and did an audition tape for Chet Collier, and they hired me to announce the 1990 Westminster Kennel Club show. I thought 'Well, this will be fun for a few years; let's see what happens.'"

For some years, Frei maintained his life in Seattle, where he ran his own public relations agency and operated two sports bars, traveling to New York annually to be the "voice of Westminster." In 2002, he took a job with the American Kennel Club as director of media relations and a

On-Air Announcer

David Frei's position as an announcer for the Westminster Kennel Club Dog Show and the National Dog Show requires some special skills. Delivery, appearance, and style are all important. A good announcer has a pleasant, well-controlled voice; good timing; excellent pronunciation; and correct grammar. Take classes in voice and diction if you have a yen to be on the air. Good technology skills help, too. You should be familiar with computers, editing equipment, and other broadcast-related devices. Finally, you'll need strong writing ability, knowledge of dogs and dog shows, the creativity to ad lib all or part of a show, and the discipline to meet deadlines.

To be ready to take on that once-in-a-lifetime offer, as Frei did, it's a good idea to study broadcasting in college or at a technical school. A bachelor's degree in broadcasting, communications, or journalism is useful. Take courses in English, public speaking, drama, foreign languages, and computer science, as knowledge in all of these subjects can be valuable in this field.

year later accepted what he has described as his dream job, director of communications for the WKC. One of his missions there includes being president and CEO of Angel on a Leash, founded in 2004 as a charitable activity of the WKC.

In addition to issuing press credentials for the annual Westminster Kennel Club dog show, writing press releases, and overseeing the arrival and counting of the Westminster entries, Frei travels around the country to promote the benefits of therapy dogs. The 2008 WKC Best in Show winner, Uno, perhaps the best-known Beagle in America, often accompanies Frei. It's a unique job that he never could have imagined when he acquired that first Afghan Hound puppy in the late 1960s.

MAF Communications Director

Heidi Jeter holds a more conventional communications director position for the nonprofit Morris Animal Foundation (MAF) in Denver, Colorado. Her primary responsibilities involve any of MAF's publications, including its newsletter, annual report, and collateral materials such as brochures; writing for or editing the organization's Web site; and media relations, helping reporters find sources for interviews. Like Frei, she says she is often doing something different every day, which is one of the things that she likes best about her job.

Jeter has undergraduate and graduate degrees in journalism and has held jobs in public relations and journalism throughout her career. "I worked for a small newspaper initially and then in the news office of a state university in Wisconsin before I went to grad school," she says.

When a layoff ended her job at a weekly publication for the wireless communications industry, Jeter spend four months thinking about what she wanted to do and where her interests lay. In the meantime, she began volunteering at a local animal shelter.

Portrait of a Communications Coordinator

At the American Animal Hospital Association (AAHA) in Lakewood, Colorado, Jason Merrihew's job as communications coordinator consists of media relations, Web site management, and communications with both AAHA members and pet owners. Merrihew also helps AAHA members market and promote their individual practices.

When Merrihew was hired by the AAHA, he had been looking for a job with a nonprofit organization but had only limited knowledge of animals. That's not a drawback as long as you have the ability to research, absorb information, and ask questions so you can become comfortable and knowledgeable in the field, he says.

"I recommend getting involved to understand animal-related issues by volunteering at or working with an animal shelter, animal welfare organization, or hospital," Merrihew says. "This firsthand experience also provides invaluable networking opportunities with leaders in the industry."

His efforts to learn more about companion animals paid off in other ways: he's now owned by two wonderful cats, Rinaldo and Rembrandt.

A communications coordinator needs exemplary verbal and written communication skills, and a bachelor's degree is necessary to obtain this type of position. Merrihew holds a degree in journalism with minors in business and English. Qualities that are important to success in his job are attention to detail, the ability to solve problems, and a willingness to research answers to difficult questions.

One of the more difficult aspects of Merrihew's job is monitoring animal abuse stories that are covered in the media, but that is outweighed by other considerations, he says. "It is disheartening to know that we have people in our society who do not value animal lives or their positive contributions to our world, but I love my job because I get to help promote the human-animal bond while encouraging better health care for pets."

"I thought, 'I could probably do something with my skills and work in the animal industry,' so that's what I started looking at. I was focusing on nonprofits, and when I found the job here, it seemed like the perfect fit for me. I was able to combine my background in writing

and editing with the passion I have for animals."

Her work-related travel can take her to interesting sites, including the veterinary school at Colorado State University, the National Zoo, and the Conservation League and Research Center at the Smithsonian Institution. Jeter's position involves travel several times a year to veterinary conferences, meetings of pet writers, and other media events.

"The great part about being director of communications is that I can have a little bit of a hand in everything, so it's not just working on the Web site or just working on direct mail," she says. "

Jenn Armbruster and her rescued Boxer, Domino Harvey, take a break from press releases at the park near ACVIM headquarters.

NSL Director of Communications

Although such positions are rare, specialized organizations and museums also have a need for people with communications skills. Elizabeth Tobey was working on a doctorate in Italian Renaissance art at the University of Maryland when she discovered the National Sporting Library (NSL)—a repository of books, papers, archives, and more on equine and field sports. It has a rich manuscript collection that includes the archives of the National Beagle Club and the Piedmont Foxhounds, hunting diaries, the pedigree book of the Walker hounds, and books on other types of sporting dogs, such as gundogs. Tobey's scholarly interests frequently focused on horses, and she began doing research at the library regularly. Because she had done scholarship in the areas of equestrian studies and had previous experience working for museums, she eventually helped the NSL develop and publicize its John H. Daniels Fellowship Program. When the position of director of communications became vacant, her work there was expanded to encompass it, and she is now the NSL's director of communications and research.

"I wear many hats. I do all the public relations for the NSL. I edit our newsletter, write press releases, manage our Web site, manage the fellowship program, and plan our public lecture series. I also organize an annual symposium, a day of lectures and learning about a topic in horse and field sports," Tobey says.

ACVIM Communications/Media Relations Manager

Jenn Armbruster loves her job at the American College of Veterinary Internal Medicine (ACVIM), which is based out of Lakewood, Colorado. As the communications and media relations manager for the ACVIM, she combines the two passions of her life—words and animals. Not only is Jenn able to help animals and their owners by creating public awareness of board-certified veterinary specialists (such as cardiologists, oncologists, neurologists, and internists), but she is able to do so with her best friend at her feet. As she says, "Every day is Take your Dog to Work Day at the ACVIM!"

Portrait of a PR Professional

Lea-Ann Germinder, president of Germinder & Associates, Inc., was among the first public relations professionals to be academically trained. Before that, most PR people were former reporters or publicists who learned on the job. In high school, Germinder enjoyed writing and the creative arts, interests that are a big part of a public relations career. At Ohio's University of Dayton, she earned a bachelor of communication arts degree in public relations and became an accredited fellow of the Public Relations Society of America.

Originally, it wasn't Germinder's intention to go into the pet field. Public relations in its own right was her primary interest. The decision to focus on the pet industry came after some experience with animal-related businesses.

"I had worked in the pet field prior to joining an agency that worked with veterinarians," Germinder says. "I enjoyed it so much that when I started my own business I decided to focus on animal health marketing and public relations, and it has been very rewarding, especially now that pets are a focus of so many businesses."

Public Relations Professional

Public relations professionals who work with dog-related businesses clarify or justify a firm's or an organization's point of view on canine health or nutritional issues to pet owners or special-interest groups such as dog breeders. They track social, economic, and political trends that might affect the company they represent, and they make recommendations to boost a business's or organization's image on the basis of those trends. They are often involved in producing internal company communications and reports. They assist executives in drafting speeches, arrange interviews and other forms of public contact, oversee company archives, and respond to requests for information. In addition, they may handle special events, such as dog-show sponsorship, parties to introduce new products, or other company activities intended to gain public attention without advertising directly.

PR jobs range from entry-level positions, such as account executive, to vice president to company owner. At all levels, the job of a public relations professional is to build relationships, communicate information about his or her company or organization, and promote the issues important to interest groups, businesses, or associations.

Entry-level *account executives* develop and place stories with national and local media, organize special events, and write press materials for clients. *Account supervisors* may be responsible for developing and managing publicity initiatives, launching new products, conducting media relations campaigns, and conducting consumer research studies. At higher levels, the job of a *vice president* includes such duties as leading a team responsible for communications strategy and planning, media relations, advertising, events, Web content, and public-education programs; developing licensing and public-service campaigns to cross-promote products; creating public-awareness, publicity, and community-education campaigns; commissioning and conducting research and surveys; developing marketing communications campaigns for large public events; and serving as spokesperson for a company or an organization.

Pet Radio-Show Host

Well-known traditional pet radio-show hosts include Steve Dale, who has two nationally syndicated radio shows—*Steve Dale's Pet World* and *The Pet Minute*—as well as *Steve Dale's Pet World* at WLS Radio, Chicago; Tracie Hotchner, who broadcasts on a public radio station and the Martha Stewart Channel of SiriusXM satellite radio; Shawn Messonnier, DVM, whose

show *Dr. Shawn, The Natural Vet*, is also broadcast on the Martha Stewart Channel; and Warren Eckstein of *The Pet Show*.

Pet Life Radio (PLR) is a three-year-old podcast radio network that features thirty-three shows hosted by well-known experts, authors, and radio and television personalities in the world of animals and pets. Listeners can download or stream PLR's shows from the PetLifeRadio.com Web site, or they can subscribe to podcasts in iTunes, Podcast Alley, Odeo, and other podcast portals. Journalist, author, and pet "edu-tainer" Arden Moore of Oceanside, California, is the host of *Oh Behave!*, a weekly half-hour show on PLR. Fellow PLR hosts include trainer and author Liz Palika and behavior consultant and author Amy Shojai.

Television-Show Host

The same skills needed for hosting a radio show apply to television. Amy Shojai does a twice-monthly live television segment, "Pet Talk," on her local CBS affiliate, and she has appeared as a guest or source on many other local or national broadcasts, including debating with Bryant Gumble about whether dogs or cats make the better White House pet on *Good Morning America*.

On "Pet Talk," she is the pet care/behavior expert, and the news anchor hosts the segment. Each segment lasts two to five minutes, and Shojai chooses the topics and suggests questions for the host to ask her. Because of the time constraints, her answers must be concise and structured in an entertaining way.

The pacing is different, too. On a television show, the most important information must be shared within the first thirty seconds. Knowing what "reads" well on camera and the flexibility to handle unscripted occurrences are skills for an aspiring TV host to cultivate. With television, there's more chance of visual bloopers, especially when pets are involved.

"I've often appeared on live television with pets, and they tend to do the unexpected," Shojai says. "More than once, I've had the staff bring their personal pets, and the animals simply weren't ready for prime time. On *Good Day New York*, the producer's cat left the set just as the cameras went live. A kitten at a Fox News station in Indianapolis climbed onto the host's shoulder and head and removed his toupee."

One difference between radio and television is that for TV, Shojai's appearance is important. Her radio show can be done while she's bleary-eyed, barefoot, and wearing a bathrobe if an interview is scheduled early in the morning, but television requires attention to wardrobe and an alert expression.

Moore added radio hosting to her considerable communications résumé after more than twenty years as a newspaper reporter, freelance writer, and newsletter editor. The skills she had developed in those areas helped her transition to radio.

What Radio Hosts Do

Hosting a radio talk show about pets requires a lot of behind-the-scenes work before the show ever goes on the air. Besides setting the format and

Pet radio host Steve Dale and his feline cohost broadcast a segment of the *Steve Dale's Pet World* show in the studios of WLS in Chicago.

tone of the show, the host chooses the topics and guests, scripts the questions, and coordinates the interview schedule. Coordinating the show can be a challenge when the producer lives in one time zone, the host in another, and the guest in yet another. Being able to work around conflicts is an essential element of being a radio host.

Shojai's show, *Pet Peeves*, is about "anything that hisses you off" about pets. Topics range from the silly (pet pampering) to the serious (dog bites and breed bans). The subject matter offers a wide-open field in terms of potential topics and guests. Shojai has covered everything from clicker-training goldfish to play basketball to cloning pets to ethical dog training and everything in between. Sometimes the topic drives the show, and Shojai must find an expert to speak about it; other times, the guest is the focus because he or she has written a popular book or has a cause to promote.

Once a topic and guest are scheduled, Shojai writes a script, a basic outline of the show that includes an introduction of herself and the person she's interviewing, as well as the questions for the guest to answer.

Freelance writer, editor, and radio host Arden Moore poses with Chipper (*left*) and Cleo.

"While it can vary somewhat, I always include a short 'rant of the week' at the top of the show that introduces the topic," she says. "These vary from tongue-in-cheek, off-the-wall crazy to deadly serious commentary and serve as the 'tease' that keeps listeners tuned in through the commercials to hear the guest. The questions are asked in a particular order to structure the interview. Part of a host's job includes knowing many of these answers in advance to help focus the interview and keep it from rambling off target."

Moore and her producer, Mark Winter, compile research for each show, pull together each guest's biographical information and photo to post on PLR's Web site, and schedule and promote episodes. The latter task has Moore appearing at pet-related events all over North America, often with her dogs or cats. She also spends a lot of time keeping up with the latest news in the world of pet behavior, medicine, trends, and products as well as participating in activities with her pets—everything from dog surfing to camping and houseboat trips to dog-and-human fitness classes.

Moore's show is all about achieving harmony in the household between people and pets, and her guests range from A-list actors participating in pet causes or starring in movies with pets—think Jennifer Aniston in *Marley and Me*—to pet experts such as "America's Family Veterinarian" Marty Becker to people with compelling stories to share, such as disabled high-school surfer Patrick Ivison, who tandem surfs with his dog, Ricochet.

Who Radio Hosts Are

For radio to work, the topic or the host—ideally both—must prompt an emotional response, and to keep listeners tuned in, the host and guests must be entertaining. Moore says that hosting a radio show requires better than average interviewing skills.

"The challenge with radio is that you need to be able to keep the conversation lively and engaging so listeners want to tune in each week. You also need to research your guests and pluck out fun and fascinating facts about them during the show. Finally, you need to recognize that your role is to showcase your guest to your audience, not to use the show to promote yourself or your books or other pet products."

It can also be difficult to contend with guests who don't have much to say or are more interested in promoting themselves than in actually caring about pets or wildlife. Other challenges include early morning interviews, the occasional bad telephone or Internet connection, and the rare occasions when a guest cancels unexpectedly or isn't well prepared. A good radio host is prepared for all eventualities, able to fill in awkward silences, draw the guest out, or pull a replacement guest out of a hat.

Education and Training

It used to be that you could learn on the job in the fields of communication, public relations, and broadcasting, but these days employers prefer to see a college degree in public relations, journalism, advertising, or communication. For management positions, some employers look for a master's degree in communications, public relations, or journalism.

In pursuit of a PR degree, you may take courses on topics such as public relations principles and techniques, PR management and administration, how to write news releases, proposals, annual reports, scripts, and speeches; visual communications, including computer graphics; social science research; and survey design and implementation. Other courses that can be useful are those in business administration, creative writing, finance, psychology, public

Barkworthy INSIGHT

REWARDS OF RADIO

For Arden Moore, the best part about her radio gig is the opportunity to chat one-on-one with some of the biggest names in veterinary medicine and behavior, not to mention Hollywood. "I enjoyed the wit of Lily Tomlin and Fred Willard and admired them for their respective causes in the world of companion animals and wildlife," she says. "I also like discovering up-and-coming talents who will soon become household names, like Zak George, host of the new show on Animal Planet called *SuperFetch*. Remember his name." Amy Shojai feels the same way. "The best thing about radio and TV," she says, "is meeting and talking to the most incredible, interesting people who share my passion for pets."

speaking, sociology, and creative writing. It helps to have experience in electronic or print journalism or training or experience in a field related to the business or organization, such as pet health care, welfare, or nutrition.

For all three of these fields, it also never hurts to learn a foreign language. The ability to communicate in a foreign language may open up employment opportunities in many rapidly growing areas around the country such as New Orleans, Louisiana; Round Rock, Texas; and Irvine, California, as well as the opportunity to work overseas, especially in countries where pet ownership is gaining in popularity.

Involvement in the canine world is always a plus, because it's how you meet other dog people who may be able to help you achieve your goals. Showing dogs, writing about dogs, and participating in dog sports are all avenues to the experience you need to have should the opportunity for such a job cross your path one day.

For radio or television, a degree in broadcast journalism is a plus. Both Moore and Shojai, as well as many other pet radio (and TV) hosts, moved into the field from a background in print journalism. Shojai earned her broadcasting chops on the other side of the microphone, being interviewed on radio and television while promoting her books, but she also had previous stage and speaking experience, including improv, and was comfortable working before a live audience. She says that being a guest on local radio and television shows, including college or high-school student-run productions, is a good way to practice the skills needed to be successful on the air. Look for other opportunities to speak in public as well, such as at church or club events or in community theater.

One of the challenges in a communication, public relations, and or course, broadcasting career is keeping pace with the rapid changes in technology. That's essential if the professional is going to be successful in disseminating important content about pets. That, of course, is the appeal of this career to someone who loves dogs and cats.

"You can help millions of dogs and cats by getting out good information that their owners can read about," PR professional Lea-Ann Germinder says. The continued evolution of the Internet as a communication channel will only bring more opportunities for disseminating news and information, she believes. "It will make public relations one of the most exciting careers that you can have."

Employment

Median annual wages for salaried public relations specialists were $51,280 in May 2008. The middle 50 percent earned between $38,400 and $71,670; the lowest 10 percent earned less than $30,140, and the top 10 percent earned more than $97,910. Depending on years of experience, size of employer, and field of employ, the salary for a communications director may start at $34,943 and go as high as $156,000 or more.

Radio is a generally low-paying field. Salaried radio-show hosts can earn starting paychecks of $15,000 to $46,000 per year. A syndicated radio host's income varies depending on how many radio stations carry the show and how much the stations pay for the show.

Whether pet experts can make money from audio and video podcasts and Internet radio shows remains to be seen. Right now, it's most useful as a way to communicate, establish, or consolidate a name and promote a brand. Potential sources of income include advertisements, subscriptions, and micropayments from listeners who download individual podcasts.

COMMUNICATIONS, PR, AND BROADCAST RESOURCES

- Colleges for Communications, http://weducation-portal.com/colleges_for_communications.html
- Colleges for Public Relations, http://education-portal.com/colleges_with_public_relations_majors.html
- International Association of Business Communicators, www.iabc.com
- National Communication Association, www.natcom.org
- Pet Life Radio, www.petliferadio.com
- Public Relations Society of America, www.prsa.org
- Steve Dale's Pet World, www.stevedalepetworld.com
- Women in Communications, www.womcom.org

SECTION 7

Animal Welfare Careers

Just about everyone likes the idea of helping animals, but it takes a special person to work in the field of animal sheltering or animal control. Jobs in these fields can bring the personal satisfactions of placing pets in good homes, reuniting lost pets with their people, and educating people about pet care and welfare, but the work can also be physically and emotionally demanding. People in this field run the risk of being bitten or scratched by the very animals they are trying to help. But for people who are committed to animal welfare, there are few callings as satisfying.

Adopted

Hold your horses

KENNEL CARD
City of Mission Viejo Animal Shelter
PUMPKIN
A121605
Intake Date: 2/12/10
Cage #: 19
Available: 2/19/10
Breed PIT BULL
Type STRAY
Color TAN/WHITE
Age 0 / 10
Sex Female
Special Conditions

CONTROL

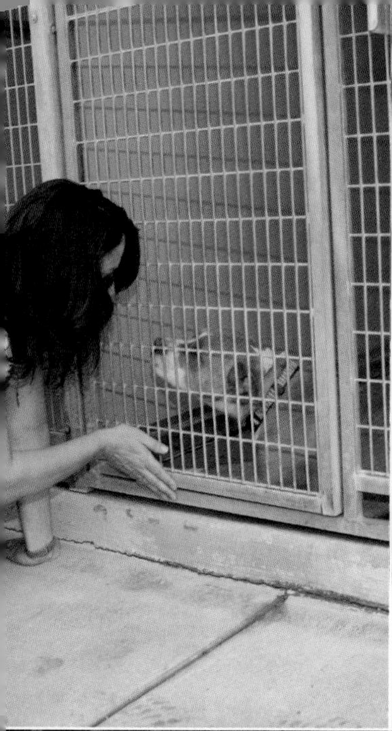

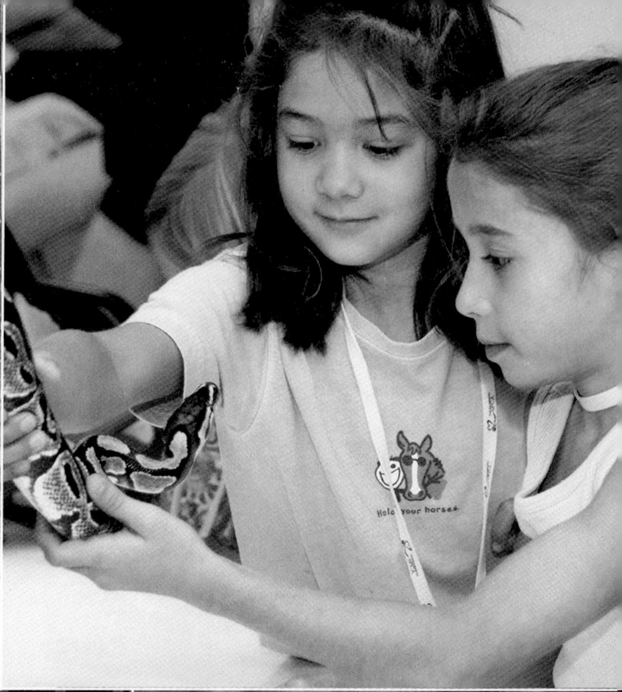

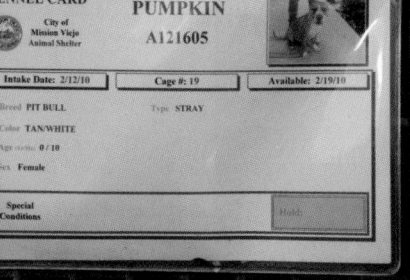

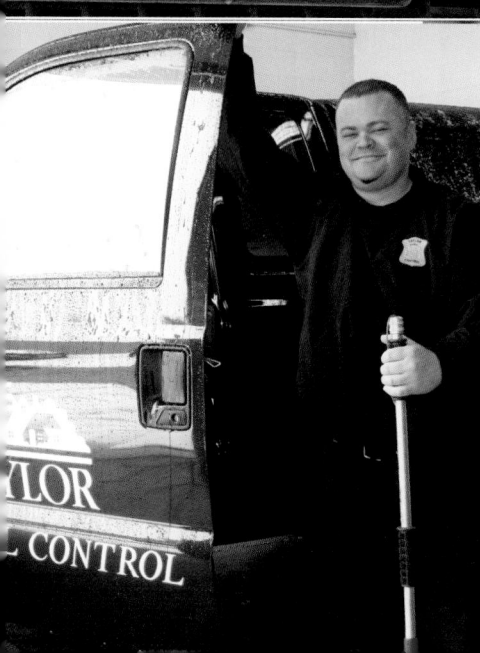

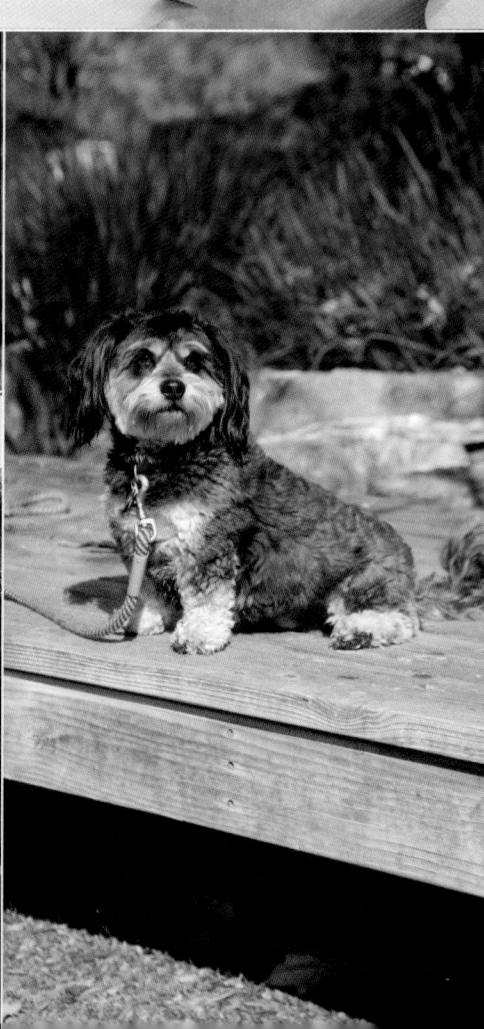

CHAPTER 20

Shelter Employees

There are many types of management or supervisory positions found at shelters, sanctuaries, and humane organizations. At the top of the list is the chief executive officer (CEO) or director, who focuses on leadership, fund-raising, and "big-picture" management. Under the CEO are various managers (depending on the size of the shelter), who oversee everything from adoptions to daily care of the animals to community programs.

Some animal shelter employees interact with the public, answering telephone inquiries, screening applicants for adoption, or educating students, adopters, and the public on neutering and other animal health issues. Entry-level jobs may involve manual labor such as cleaning animal cages or carrying heavy bags of pet food or other supplies. Kennel attendant is an entry-level job with room to branch out.

One of the most rewarding jobs in animal welfare is that of adoption counselor. Matching the right pet and person gives every adoption counselor a feeling of accomplishment and pleasure. If you love dogs and cats, enjoy interacting with people, and have great customer service and sales skills, this may be the right job for you.

Shelter Chief Executive Officer or Director

The tasks of a CEO or shelter director may involve oversight of a shelter's finances, fund development, or collaborating with community groups or

NO SMOKING

Francis Battista is cofounder and director of Best Friends Animal Society in Kanab, Utah, the nation's largest animal sanctuary.

veterinarians to improve animal welfare locally or build support for the shelter. If someone is hired into this position by a shelter that is in the process of expanding, he or she may serve as a project manager for the new construction.

Shelter executives come from many different backgrounds. Robin Starr, executive director and CEO of the Richmond SPCA in Virginia, was formerly an attorney specializing in mergers and acquisitions. Bonney Brown, director of the Nevada Humane Society, has a fine arts degree from Boston University and spent ten years in retail buying and management before moving to the field of animal welfare. And Susanne Kogut, executive director of the Charlottesville-Albemarle SPCA in Virginia, held corporate finance positions at several institutions.

The animal shelter world is in a state of flux, and executives must be prepared to meet their communities' calls for kinder, more effective ways of caring for and placing animals so that all have an opportunity to find homes rather than be euthanized.

Francis Battista, a founder and director of Best Friends Animal Society in Kanab, Utah, the nation's largest animal sanctuary, says that leadership and good negotiation and collaboration skills are essential for the shelter CEO of the future.

"Animal issues are really about social change," he says. "It's not simply about how to run a shelter or how to run an organization; it's about how to work within the community, with other stakeholders, and move forward to bring about social change. Shelter directors and nonprofit directors of animal organizations need to be skilled in a whole variety of things, but social networking, communication, negotiation and coalition building are at the top of the list."

Shelter Manager

Patty Hegwood is a manager for Best Friends. As director of animal care, she oversees, among other things, the Best Friends clinic, the volunteer department, adoptions, and the daily care of more than 1,700 animals. Her colleagues include Jeff Popowich, animal care operations manager, who oversees day-to-day operations involved in the care of the animals at Best Friends and works with all animal departments to ensure that the best practices are being used for animal care, enrichment, and housing. Hegwood also works with adoptions manager Kristi Littrell, volunteer manager Kalene Sattler, and director of community programs and services Julie Castle.

Managers such as Hegwood and her colleagues are more involved in the day-to-day running of the shelter than is the CEO. They supervise employees and must be able to manage a budget. Their jobs may involve implementing creative educational programming, directing volunteer activities, supervising adoption counselors, managing animal care, and ensuring compliance with local and state regulations. They manage rabies-control programs, evaluate dogs with respect to dangerous-dog or other related ordinances, provide court testimony on animal behavior,

DO YOU HAVE WHAT IT TAKES?

SHELTER CEO/ MANAGER

Shelter CEOs and managers should have the following characteristics:

- ○ Managerial skills
- ○ Fund-raising abilities
- ○ Interpersonal skills
- ○ Excellent verbal and written communication skills
- ○ Negotiating ability
- ○ Compassion for animals and people
- ○ Creative thinking

Animal-Control Director

The job of an animal-control director is to safeguard public health and safety, enforce animal-related laws, and protect pets and people. A good animal care and control program also encourages responsible pet ownership and humane care and treatment of animals through public education. Says Taylor, Michigan, pound master John Grove (*above*), "Educating people is a big part of this job."

Animal-control directors usually work for the city or county. Most positions require a college degree in animal science, biology, or a related field. Courses in veterinary science or administration of animal services are useful. People who achieve this type of position generally have at least five years' experience managing animal services programs, supervising others, and creating and meeting annual budgets.

develop and implement programs to reduce pet overpopulation and euthanasia through spay/neuter initiatives and public awareness campaigns, and speak at civic functions. Some managers must be certified as having the ability to properly euthanize animals. Shelter managers may work for private organizations such as Best Friends or for municipal or county shelters as animal-control directors.

Shelter Adoption Counselor

Adoption counselors get to know the animals in the shelter so they can make good recommendations for people who are looking for pets. The counselors review adoption applications, interview applicants, and guide people through the adoption process, sharing information about pet care and behavior. When adoptions are completed, the counselors may photograph the happy new family members and write up their stories for the shelter newsletter or Web site. They follow up by phone or sometimes with a home visit to make sure that everyone is adjusting well. That's the fun, easy part.

It's not so easy when an adoption application has to be denied. Good adoption counselors are able to communicate the decision in a courteous and friendly way, without making potential adopters feel angry or rejected. They may also spend time advising people who are having problems with their pets or who want to surrender them to the shelter. Ideally, a counselor's advice will help an owner resolve his or her pet's behavior problems so that the pet can be kept in the home.

Adoption counseling is more than just playing with pets and talking to people. Other tasks may include answering phones and performing administrative tasks; cleaning animal and public areas during shelter hours; transporting animals, cages, and other equipment to and from off-site events; monitoring the health of animals and reporting any problems as soon as possible; and helping out at special events. This is generally not a supervisory position, although adoption counselors may work with volunteers to help place more animals. The best person for the job enjoys doing a lot of different things and is pitching in where needed.

A shelter worker gives much-needed attention to one of the shelter's charges. Kennel attendants often provide homeless animals with emotional as well as physical care.

Adoption counseling is all about people skills—and pet knowledge, of course. Would-be adoption counselors are willing to learn about cat and dog behavior, ways to recognize good matches, and techniques for resolving problems. They enjoy talking to people, can say no in a nice way, and remain calm and professional even in stressful situations.

Kennel Attendant

Kennel attendants perform basic tasks, such as cleaning cages and dog runs, filling food and water dishes, and exercising animals. Experienced attendants may provide basic animal health care, as well as bathing animals, trimming nails, and attending to other grooming needs. Their job may involve keeping records or administering vaccinations under the supervision of a veterinarian or vet tech.

Sometimes they answer phones or meet with the public, interviewing prospective adopters or providing information to the public about

neutering or other pet health issues. Depending on where they work, kennel attendants may be promoted to kennel supervisor, assistant manager, or manager.

Education and Training

People who work at shelters come from all types of backgrounds. Those with administrative, managerial, or executive positions may have college degrees in such disparate areas as history, psychology, philosophy, English, public administration, animal science, and business.

A position at an animal shelter may call for some type of specialized training, such as knowledge of anticruelty and animal-control laws or standards of animal care. A person interested in such a position may get the necessary training from a humane organization, such as the American Humane Association, American Society for the Prevention of Cruelty to Animals, Best Friends Animal Society, or National Animal Control Association.

These organizations offer programs and workshops aimed at shelter employees. Topics include procedures for conducting cruelty investigations, appropriate ways to capture animals, techniques for preventing or dealing with problems involving wildlife, appropriate methods of euthanasia for shelter animals, and ways to work with the public.

Public-relations skills are vital for people who work in the field of animal welfare. Welfare workers deal with people whose emotions range from the depths of sadness to the heights of anger. They need excellent communication, sensitivity, and patience.

DO YOU HAVE WHAT IT TAKES?

KENNEL ATTENDANT

A good kennel attendant should have the following characteristics:

- ○ Good record-keeping skills
- ○ Good animal-care skills
- ○ Good cleaning skills
- ○ Ability to lift up to 50 pounds
- ○ Compassion for animals

Becky Swayze (*left*) and Laura Jensen work at the Woodhaven Animal Control, in Trenton, Michigan. Both decided upon this career after volunteering at humane societies.

The primary educational requirement for an adoption counselor is a high-school degree or GED, although it never hurts to have additional education in subjects such as psychology, biology, animal science, or English, all of which can be useful in working with people or animals. And almost any office job these days requires some computer literacy and typing ability.

Applicants who are familiar with animals and their behavior or who have experience volunteering or working with rescue groups, humane societies, or other animal welfare agencies will have an advantage when it comes to this type of employment. Experience working with the public is also a plus.

The position of kennel attendant requires little training, and most often this work is learned on the job. A high-school diploma or GED may be required. Although kennel attendants learn on the job, it's always helpful if they have had some experience with animals, even if it is from caring for their own pets.

Portrait of a Shelter Revolutionary

Rich Avanzino didn't start out intending to revolutionize the world of animal sheltering. In fact, his somewhat unconventional career path began with degrees in both pharmacy and jurisprudence. His career then took an even more surprising turn when he took over as president of the San Francisco SPCA in 1976.

Avanzino took the organization from the verge of bankruptcy to one of the best-funded animal shelters in the country. More importantly, during his more than two decades at the SF/SPCA, Avanzino led the city and county of San Francisco to implement an "Adoption Pact" that guaranteed that all healthy animals would be adopted and that also saved most of the sick and injured animals. The pact brought San Francisco's euthanasia rates down to the lowest of any urban area in the United States.

"It wasn't me who accomplished that," Avanzino says. "It was the good people of San Francisco, who demanded more for the animals in the City of St. Francis than death. I believed we could find a better way, and with the help and compassion of our community, we did."

Modesty aside, Avanzino's accomplishment in San Francisco led PeopleSoft and Workday founder David Duffield and his wife, Cheryl, to tap Avanzino to lead Maddie's Fund, the $300 million foundation they created to honor the memory of their dog, Maddie. Maddie's Fund seeks to end the killing of dogs and cats in shelters and make the United States a no-kill nation.

His background in law as well as his experience transforming the finances of the SF/SPCA taught Avanzino a critical lesson: animal welfare organizations need to learn to operate like businesses if they want to succeed in saving animals' lives and keeping their bills paid. "Just like any successful business, shelters need to provide good customer service, be clean and welcoming, have convenient hours and locations, and create goodwill and support in their communities," he says.

Transparency and accountability are two more business concepts that he says are essential in the animal welfare world. "In the business world, transparency usually refers to finances, and that's important in shelters, too," he said. "But what we're really talking about is shelter data, tracking and reporting the outcome of every live dog or cat who enters that facility."

KENNEL CARD PUMPKIN

♥ PUMPK
sweet & loving
gives kisses
submissive · p
walks well on a lea
very mellow
3/19 9:36

A visitor to a shelter in Mission Viejo, California, talks to Pumpkin.

Employment

Job opportunities vary in this area, but there is frequent turnover in the overall field of animal care, so the Bureau of Labor Statistics predicts that employment of animal care and service workers will grow by about 21 percent through 2018. The demand for animal care and service workers in animal shelters is expected to grow as communities across the country increasingly recognize the connection between animal abuse and abuse toward humans.

Animal-control employees also help to protect the health and safety of people and pets, a job that is increasingly essential when it comes to diseases that are spread between humans and animals. Many animal shelters work hand-in-hand with social service agencies and law-enforcement teams. Job opportunities will be best in midsize and metropolitan areas.

Executive and managerial salaries vary based on such factors as geographic location, the size of the agency, and the administrator's level of experience. For a shelter manager or animal-control director, salaries range from as little as $12,000 in a small community to $85,000 or more in a metropolitan area. The chief executive officer of a national humane organization may earn $150,000 or more.

While the emotional rewards of being an adoption counselor can be great, the financial rewards are not. Depending on geographic location and the financial resources of the shelter, adoption counselors may earn from $7.50 per hour to $17.50 per hour. Benefits such as health care or a retirement plan may or may not be included.

Kennel attendant is a job with a high turnover rate, so positions are frequently available. It's a good choice for people with little experience who want a flexible work schedule or temporary or part-time work. Wages are low in this field, ranging from $15,140 to $31,590, but if you're interested in working for a shelter, this position is a good place to start.

SHELTER EMPLOYEE RESOURCES

- American Society for the Prevention of Cruelty to Animals, www.aspca.org
- Best Friends Animal Society, www.bestfriends.org
- Law Enforcement Training Institute, http://leti.missouri.edu/
- National Animal Control Association, www.naca.org
- University of Florida Veterinary Forensic Science Program, www.ufsheltermedicine.com/animalForensicsCrueltyAbuse.html

CHAPTER 21

Humane Educator and Humane Investigator

You've seen them on Animal Planet's *Animal Cops* show. Known also as cruelty investigators or simply as animal-control officers, humane investigators look into crimes against or abuse of animals. In many communities, their duties are similar to those of the police; they may even be part of the police force. They rescue animals in harm's way, protect them from abusers, save them from starvation. Not every day in a humane investigator's life is TV-worthy, but people in this field gain much satisfaction from their work, which includes the ability to protect pets and people, prosecute people who abuse or torture animals, and return lost animals to their homes or adopt them out to new homes. Every day is different, and there are always challenges.

As the work of humane investigators proves, there a great need to educate the public about kindness and compassion toward animals. That's the job of humane educators. It is a job that is not only enjoyable and rewarding but also essential to developing the caring pet owners of the future.

Humane Investigator

A humane investigator enforces city and state animal laws, investigates reports of animal abuse and neglect, and inspects pet stores, zoos, and other facilities. If a humane investigator has police powers, the job may entail obtaining search and seizure warrants, executing search and arrest

warrants, filing complaints with county attorneys, and documenting evidence with photos or videos in preparation for criminal trials. Animal-abuse cases range from neglect and abandonment to animal hoarding and dog fighting. Humane investigators often speak to the media about cruelty cases and must be comfortable being interviewed by print, television, and radio journalists.

In addition to investigating possible crimes, a humane investigator's day can include picking up stray dogs and returning them to their homes, transporting animals to shelters, presenting information about animal welfare to schoolchildren, and responding to calls about injured or at-risk animals. Those calls may involve retrieving an animal from the freeway or breaking a pet out of a hot car before the animal dies. The job can be physically demanding. Some shelters, such as Boston's Animal Rescue League, have humane officers certified in technical animal-rescue skills, including ice rescue, high-angle climbing, technical ropework for rescuing cats in trees, swiftwater rescue, large-animal rescue, chemical capture, and disaster response.

Humane officers may find themselves helping people as well as animals. Some humane officers are cross-trained so that they are able to recognize not only animal abuse but also child abuse, domestic violence, and sexual abuse. It's common to see a link between animal abuse and violence toward people, so it's important for humane investigators to be able to recognize the signs. Throughout their careers, humane investigators may take classes on such topics as dog fighting, cock fighting, protection of animals in motion pictures, animal care, and euthanasia. Often, their only weapons are education and diplomacy.

DO YOU HAVE WHAT IT TAKES?

HUMANE INVESTIGATOR

A humane investigator should have the following characteristics:

- ○ Written and verbal communication skills
- ○ Leadership and teaching skills
- ○ Knowledge of laws and regulations on animal welfare and cruelty
- ○ Ability to deal with the public in crisis situations
- ○ Patience
- ○ Physical ability to lift, hold, or restrain animals
- ○ Problem-solving skills
- ○ Ability to cope with emotional distress

Portrait of a Rapid-Response Manager

Until recently, Richard Crook was rapid-response manager for Best Friends Animal Society, a job that involves developing and managing large-scale field projects such as Hurricane Katrina-type rescues and rescuing animals after puppy-mill or hoarding busts. Before he joined Best Friends, Crook was a firefighter trained in emergency management, disaster preparedness, and urban search and rescue. He owned and operated several businesses and worked as an environmental services director for a long-term-care facility. Everything in his background has contributed to his work in the field of animal welfare.

"I can attribute much of my success in animal welfare to my firefighting and long-term-care backgrounds," he says. "You have to be firm, safety-oriented, and organized in the field yet have the ability to understand and meet the needs of the many personalities you encounter. Being successful in animal welfare isn't about managing animals; it's about managing people."

Crook recently moved on to a new interest that makes similar use of his skills: he is chairing a best-practice working group sponsored by the USDA and is involved with a second such group sponsored by the Animal and Plant Health Inspection Service. The work will involve integrating animal search and rescue (that is, searching for lost animals) with human search and rescue.

Dedication and commitment to animal welfare and public well-being are essential for a long-term career in this type of work. So is a resilient attitude. Humane investigators work with the public as well as with animals, so good interpersonal and communication skills are important. People in the field are knowledgeable about dog and cat breeds and behavior as well as animal welfare policies and legislation. Other qualities they need are accuracy, organizational skills, and problem-solving ability.

Humane Educator

For a humane educator, each day can be different, which is part of the appeal of the work. During the summer, shelters may offer day camps for kids. At the Sacramento SPCA, there are six week-long sessions for children ages seven to nine, ten to twelve, and thirteen to fifteen; there are approximately twenty-five campers per session. Humane education specialist Dee Dee Drake supervises one employee and two to four teenage volunteers. For Drake, a typical day at camp starts at 7:30 a.m. with prep work for camp, followed by activities for campers such as helping to socialize adoptable kittens or creating craft projects. Sometimes guest speakers do presentations. Throughout the year, Drake keeps busy with educational presentations for schools or community groups and serves as managing editor of the SPCA's quarterly magazine.

"As at most nonprofit organizations, employees wear many hats here," she says. "I like the variety it provides. Every day is different."

Another benefit is that Drake's two Pugs, Rhoda and Marlee, come to work with her every day. Marlee is also an "employee," serving as Drake's demo dog for educational presentations. Marlee adores children and loves doing classroom visits. Of course, a love of animals is a necessity for a

During a day camp session at the Sacramento SPCA, three campers lavish attention on one of the shelter's dogs.

humane educator, but so are good people skills. In her job, Drake works with children and adults, including seniors and people with developmental disabilities. It's important to be able to present information at each group's level.

"You have to have extensive knowledge about your shelter's particular policies, procedures, and philosophies, as well as a strong knowledge of animal-welfare issues in general, because when you're doing educational presentations, people will want to ask questions about everything related to animals and the world of sheltering," she says. In addition, she is trained in children's first aid and CPR, a certification that must be renewed every two years. She attends conferences and workshops to stay up to date in the field.

DO YOU HAVE WHAT IT TAKES?

HUMANE EDUCATOR

A good humane educator should have the following characteristics:

- Enjoy working with all kinds of people
- Teaching ability
- Public speaking and presentation skills
- Strong knowledge of animal care and behavior

Education and Training

Entry-level positions in humane investigation call for a high-school diploma or GED certificate. To move up in this field to an administrative position, however, a college degree is helpful. Some humane investigators are trained as veterinary technicians and then move into the field of law enforcement. Investigators are often required to become certified in areas such as defensive use of aerosol sprays, animal first aid and CPR, and euthanasia.

College

Areas of study to consider for humane investigation include animal science, biology, business, computer science, criminal justice, English, psychology, sociology, and zoology. A newly established veterinary forensic science program offering undergraduate, graduate, and continuing education at the University of Florida in conjunction with the ASPCA will benefit future humane investigators. The undergraduate and postgraduate courses are available to law-enforcement personnel and animal-control officers as well as veterinarians. Courses include forensic entomology, buried-remains excavation, bloodstain-pattern analysis, bite-mark analysis, and animal crime-scene processing. In one course, students will have the opportunity to participate in a mock trial of an animal cruelty case, gaining valuable courtroom experience. Training takes place in the classroom, online, and through the newly formed International Veterinary Forensic Sciences Association.

A college degree in one of the liberal arts or social sciences (English or psychology, for instance) or experience as a teacher is a good background for anyone who

SPCA humane education specialist Dee Dee Drake and pug Marlee teach the public how to interact with animals.

wants to become a humane educator. In high school and college, build a solid foundation for yourself by working with children or other groups of people and volunteering for a shelter or rescue group. Polish your public speaking and presentation skills. It's also a good idea to stay current on animal-related legislation as well as the latest information on animal care and behavior.

Certification

For humane investigation, ongoing specialized training is usually required to become certified in such techniques as chemical capture or euthanasia. Certification as an animal-control officer by the National Animal Control Association is also available.

Many investigators hold certifications from the Law Enforcement Training Institute of the University of Missouri's Cruelty Investigation School. Courses there address such topics as animal law, written and photographic documentation, commercial animal sales, hoarders, and disaster planning.

Henry Bergh: America's Protector of Animals

An icon from the nineteenth century, Henry Bergh makes the history books for being the man who founded the American Society for the Prevention of Cruelty to Animals (ASPCA) in 1866. Born into a wealthy New York family in 1813, he wrote plays and poetry, and for a while attended Columbia University, from which he dropped out to travel in Europe. In 1863 Bergh was appointed to a Russian diplomatic post to Czar Alexander II. In Russia, Bergh witnessed the poor treatment of animals by the peasants and was greatly moved. In 1865, while in England, he met the Earl of Harrowby, the president of the Royal Society for the Prevention of Cruelty to Animals. So influenced was Bergh by this meeting that he decided to dedicate his efforts to animal-protection causes in the United States. His dedication to this cause and his contacts with the elite of New York City led to the founding of the ASPCA, whose charter was incorporated by the New York Legislature. Bergh's moral movement was launched.

The society's original purpose was to police animal cruelty in New York City, including dog fights, drowning stray dogs in the East River by dog catchers, and the abuse of working dogs and horses by their owners. His intention was that his society would be a national society, hence the word *American* in its title. New York laws did not provide for that, but by the time Bergh died in 1888, nearly all thirty-eight states had adopted laws similar to those in New York. The fact that there are so many humane societies in our cities and towns today is a living testimony to the courageous and unyielding work of Henry Bergh, "whose ideas gave kindness a new dimension," in the words of Gerald Carson of the *American Heritage*.

Training in recognizing animal abuse is available from the American Society for the Prevention of Cruelty to Animals. The standards of investigations and the science used to document animal-related crimes are high—and getting higher.

Other Qualifications

Because a humane investigator is a law-enforcement officer, expect to face mandatory drug screening and background checks. A valid driver license is also a job requirement. Other qualifications depend on the state or the organization. In Texas, for instance, a humane investigator must have a basic peace officer certificate from the Texas Law Enforcement Academy and must meet the requirements to be commissioned as a law-enforcement officer; he or she also must have one year of related experience in law enforcement, the military, or security work. It goes without saying that experience with and compassion for animals is essential.

Employment Outlook

Sadly, work in the field of animal control and welfare is generally not high paying. It can start at minimum wage for entry-level positions. The pay increases based on level of experience, education, and certification. Salaries also vary by geographic area and community size.

Investigators may earn as little as $12,000 in small communities and as much as $85,000 in cities, with salaries falling somewhere in the middle in midsize communities. In one small midwestern city, for example, the pay scale is $13.85 to $18.64 per hour, approximately $28,800 to $38,771 per year.

A day camper at the Sacramento SPCA is helping to socialize a pair of tabbies so they can be adopted out.

Barkworthy BITE

GAINING EXPERIENCE
"The four years I spent at the San Francisco SPCA working in the Hearing Dog Program exposed me to nonstop dialogue about dog behavior, training techniques, and sheltering issues. I soaked it all in, even though I wasn't a trainer myself. So when the time came to apply for the humane ed job at the Sacramento SPCA, I had a few years of animal-related employment under my belt."

—Dee Dee Drake, humane education specialist

Humane education jobs are uncommon. You may need to take another job with the organization you're interested in just so you'll be on hand if something opens up. Many shelters and humane groups don't have humane education programs, but they may be interested if you offer to create one from scratch.

On the downside, humane educators work long hours, for low pay. A typical salary range is $11 to $24 per hour, although large shelters or humane organizations in major cities may pay more. A managerial position in a large city may pay as much as $125,000. Job security can also be a concern. When budget cuts must be made, it's all too easy for an administrator to say that humane education programs aren't essential to a shelter's day-to-day operation.

But the enjoyment factor and the belief what you're doing can make up for a lot, Drake says. For someone who loves working with people and animals, this can be the ideal career. "It's an awful lot of fun, and I'm one of the only people I know who doesn't dread going to work every day," Drake says. "I love my work, I work with terrific people, I get to play with kids, and my dogs come to the office with me every day."

HUMANE INVESTIGATOR AND EDUCATOR RESOURCES

- American Society for the Prevention of Cruelty to Animals, www.aspca.org
- Best Friends Animal Society, www.bestfriends.org
- Federal Emergency Management Agency, http://training.fema.gov
- Institute for Humane Education, http://humaneeducation.org/home
- Law Enforcement Training Institute, http://leti.missouri.edu
- National Animal Control Association, www.naca.org
- National Humane Education Society, www.nhes.org
- University of Florida Veterinary Forensic Science Program, www.ufsheltermedicine.com/animalForensicsCrueltyAbuse.html

---

SECTION 8

Petrepreneurs and Associated Careers

Owning a business is many people's dream. With some pet-related careers, that dream can come true. Examples include owners of pet boutiques or other retail businesses, dog walkers and pet sitters, and pet detectives. Other careers that lend themselves to the dream but are covered elsewhere in this book include artist, pet massage therapist, dog groomer, photographer, writer, and veterinarian.

Successfully running a pet business calls for more than a love of animals, though; it also takes strong business skills and planning. You'll need to decide its legal structure (sole proprietorship, partnership, or corporation), learn about zoning and licensing requirements in your area, purchase sufficient property and liability insurance, write a business plan, put up your own money or obtain financing to get started, and talk to a CPA about tax planning.

CHAPTER 22

Animal Communicator and Caretakers

People today worry about the emotional and physical well-being of their companion animals, especially when there seems to be less and less time to spend with their pets, attending to their needs. To help keep their dogs happy and healthy, owners turn to professionals in the pet world, from animal communicators to dogs sitters and walkers. Those concerned that their beloved pooches are turning into couch potatoes are even taking their dogs to special fitness trainers.

Animal Communicator

When owners sense that their pets are in emotional distress but have no idea what could be wrong or how to help, they will sometimes consult an animal communicator. An animal communicator, sometimes known as a pet psychic, reads or senses what pets are feeling and relays that information to their people. Animal communication has been described as the ability to make a connection with an animal telepathically, usually through sensing their feelings or visualizing images. A communicator's insights can help people develop a deeper relationship with their companion animals.

Animal communicators may meet animals face to face or work by telephone. Some animal communicators even commune with pets who have died, bringing comfort to their former owners. Well-known animal communicators include Sonya Fitzpatrick, who hosted Animal Planet's

The Pet Psychic in 2002; Lydia Hiby, author of *Conversations with Animals* (NewSage Press, 1998); Carol Gurney, author of *The Language of Animals: 7 Steps to Communicating with Animals* (Dell, 2001); and Los Angeles pet psychic Jackie Cronin.

Whether you believe in the ability to communicate with animals or not, it is becoming a popular career for people who love animals, who are good at observing and understanding their behavior, and who have a rapport with people. Cronin, for instance, finds out from the owner how the animal behaves—from chewing on shoes to hiding under the bed—and then asks the pet what he or she has to say about the situation.

Carol Gurney, founder of the Gurney Institute, which teaches others how to develop their own animal communication skills, relaxes with her Golden Retriever, Spirit.

Animal communicators say that their efforts help foster better understanding between people and pets, and that's never a bad thing. Through their observation and communication skills, they may be able to help improve behavior problems or identify the presence or location of health problems, which can then be verified by a veterinarian. Some animal communicators even help locate missing pets.

Barkworthy INSIGHT

DEVELOPING ABILITIES

If you prefer to develop your animal communication abilities on your own, it's a good idea to study both psychology and animal behavior. Working with pets as a trainer, behaviorist, dog walker, groomer, vet tech, or pet sitter is also a good way to build your knowledge of animals as well as your observational skills.

Education and Training

There is no single route to becoming an animal communicator. Some people, including Sonya Fitzpatrick and Jackie Cronin, recognize their ability to communicate with animals at an early age. Fitzpatrick avoided using her ability for many years because she felt physical pain when her animals were hurting, but Cronin frequently used her ability to help solve problems with animals she encountered while working as a dog walker and trainer. Lydia Hiby, who was trained as a veterinary technician, apprenticed with animal communicator Bea Lydecker.

Gurney consulted an animal communicator about her ailing cat and was so impressed by the help she received that she began studying the technique herself some thirty years ago. Now she has opened the Gurney Institute to train others to develop their animal communication skills.

Students can usually complete the 300-hour program—which includes twenty-two class days, sixty-four case studies, twenty hours of community service, and attendance at a two-day workshop—in one and a half to two years. Course topics include how to resolve behavioral issues, how to locate lost animals, and how to help people and animals work through the dying process. Workshops are available for people who simply want to learn the basics of animal communication before deciding whether to take their education further.

Employment Outlook

This is a relatively new profession, so it's hard to say what its future will be. Anyone who can help pet owners better understand and communicate with their animals is likely to be successful, however. Most communicators charge a per-session rate, with additional fees for more than one pet. Sessions may range from fifteen minutes to ninety minutes, and depending

---

DO YOU HAVE WHAT IT TAKES?

ANIMAL COMMUNICATOR

A pet communicator should have the following characteristics:

- ○ Sensitivity to the feelings of people and animals
- ○ Knowledge of animal behavior and body language
- ○ Problem-solving ability
- ○ Good verbal communication skills
- ○ Ability to focus
- ○ Integrity
- ○ Excellent listening skills

on the length of the session, rates range from $40 to $190 or more. Cronin was once flown to the East Coast and paid $2,000 to do a reading for a horse and three dogs.

Dog Walker

Walking dogs for a living is a great way to help improve a dog's quality of life, help people who want to take good care of their canine companions but just don't have the time or lack the physical ability to do so, and simply spend lots of time outdoors with many different types of dogs.

There are few requirements laid down for dog walkers, but the city of San Francisco's Animal Care and Control department suggests certain guidelines for dog walkers to follow. They include not walking more than six dogs at a time, ensuring that each dog is wearing a current dog license and identification, verifying that each dog is current on vaccinations, and always carrying cleanup bags for removal of dog feces.

What Dog Walkers Do

Dog walkers may take their charges to places where they are allowed to run loose, but otherwise the dogs in their care should always be leashed. Because they may transport clients' dogs in their cars, dog walkers should always have a way of safely securing each dog, such as a crate or a canine seatbelt.

A dog-walking session can last from fifteen minutes to an hour or more. Some dog walkers take several dogs out at once, letting them play together in a safe area such as a dog run or enclosed park where dogs are permitted off leash. Good dog walkers only do this with dogs they know get along, and they must always keep an eye on the dogs' play to make sure roughhousing doesn't get out of hand. Smart dog walkers make separate trips for dogs of different sizes or those with special needs.

Dog walking calls for good handling skills, a reasonable amount of physical strength, and the ability to think quickly in an emergency in case a dog gets loose or a fight breaks out. On rainy days, be prepared to clean up wet, muddy dogs before leaving them, worn out and happy, in clients' homes. You'll also need to do your own scheduling, billing, and marketing unless you can hire someone to do those tasks for you.

Education and Training

Anyone can become a dog walker by printing up some business cards and soliciting clients, but there is a training program available for people

A dog walker and her Boxer charge stroll down a city street.

interested in earning certification. A company called dogTEC, based in Sixes, Oregon, helps would-be pet professionals set up their businesses and offers a four-day dog-walking workshop that covers management of a group of dogs, dog communication and body language, safety and fight protocols, how to teach polite leash behavior, the screening process for clients and dogs, public-relations techniques, and more. The course is taught through lecture, video analysis, demonstrations, hands-on exercises, and field trips. Three of the workshops are held in California and one is held in New Hampshire. A ten-week telecourse is also available.

A number of dog walkers are also pet sitters and may be licensed, bonded, and insured or certified by the National Association of Professional Pet Sitters or Pet Sitters International. Some have pet first-aid or CPR skills. Becoming a dog walker may require getting a business license from your city, county, or state, especially if you hire employees. Check with your city or county clerk to make sure that you don't overlook any requirements.

Employment Outlook

Because dog walking is primarily a business of self-employment, there are no statistics on the job outlook or salary range for dog walkers. They are likely to thrive, however, in urban and suburban areas with high numbers of busy professionals who need help caring for their animals.

A dog walker's rates and income depend on his or her locale, the number of clients, and the length and frequency of the walks. A dog walker in Seattle or Portland might charge $20 for a single thirty-minute walk; $15 for a fifteen-minute walk for puppies or older dogs; and $35 for an hour-long walk for an energetic dog. In the South or Midwest, a dog walker's fees may range from $10 to $25 per hour. There may be additional fees

for multiple dogs, walks on holidays or walks during inclement weather. In most regions, group walks are charged at lower rates per dog than are private walks. Most dog walkers offer packages with discounts for multiple weekly walks. For instance, a dog walker who charges $20 for a half-hour walk may charge $85 for half-hour walks five times a week.

Pet Sitter

When a pet's owners are away, a pet sitter may care for the animal in the home, visiting once or twice daily; may stay in the owner's home full time; or may care for the animal in his or her own home. A pet sitter's duties include feeding and walking, giving medication if needed, and cleaning up after the animal. He or she may also bring in mail, water plants, or do other small tasks around the home, depending on the arrangements between sitter and owner.

What Pet Sitters Do

A typical day for pet sitter Terry Albert involves getting up early to care for dogs who are staying in her home. Then she is busy all morning making visits to pets she is caring for at their own homes. At dinner time, she repeats the morning routine, including visits to pets in other homes. Some clients require late-night visits to bring their dogs in for the night. When she's not caring for animals or making visits, Albert is cleaning—cages, crates, floors—or waiting for people to pick up or drop off dogs for boarding. New clients must be interviewed about their needs and schedules.

Difficult issues that pet sitters face include aggressive animals, fence jumpers and other escape artists, unhouse-trianed or destructive pets, dogs who don't get along, and poorly cared for pets. Some clients are slow to pay or are dishonest about a pet's behavior problems.

Maintaining a work/life balance can be difficult for pet sitters. It's not always easy for them to make time for themselves, even though they are self-employed and work out of their homes. Late-night emergencies are common, and holidays are usually spent caring for other people's animals rather than spending time with family and friends.

It's essential for pet sitters to set boundaries with clients from the very beginning. Be firm about the hours during which you are willing to take calls and make visits, as well as the circumstances under which you will pet sit. Some pet sitters won't care for dogs or cats who are outdoors

Portrait of a Pet Sitter

Terry Albert of Poway, California, turned to pet sitting after seventeen years in a corporate advertising career. Her experience with pets included working at a boarding and training facility for dogs and fostering rescue dogs, as well as caring for her own pets. Her bachelor's degree in fine arts didn't contribute much to her skills as a pet sitter, but she did take a pet first-aid class and had management experience from handling a $17 million advertising budget for Pep Boys Auto Parts. She makes visits to homes and boards animals in her own home. It's not unusual for her to visit a dozen homes per day or to care for up to eight dogs in her home.

"Pet sitting is more than just a fun job," says Albert. "There's lots of responsibility, and it requires professionalism, business sense, and customer-service skills."

For Albert, the most challenging aspect of starting her new business was building a clientele that was big enough for her to make a living. She ran an ad in the local paper and relied on word of mouth.

Making time for herself is also often problematic. "I have to book vacations months in advance," Albert says. "In May, I booked a trip for the end of August, and I don't have a day off until August 26. I sometimes pay someone else to come in and spend time with my boarding animals so I can get away for a day."

While pet sitting can be a difficult way to make a living, it has its rewards, Albert says. "I get to be at home and don't have to work in an office. I'm outside a lot, which I love. And I love animals, so it is fun to just hang out with them."

only, for instance, or for dogs who are untrained and thus difficult to walk or handle.

Savvy pet sitters purchase liability insurance and may become bonded. They usually do their own scheduling, billing, and marketing, although some pet sitters are employed by companies that perform those tasks for them. Pet sitting is a career that also sometimes calls for reliance on others. A pet sitter may need help when a family emergency comes.

Education and Training

A high-school education can provide the basic business skills a pet sitter needs, but it never hurts to take courses in accounting and marketing if you plan to run your own business. Some pet sitters are trained as vet techs or have taken a pet first-aid class through the American Red Cross or a local veterinary hospital.

Pet sitters can also become certified through the NAPPS, which offers an educational program that covers pet care, health, nutrition, behavior, a pet first-aid course, and business development and management. Pet sitters who take the course must pass an online exam with a minimum score of 75 percent. According to the NAPPS, the course takes approximately sixteen weeks to complete.

Employment Outlook

Like dog walkers, pet sitters are primarily self-employed, so there are no statistics on the number of jobs available, salary levels, or predictions for future employment. The need for pet sitters in a given area varies according to the size of the community, the number of pets in the area, and the income levels of the residents. Pet sitters often face competition

A pet sitter and her two charges lounge comfortably on the couch. A good sitter should be able to bond with her or his charges quickly.

from a potential client's neighbors or local high-school or college students, who may perform the work at no charge or for lower rates.

Making enough money can be a challenge for a pet sitter, whose income can vary widely from month to month. Pet sitters may charge by the number of visits they make, the number of animals they care for, or both. Separate fees apply for living in or for boarding animals. Depending on the area of the country, pet sitter rates can range from $15 to $25 per home visit. In-home rates may be $30 to $135 per day. Boarding rates range from $10 to $55 per dog per day, sometimes with discounts for multiple dogs.

Fitness Trainer for Dogs and People

For dog owners who are worried that their animals are getting too pudgy and out of shape, there are workout programs, yoga classes, and even some gyms that now incorporate dogs into their fitness activities. Personal trainer Dawn Celapino of San Diego, California, loves to do things with her dog, Jack, and in 2009 she turned their outdoor play into a business: Leash Your Fitness.

What Fitness Trainers Do

Celapino and her fellow trainers lead people and dogs through hour-long workouts that involve cardio, stretching, balance, strength training, and dog training. Some classes focus on trail running, yoga, or special activities such as kayaking or camping. All include dogs as active participants. An exercise class with dogs has multiple benefits, Celapino says. When people and dogs walk or run together, they get only a cardio workout.

"In a class, they're getting upper and lower body strength; they're getting core balance; they get a lot of stretching. To benefit the dog, we're also doing dog obedience. Instead of just walking and not having to think about anything, during our class the dogs have to stop and sit, stop and lie down, heel. They're being challenged mentally so it tires them a lot faster."

Celapino isn't the only trainer jumping on the dog/human fitness trend. Amy Stevens (*pictured on page 321*) of Scottsdale, Arizona, has produced a DVD called *Yoga 4 Dogs*, a half-hour workout for people and dogs. Stevens includes two routines, depending on the size of the dog. She says she has seen increased interest in yoga with dogs over the past two years. "People are intrigued by it, they're interested, they ask lots of questions," she says.

Education and Training

Fitness trainers and yoga instructors should be able to plan and lead a class and be certified by an organization accredited by the National Commission for Certifying Agencies. Requirements for certification as a fitness trainer usually include possession of a high-school diploma, certification in cardiopulmonary resuscitation, and successful completion of an exam, which may have both written and practical sections. Exams may test knowledge of human physiology, understanding of proper exercise techniques, assessment of client fitness levels, and development of exercise programs. Some fitness instructors have earned

DO YOU HAVE WHAT IT TAKES?

FITNESS TRAINER

A fitness trainer for dogs and people should have the following characteristics:

- ○ An outgoing personality
- ○ Excellent communication skills
- ○ Ability to motivate people
- ○ Excellent health and physical fitness
- ○ Strong sales skills
- ○ Ability to attract and retain clients
- ○ Knowledge of human and canine physiology

In this fun image, Dawn Celapino's Cairn Terrier, Jack, appears ready to follow his fitness trainer owner's every move.

a bachelor's degree in exercise science or physical education, but certification is usually required even with a degree. Yoga instructors should have specialized training. Programs range from a few days to more than two years.

In addition to being knowledgeable about human physiology and kinesiology, trainers who wish to include dogs in their classes should become educated about canine physical needs and trained in animal CPR and first aid.

Celapino and her fellow trainers are all experienced at working with people and dogs. Celapino is an ACE-certified group and personal trainer with twelve years' experience. She has a bachelor of science degree in kinesiology and has taken certification classes in posture, gait, muscle balancing, and nutrition. She and her Cairn Terrier, Jack, enjoy doing anything outdoors, including yoga, hiking, biking, kayaking, swimming, and surfing.

Employment Outlook

This is a new field, but Celapino and Stevens have both seen increased interest from dog owners. Celapino's business has grown rapidly. It began with one location in 2009 and now has four.

Employment of fitness workers in general is expected to increase by 29 percent through 2018, much faster than the average for all occupations, according to the BLS. Trainers who offer dog-friendly workouts may be more in demand. This is a career or business with opportunities to work full time or part time.

COMMUNICATOR AND CARETAKER RESOURCE

- *Animal Communication,* by Jacquelin Smith. Galde Press, 2005.
- *Animal Talk: Interspecies Telepathic Communication,* by Penelope Smith. Atria Books/Beyond Words, 2008.
- *Conversations with Animals,* by Lydia Hiby. New Sage Press, 1998.
- Dear Labby, blog for pet sitters, www.DearLabby.blogspot.com
- DogTEC Dog Walking Academy, www.dogtec.org/dog-walking-academy.html
- Gurney Institute of Animal Communication, www.gurneyinstitute.com
- *Learning Their Language: Intuitive Communication with Animals and Nature,* by Marta Williams and Cheryl Schwartz, DVM. New World Library, 2003.
- National Association of Professional Pet Sitters, www.petsitters.org

- Pet Sitters Associates LLC, www.petsitllc.com
- Pet Sitters International, www.petsit.com
- San Francisco Professional Dog Walkers Association, www.sfprodog.org
- Six-Figure Pet Sitting Academy, http://networkedblogs.com/p24597640
- *The Dog Walker's Startup Guide: Create Your Own Lucrative Dog Walking Business in 12 Easy Steps,* by J. D. Antell. Novus Markets, 2009.
- *The Language of Animals: 7 Steps to Communicating with Animals,* by Carol Gurney. Dell, 2001.
- *The Language of Miracles: A Celebrated Psychic Teaches You to Talk to Animals,* by Amelia Kinkade. New World Library, 2006.

CHAPTER 23

Pet Hosts

Hospitality isn't limited to human guests at fancy resorts or bed-and-breakfasts anymore. Whether their animals are being boarded, having supervised playdates, or traveling with them, owners expect their pets to be welcomed and cared for just like any other member of the family. The up-and-coming field of pet hospitality holds several business and career opportunities for animal lovers.

Boarding Kennel Owners and Employees

You may think of it as a boarding kennel, but the modern petrepreneur often regards his or her property as a resort for dogs and the business as providing pet hospitality. A boarding kennel these days is much more than a place for a pet to stay while his people are on vacation. Many boarding kennels offer day care, training, and grooming services as well. In recognition of that transition, what was once the National Boarding Kennel Association is now known as the Pet Care Services Association (PCSA).

Boarding kennel managers and staff are often drawn not only from the ranks of veterinary technicians and groomers but also from those of hospitality and restaurant employees, says Dennis Dolan. Dolan is the president and the chief executive officer of Best Friends Pet Care, a chain of forty-three pet resorts, including four of them at Walt Disney World Resort in Orlando, Florida.

What Boarding Kennel Owners and Employees Do

Keeping pets happy is entwined with keeping pet owners happy. Communicating about pets with customers is important. "If you leave your pet with us, when [he's] doing activities we take a picture and e-mail it to you so you can see your pet is happy and busy at Best Friends," Dolan says.

Some kennels have webcams in some or all of their suites, but given that lots of dogs spend much of their day sleeping, that can backfire in an amusing way. "We've had owners who call and say their dog is dead, and we have to go in and show that the dog is alive and moving," Dolan says. "Sometimes they call again the same day to say that the dog is dead."

In addition to their primary responsibilities of pet care, safety, and happiness, boarding kennel owners and managers have a wide range of other duties, including facilities management (appearance, cleanliness, and safety); record-keeping (immunization forms and pet care agreements); compliance with employment law, business licensing, and zoning regulations; and employee hiring, training, and supervision. Finding good employees, increasing market awareness, and training staff to recognize pet behavioral and health issues are just some of the challenges

Heidi Ganahl:
Founder of Camp Bow Wow

Heidi Ganahl transformed her passion for dogs into a $40 million franchise known as Camp Bow Wow, one of the fastest growing businesses in the United States, according to *Inc 500* and *Entrepreneur Magazine*. The original Camp Bow Wow opened in Denver in 2000; today there are more than 200 locations in forty states and Canada. Ganahl credits man's best friend with inspiring her to create her business, and she's returning the favor with the Bow Wow Buddies Foundation, a nonprofit dog welfare organization she founded to rehome the homeless and to raise funds for health research. In 2010
Ganahl released her first book, *Tales from the Bark Side* (Heidi Inc.), and devotes some of her time to inspirational speaking engagements geared toward entrepreneurs, business students, and start-up dog-business folk.

faced by boarding kennel owners and managers. Projecting an image of caring—and providing the reality of it, of course—is also paramount. Seemingly simple gestures, such as always greeting pets by name, can mean the difference between one-time and repeat customers.

"The level of expectation of the customer is much higher today than it was even five years ago, so you're always working to deliver more," Dolan says. "It's not only important that you do a good job taking care of pets but also that you project that to your customers, because if [you do] not, they don't know."

Because Best Friends Pet Care is a national chain, it also has regional managers, who oversee seven to twelve centers in a specific area. Regional managers, all of whom were once center managers, make regular visits to the kennels under their supervision and work with them to resolve challenges or take advantage of opportunities.

Who Boarding Kennel Owners and Employees Are

Dolan says that Best Friends Pet Care likes to hire people who have been trained as vet techs because of their background in pet health. Even though the kennels are not veterinary hospitals, they care for hundreds of thousands of pets every year.

"If they do get sick while they're with us, we want to catch it at the earliest possible time," he says. "We have also found people from the hospitality business—hotels, restaurants, and some in retail."

No matter what their background, Dolan says, all staff members need to have a great affinity for people and for pets, or they won't be successful.

Education and Training

The skills necessary can be learned on the job or through industry or company training programs. Everyone hired at Best Friends Pet Care for any position must become certified through the company's training

Best Friends Pet Care president and CEO Dennis Dolan and Clancy look ready to welcome canine guests (and their humans) to one of the Connecticut resorts.

program. "Our managers are required to be certified in all positions within the center, whether it's animal care, day camp counselor, customer service manager, or customer service representative," Dolan says. "We also have a training program, a week-long class held at our home office, just for managers and those whom we believe have the potential to be managers."

The PCSA offers a three-stage home-study program for individuals interested in pet care. The first two stages address basic and advanced principles of animal care, facility management, and customer service. The third stage, which leads to the title of certified kennel operator and requires three years of experience and employment as a pet-care service manager, focuses on management and professional skills.

Employment Outlook

The BLS predicts that employment of animal care and service workers will grow by 21 percent through 2018 and says that pet owners are expected to increasingly purchase pet-related services, including daily and overnight boarding.

A boarding kennel manager at Best Friends may earn a salary in the $40,000 range, with the potential for bonuses for such accomplishments as bringing in new customers, increasing revenue, or reaching certain

Pet Friendly Hotel

Happy hour at Hotel Indigo in San Diego's Gaslamp Quarter is on Tuesdays from 5 p.m. to 8 p.m., with live music, great cocktails, cozy seating by the fire pits, and treats for the dogs. Dogs? At happy hour? Get used to calling it "yappy" hour.

Dogs are the new VIP guests. Hotels, resorts, and bed-and-breakfast inns don't just permit pets anymore; they offer them amenities from made-to-order meals to sessions with a pet massage therapist or groomer. They offer designer dog beds, in-room food and water bowls, playrooms, fenced outdoor areas where dogs can run, pet-friendly dining areas, and even dog walking and day care provided by the resort staff. According to a 2008 survey by TripAdvisor, 61 percent of respondents have traveled with their pets, and 46 percent said they would stay only at pet-friendly hotels.

If you're considering opening a pet-friendly place, the most important aspect to think about is the financial outlay it requires. Unless you're turning your home into a bed-and-breakfast, you'll need to purchase a property in an attractive area that people will want to visit, furnish it attractively with fabrics and other materials that are easy to keep clean, hire employees, and purchase insurance to protect your six- to seven-figure investment. Be prepared to offer something special if you want to attract dog owners to your place—think hayrides or guided dog-friendly hikes. Hone your hosting skills while you're at it, as a great bed-and-breakfast or inn is known for its food and friendly service.

customer-satisfaction levels. Some salaries are higher based on the size of the market or facility. Managers at independent kennels, kennels in small towns or cities, or veterinary clinic kennels may make $24,000 to $32,000.

Dog Day-Care Owner

If you would rather have dogs come to you on a set daily schedule and want to offer a service that caters to busy but devoted pet owners, you may find opening a dog day-care center to be fun and fulfilling. Caring for pets during the day while their people are at work can take several different directions.

What Day-Care Centers Offer

Some pet day-care centers offer simple, basic care with plenty of playtime and attention for the dogs but no luxuries; some bill themselves as dog camps, with lots of activities and games; and some go all out and offer training, spa (read: grooming) services, and high-end toys, treats, beds, and foods in their pet boutiques. Whatever its style, a well-run dog day-care center in the right location can attract many clients.

Amy Nichols, founder of Dogtopia, started a day-care service for dog owners in 2002, after tiring of the telecommunications industry. Now she owns three centers and has branched out into selling franchises of the business, 34 so far. She hopes the business will expand to 200 day cares by 2015.

Getting Started

When it comes to starting a dog day-care center, you have two choices: create a unique business or franchise an existing one. There are pros and cons to franchising. Buying a franchise gets you guidance on getting started, from floor design to party planning to product placement; assistance with marketing and advertising; instruction on dog training and on business management; on-site support before opening; and follow-up visits for operational assistance. You may also have the advantage of starting out with the recognition value of a nationally known name.

In a day-care playroom at the Bark 'N Lounge in Keller, Texas, Kristy Pierce gives one of her charges some extra attention.

DAY-CARE OWNER

A dog day-care owner should have the following characteristics:

- ○ Determination
- ○ People skills
- ○ The ability to "sell" clients, vendors, and investors on your business
- ○ An excellent credit record and enough collateral to back up a bank loan
- ○ The chops to get financing for and run your own business

Expense is one of the largest drawbacks of franchising. Dogtopia charges a franchise fee of $40,000, and then there are the costs of leasing and furnishing a space, buying insurance and supplies, hiring employees, and marketing the business. A franchised dog day-care business can have start-up costs ranging from $243,000 to $458,000, depending on how many services you offer and the size and location of the business. Dogtopia franchisees have an ongoing cost in the form of a franchise "royalty" of 7 percent of gross sales, payable weekly.

A franchise isn't essential for success in the dog day-care business. If you choose not to franchise and are working out of your home or even leasing commercial warehouse space, your start-up costs can be much less. You may consider opening up a dog day-care center on your own if you already have excellent marketing or sales skills, retail experience, and good management skills when it comes to both dogs and people. Management and training are alike in many ways, after all.

Whichever way you go, be aware that opening a dog day-care business requires a lot of work upfront. You'll need to learn about zoning laws, health requirements, operating permits, and insurance needs. If balancing the books isn't your forte, you'll need to hire an accountant to help you stay in the black. And, of course, you should not only love dogs but also be knowledgeable about their behavior, training, and activities.

Be smart about location. Studying the demographics of your area will help you decide whether a day-care business is feasible. Nichols opened her first day-care center in a business park, which makes it convenient for pet owners to drop dogs off and pick them up on the way to and from work.

Successful dog day care operators always put the customers—canine and human—first. That can mean anything from allowing the dog to have a favorite recliner from home to installing webcams so owners can see how much fun their dogs are having during the day. Some pup camps offer

Joseph Sporn: Inventor of Dog Day Care

Joseph Sporn opened the world's first dog day-care center in 1987—the Yuppie Puppy, located on West 86th Street in New York City. The business offers grooming and boarding in addition to day care. Originally a certified groomer, Sporn is the petpreneur behind one of the nation's fastest growing pet businesses. He continues to enjoy the career that he's created for himself. "Having invented day care for dogs is a crowning achievement for me. No money or accolade could match the sense of satisfaction and joy of having started something that would turn into something so huge and so pervasive around the world." *Pet Product News International* reported in 2010 that more than a million Americans take their pooches to day care each year. In 1999 the Sporn Company was established after the success and popularity of the Sporn Training Halter, invented at the Yuppie Puppy Pet Care Center in Manhattan in 1992, the only harnesses the ASPCA recommends to control pulling.

lavish amenities, such as swimming pools, pet videos for their dogs' viewing pleasure, and taxi service to the veterinarian.

Talk to other people in pet-retail and pet-care businesses, including pet day-care owners. Consulting a business coach, especially one with experience in pet businesses, may also be a worthwhile investment of your time and money. The cost of consultations can range from $75 for a thirty-minute phone chat to nearly $9,000 for seven days of on-site advice.

Training

Before you jump into a dog day-care business, consider getting a taste of the action first. Lucky Dog Resorts and Training School in Colorado Springs, Colorado, owned by Debi Ropes, is a canine activity center that offers day care, boarding, training, agility, and grooming. For people, it offers a chance to visit the resort through Vocation Vacations, a company that offers "dream job holidays," and experience five days in the life of a dog day-care owner. During your stay, you'll introduce dogs safely in a

Barkworthy INSIGHT

A BRIGHT FUTURE

The pet hospitality category has a bright future, Dennis Dolan believes, especially in metropolitan areas, and the day-camp segment has experienced growth even in times of recession. "The opportunity for dogs to play with other dogs has become much more prominent among pet owners the last five or six years. All of our new places will have day camps."

play group setting; learn about employee education and management and customer service issues; learn about health, behavior, and safety issues; practice dealing with stressful situations; and study kennel software.

A similar opportunity is offered by a company called Doggie View, based in Austin, Texas, and run by Barbra Waldare, who bills herself as a dog day-care consultant. Her three-day Doggie View School course is available in a number of locations across the country and offers hands-on experience working in a dog day-care center. Each class is limited to three people to ensure that each student gets plenty of attention.

Employment Outlook

The environment for pet businesses is healthy. Even in a tough economy, people are still spending money on their animals. Bob Vetere of the American Pet Product Association (APPA) says that he expects expenditures in the field to continue to rise. A petrepreneur's income is highly variable, dependent on the economy and on what the market will bear in your area. Be sure that your budget is lean enough to survive those months or years when income is low.

PET HOSPITALITY RESOURCES

- Best Friends Pet Care, www.bestfriendspetcare.com
- CentralBark, www.centralbarkusa.com/franchising.html
- Cornell University School of Hotel Administration, www.hotelschool.cornell.edu
- Doggie View, www.doggieview.com
- Dogtopia, www.dogdaycare.com
- Florida International University School of Hospitality and Tourism Management, http://hospitality.fiu.edu
- Hospitality Schools, www.hospitalityschools.com
- International Franchise Association, www.franchise.org
- Lucky Dog Resort and Training School, www.bealuckydog.com/other services.html
- North American Dog Daycare Association, http://finance.groups.yahoo.com/group/nadda
- Northern Arizona University School of Hotel and Restaurant Management, http://home.nau.edu/hrm
- Pet Care Services Association, www.petcareservices.org

CHAPTER 24

Other Pet-Business Owners

There are many other kinds of pet-related businesses that you can set up. One exciting and satisfying career is that of pet detective, helping people find the precious four-legged members of their families who have gone missing. Another type of business is a pet boutique, which allows you to satisfy the needs of pet owners through products chosen to match your own distinct style. Other businesses, such as a pet cemetery, allow you to help other animal lovers in their time of grief. Then there are the businesses for those who don't mind dealing with the least attractive part of owning a dog!

Pet Detective

Thousands of pets go missing every year. Pet detectives use their knowledge of dog behavior and their investigative skills to track down lost pets and return them. People hire pet detectives for many reasons; for example, they or their family members may not be able to conduct a thorough search. A pet detective can post flyers, check shelters and rescue groups, perform Internet searches, post information on lost-pet Web sites, interview neighbors and follow up on potential sightings, set humane traps to capture a panicked dog, or even follow a trail using trained search dogs.

After compiling information about a missing pet, pet detectives will use these various techniques as well as networks of paid and volunteer

Detector-dog Rachel has tracked down "lost" cat Yogi during a training exercise conducted by pet detective Kat Albrecht.

searchers to track down the missing animal. They send posters to veterinarians, kennels, groomers, medical research labs, police agencies, humane societies, animal-control agencies, and pet-supply stores not only in the city or county where the pet was lost but also in the surrounding areas. Many pets are found more than 30 miles from home.

Postcards with the pet's photo may be sent to residents in the immediate neighborhood, as well as to veterinary hospitals within 10 miles and animal shelters within 30 miles. The idea is to create a network of individuals—the mail carrier, neighborhood kids, garbage collectors, utility workers—who will keep an eye out for the dog. Ideally, all of this is done within the first twenty-four hours of the dog's disappearance.

Understanding Why Dogs Go Missing

A good pet detective understands why dogs go missing. Sometimes they're stolen out of yards, but Kat Albrecht, former police officer, pet detective, and author of *The Lost Pet Chronicles* (Bloomsbury USA, 2005), says the three most common reasons that dogs become separated from their people are wanderlust, opportunistic journey, and blind panic. Wanderlust is a common problem in intact male dogs of any breed, as well as in both sexes of certain types of dogs (for example, scenthounds). They attempt to escape yards or homes by climbing over, digging under, or wiggling through a fence; bolting out an open door; or pulling free from a loosely held leash. "These dogs want to explore, follow a scent, find a particular person, mark their territory, find other dogs to fight or play with, or mate," say Albrecht.

Opportunistic dogs take advantage of unexpected chances to go

Microchipping

During a visit to the home of their owner's son and daughter-in-law, two Cavalier King Charles Spaniels escaped out of an unlatched screen door and went on an expedition. When the two miscreants decided it was time for a hearty snack and a nap, they ran through a backyard and made their presence (and demands) known at the nearest door.

The young couple who lived there were surprised when the two dogs came sauntering in, wagging their tails, and made themselves at home. The dogs' rabies tags weren't of assistance in contacting the owner, but the tech-savvy couple took the dogs to the nearest veterinarian, where they were scanned for a microchip. Bingo! The breeder who'd had them microchipped as puppies was contacted, she got in touch with the owner, and the dogs were returned safely.

Barkworthy INSIGHT

NOT ABUSED, JUST SCARED

Lost dogs with xenophobic temperaments—those that are shy, skittish, or fearful of anything new or different—can face difficulties getting back home once they're found. "Many people who find stray xenophobic dogs believe that, based on how the dog cowers in fear, the dog was 'abused,' " says pet detective Kat Albrecht, "and they refuse to return these dogs to their owners, even when the dog has a collar and ID tag."

exploring. While some dogs who go out an open door or gate may remain in their yards, most can't resist the temptation to follow their noses on journeys that can take them blocks or miles from home.

Firecrackers, thunderstorms, and other fear-inducing situations can cause blind panic. Noise-phobic dogs have been known to break through plate-glass windows, chew through screens, push boards loose on fences—whatever it takes to try to escape from a scary sound. These dogs are at high risk of being struck by cars or running many miles away from home.

Education and Training

The main requirements for becoming a pet detective are investigative skills and knowledge of animal behavior to predict such things as how far lost pets can travel or where they might go. Many colleges and universities offer animal behavior classes. Useful skills that can be obtained through criminal justice courses in research methods include investigative techniques such as deductive reasoning, search probability theory, and deception detection. Learn how to use equipment such as search cameras, amplified listening devices, and humane traps with baby monitors. Try to gain experience working with and handling as many different dogs as possible. Knowing how to approach and calm a frightened animal is an important part of this job. One way to learn this skill is by volunteering at an animal shelter.

Employment Outlook

This is a career that is still in development. Fees will vary depending on such factors as locale, length of time the pet has been missing, the required services, and whether any travel is necessary. Fee-based services that pet detectives may offer include use of a trained detection dog to locate lost dogs or cats, use of traps to capture lost animals, behavioral

Detector-dog Rachel learns to track under the direction of Kat Albrecht, who learned her own tracking skills as a police officer.

profiling consultations, use of detection and surveillance equipment, distribution of posters or flyers in target search areas, interviews with neighbors and other potential witnesses, and animal-shelter searches.

The charge for a phone or on-site consultation may be $150 to $200 an hour. To put up large posters and banners, plus advice on how to respond to callers, a pet detective may charge $375, plus the cost for materials. A half-day search using a trained detection dog could be billed at $2,000, depending on the terrain and the length of the search. Hourly rates for searches, including shelter checks, range from $25 to $65 or more, based on the type of search. Fees for setting out one or more humane traps may be $25 per hour, plus mileage and the cost of trap rental.

Pet Boutique Owner

A pet boutique is no ordinary pet store. Its clients seek unique or high-end products for pampering their pooches, exclusive or artsy items that aren't found on every pet-store shelf. In addition to top-shelf foods and treats, designer collars and leashes, and salon-quality shampoos and grooming equipment, a boutique may carry handmade jewelry, hand-knit dog sweaters, hand-thrown dog dishes, or original work by local pet artists.

Getting Started

It's not unusual for pet boutiques to be started by people who have a love of pets and an entrepreneurial bent, or who are disappointed by the items they find in their local pet-supply stores. Like Holly Hoenes, founder and president of Yuppy Puppy Pet Boutique in Ellicott City, Maryland, they utter the words "I should open a pet boutique." The next thing they know, they're in business. A few days after her fruitless shopping trip, Hoenes saw a property for lease. She signed the papers for it just days later, and within a week was on a flight to Chicago to a pet-product trade show. Her shop opened a month after she signed the lease.

Molly receives a much-appreciated treat on a visit to Salty Paws Homemade Biscuits and Store in Kitty Hawk, North Carolina.

Write a business plan that spells out all the details of your business so you don't forget anything important. If you need financing, your bank will want to see projections for costs and potential income. Other factors to consider include location, initial and ongoing costs, type and quality of merchandise, and your target customers and how to attract them.

Location: As with any business that involves real estate, the cardinal rule is location, location, location. Choose an area with lots of foot traffic and with the demographics to support the type of store you want to open. The area surrounding Red Bank, New Jersey, for instance, where luxury pet boutique Paw Palace is located, is home to celebrities and wealthy families who want and can afford the best for themselves and their pets, as well as middle-class people who are willing to splurge occasionally on something special for a pet, even during a recession. Yuppy Puppy's locale of Ellicott

City is a historic area with a charming character, and Hoenes's boutique is attractive to locals and tourists alike.

Costs: Depending on the brands you carry, the size of your shop, and the cost of real estate in your location, expect to spend $25,000 to $50,000 up-front to lease and stock a shop with unique, high-end items. Try to negotiate new-customer and repeat-order minimums. Companies may be more willing to deal in times of recession.

Consider venturing into business online before opening a brick-and-mortar store. That's what Dana Ujobagy did before opening Paw Palace. This allows you to test your concept and is a less expensive way to get started. An online business has the potential to reach a bigger market, and you'll spend less on inventory, rent, display racks, and employee salaries and benefits. Ujobagy started by stocking luxury pet items, such as clothing, decorative collars, and treats worthy of canine foodies, and soon expanded to carry natural dog foods and offer grooming services.

Merchandise: Buy the highest quality items you can afford, and try to select stock that will sell well in your area. If your best friend or next-door neighbor is an interior designer or a sales associate in an upscale women's boutique, don't be shy about asking for her advice. She will know what colors and styles are popular for your locale. To keep customers coming back, plan to have new merchandise coming in at least twice a month, and set aside a percentage of every sale to purchase inventory that you might otherwise not try.

Customers: Stay in tune with your customers' desires. Ujobagy surveys customers annually via e-mail to find out what they're interested in, and she added grooming services after three years of always referring customers to other businesses for their pets' bathing and blow-drying needs. Your customers and their pets are your best consultants.

Employment Outlook

According to the National Retail Federation, signs point to an improved economy and consumers with more

DO YOU HAVE WHAT IT TAKES?

PET BOUTIQUE OWNER

A pet boutique owner should have the following characteristics:

- ○ A sense of style
- ○ Retail experience
- ○ Good people skills
- ○ An entrepreneurial spirit
- ○ Good credit to obtain financing
- ○ An eye for unique or attractive pet products

Sea Breeze Pet Cemetery in Huntington Beach, California, offers cremation and lawn-burial services, granite markers, flowers, and other services for pet owners.

confidence. Combined with the expectation of continued growth in the pet industry by the APPA's Bob Vetere, that likely means good news for retailers who specialize in pet wares.

Pet Cemetery Owner

Stephen King's creepy novel *Pet Sematary* (Doubleday, 1983) may have given the business a less than appealing reputation, but the more than 600 active pet cemeteries in the United States provide an important service for pet owners who would like the option to cremate or bury their pets and inter their remains in a beautiful, peaceful resting place. A pet cemetery is a burial ground for pets. Other options are pet crematories, which may include a resting place for the cremains, and pet memorial centers, which can be simply a place to hold a memorial service for a pet—much like a funeral home—or can be associated with a cemetery or crematory.

Getting Started

The pet-cemetery business requires not only a compassionate heart but also an eye for beauty and a head for business. The first thing pet owners will notice is whether the grounds are well kept. Nobody wants to bury a pet or visit a pet memorial in a place that is overgrown with weeds. A pet cemetery should reflect the owner's long-term commitment to its upkeep. Factors you should consider include cost, services to be offered, and location.

Costs and Planning

Expect to spend $100,000 to $250,000 or more to start up a pet cemetery, pet memorial center, or crematorium. How much you spend depends first on the cost of land where you want to open your business and the square footage of your buildings.

Other expenses include equipment such as mowers, trimmers, and a backhoe for digging graves; vehicles for getting around the property and transporting caskets and headstones; supplies; construction, installation, and landscaping of an office, a chapel, and the grounds; a crematory, if desired, which costs $35,000 to $80,000 for a single machine; watering systems; gardens; and plots. It costs money to acquire permits or business licenses from your city, county, or state. You will need to pay a lawyer to draw up a perpetual-care deed and set up a fund for upkeep of the plots. There will also be expenses associated with the hiring of a writer, a designer, and a printer to create and produce brochures, business cards, and various other materials. You'll also need a relationship with a monument or marker company or the materials and machinery to cut and engrave granite for headstones. Urns, caskets, jewelry, and artwork are other items you will need to purchase. Employees will include groundskeepers and salespeople to inform pet owners of the services offered.

If you need financing, your bank will want to see a business plan showing anticipated costs and potential income. That means figuring out how much room you have for plots of varying sizes, known as "tracting" the land, as well as storage space for urns of cremated animals, and how much to charge for each. You'll need to estimate how many clients you

Flowers grace the final resting places of beloved pets at the Sea Breeze Pet Cemetery. Each burial site has a granite marker.

can anticipate based on the pet-owner demographics of your area.

As with any other business, you should anticipate a startup period of three to five years, says Coleen Ellis of Indianapolis, Indiana, a consultant and founder of Two Hearts Pet Loss Center.

Services

Most pet cemeteries offer a variety of services, enabling pet owners to choose a cremation, burial, or memorial that meets their emotional and financial needs. Some of the pet cemeteries are stand-alone operations, while others operate alongside other pet-related businesses, such as boarding kennels or veterinary hospitals, or are affiliated with cemeteries for people, where a section of the grounds have been set aside for pet burials. Recently, some funeral homes have begun to offer their services for pets as well as people. For someone with a kind nature who loves pets and people, this can be a satisfying and different career.

Become familiar with companies that make pet memorial stones, urns, and coffins. You will need to advise grieving pet owners about what is available for holding their pets' remains or marking their graves. Some pet cemeteries and crematories offer a place for memorial services and someone to lead them, if desired.

Another service you can offer is pick-up of deceased pets. This is a boon to the person with a large dog or someone who simply can't face bringing the pet in for burial or cremation. Some pet cemeteries provide temporary storage of the animal's body until burial can be arranged at another time or another place.

Long-Term Commitment

People will want to know whether the cemetery will still be there in five or ten years. Some pet cemeteries are deed-restricted, meaning that they cannot be used for any other purpose, such as development. You should own the land, usually 5 to 10 acres, on which the cemetery is built and maintain a care fund for the upkeep of the grounds. If areas surrounding the cemetery are developed, it will be necessary to ensure that there is still access to the grounds. The ideal spot is a rural location, where nearby residents or businesses won't be disturbed by the proximity of a pet cemetery.

Professional Associations

Membership in the not-for-profit International Association of Pet Cemeteries and Crematories (IAOPCC) will give your business credibility. The IAOPCC upholds business ethics and practices, maintaining a strict code of ethics by which all members must abide. The organization has extensive information on starting up and operating a pet cemetery or crematory, offers management consulting at no charge, and holds an annual convention that includes a seminar for prospective owners of pet cemeteries and opportunities to meet with providers of supplies and services as well as other people who run pet cemeteries. A bimonthly publication, *News and Views*, features articles about pet cemeteries and crematories, and a public relations service will mail press releases for members.

Grief Counseling

If you are not prepared to lead memorial services or offer grief counseling yourself, seek out a pet-loving minister, priest, psychologist, or social worker in your area who may be interested in reaching out to grieving owners. Look for someone with good speaking skills, a soothing manner, and a way with words and ceremony. Your clients should never hear the insensitive phrase "Even though Max was just a pet." Concern for the afterlife of a pet is common, so the grief counselor should also have the philosophical and theological sophistication to address the idea of life after death for pets and the different cultural conceptions of pets in an afterlife. Ideal candidates have experienced pet loss themselves and can empathize with pet owners.

A new organization, the Pet Loss Professionals Alliance, provides education and opportunities for professional growth for people in the field. It will also help to educate consumers on their options and help them find related businesses in their area that have the services they need.

Employment Outlook

Doyle Shugart of Atlanta, Georgia, a member of the IAOPCC's board of directors, sees a bright future for the pet cemetery business in places that aren't already served by one or that have the demographics to support growth. He also notes that some human funeral homes are recognizing the need for pet funeral services, burials, and cremations and expanding to meet those needs.

Pet cemetery ownership ranges from small "mom and pop" operations with income of up to $100,000 per year to large pet cemeteries with a hefty investment in equipment, employees, and landscaping that may bring in several million dollars per year, Shugart says.

Waste-Disposal Business Owner

Most of us don't see dollar signs when we look at a pile of dog poop. For people who can stand a little odor, have a passion for owning their own business, and are interested in an easy, inexpensive start-up opportunity, scooping poop for pet owners can be a profitable line of work. The only equipment you need is a shovel, plastic bags, garbage pails, gloves, rubber boots, face masks, and reliable transportation.

Getting Started

Of course, as with any business, there's a little more to it than that. Factors to consider include your physical fitness for the job, how to market your services, where you're willing to work, how and where to dispose of waste, weather conditions, and when and whether to hire employees.

DO YOU HAVE WHAT IT TAKES?

WASTE-DISPOSAL BUSINESS OWNER

A waste-disposal business owner should have the following characteristics:

○ Entrepreneurial spirit
○ Good people and dog skills
○ Physical fitness
○ Marketing know-how
○ Familiarity with waste-disposal ordinances
○ A less-than-keen sense of smell

Companies that offer poop-scooping services do more than rid your yard of dog waste. They use a number of methods to help your yard look and smell fresh. Besides bagging waste and either placing it in your trash can or hauling it away, they may treat the yard with enzymes to reduce the appearance of ugly yellow urine stains on grass, apply deodorizers or disinfectants to reduce odor or kill germs in the yard, use a hose to clean off decks or patios, install training aids to encourage dogs to eliminate in a particular area, and even scoop litter boxes.

Physical Demands

Lift and toss. Tote that bag. All day long. Scooping poop isn't easy. The gloves you wear aren't just to protect you from coming in contact with the stinky stuff; they also help to prevent blisters, calluses, and possible injuries. Between bagging and hauling, your hands, wrists, arms, and back all take a beating. You may want to have a good massage therapist on call if you take up this line of work. On the plus side, rhythmic shoveling and scooping can put you into a Zen state of mind, and many visits don't take more than ten minutes to complete.

Consider hiring other people to do the physical labor, paying them hourly or per yard, while you manage the business end of things. Be sure you meet legal requirements as far as paying employment and other taxes. Liability insurance, workers compensation, and bonding are other potential expenses.

Costs

Start-up costs can be low for a poop scoop business. You need reliable transportation to get to customers'

From left to right: Steve Lewis (manager), Tom LaBriola (owner), and Tony Evans (manager) of Doggy Duty, a scooping business in Tracy, California.

homes and, if necessary, to haul away waste. Assuming that you already have an appropriate vehicle, it should not cost more than $500 to purchase the necessary equipment such as a shovel, plastic garbage bags, sturdy gloves, and rubber boots, plus office supplies and a cell phone. Expect to spend another $1,000 to $2,000 in marketing and advertising expenses.

Costs will be higher if you choose to go the franchise route. Doody Calls charges a $34,500 franchise fee, plus a 9 percent royalty and estimates start-up costs at $39,730 to $63,920. The advantage is support in the form of training, marketing materials, and a call center. Franchises can also offer greater name recognition.

Climate and Service Areas

Take your climate into account when deciding if this is the right business for you. Sometimes you'll be doing your business on lovely, moderate days with a light breeze and not too much sun, but in general, working outdoors means that more often than not you're going to be hot, cold, or wet, depending on the season. Weather also affects your working conditions. Poop will stink more in summer heat, be more difficult to find beneath fall leaves and mounds of winter snow, and be slick and heavy after a rain shower.

What areas will you serve? The more you have to drive, the more you'll have to spend on fuel and vehicle maintenance, which can cut into your profits. In deciding where to market your business, figure out how many yards per hour you can clean, how far you want to drive, and how much time you'll need to spend on other business-related chores, such as billing, marketing, and customer care. Start small and then decide if and where you want to expand.

Disposal

Now that you have all of this dog poop, what are you going to do with it? Your service can offer customers one of two options. The first option is simply to bag the waste and place it in the customer's trash can for pickup by the garbage collector. The second option is to haul the waste away and dispose of it yourself by taking it to a landfill or sewage plant, which will levy a fee based on the size of your load. Be sure to build those costs into the rate you charge. Check with your city or county to see what ordinances apply to pet waste disposal.

Employment Outlook

If you'd like a little help getting started and are willing and able to make more of an investment, franchise opportunities are available. There's also an organization for professional poop scoopers, the Association of Professional Animal Waste Specialists. Their code of conduct includes requirements for member businesses to treat animals with respect, be mindful of the client's security, disinfect tools and shoes between each visit to prevent the spread of parvovirus and other diseases or parasites, dispose of waste according to state and local laws, and obtain and maintain commercial liability insurance.

Most poop-scoop businesses charge a flat monthly fee of $50 to $60 or more to come by weekly and clean up customers' yards or their businesses. Rates can depend on the number of dogs, the frequency of visits, and whether the service is year-round or seasonal. Some poop-scoop businesses offer other services, such as litter-box cleaning, leaf raking, or kennel sanitizing, for an additional charge.

OTHER CAREER RESOURCES

- American College of Veterinary Internal Medicine Foundation, www.acvimfoundation.org/petloss
- Association of Professional Animal Waste Specialists, www.apaws.org
- Delta Society, www.deltasociety.org
- *Dog Detectives: Train Your Dog to Find Lost Pets,* by Kat Albrecht. Dogwise, 2007.
- Doody Calls, www.doodycalls.com
- International Association of Pet Cemeteries and Crematories, www.iaopc.com

- Missing Pet Partnership, www.missingpetpartnership.org
- Pet Butler, www.petbutler.com
- Pet Loss Professionals Association, www.myplpa.com
- Pinellas Animal Foundation, www.pinellasanimalfoundation.org/index .php/programs/pet-loss-support
- Poop Butler, www.poopbutler.com
- Pooper Scooper, http://pooper-scooper.com

Recreation, Events, and Judging

The world of dog sports has seen unprecedented growth since 1990, when agility and the Canine Good Citizen test began to gain in popularity. Because so many more people are participating in events such as conformation shows, agility, obedience, and rally with their dogs, there is a greater need for handlers, judges, and show superintendents, not to mention more business for companies that make equipment for use in canine sports. Outside the world of dog shows and events are other athletic endeavors involving dogs; among them are foxhunting and dog sledding.

BEST IN SHOW

CHAPTER 25

Breeder and Professional Handler

The first thing to know about breeding dogs is that it's not a true career. That is, when done correctly, it's not an activity that will support you if you have a family to raise and a mortgage to pay. In fact, the closest relationship dog breeding has to a career is that you have to have a career to support the habit. But if you love dogs, care about their futures, and have a nurturing, caring, dedicated nature, it's a hobby that can bring a great deal of pleasure and satisfaction.

There are more opportunities to make a living as a professional handler than as a breeder. However, showing dogs means much more than just running them around the ring in front of the judge. It is a difficult job, requiring dedication to the dogs and to the effort required to show them.

Breeders

Breeding dogs is not about churning out puppies to sell. A good dog breeder has the intent of bettering the breed by producing dogs who are good, healthy representatives of their breed, both physically and mentally. Doing so is time-consuming and expensive. Breeding-quality dogs earn their status through being shown to their championships, then vetted for good health and temperament before breeding. That's just the beginning of the expenses incurred by breeders.

Standards and Health

What does it mean that a dog is a good representative of his breed? Every breed has a standard, a written description of the ideal appearance and temperament for that breed. The breed standard is what keeps Labs looking and acting like Labs and Rottweilers looking and acting like Rottweilers. There is no such thing as the perfect dog, but the breeder's goal is to breed dogs who resemble the description in the breed standard as closely as possible. Breeders show their dogs in conformation (dog shows) so they can be evaluated as to how well they stack up against the breed standard.

Joanne Nash, shown here with one of her Dalmatians, is a longtime breeder of Dalmatians and Cavalier King Charles Spaniels.

The other side of being a good breeder is producing healthy dogs with few or no genetic problems. Doing so is an expensive endeavor. Just like people, all dogs, even mixed breeds, can be susceptible to certain genetic health defects; for instance, hip dysplasia, eye disease, or heart problems. Good breeders obtain health certifications for all of their breeding stock to reduce the risk that puppies will be born with health problems or develop them later in life.

Expenses

According to Joanne Nash of Los Altos, California, who has been breeding Dalmatians and Cavalier King Charles Spaniels for more than twenty-five years, you will also need to be prepared to spend a lot of money before puppies ever appear. Among the initial expenses are prebreeding health tests for the bitch to ensure she is in good health, including a test for brucellosis, which is a sexually transmitted disease. In some cases, there may also be one or more progesterone tests to pinpoint the time of ovulation.

Do You Have a Market?

Besides taking into account the time, money, and energy that it takes to raise a litter for eight to twelve weeks—the typical amount of time before puppies are ready to go to their new homes—you must also consider whether there is a realistic market in your area for your breed. If you want to breed Great Pyrenees but live in New York City, you may discover that it's difficult to find people who want to purchase your puppies. Before you start breeding, do your homework and determine whether you will have a market for your dogs. You may need to decide whether you are willing to ship puppies to buyers across the country or will require them to come pick up their puppies in person.

After that come the costs associated with the breeding itself. Different breeds can have a different range of stud fees, from a few hundred dollars to $1,000 or more. And the right stud dog is not always the Lab next door. Breeders seek out the stud who will best complement the attributes of the bitch and who has undergone equivalent health testing.

The perfect stud may be on the other side of the country, which means the expense of either shipping or driving your bitch to the stud. Dog breeding etiquette calls for the bitch to go to the stud—and paying the owner of the stud dog for her keep while she is there. Some dogs don't breed easily and require artificial insemination—often more than once—another expense.

Once the bitch is successfully bred and shipped back home, she will need special care during the sixty-three days of her pregnancy. That means feeding her a puppy diet to ensure that she gets all the nutrients she needs while the puppies are developing. The breeder may also elect to run a hormone test or schedule an ultrasound exam to confirm the pregnancy and, later, a radiograph to determine the number and positioning of the puppies.

There are the costs of a whelping box, bedding, and other equipment, along with extra food for the dam (mother). The breeder will also have the expense of a higher heating bill because of the need to keep the puppies warm. Later for the puppies, the breeder must pay for dewclaw removal or tail docking by the veterinarian if desired, puppy vet checks, deworming and

DOG BREEDER

A dog breeder should have the following characteristics:

- ○ A desire to improve your breed
- ○ A nurturing personality
- ○ Good observation habits
- ○ An interest in and understanding of genetics
- ○ Good record-keeping skills
- ○ Lack of squeamishness

first vaccinations, and microchipping for puppy identification purposes. The breeder will also need to buy supplies for raising the puppies, which can include a scale for weighing the puppies, a heating pad, washcloths, house-training pads for the use of mother and pups, a bulb syringe, milk substitute for puppies, a feeding tube, and antiseptic solution. Registering the litter with the American Kennel Club (AKC) is another expense.

Unforeseen events can occur, too: a late-night trip to the veterinary emergency clinic if something goes wrong during whelping, a Caesarean section if the mother is unable to give birth naturally, or the death of the mother or one or more puppies due to various complications. If a dam is unwilling or unable to care for her puppies, they will need to be tube- or bottle-fed by the breeder. Sometimes, smaller puppies in a large litter must be supplemented with a feeding tube or bottle to ensure that they get enough nutrition. And even with health testing, a puppy may develop a serious unexpected genetic problem as an adult.

Time

Breeding is not only expensive but also time-consuming. Breeders who hold down regular jobs should be prepared to take time off to deal with the types of situations previously discussed or have an experienced person lined up who can help. Even under normal circumstances, they may need to take time off for the birth and puppy-raising. Don't forget to make time in your schedule for such things as veterinary visits, socializing and house-training the pups, and talking to prospective buyers.

There's also a lot of record-keeping to be done: tracking the weight of the puppies weekly to ensure that they are growing at the proper rate, measuring their heights and body-lengths and making observations about their behavior and temperaments. All of this information helps you build the store of knowledge that you need to evaluate future litters. And all of this takes time.

Julia Gasow and Patricia Craige Trotter: Peerless Breeders of Perfect Show Dogs

Many breeders produce countless champions and near-flawless specimens of their chosen breeds, but few breeders are able to "stamp" a breed so profoundly that the breed is forever changed. Among the few are Julia Gasow (*shown at right*) and Patricia Craige Trotter (*shown below*), both of whom elevated their chosen breeds to a new level of competition in the show ring. Gasow is the famed matriarch of the Salilyn English Springer Spaniels, the elegant, full-coated American-type Springer with a distinctively chiseled head. Trotter is the master breeder behind the Vin-Melca Norwegian Elkhounds, sometimes fondly called Craige-hounds. Gasow's breeding program was established in the 1930s, and her dogs have won no fewer than 400 Best in Show awards, including three Westminster winners. Her dogs consistently vied for the Top Dog spot for six decades.

Trotter not only bred great dogs but also showed them herself, including ten Hound Group winners at Westminster, among the nearly thirty dogs she campaigned into the top ten Hounds. While the elusive Best in Show at Westminster

has yet to be won by Trotter, she's judged there several times and holds the record for most Groups won by an owner-breeder-handler. Without a doubt, she's the top owner-breeder-handler in the history of show dogs. Gasow's Ch. Salilyn Aristocrat lays claim to the title Top Producing Sire of all time with 188 AKC champions, and Trotter's Ch. Vin-Melca's Howdy Rowdy, in second place, was not far behind with 166. Both Trotter and Gasow were inducted into the Hall of Fame, in 1990 and 1986 respectively.

Trotter has also left her mark on the dog fancy as an author. Her *Born to Win: Breed to Succeed* (2nd ed., Kennel Club Books, 2009) demonstrates her prowess as a master breeder and a teacher, her "real-life profession" for forty years. The book is regarded as one of the most important works on breeding and showing dogs.

Basset Hound breeder Claudia Orlandi believes an understanding of genetics is essential to producing healthy dogs with nice temperaments.

Because they take breeding dogs so seriously, good breeders want only the best for their puppies. They carefully screen potential puppy buyers to ensure that each pup will go to a caring home. A good breeder requires buyers to a sign a contract agreeing to return the dog to him or her if for some reason they can no longer keep the dog. That's a big commitment, but it's one that every responsible breeder should make.

BE PREPARED

Whether they are new or experienced, breeders should always be prepared for surprises, says breeder Joanne Nash. Reading about breeding and talking to experienced breeders will help. "What's typical for us is something new and different with each litter, sometimes something good and sometimes a disaster."

Education and Training

Becoming a dog breeder is mainly a matter of learning on the job or apprenticing with an experienced breeder. An animal science background is useful but not essential. There are many books on the subject and seminars that you can attend. Top Basset Hound breeder Claudia Orlandi, PhD, offers a home-study program that covers genetics, breeding systems, pedigrees, selection, anatomy, and genetic defects. Orlandi is a teacher by profession, and her skill at imparting information shows in her lectures.

When it comes to breeding dogs, finding a mentor is a good first step. Look for someone in your breed if possible; the breeder of your own dog may be just the right person, especially if he or she lives nearby. You will also want to spend time looking at the litters of other breeders and talking to them about their experiences. For additional guidance, look to some of the top books on breeding dogs (see the resource list at the end of this chapter).

Employment Outlook

Given all the expenses, it's rare for most dog breeders to make any kind of profit, let alone a living. Most serious breeders have only one or two litters a year at most.

"To make a living, one would need quite a few females to breed, and the days of large show/breeding kennels are basically over, with a few exceptions," Nash says. "To be a responsible breeder, one needs to plan each litter and spend what's necessary to raise it well. By the time you factor in all the expenses, to say nothing of all the time required, the 'profit' from the litter isn't enough to live on. For most breeders, breeding is an expensive hobby that may occasionally be somewhat profitable, although they can't count on that. There are a few opportunities for a dog lover to be employed by a large show/breeding kennel, but those few jobs usually go to dog people with both show and breeding experience."

Grahm Swayze perfectly presents a Whippet. Once a top-winning Junior Showmanship handler, Swayze has gone on to become an accomplished professional handler.

Pyrenean Shepherd breeder Patricia Princehouse estimates that serious breeders probably lose about $10,000 per year.

Nonetheless, Princehouse and Nash enjoy the challenge of breeding good dogs and watching puppies grow and develop to be nice representatives of their breed. Making new friends and helping new breeders are also positive aspects of breeding dogs.

Professional Handlers

A handler's life is physically taxing. Handlers are frequently on the road, traveling to shows, as many as 100 to 200 annually. Handlers load and unload dogs and gear for transport, usually in a van, SUV, or recreational vehicle; lift dogs onto and off grooming tables; shampoo, blow dry, clip, and trim their canine charges; and run, jog, or swim with their dogs to keep the dogs in top physical condition. They may attend shows as many as five days a week, including every weekend, during the busy show season.

What Handlers Do

When handlers are home, they are still busy caring for the dogs or researching judges who will be at upcoming shows and deciding which dogs to enter in which classes in future shows. An experienced handler sometimes becomes a breeder as well, or works in partnership with a breeder, and is able to look at a litter of young puppies and know which ones have the "it" factor: that special something that will take them to the top in the conformation world.

Not all handlers work in the conformation ring. Some are professional field trialers who train and handle retrievers and other sporting dogs for competition in high-stakes and highly competitive field trials. A field trial is a practical demonstration of a dog's ability to do the work

Fashion Sense

One thing a handler needs is fashion sense. You can't walk into the show ring wearing just any old thing. A handler's clothes should set off the dog while not drawing attention to the handler. For instance, solid-colored clothes work best with spotted, patched, or brindle dogs. The color should complement the dog and help ensure that he stands out. That means, for example, if you're showing a white dog, don't wear white.

It's also important to wear clothes in which you can bend and move easily. Smart handlers avoid anything flowing that they might trip over or that the dog could step on as well as anything revealing that they might . . . er . . . fall out of as they run around the ring. Whatever they wear must have pockets for holding bait—usually liver—or the dog's favorite toy, which is useful for getting his attention when he needs to strut his stuff.

Frank Sabella: Artist on the End of a Show Lead

Like his mentor Anne Rogers Clark, Frank Sabella is a native New Yorker, a former professional handler, a Poodle person, and one of the few who has won and judged Best in Show at the famed Westminster Kennel Club. A former ballet dancer, Sabella brought his own brand of finesse and showmanship to the world of professional dog handling. He wrote the definitive book on handling: *The Art of Handling Show Dogs* (B&E Publications, 1980). During his twenty-year handling career, he handled three Top Dog All-Breeds as well as many number-one dogs in their breed. His specialty was always coated breeds, and he and judge Richard G. Beauchamp share credit for "inventing" the clip that is now universally used for the Bichon Frise breed. His Westminster triumph was with a white Standard Poodle in 1973, and he judged Best in Show there in 1990. Sabella's judging career has taken him around the world, and his popularity and authority seem to know no bounds or borders. In the United States, he is licensed to judge all breeds in four groups as well as many others. He was inducted into the Anne Rogers Clark Hall of Fame in 2010.

for which he was bred, whether that is finding, flushing, pointing, or retrieving game. There are different types of field trials for pointing breeds, retrievers, spaniels, scenthounds, and terriers. Successful professionals may handle as many as twenty to thirty dogs and are paid based on how successful they are, which can add up to a healthy income for someone who is skilled at training and coaching dogs to bring out their best.

When they're not showing dogs, handlers can often be found judging matches and sweepstakes, organizing grooming and parking at dog shows, taking their dogs to nursing homes or children's hospitals for pet-visitation therapy, or speaking to pet owners about care or animal welfare.

Chris Grisell of Fairland, Indiana, breeds Weimaraners and handles other sporting breeds and hounds. Before she takes on a new client's dog, she has the dog live with her for at least two weeks, even if he is local and won't be boarding with her.

"You really need to know each and every individual dog," Grisell says. "So I want the dogs to live with me, even if they're from this area, for a minimum of two weeks so that I can get to know the dog and see what his flaws are and what his personality is like. I think that has helped me more than anything else. If they don't want me to keep the dog and I can't figure the dog out without his living with me, then I just don't handle him because I'm not going to do a good job."

To be successful, handler and dog must have confidence in, trust in, and respect toward each other.

Who Handlers Are

Great handlers love dogs, are honest with their clients, and set realistic goals for the dogs they are showing. To present dogs at their best, handlers must have superb artistic and presentation skills.

Some successful handlers have certain styles in the ring. Some go in with the attitude of a showman, while others have a more low-key manner. Some handlers are known for specializing in large, athletic, or "difficult" dogs or in particular groups or breeds, such as terriers or Poodles. Others take an all-around approach, showing everything from Chihuahuas to Mastiffs.

A professional handler who belongs to the Professional Handlers Association (PHA) is expected to follow a code of ethics that spells out appropriate behavior. Beyond the courteous and professional demeanor that defines good sportsmanship, professional handlers should not steal clients, maliciously criticize other handlers or their dogs, or berate or belittle judges. Handlers are expected to properly care for the dogs entrusted to them and to promptly notify clients of show results and provide them with any ribbons, trophies, or prizes if the contract calls for awards to go to the owners. Last, but definitely not least, a handler needs a good head for business—or the sense to hire someone who has one. Part of being a handler involves sending out itemized and timely billing statements for fees owed.

Getting Started

Setting up as a professional handler isn't inexpensive. A handler needs a home with a kennel to board the dogs in his or her care as well as a great deal of equipment and appropriate transportation. A handler also needs a good contract, which provides clients with a written agreement that spells out the responsibilities and expectations for both client and handler as well as a fee schedule.

A Kennel

According to the PHA, the kennel should have permanent housing indoors with room for the dog to walk around, plus outdoor exercise areas. Kennels must be heated and cooled according to the weather, and there should be a large, clean grooming area to prepare the dogs before the show. Handling without a kennel setup is unfair and cruel to the dogs in the handler's care. Dogs should never be expected to live in crates for the majority of the time spent with the handler.

Grisell has a 21-acre property in Indiana with large runs and five fenced, 1-acre yards. Plenty of space for free exercise is good not only for

A second-generation dog show man, Michael Scott (*pictured with a Pointer*) has proven his versatility as a professional handler by winning top dog of the year in four different variety groups.

a show dog's physical condition, keeping him lean and well muscled, but also for his mental state. Good handlers want and need their dogs to be happy and well conditioned.

Equipment and Transportation

Must-have equipment includes crates, crate pads, crate fans, cooling mats, grooming tables, professional blow dryers, scissors, combs, brushes, shampoos, conditioners, spray bottles, show leads and collars, a tack box or bag in which to pack such items, bait, a cooler for food, a first-aid kit, towels for cleanup, and dollies on which to haul everything. There are expenses as well for upkeep—having scissors sharpened, for instance—and replacement as items wear out or are used up.

A professional handler also needs reliable transportation for canine clientele. This is usually a large van, such as a Freightliner Sprinter, or a fully equipped recreational vehicle. The vehicle must be able to hold crates, exercise pens, grooming equipment, and food and water. With a motor home, the handler has lodging on wheels and can keep the dogs under a watchful eye while avoiding hotel expenses.

Education and Training

Many dog handlers begin their careers at an early age. They grow up in families that show dogs or they get dogs as youngsters and begin showing in 4-H or Junior Showmanship. Handling is a career that develops on the job. Watching other handlers teaches beginners how to prepare for showing dogs, from proper grooming to arriving at the ring on time to presenting their dogs to the judges. Young handlers often apprentice at the kennels of breeders or experienced handlers, where they may have the opportunity to groom, train, and handle many different breeds. They go to dog shows every week and learn how to bring out the best in every dog.

Employment

Only about 250 people make a living as full-time handlers in the United States. Others may begin handling dogs part-time as a hobby or for extra income and may move into full-time handling if they build up large enough client bases or retire from other jobs.

"Probably only 5 percent of all professional handlers, maybe a little more, make a real decent living," Grisell says. "I think most of the professional handlers have started in another career and bought a kennel and then [gone on] to professional handling. I have 21 acres, and there is no way I could have made the money handling to buy this place." A rare few who are at the top of their game can earn more than $100,000 a year.

BREEDER AND HANDLER RESOURCES

- *ABC's of Dog Breeding: What Every Breeder Should Know!* by Claudia Orlandi. www.abcsofdogbreeding.com
- *The Absolute Beginner's Guide to Showing Your Dog,* by Cheryl S. Smith. Three Rivers Press, 2001.
- *Canine Reproduction and Whelping: A Dog Breeder's Guide,* by Myra Savant-Harris. Dogwise Publishing, 2005.
- *The Complete Book of Dog Breeding,* by Dan Rice, DVM. 2nd ed. Barron's, 2008.
- *New Secrets of Successful Show Dog Handling,* by Peter Green. Alpine Publications, 2002.
- Professional Handlers Association, www.phadoghandlers.com
- *Show Me!* by D. Caroline Coile. Barron's, 1997.
- *Successful Dog Breeding,* by Chris Walkowicz and Bonnie Wilcox, DVM. Howell Book House, 1994.
- *The Whelping and Rearing of Puppies,* by Muriel P. Lee. TFH Publications, 1997.
- *The Winning Edge: Show Ring Secrets,* by George Alston. Howell, 1992.

CHAPTER 26

Dog Show Judge and Superintendent

D og show judges evaluate dogs in the conformation ring. They must know the breed standard—a written description of the perfect dog, including head, eyes, ears, body type, coat, color, and gait—for each breed that they judge, and they must determine which dog most closely meets the breed standard on that particular day. Judges are licensed by the American Kennel Club after meeting a number of qualifications, including a minimum number of years showing and breeding dogs.

Judges are also needed for dog sports such as agility, obedience, and rally. Like conformation judges, they must meet strict requirements regarding experience, knowledge of procedures, and ethics. And while conformation shows and obedience trials have a relatively straightforward routine, agility and rally trials call for judges who can design appropriate courses for each level of competition.

A show superintendent is hired by a dog club's show committee to oversee the production of a dog show—and it is a production—everything from taking entries and printing the show catalog to managing the setup and teardown of all of the tents, tables, rings, and other structures required to put on a dog show. The business of superintending dog shows ranges from small family outfits to large companies. They may operate only in a certain area or have the capacity to manage shows across the country.

Dog show judge Chris Walkowicz awards Best in Show to the Standard Poodle Ch. Brighton Minimoto at the Cen-Tex Kennel Club Show in November 2007.

Dog Show Judges

Chris Walkowicz of Sherrard, Illinois, has been judging dogs in conformation since 1995, after thirty years of training, showing, and breeding German Shepherd Dogs and Bearded Collies. Like many other people who decide to become judges, Walkowicz wanted to advance in the sport, and judging seemed like a natural progression.

"I thought it would be physically easier to stand in the middle than to run around a ring," she says with a laugh, adding, "it's not."

What Dog Show Judges Do

A conformation judge may spend two to five days preparing for a show. Besides reviewing the breed standards, he or she must make reservations, pack, and travel to the show. Once there, the judge hopes the ring steward works efficiently as far as sending the dogs into the ring in a timely manner and having everything the judge needs readily at hand, goes over the dogs in the ring, and faces the mental challenge of selecting the best dog.

Anne Rogers Clark:
America's Legendary Dog Show Judge

Born January 6, 1929, Anne Hone Rogers (later Mrs. James Edward Clark) is the most iconic figure in the American purebred dog world. She was a poodle breeder, a professional handler, an AKC all-breed judge, and a mentor to hundreds of other breeders, handlers, and judges. She was described by dog show historian Bo Bengtson, one of her students, as "legendary." She won her first Best in Show when she was just twenty-one years old, with her mother's English Cocker Spaniel. As a professional handler, she soared above all others, winning Best in Show at Westminster three times (1956, 1959, and 1961), each time with a poodle. She was the first female professional handler to win the show. In 1967 she became an AKC judge and retired from handling.

At six foot two, she cut an imposing and immediately recognizable figure in the ring. She judged Westminster a record twenty-two times and was the only judge in history to judge all seven groups. *The New York Times* referred to Clark as "for six decades a fixture at Westminster." By judging Best in Show at Westminster in 1978, she became the only woman in history to have won Westminster as well as have judged its finale. Few judges in the history of the dog sport are as revered as Clark. Her success as a breeder was less trailblazing, though she did breed a Miniature Poodle who won Best in Show at Westminster, adding to her long list of unique accomplishments. Arguably Clark was the only bona fide superstar in the sport of dogs, and the AKC's Hall of Fame was renamed to the Anne Rogers Clark Hall of Fame in 2007, the year after her passing.

An agility judge has more responsibilities than simply judging each dog's performance. Before the trial, he or she must design a course and submit it to the show-giving club for approval. On the day of the show, the judge ensures that the course is built correctly and doesn't have any safety hazards. Before competition begins, he or she must measure any dog whose height hasn't been established to make sure his is entered in the correct height division. The judge decides and controls the procedures for entering and exiting the ring and running the course; verifies that scores, course yardages and standard

DOG SHOW JUDGE

A dog show judge should have the following characteristics:

- ○ Integrity and impartiality
- ○ Knowledge of breed conformation, gait, and temperament
- ○ Knowledge of a sport's rules and regulations
- ○ Good record-keeping skills
- ○ Experience in showing and breeding dogs or putting sports titles on dogs
- ○ Strength of character

course times are recorded accurately; and signs and initials the official catalog to certify it. Last but definitely not least, it is the agility judge's job to instill an atmosphere of fun for dogs, handlers, and spectators.

Obedience judges have similar responsibilities. They set up the ring or instruct the ring steward on how this should be done, explain the procedures they want used when obedience teams enter and exit the ring, ensure that the ring size is correct, check the equipment to make sure it is in good condition, and decide the placement of the gate and the judge's table. Judges check to make sure ring conditions are acceptable with good footing and level ground and that an indoor ring is well lit. If the obedience trial is held outdoors, the judge should make sure the sun won't be in competitors' eyes. The judge is also responsible for designing a well-thought-out heeling pattern and measuring dogs to make sure jump heights are set correctly for each.

In a rally competition, the judge arrives early to inspect the ring and make sure it meets the requirements outlined in the regulations and posts the course or courses outside the ring. During the ring inspection, the judge examines signs and sign holders for proper and secure placement, makes sure distractions can be seen and smelled but not swallowed, and measures the jumps to ensure they are at the designated height. Before beginning, the judge reviews the entry list, goes over procedures with the ring steward, and decides how to arrange the entries, such as low jump heights to high.

On a typical multi-breed or multi-event show day, a judge rises early, catches a shuttle to the show from the hotel, judges for three to four hours, then takes a break for lunch. Afterward, he or she completes the Breed judging assignment and then views or judges the Groups. At breakfast, lunch, and dinner, the judge can be found talking dogs with colleagues. Collapsing into bed early is the usual end to the day.

For Walkowicz, the best part about judging is learning about many different breeds, as well as the mental challenge of evaluating the dogs. So is finding a great dog— "Especially if I'm the first one to do it," she says.

Although finding the best dog is stimulating and exciting, it's not always easy. "Sometimes we must plow our way through mediocrity or disappoint a friend or a child," Walkowicz says. "That's hard, but we're there to reward the best dog, not to please people."

Training and Experience

No particular degree is required, although most judges have a college degree or at least a high-school diploma. What they need most, however, is experience in showing and breeding dogs or, for dog sports, training and putting advanced titles on dogs.

Breeding and Raising Champion Dogs

To become a conformation judge, a person must have shown dogs for at least a dozen years and bred five litters on his or her own premises. In

Judge Sari Brewster Tietjen awards the 2009 Best in Show at the Westminster Kennel Club to Sussex Spaniel Ch. Clussexx Three D Grinchy Glee ("Stump"), the oldest dog to ever win the show. Stump's handler was Scott Sommer.

Portrait of a Dog Show Judge

Sari Brewster Tietjen has been "in dogs" since she was a child. By the time she reached adulthood, she had bred, raised, and showed more than a dozen different breeds. Tietjen has judged dogs for more than forty years and in 2009 reached the pinnacle of her career when she judged Best in Show at the Westminster Kennel Club Dog Show. Prior to that experience, she had judged Breeds and Groups, including the 2009 Toy Group, at Westminster nine times.

How does one prepare for that kind of assignment?

"Pray a lot!" says Tietjen, who was thrilled and deeply honored when she was offered the Westminster Best in Show assignment. "Seriously, at that level, you know you are going to have some beautiful dogs in the ring. You have to keep your wits about you, evaluate each dog against its breed standard, and then how it measures up against the other dogs in the ring."

other words, you can't just breed in partnership with someone else who does all the work. You must have hands-on experience with breeding, whelping, and raising a litter. In addition, prospective judges must have produced four champions from those litters before they can apply for a license. Those are just the minimum requirements. Most would-be judges have much more experience. Be sure to document all your experience in writing, Walkowicz advises.

Applicants who do not meet the litter or champion requirements may qualify by documenting any combination of the following requirements: breeding and raising four litters in each breed requested; breeding at least two champions in each breed requested; owning at least one dog who has sired four champions in each breed requested; owning or maintaining four dogs who earned championships during that time in each breed requested; personally exhibiting four dogs to their championships, earning all fifteen points and both majors, in each breed requested; personally exhibiting two dogs as specials for at least two years in each breed requested; or documenting twenty-five years of experience exhibiting dogs in conformation. Participating in club activities or serving as a club official also helps in meeting judging requirements.

Putting Sports Titles on Dogs

Depending on the sport you apply to judge, you must have three to six years of experience in competition. Agility judges are required to have at least five years, obedience judges six years, and rally judges three years, with a gradual increase to six years. Would-be agility judges must earn at least two types of agility titles; obedience judges must train and put a Utility Dog title on one dog of their own, plus put a Companion Dog title on at least one other dog; rally judges must have earned a Companion Dog Excellent title on their own dogs and trained and titled at least one dog to a Rally Excellent title. Other experience requirements include working as a timer, a scribe, and a course builder at a licensed AKC agility trial; acting as a ring steward at a licensed AKC obedience or rally trial at least ten times; and serving as a trainer or assistant trainer in a dog training club.

Passing Tests

Other hurdles for conformation judges include passing open-book tests on anatomy and judging procedures, as well as passing tests and having an interview with an AKC executive field representative on each breed

Scott Sommer (*pictured*) from Houston, Texas, has handled two Westminster Best in Show winners: a Bichon Frise named Ch. Special Times Just Right! ("J.R.") in 2001 and a Sussex Spaniel named Ch. Clussexx Three D Grinchy Glee ("Stump") in 2009.

for which you are applying. Judging applicants must also have completed six stewarding assignments (stewards at dog shows manage the ring by ensuring that exhibitors enter the ring in the correct order, that the judge has everything he or she needs, calling for cleanup if necessary, and other such tasks) at AKC member or licensed shows in the three years prior to their application and six judging assignments at AKC-sanctioned matches (practice shows), specialty matches, sweepstakes, or futurities. Applicants must also attend an AKC basic judging institute. Prospective judges will be approved upon first application only for those breeds in which they have documented experience in owning, breeding, and exhibiting, according to the AKC. They may apply for further breeds as the requirements are met.

Dog sports judges must also meet requirements for practical judging experience, such as judging sanctioned matches, and attend judges seminars in their chosen sports and pass the required tests. For instance, applicants to judge agility must pass a two-part course analysis test and show that they can successfully design all levels of courses. Complete requirements are found on the AKC Web site at www.akc.org.

Employment Outlook

As of 2009, there were 3,200 AKC judges and an average of five to six new applicants every month. They work some 1,500 all-breed shows, plus more than 2,200 specialty shows. A new judge who is pleasant, does a good job, and makes an effort to continue learning about breeds can gradually become in demand.

Judges may be paid per dog or may be given a fee plus expenses. Beginning judges are usually paid $3 to $4 per dog. Judges who are AKC delegates are not allowed to charge fees and are limited to expenses. Most judges who are approved for one or more Groups charge a fee plus expenses. The fee is based on the number of breeds they judge.

Dog Show Superintendents

Among the many duties and responsibilities of an AKC-licensed superintendent are to hold shows under the rules and regulations of the AKC and to enforce all such rules applying to dog shows. The superintendent assists and advises the club in all matters pertaining to its show and serves as trustee of a show-giving club's income from entry fees.

What Show Superintendents Do

The superintendent accepts and processes entries and prepares and mails the premium lists (which provide the details of the show) as well as the judging programs and show catalogs. The superintendent furnishes the club with a copy of the official results of its show, tabulates the official results of the judging, and forwards the results to the AKC within a set time frame. Superintendents may also set up or maintain mailing lists or membership databases for clubs or advise clubs on planning and promoting national specialties, group shows, or seminars.

Back in the day, a dog show superintendent's job involved typing IDs on a manual typewriter and hand-stamping armbands. Catalogs were typeset by hand on a linotype machine. Things change, and in this case, for the better. Today, everything is faster, automated, computerized. Telephones, fax machines, and e-mail facilitate last-minute entries or changes. Large presses capable of printing 9,000 sheets per hour produce catalogs and brochures, with the aid of machines that fold, stitch, trim, and bind the printed matter that is necessary for following what's happening at a dog show. A desktop publishing system allows the superintendent to generate camera-ready copy for its publications, and a Web

Show superintendents, such as the one shown here at Westminster Kennel Club, ensure that a dog show runs smoothly from beginning to end.

site allows exhibitors to go online and find premium lists, a schedule of upcoming shows, judging schedules, entry blanks, mailing list request forms, cancellation forms, and show results.

On the day of a show, the superintendent and staff members begin work early. They arrive at the show site by 7 a.m. to set up and get ready for transfers to Best of Breed. They prepare judges' books, ribbons, and armbands, packing them neatly into tote bags for the ring stewards to pick up. If they are setting up the rings, they arrive a day or two before the show to get the work done. Once the show begins, they answer questions and solve problems for exhibitors; this can range from interpreting rules or explaining the point schedule to answering questions from the public about how dog shows work. In the meantime, they're also dealing with lost children, settling exhibitor disputes, accepting entries to upcoming shows, or marking catalogs for the show-giving club. When the show is over, they pull everything down and store it until it's needed for the next show.

Education and Training

No particular educational degree is required to work in this field. A high-school diploma and a college degree are helpful but not required. Some people in this field have college degrees in such areas as history and political science or a background in the military. In most cases, this type of work is learned on the job. As mentioned, sometimes it's a family business that people grow up in or marry into.

At MB-F in Greensboro, North Carolina, would-be superintendents must apprentice for a minimum of six months to learn the duties required. They must have at least ten years of dog-show experience as an exhibitor, handler, judge, or active dog club member. Show superintendents and their family members cannot actively show dogs. To find

Barkworthy INSIGHT

ORGANIZATIONAL TALENTS

Good dog show superintendents need the organizational talents of a Border Collie to ensure that shows—which may have 2,000 or more dogs entered—run smoothly. They must cope with back-to-back shows, three-day shows, and circuits of many shows. New people entering the sport, who need help learning the ins and outs of the game, as well as the increasing number of obedience rally and agility competitions at dog shows, add to the challenge.

out more about this career, visit a dog show and track down the superintendent, or contact companies that do this work and set up an informational interview.

Employment Outlook

Superintending a dog show is a specialized business that is done more for love than money, according to Fred J. Lyman, treasurer of MB-F. "With the decrease in the number of dogs being shown in shows currently, most superintendents hope that they can break even or make a very small profit on a show. When I say 'a very small profit,' [I am] talking about $200 to $300 average per show. In many cases with small shows, superintendents actually lose money. Contrary to what most people believe, dog show superintendents do not make lots of money." Show superintendents generally are paid a flat fee, plus a certain amount for each dog entered.

JUDGE AND SUPERINTENDENT RESOURCES

- AKC judging guidelines, www.akc.org/pdfs/rjl003.pdf
- BaRay Event Services Inc., www.barayevents.com
- Bob Peters Dog Shows, www.bpdsonline.com
- *Dog Show Judging: The Good, the Bad, and the Ugly,* by Chris Walkowicz. Dogwise Publishing, 2009.
- Dog Show Superintendents Association, www.dogshowsupers.org
- *An Eye for a Dog: Illustrated Guide to Judging Purebred Dogs,* by Robert Cole. Dogwise Publishing, 2004.

- Garvin Show Services LLC, www.garvinshowservices.com
- Jack Bradshaw Dog Shows, www.jbradshaw.com
- Jack Onofrio Dog Shows LLC, www.onofrio.com
- MB-F Inc., www.infodog.com
- McNulty Dog Shows Inc., www.mcnultydogshows.com
- Rau Dog Shows, www.raudogshows.com
- Roy Jones Dog Shows Inc., www.royjonesdogshows.com

CHAPTER 27

Other Jobs in Dog Sports

The sport of foxhunting in America focuses on the joy of the chase: riders on horseback following the hounds as they scent out their quarry of fox or coyote. The wild hunt ends when the quarry goes to earth, escaping to run another day. Foxhunting is organized and governed by means of hunt clubs and the Masters of Foxhounds Association (MFHA). Hunt clubs may be run by volunteers who do all of the work necessary to manage the hounds and the land over which members hunt, or they may hire professional staff.

Far from the green fields of the fox hunters are the frozen white fields of the mushers. Professional dog mushers are rare. People who race sled dogs for a living rely on winnings from races, money earned from selling dogs they breed, and in rare cases, endorsement income from pet-food manufacturers or other related businesses. The pickins, as they say, are slim. Mushers live and train in harsh environments, for the most part, and run the risks of accidents or injuries on the trail, either to themselves or their dogs.

Hunt Staff

Professional hunt staff members include huntsmen, whippers-in, and kennelmen. Whether they are professionals or amateurs, all are essential to the smooth running of the hunt club.

Huntsman

The term *huntsman* applies to men or women who are employed by hunt clubs to direct the hounds (which are usually American or English Foxhounds) during the hunt, care for and train the hounds, and breed new litters as required. The huntsman plans the strategy for each hunt; carries the horn; controls the hounds, indicating where he or she wants them to draw a fox or a coyote; and ensures that the hounds chase the quarry as a cohesive pack.

Making a pack requires the huntsman to choose hounds who can work together to contribute to the hunt's success. A huntsman must be able to accurately assess essential talents and abilities in the dogs, such as

Huntsman Lynn Lloyd of Red Rock Hounds leads an event.

striking, marking, honoring, cold tracking, giving voice, quartering, casting, and identifying scent, as well as characteristics such as toughness, bravery, drive, and speed.

The huntsman acts as a sort of conductor, orchestrating the movement of the hounds, encouraging the tail hounds, steadying the lead hounds as needed, and controlling all of them by voice, mannerisms, and horn. It's been said by Reg Spreadborough, huntsman for Orange County Hounds, speaking at the 2010 MFHA hunt staff seminar, as reported by Full Cry, a hound blog written by Glenye Oakford, that there should be a "golden thread" of communication not only between huntsman and hounds but also between huntsman and staff.

Huntsmen choose hounds based on the terrain over which they hunt, but also according to which hounds suit the huntsmen's own personalities. Huntsman Lynn Lloyd of Red Rock Hounds in Nevada has a pack of 150 Walker Hounds. That's a larger than normal pack, but she counts her acreage in the hundreds of thousands. Walkers, which descend from English Foxhounds, are fast, agile, and tireless, well suited to baying up the coyotes, bobcats, and mountain lions in Lloyd's territory.

Besides being knowledgeable about hounds, a huntsman must be an expert foxhunter, well grounded in the arcane conventions of the sport. Being a huntsman also calls for quick decision-making skills and strong leadership ability. If a season is successful, the huntsman wins the praise for it; if it is not, he or she takes the blame.

Whipper-in

Whippers-in, also known as whips, assist the huntsman in managing the hounds. They ride off to the sides of the hunt to ensure that the hounds don't stray; discourage the hounds from unwanted quarry; turn the hounds back or encourage them forward as needed; and keep the huntsman informed about the whereabouts of the hounds and the movement of the fox. A good whip is an experienced foxhunter who knows the hounds and has the riding ability and stamina to keep up with them and keep them in line. Whips may also help the huntsman with other tasks related to the hunt. After a hunt, they help count the hounds to make sure all are accounted for, check their conditions as they are loaded up into a truck or trailer for transport back to the kennel, and report to the huntsman any signs of unsoundness or unusual behavior.

At the kennels, the whippers-in may help to choose hounds for a hunt, feed and water the hounds, provide basic care for injuries, and clean the kennels. They know the hounds well and are familiar with the social structure of the pack, so their opinions are valued by the huntsman and Master of Hounds. Many huntsmen often begin their careers as whips.

DO YOU HAVE WHAT IT TAKES?

HUNT STAFF

A huntsman should have following characteristics:

- ○ Strong leadership skills with both dogs and people
- ○ Good decision-making ability
- ○ Excellent horseback-riding skills
- ○ Knowledge of hounds
- ○ Physical strength and stamina

A whip should have the following characteristics:

- ○ Good verbal communication skills
- ○ Strong leadership ability
- ○ A responsible nature
- ○ A quiet and relaxed attitude toward the hounds
- ○ Physical stamina
- ○ Excellent riding skills

Kennelmen

The huntsman oversees the kennelmen, who feed the hounds and clean the kennels. The job of a kennelman (who may certainly be a woman) may encompass preparing the hounds' meals, cleaning food and water troughs, and cleaning the hounds' living areas. Kennelmen provide the hounds with basic care such as grooming and deworming, and pick up dog waste. Kennelmen help to exercise the hounds, either in the

A foxhound leaps into the chase. Whippers-in manage the dogs on the field, while kennelmen take care of them off the field.

field or turning them out into paddocks on the days they don't hunt. Some positions require kennelmen to exercise the hunt's horses. The job may also involve raising and training puppies, driving the hound truck or trailer, clearing trails, building jumps, repairing fences, setting out meat laced with dewormer for the local foxes, helping foxes in trouble, and setting up for social events or steeplechase races. A kennelman works six days a week and is generally paid a salary with benefits.

Education and Training

Hunt staff usually come to their positions through experience or apprenticeship; there are no schools that teach huntsmanship, whipping-in, or kennel management. They are skilled outdoorspeople whose talents range from reading the weather to predicting the behavior of the quarry. Huntsmen, whips, and kennelmen must also be knowledgeable about the use of radios and tracking collars on the hunt field. When they aren't working with the hounds, they are busy maintaining the land over which their club hunts.

Some hunt clubs have a junior whip program to train young people who may one day become honorary (volunteer) or professional whips. At Glenmore Hunt Club in Staunton, Virginia, juniors who want to learn to be whips must walk out with the huntsman five times, attend one Glenmore hunt staff seminar, know at least five couples (ten) of entered hounds by name, and complete five scheduled hunts, riding as an assistant whip on at least one of the hunts.

Hunt clubs may hold cubbing camps for children to teach them the basics of the hunt, or clinics or workshops that are open to all members or even the public. Young people who are interested in pursuing a career or avocation with a hunt may want to attend a college with a good equestrian program such as Sweet Briar College in Virginia, the University of Maryland, Stephens College in Missouri, and Pennsylvania State University. Many of the courses such schools offer in their equine programs—farm management or principles of nutrition, breeding, and disease, for instance—would be useful to someone who wants to work as a huntsman or a whip.

The MFHA has a professional development program to enhance and improve the skills of hunt professionals. Huntsmen, whippers-in, and kennelmen can apply to the year-long program. Activities and benefits include

Huntsmen must manage people and dogs as Lynn Lloyd does with this pack of hounds. Lloyd has a pack of 150 Walker Hounds.

attending the Virginia Hound Show (a conformation show for American, English, and crossbred Foxhounds) and working in the four rings, offering a chance to observe the judges and study their decisions; personalized guidance in such areas as hound nutrition, kennel management, breeding and whelping, and hunt country management; access to an extensive reference library of books and DVDs; and assignment of a mentor. Apprentices must pass a test to graduate from the course.

Employment

Because foxhunting is an uncommon activity, few positions are available. The sport is limited to certain parts of the country, with foxhunting clubs found mainly on the Eastern Seaboard and in the South. There are only 171 MFHA-recognized hunt clubs in the United States and Canada. A huntsman's salary is commensurate with experience and the club budget; it usually ranges from $24,000 to $50,000. It may include housing, health insurance or coverage through workmen's compensation, livery, and horses. The average huntsman makes between $28,000 and $35,000, plus perks. Some huntsmen, such as Lloyd, run their own packs and have other income.

Most whips are honorary, meaning they volunteer their time to the club. A rare few whips are professionals who earn a salary for their work. The salary of a whip varies depending on the whip's experience and the club's budget. Professional whips are paid $18,000 to $34,000 annually and may receive perks such as housing, clothing, and horses.

Musher

The life of a musher is difficult, jobs are rare, and the financial rewards are uncertain, but the upside is the opportunity to spend your days outdoors with dogs. One lucky dog sledder is employed by the federal government. The National Park Service hires a kennel manager for Denali National Park and Preserve in Alaska. The job involves running a thirty-one-dog kennel, patrolling the wilderness park by dog sled, going out on search and rescue missions, and conducting educational programs and community outreach.

During the summer, the kennel manager can expect to present three daily hour-long interpretive programs.

The job is physically demanding and calls for strong leadership skills, not to mention time spent caring for canine colleagues. Denali's kennel manager must feed the dogs, plan and carry out breedings and whelpings, train the dogs, and give vaccinations. There's also the chance to work outdoors, in the company of dogs, in the midst of one of America's grandest wilderness areas.

Education and Training

No particular degree is required to become a musher, only a high level of skill and determination. Mushers learn by doing, usually after they first experience the thrill of being behind a team of dogs.

Musher Becky Swayze, owner of Trail Boss and Kennel and Dog Sled Equipment, unloads her dog sled. She works a team of seven Siberian Huskies, all of them rescue dogs.

Susan Butcher: First Lady of the Iditarod

A vet tech by profession, Susan Howlet Butcher became the second woman ever to win Alaska's famed Iditarod Trail Sled Dog Race (a 1,152-mile wilderness trek through rugged terrain), following the historic win of Libby Riddles in 1985. Never one to shy away from a challenge, Butcher mushed her way to Iditarod victory for three consecutive years, starting in 1986. She was hailed nationally for her sled-dog accomplishments— "the best competitive dog racer in the universe"—and remains the only woman to have won the Iditarod four times, the fourth in 1990. Butcher's determination, natural talent, and strenuous training regimen for herself and her huskies, along with her single-minded focus on that faraway finish line, made her legendary in the sport of dog mushing. Few athletes have ever become so synonymous with a sport as has Butcher with mushing. In 2008, the state of Alaska honored Butcher, two years after her death from cancer at age fifty-one, by naming the first Saturday of every March in Alaska Susan Butcher Day. Butcher was also been inducted into the Alaska Sports Hall of Fame in 2007. Her husband, David Monson, and her family honor her memory through the Susan Butcher Family Center at Providence Alaska Medical Center in Anchorage, a haven for families affected by cancer.

The park ranger position at Denali, however, is quite a bit more demanding, calling for a bachelor's degree with a high grade-point average in one of the natural or earth sciences, history, archaeology, anthropology, or park and recreation management. The position also requires at least one year of experience in one of the following: a park guide or tour leader position, recreational management, archaeological or historical preservation research work, or work in another scientific field.

Employment Outlook

Like foxhunting, mushing is not a common activity; it requires a rural locale with lots of snow in the winter and roads or trails where training can take place during the summer.

The handful of people who make a living as professional dog mushers are lucky to earn a few thousand dollars a year. Only a top few earn enough money through winning races and breeding dogs to keep themselves and their furry charges fed and sheltered.The lone government job

A National Park Service ranger and musher runs dogs through Denali National Park and Preserve in Alaska.

as a dog musher has a pay range of $33,477 to $66,542, depending on experience. That job includes benefits such as health insurance and paid vacation time, as well as a cost-of-living allowance. The salary alone, even at the lowest level, is much more than most mushers earn in a race season. If you plan to become a dog musher, expect to hold a second job or have some other source of income.

HUNT STAFF AND MUSHER RESOURCES

- *Dog Driver: A Guide for the Serious Musher*, by Miki Collins. 2nd ed. Alpine Publications, 2009.
- *Foxhunting: How to Watch and Listen*, by Hugh J. Robards. The Derrydale Press, 2006.
- Foxhunting Life with Horse and Hound, www.foxhuntinglife.com
- *Foxhunting with Melvin Poe*, by Peter Winants. Derrydale Press, 2002.

- International Federation of Sleddog Sports, www.sleddogsport.net
- International Sled Dog Racing Association, www.isdra.org
- Masters of Foxhounds Association of America, www.mfha.com
- *MUSH! Revised: A Beginners Manual of Sled Dog Training* by Charlene LaBelle. 4th ed. Barkleigh Productions, 2007.

Working-Dog Handlers

Several careers offer the opportunity to work with dogs and help people at the same time. Some of these are in law enforcement; for example, police officers and federal agents use dogs to sniff out drugs, evidence of arson, and explosives. Other people handle search and rescue dogs. Dogs can also be trained to detect bed bugs, gas pipeline leaks, gypsy-moth egg masses, toxic mold, termites, and the scat of endangered wildlife, to name just a few of the ways in which their keen sense of smell is put to use. They are even being trained to detect peanuts in an effort to help people with potentially lethal peanut allergies. There is an extraordinary bond between handlers and their canine partners. That close relationship is essential to developing a strong and beneficial working partnership.

CHAPTER 28

Law-Enforcement Dog Handlers

Like any law-enforcement officer, those who work with dogs have duties that involve maintaining regular patrols, responding to calls for service, and doing paperwork. Depending on the size of the agency, they may be assigned to a specific type of duty or they may do a little bit of everything. Officers who patrol specific areas with their canine partners must become familiar with their patrol areas so that they immediately recognize anything unusual, such as suspicious circumstances or hazards to public safety. They may identify, pursue, and arrest suspected criminals or resolve disputes within the community.

Some police officers work with special units that make use of their dogs' skills. These can include arson, bomb-detection, and drug-detection work. They work fire scenes; public transportation venues, such as subway stations, train stations, or airports; and large public events that may be the subject of bomb threats. They may also check vehicles or buildings for drugs or other contraband.

Many urban police agencies promote community policing, encouraging officers to build relationships with citizens in the neighborhoods they patrol. Part of this work may include doing presentations with their dogs at schools or other public events.

Federal agencies that may have patrol- or detection-dog handler positions include the Central Intelligence Agency; the U.S. Postal Service;

the Secret Service; the Drug Enforcement Administration; the Federal Aviation Administration; Customs and Border Protection; the State Department; the Bureau of Alcohol, Tobacco, and Firearms; the U.S. Marshals Service; and the U.S. Department of Agriculture. Many states also have a variety of detector-dog programs. Here's a sampling of what you can expect if you are interested in becoming a law-enforcement dog handler.

Arson Dog Handler

Arson dogs, also known as accelerant-detection K9s, are trained to sniff out the slightest traces of accelerants, substances used to set fires. The overwhelming majority of arson dogs are Labrador Retrievers or Labrador mixes, whose scenting ability, desire to please their people, and trainability are among the traits that make them ideal for the job. These dogs partner with specially trained law-enforcement officers whose job it is to investigate fire scenes and determine a fire's cause. More than 200 arson dog teams are presently at work in the United States and Canada. When they're not working fire scenes, they're practicing their skills so that they'll always be at the top of their game.

What Arson Dog Handlers Do

Arson dog handlers must have complete trust in their canine partners, but they can't rely solely on their dogs. Once the dog alerts on a scent, it's the

New York investigator Dale Moone and his late Golden Retriever partner, Alex, inspect the scene of a fire, looking for signs of arson. Alex was trained to alert on certain scents.

handler's job to investigate further. "We use them as a tool," says Dale Moone of the Arson Bureau, part of the New York State Department of State Office of Fire Prevention and Control. "Just because they indicate does not mean that it's arson. When the dog indicates, I can't reach down and pull up a tangible item; plus, how do we know he's not indicating on a decorative lamp that might contain kerosene? It's not illegal, for instance, to have gasoline or kerosene in your home. So those are some of the challenges. We have to clean off the floor and find a physical pour pattern or other physical evidence that can only be consistent with an ignitable liquid that has been spread out as an accelerant.

"We'll take a sample and send it to a laboratory, and more than 50 percent of the time, the laboratory will come back with a negative finding. That doesn't mean it was never there; it just means that either we weren't exactly right where we took the sample or it's burned to total completion, to where it can't be found by a laboratory but it can by a dog. It's up to me to do the digging to confirm what he is finding."

Arson-Detection Training and Certification

To be successful, trainers must establish a bond with their dogs, who will become members of their families, just like any other dog. In Alfred, Maine, dogs and their handlers attend school at the Maine Criminal Justice Academy for five weeks to learn to detect evidence of arson, the criminal setting of fires. Practicing at simulated fire scenes, they learn how to locate and identify tiny drops of accelerants, the fuels used to start fires. The challenges that face them? Wet grass, wet buildings, mud, ashes, soot, and charred debris.

Each day's training begins early in the morning with basic identification of accelerant scents—repeated at the end of each day—followed by a long

walk to help the dogs shake out the fidgets. After lunch, the teams work in a large oval space that resembles a skating rink, seeing how many drops of accelerant their dogs can identify. Accelerant drops are placed in a variety of locations, such as on steps or along walls, so teams can become accustomed to searching all types of areas. The training is videotaped to help measure each team's progress.

Handlers must also learn to identify hazards, such as dangerous debris or weakened areas, that could endanger their dogs or themselves. They also acquire the skills needed to collect samples, which are then sent to crime labs for analysis and identification. Throughout the training, teams discuss scenes and searches in a group setting. Scenes may involve simulations, controlled burns done by the local fire department, or actual fire scenes to which the class has access. Teams also learn how to search for people, living and dead.

To become certified, the dog-and-handler team must pass two evaluations, and the handler must also pass a written test. Any failure means further training. To maintain their skills, dogs and handlers must be recertified annually.

Explosive-Detection Dog Handler

Police departments, government agencies, and the military use explosive-detection dog (EDD) teams. The job of the dog-handler teams is to protect people and property from criminal or terrorist use of explosives. At high-risk places or events, such as government offices, political conventions, or the Olympic Games, they conduct routine searches of buildings, vehicles,

Hero sniffs at a bag on a New York City train, checking for explosives. The German Shepherd Dog is handled by Lieutenant John Kerwick, head of the MTA Police K9 unit.

materials, packages, and people and respond to bomb threats. Teams are on call twenty-four hours a day.

EDD Training

Training through a program such as the one at Auburn University's Canine Detection Training Center (CDTC) in Alabama prepares teams for their work. The center offers dog and handler training for explosive and drug detection, handler instruction, detection-team evaluation and refresher training, customized courses for specific needs, and canine-program supervisor and management seminars. The duration of a specific course depends on the level of competency that the team is expected to achieve.

Most students at the CDTC are already employed by federal or local police departments or private security companies, but almost anyone can attend. Independent students should be prepared to undergo background checks. Dogs and handlers who graduate from the program are employed by agencies and organizations such as the Department of Energy, the U.S. Coast Guard, the U.S. Secret Service Technical Services, and the Federal Protective Service.

Instructors at CDTC come from various canine backgrounds. "We feel the more representatives we have from the community, the stronger we become as a team," says John C. Pearce, associate director at CDTC. "When developing new canine technology, pulling information from all these different resources is extremely helpful."

Who EDD Handlers Are

Pearce says a good handler must have initiative, discipline, and a strong sense of responsibility. Learning and training aren't over after a course is completed. Dogs and handlers must practice their skills frequently.

"You must have the initiative to train as required," Pearce says. "You never know when you are going to get that call to employ the dog. It could be a life-threatening situation. If you haven't done your training, there is just no way to cram. It is conditioning, and it takes place over several training sessions and a period of time."

John C. Pearce is the associate director at Auburn University's Canine Detection Training Center in Alabama.

Police Dog Handler

Canine handlers are charged with caring for a law-enforcement tool that is not only expensive but also thinks for itself. Unlike a gun, you can't take a dog home, lock it in a safe, and forget about it. A police K9 is a family member as well as a crime-fighting partner.

Who K9 Handlers Are

The characteristics that set apart a K9 handler are maturity and a high level of responsibility. He or she must also have a flexible schedule when it comes to a personal life. Police dog handlers don't just work regular patrol hours; they must be available for after-hours "call-ins."

Police K9 handlers develop a strong relationship with their dogs, but they must also be willing to put them in harm's way. "The officer knows that when he goes to work, the dog will be in harm's way," says Lieutenant

A K9 handler and his German Shepherd Dog partner get ready to go on patrol in the city of Harrison, New York.

John Kerwick, a member of the U.S. Police Canine Association. "If the choice comes down to risking fellow officers' lives or the dog's, the choice will be the dog, a very hard decision."

Police K9 handlers don't come straight out of the academy. The more law-enforcement experience a candidate has the better he is suited to the work, Kerwick says.

In addition to work experience, potential K9 officers must show affection toward animals, possess the ability to work independently at major events, and be willing to devote a lot of off-duty time to caring for their four-legged partners. Public speaking skills are also an advantage. Police K9 officers frequently do presentations at schools and other public events.

Law-Enforcement Dog Handler Training

Coursework to become a law-enforcement dog handler includes learning to choose and train a dog; working the dog in an open-area, vehicle, and building searches; becoming familiar with apprehension techniques; presenting courtroom testimony; and caring for the dog. Attendees also learn management skills, such as how to establish a K9 unit or make better use of one that already exists.

Patrol-dog training takes approximately sixteen weeks. Detector-dog training usually takes twelve weeks, and police canine handlers generally attend a six- to eight-week course.

All of the skills and concepts learned in the courses must be reinforced on a regular basis; training is ongoing. The industry standard is about four hours per week of supervised training for each discipline—narcotics or explosives, for instance—for which the dog is trained.

For the handler, training is demanding, but for the dog, it must be fun. Most handlers try to make training exercises into games that the dog will be excited to play.

"Most of the training starts out simple and gets more detailed as the team progresses," Kerwick says. "Before the team can move on, the foundation must be clearly understood by the handler and the dog."

The training techniques used with law-enforcement dogs have evolved from sharp leash corrections in the 1960s and 1970s to the more progressive methods of the present. Positive reinforcement, using play as rewards, is the most common method of training, Kerwick says, although some detector-dogs may earn food rewards.

"I believe that every dog is different, and therefore each dog should be treated as a individual," Kerwick says. "We and they all learn differently and

A handler-dog team with the Harrison Police K9 Unit check out a parked car. No matter how close the bond, a K9 handler must be willing to put his or her dog in harm's way.

at different rates. I get around a lot and I know of no unit that would permit being harsh toward an animal. There is always a better way to teach."

To be successful, handlers of working dogs must have an understanding of canine physiology and motivation. After all, you can't force a dog to use his nose. The dog must want to do the work for which he's being trained, and motivating the dog calls for a handler to have skills in positive reinforcement.

The best trainers in any field know what rewards work for each dog so that the dog's efforts are worth his while. A detection dog will work for hours hunting the scent of drugs, explosives, or other contraband, all for the reward of chasing a tennis ball or tugging on a towel—or whatever the dog enjoys most—for a few minutes.

Trainers must know what each dog responds to in training and what reward makes each dog excited. For instance, instructors for the National Detector Dog Training Center in Newnan, Georgia, may work with five or six dogs at a time, so they must be able to respond quickly to an individual dog's quirks, remembering which one reacts better to gestures, which one calls for a speedy response, and so on.

Besides being creative in finding rewards, trainers must also be creative in solving problems. Yelling at a dog when he does something wrong is easy, but it doesn't move the training process forward. Good trainers must constantly find positive, creative ways to motivate dogs as well as to prevent them from failing.

Working-dog handlers should enjoy interacting with people and meeting the public. Important character traits are honesty, sound judgment, integrity, and a sense of responsibility. In some agencies, candidates are

A dector dog and law-enforcement handlers check luggage for evidence of explosives or contraband such as foods and plants banned from import.

interviewed by psychiatrists or psychologists or given personality tests. Most applicants are subjected to lie-detector examinations or drug testing. Some agencies subject sworn personnel to random drug testing as a condition of continuing employment.

Work Environment

Law enforcement can be dangerous and stressful. In addition to the obvious dangers of confrontations with criminals or dealing with situations such as bomb threats, police officers and detectives must be constantly alert and ready to deal appropriately with threatening situations. Many law-enforcement officers witness death and suffering resulting from accidents and criminal behavior. A career in law enforcement may take a toll on a person's private life.

Uniformed officers, agents, and inspectors are usually scheduled to work forty-hour weeks, but paid overtime is common. Shift work is necessary because protection must be provided around the clock. Junior officers frequently work weekends, holidays, and nights. Police officers are required to work whenever they are needed and may work long hours during investigations. Officers in most jurisdictions, whether on or off duty, are expected to be armed and to exercise their authority when necessary.

Education and Other Qualifications

Qualifications for the appointment of police and detectives are usually governed by civil-service regulations. The minimum education required to join a police force is a high-school diploma, but some departments may require one or two years of college coursework or, in some cases, a college degree. Many junior colleges, colleges, and universities offer programs or degrees in law enforcement or administration of justice, and officers with degrees in those subjects usually earn higher salaries.

Graduation from an agency's own academy or training course is also required, followed by on-the-job training. Agencies may pay all or part of the tuition for officers working toward degrees in criminal justice, police science, administration of justice, or public administration, and they pay for the training required to become a K9 handler.

Training Law-Enforcement Dogs

Wherever they work, most law-enforcement dogs are trained at facilities before they are matched with their new partners. One such training school is Adlerhorst International Police K9 Academy in Riverside, California, founded in 1976, which obtains, trains, and sells police dogs. Adlerhorst has trained thousands of dogs over the years, placing them in jobs at airports and with more than 500 police departments nationwide.

The trainers at Adlerhorst are retired police K9 handlers. The dogs, mainly German Shepherd Dogs and Belgian Malinois, are imported from Europe when they are approximately two years old. Besides being physically sound, they must have successfully completed programs that ensure a particular level of socialization and training, such as Schutzhund I or KNPV I certification (KNPV is the acronym, in Dutch, for the Royal Dutch Police Dog Association). The dogs learn skills such as "guard and bark" techniques, search and rescue protocols, and explosive detection. Once trained at the facility, they are paired with police officers who then complete the appropriate training programs with them.

Factors that can determine whether you are accepted for K9 handler training include previous education and experience and good performance in tough written tests. Other requirements, depending on the job, include U.S. citizenship, being at least twenty years old, and being in excellent physical condition.

For instance, police or firefighter applicants must pass physical exams that test vision, hearing, strength, and agility. Playing team sports and participating in other forms of physical activity are good preparation for this type of work because they help to develop competitiveness, teamwork, quickness, and stamina. Knowing a foreign language such as Arabic, Chinese, Spanish, or Vietnamese can also be an asset, especially in working for an urban police or fire department or a federal agency.

Employment Outlook

Working-dog handlers may find employment with local, state, or federal agencies or with private security firms. Job opportunities in most local police departments are expected to be excellent for qualified individuals, although the best-qualified applicants will have an edge. A more security-conscious society and population growth will probably contribute to an

K9 state trooper Devitt gets ready to spring into action. The Canine Unit of the New York State Police grew from three handler-dog teams in 1975 to sixty-six in 2010.

increasing demand for police services. There is greater competition for jobs in state and federal agencies, and only average employment growth is expected in those areas.

According to the U.S. Bureau of Labor Statistics' *Occupational Outlook Handbook*, applicants with military experience or college training in police science will have the best opportunities in local and state departments. Applicants who have a bachelor's degree and have had several years of law-enforcement or military experience, especially investigative experience, will have the best opportunities for obtaining positions in federal agencies.

Salaries for law-enforcement officers who are dog handlers vary depending on such factors as locale and length of service. Federal employees who serve in law enforcement have special salary rates.

Police and sheriff's patrol officers had median annual earnings of $51,410 in May 2008. The lowest 10 percent earned less than $30,070, and the highest 10 percent earned more than $114,300. They may also earn overtime. Median annual earnings of fish and game wardens, who often conduct search and rescue operations, were $48,930. The lowest 10 percent made less than $30,400 and the highest 10 percent made more than $81,710.

The typical working-canine handler is eligible for a special rate of pay under the Fair Labor Standards Act, Officer Kerwick says. It usually allows for a stipend of approximately 5 percent to compensate the officer for feeding and exercising the dog during off hours. In New York City, that percentage comes to approximately $6,000 per year, but it can be considerably less in other parts of the country.

Common benefits for any police officer or local, state, or federal agency employee include paid vacation, sick leave, and medical and life insurance, as well as allowances for uniforms.

LAW-ENFORCEMENT RESOURCES

- Adlerhorst International Police K-9 Academy, www.adlerhorst.com
- All States K9 Detection, www.allstates-k9.com
- Auburn University's Canine Detection and Training Center, www.vetmed.audurn.edu/cdri
- Canine Scent Investigations LLC, www.csidogs.com
- Southern Star Ranch, www.southern-star-ranch.com
- U.S. Police Canine Association, www.uspcak9.com
- Work Dogs International, www.policedogtrainers.com

CHAPTER 29

Other Working-Dog Handlers

There are other working-dog handlers who don't work directly for law-enforcement departments or governmental agencies. Among them are search and rescue (SAR) dog handlers, who are trained to help to find or rescue people who are lost or are victims of natural or man-made disasters such as avalanches, earthquakes, or explosions. They can ply their skills in any part of the country, and many travel the world, helping save lives when disasters occur. Often, they are police or firefighters who do SAR work as part of their jobs, but they may also be civilian volunteers. Unless you are planning a career in police work, firefighting, or a first-responder-type job such as emergency medical technician, search and rescue work will probably not enable you to make a living.

Some handlers and their dogs are employed by businesses to sniff out bedbugs, toxic mold, or termites in buildings and private residences. They and their handlers undergo the same type of training as other detection dogs, but for different scents.

Search and Rescue Dog Handlers

In 1991, just after they became engaged, Heather Houlahan and her husband acquired a German Shepherd puppy. It was only a matter of days before they recognized that she would need a job to keep her busy, and that realization was to change their lives. After investigating various activities they could do

Handler Sue Bulanda (*left*) and Scout take part in a water search with the Phoenixville Fire Department Canine SAR Unit and Phoenixville Fire Department Dive Squad.

with their smart and highly active dog, they settled on what was then the little-known job of search and rescue work. Today, Houlahan is the canine director for the Allegheny Mountain Rescue Group (AMRG).

It takes a special kind of person with a certain lifestyle to become a SAR dog handler. Expect to be on call 24/7. Disasters occur at all times of the day or night and on holidays and weekends. SAR dog handlers, whether they are employees or volunteers, must be ready to go at a moment's notice. Many search and rescue personnel are self-employed or have worked out agreements with their employers that let them take time off when necessary to participate in a search. Houlahan is a dog trainer in regular life, so she has some flexibility.

"I try not to ever cancel a class for a search, but I have," Houlahan says. "In fifteen years, I've only had one objection from a client about my going on a search. A lot of AMRG's members are in public safety professions, and this does create conflicts, because if you are an emergency room physician or a paramedic on an ambulance, you cannot take off. So you may need to wait until your shift is over and find somebody to cover your next one, or you might just miss some searches. We understand that there are times when somebody's not going to be able to come, and we try to have enough redundancy in the organization to make that work."

Who SAR Dog Handlers Are

SAR dog handlers are proficient in land navigation with map and compass, radio communications, wilderness survival, and first aid. Most units require SAR handlers to be certified in advanced first aid with CPR, and that certification must be renewed annually.

You should be able to walk for long distances in all kinds of weather and carry a heavy pack that can weigh as much as 90 pounds. You must traverse all kinds of terrain and rubble with all kinds of footing, and expect to work shifts of up to twelve hours at a time. SAR teams must work effectively with many other people and dogs, and SAR handlers must have some emotional fortitude, as not every search has a happy ending. Instead of rescuing a person, you may find yourself bringing back a body or not finding the person at all.

If you are a volunteer, you must be able to bear the cost of travel and expenses yourself. You may spend a minimum of $1,500 to $2,000 per year to equip and maintain yourself and your dog. Add in mileage, fuel, cell phones, equipment, and dog costs such as food and veterinary care, and you can easily spend $8,000 to $10,000 per year.

Being able to work toward a goal patiently and consistently is essential. Too many people don't have that mindset, Houlahan says. "They love dogs and they want to do something with dogs, but they don't have an orientation toward working at something long-term and building step by step. They want it right now. Over 95 percent, and probably closer to

DO YOU HAVE WHAT IT TAKES?

SAR HANDLER

A SAR handler should have the following characteristics:

- ◯ Enjoy working with dogs
- ◯ A love of the outdoors— no matter what the conditions— and outdoors skills
- ◯ People skills
- ◯ Emotional strength
- ◯ Ability to cover expenses
- ◯ Ability to spend time training and participating in missions
- ◯ Patience
- ◯ Persistence

Timothy Lombardi and Buster, of FEMA's Urban Search and Rescue Response Systems' Ohio Task Force One, wait to be deployed with relief efforts for Hurricane Gustav in Georgia in 2008.

99 percent, of the people who call and say, 'I want to train my dog for search and rescue' will wash out. That's not primarily because the dog can't do it. It's more often a human failure."

Be aware, too, that SAR is a law-enforcement activity. You can be held to standards of documentation that can stand up in court, even if you are a volunteer. That calls for a methodical way of thinking and a fanatical devotion to record-keeping.

The most important realization for many is that SAR is not an opportunity for recognition of heroism. Most often, it is steady, plodding work with the only reward being the satisfaction of a job well done and the pleasure of working in partnership with a dog.

"Search and rescue is about deliberately and methodically doing a job as part of a large effort in such a way that all of your colleagues know that job has been done properly," Houlahan says. "You will not very often be the person who finds that lost kid. In any given search, there may be hundreds of tasks written, and if that search is productive, only one team makes that find. But every other team was able to report back that an area was searched to a high degree of confidence that no one was there, or they may have detected clues or the absence of clues, which can be a clue in itself in some circumstances. So you have to have a Zen consciousness about teamwork and not be trying to hog the headlines. That's tough, because we're asking people to be action-oriented and forward but also patient and cooperative."

SAR Training

Search and rescue work is much more than a walk in the woods. Not every dog or handler can do the work, and both require extensive training. It takes at least a year of training twice a week or more, for a dog/handler team to learn the basics, and one and a half to two years to become completely trained. Many more years of experience are necessary to learn new techniques and become an expert in a particular discipline of search and rescue. Different terrains and different scenarios require

Search Dog Foundation lead trainer Pluis Davern (*right*) works with a canine recruit. Pluis Davern is well known and respected in the field of search and rescue.

different skills, and searching for a person buried in an avalanche is not the same as searching for a person buried in the rubble of an explosion.

"[My husband and I] had a lot of outdoorsy-type skills, which is an excellent place to start," Houlahan says. "Most of the best handlers are people who are very comfortable on foot in the outdoors. But in terms of search and rescue skills, we had to start from scratch."

Types of SAR work for which a team may be trained include wilderness, airscent, scent-specific, water body recovery, human remains detection, disaster live body, and avalanche. All disciplines require specific training. General training may include but isn't limited to searches in confined spaces or collapsed structures, first-aid techniques, and site preservation.

Skills, Experience, and Personal Traits
To succeed in SAR-specific training, a SAR handler should have a strong set of survival skills, acquired before becoming involved in search and

rescue missions. One of the most crucial of those skills is navigation, including the ability to use a map and orienteering compass and navigate a search pattern. "Nowadays, people think they can get away with owning a GPS, but that is not the case," Houlahan says. "Navigation is a skill that you have to acquire and maintain at a very high level."

Other survival skills that come into play are communications and wilderness medicine. Houlahan is now a ham radio operator and is certified as a wilderness emergency medical technician and wilderness first-aid instructor.

There's another, less tangible quality that characterizes a good search and rescue dog handler: being comfortable in an independent situation. While each dog/handler team is part of a group, a search and rescue handler often performs the tasks of a mission with only his or her dog for company—which is not necessarily a drawback, by the way. When they have short-term survival skills and are confident in their knowledge, handlers are more comfortable in their work, making them less likely to wimp out when the going gets tough.

Houlahan also likes to see another personal characteristic: the potential to grow into a management position and develop other SAR teams. People who train SAR teams must be able to manage or work in a volunteer organization, teach all kinds of people and dogs, and understand search strategies and techniques as well as the behavior of lost people.

If you think you might enjoy SAR work at some time in your life, either as part of your career or as a volunteer, you'll have a head start if you develop wilderness skills early on through activities such as hiking, climbing, orienteering, skiing, snowshoeing—you name it. If it's outdoorsy,

BE PREPARED

Don't assume that having a background in dog training or competition will give you an advantage as a SAR handler. Sometimes it's even a disadvantage.

"If your background is in things like obedience or competition with dogs, you have a lot to unlearn," Heather Houlahan says. "That's probably the biggest thing that has to happen with someone who comes from a doggy background as opposed to an outdoorsy background. They need to learn how to work with dogs instead of having the dogs work for them. They don't have the $30,000 nose and the brain that is attached to it, and they need to have respect for both of those things."

Volunteer disaster worker Debbie Walters works with Calvin at Orlando's Urban Search Training Center.

it can help you prepare for this type of work.

Becoming a SAR Dog Handler

Local or national search-dog organizations offer seminars or training, and the National Association for Search and Rescue has an annual conference with seminars. Training is also available from the National Disaster Search Dog Foundation, which trains dogs for SAR work and then places them with handlers.

Expect to meet once or twice a month for training with a local group. Training sessions may last for a few hours or take up a full weekend. In addition, you'll need to train on your own, working with your dog and honing your skills in map and compass reading, survival, first aid, or radio use and communications. Members of Absaroka Search Dogs in Montana estimate that handling a dog adds as much as twenty hours per week to a normal SAR training schedule. To be successful, Houlahan says, you must commit to working with your dog daily, even after you're trained, to maintain your skills and deepen your relationship with your canine partner.

"The teamwork you have to have with other people is nothing compared with the teamwork you have to have with your dog," she says. "If you develop a high level of trust with your dog, when he is having trouble with a scent problem he will look to you and let you know, and you can help work it out because you've got the big brain and the radio and the map and other things that he doesn't. This is all about two-way communication."

Firefighter Linda D'Orsi of Chula Vista, California, works with a good-looking blond partner named Cody. She and the Golden Retriever are members of San Diego County's Urban Search and Rescue Task Force 8. Their job calls for them not only to search for lost people but also to confirm that a search is not needed. For instance, they might investigate a bluff collapse to ensure that no people are buried beneath the rubble. They also travel to disaster scenes, such as New Orleans after Hurricane Katrina. Cody was trained by the National Disaster Search Dog Foundation, which then paired him with D'Orsi.

Commercial Working-Dog Handler

Some detection dogs use their noses to sniff out problems, such as bedbugs, toxic mold, and termites, in buildings and private residences. This type of work requires a dog and handler to undergo intense training, similar to that of any detection-dog team, for the specific scent that they are trying to detect. However, handlers of commercial working dogs such as termite- or mold-sniffing dogs generally work normal hours and do not face the same stresses and dangers that law-enforcement dog handlers do.

Length of training varies depending on what the dog is being trained to search for. Termite-detector dogs are certified after eight to ten months of training. Some trainers have their dogs recertified every three months to ensure that their skills are still "up to sniff."

Some types of commercial detection dogs have restrictions on their use. For instance, dog trainer Sue Bulanda was the first person to successfully train dogs to detect toxic mold, and she holds a patent on the training and use of mold-detection dogs. Anyone who wishes to start a business in this field must

Trainer Sue Bulanda holds Riley, whom she will be training to detect arson.

purchase a license from her; to do otherwise would be a violation of her patent rights.

Employment

Search and rescue dog handlers are generally volunteers, although, as mentioned, police officers, firefighters, and other first responders can become SAR handlers as part of their jobs. There is always a need for well-trained teams in any area of the country.

Handlers of commercial working dogs often own their own businesses, and their work with dogs

Sue Bulanda trained Jib, a SAR dog, to detect toxic mold, proving a detector dog could be cross-trained.

At the age of nine, household pet Lily became the first dog trained to detect toxic mold in homes and other buildings. Sue Bulanda developed the training scent and trained Lily.

may be only a part of those businesses. While the income they bring in may vary, depending on the area of the country in which they work, dogs that can sniff out bedbugs or termites may be leased out for as much as $200 per hour or thousands of dollars annually. A dog handler who works for a pest-detection business may make $60,000 or more annually.

OTHER HANDLERS RESOURCES

- Florida Canine Academy, www.mold-dog.com
- National Association for Search and Rescue, www.nasar.org/nasar
- National Disaster Search Dog Foundation, www.searchdogfoundation.org
- National Entomology Scent Detection Canine Association, www.nesdca.com
- National Police Bloodhound Association, www.npba.com

- *READY! The Training of the Search and Rescue Dog*, by Susan Bulanda. 2nd edition. Kennel Club Books, 2010.
- *Ready to Serve, Ready to Save: Strategies of Real-Life Search and Rescue Missions,* by Susan Bulanda. Doral Publishing, 1994.
- *Scenting on the Wind: Scent Work for Hunting Dogs,* by Susan Bulanda. Doral Publishing, 2002.

Pet-Oriented Professions and Industry Careers

Many careers do not necessarily involve working directly with animals, but they can be in professions with an orientation toward animals or in pet-related industries or businesses. Such careers include animal-law attorney, librarian of a special collection, and therapists who deal with loss of animals or are assisted by dogs in their therapy work. In industry, there are careers involving selling advertising for pet-related magazines and marketing and promotions positions with companies that make or sell pet products. Many people who love animals have found their way into these positions because of a background in showing dogs or some other interest in or experience with animals.

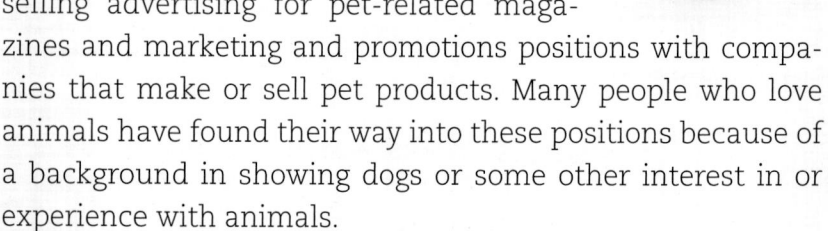

CHAPTER 30

Attorney, Librarian, and Therapists

Lawyers, librarians, physical therapists, and psychologists all have a place in the world of dogs and other animals. Lawyers shape the many laws relating to animals or prosecute animal-related cases. Librarians assemble and disseminate information about dogs. Psychologists and physical therapists work with their canine partners to help people deal with problems in their lives or to help people regain their physical faculties or work on behavioral, emotional, or learning problems.

Animal-Law Attorney

The specialty of animal law is an emerging field, but laws regarding animals have existed for centuries. Many laws affect companion animals, captive animals, food animals, and wild animals at local, state, federal, and international levels. Recent rulings, such as the 2010 Supreme Court decision that struck down a federal law banning depictions of animal cruelty, as well as legislative attempts by states and cities to mandate certain types of pet care (such as spay/neuter surgery) or prohibit others (such as declawing) illustrate how important animal law has become in our society.

Attorneys in the field of animal law work to promote animal protection and welfare through legal reform. They may fight breed-specific legislation or take cases that involve the custody of an animal, veterinary malpractice, disputes relating to pet clauses in leases or homeowners' association rules,

Phorest, owned and handled by attorney Robert Newman, wins the Hound Group at Rosa City Cluster in 2010. Newman, who breeds Pharaoh Hounds, specializes in animal law.

domestic-violence protection for pets, class action suits against commercial pet breeders, the establishment of pet trusts, or the disposition of a pet after the owner's death. Some lawyers who specialize in animal law work for humane organizations or community groups to strengthen protections for animals, either in court or as lobbyists.

Issues that animal-law practitioners can expect to face in the future are pet-food safety, breed-ban legislation, loss of companionship, regulation of complementary and alternative therapies (such as acupuncture and homeopathy), and the definition and prosecution of animal abuse. The loss of companionship issue is becoming one of the seminal topics in animal law. This is the question of whether animals are merely property or deserve greater consideration by the law as companions in the event of injury or death through veterinary or other professional negligence.

Other aspects of animal law include advising businesses such as boarding or training facilities or pet-sitting, dog-walking, or poop-scooping services on insurance, liability, and other legal matters. Lawyers draft contracts and releases, arbitrate disputes, and defend clients from lawsuits. Veterinary malpractice and custody cases are most common in the experience of animal-law attorney Robert Newman. He says that young lawyers will make the most progress in animal law. "The groundwork has been laid for changes in laws regarding animals, and those changes will come with young, up-and-coming lawyers in this area."

Education and Training

Becoming a lawyer requires a bachelor's degree, plus three or more years in law school to earn a doctor of jurisprudence degree. Before practicing, a lawyer must pass the bar exam for his or her state. Federal courts and agencies set their own qualifications for those practicing before or in them.

More than 100 law schools in the United States offer animal-law courses or seminars. Among those with programs in animal law are George Washington University Law School, Washington, D.C.; the Center for Animal Law Studies at Lewis and Clark Law School, Portland, Oregon; and the University of Virginia School of Law, Charlottesville. At Georgetown University, in Washington, D.C., the program includes a seminar on animal law and wildlife protection and externships with humane organizations.

Employment

Although interest in animal law is growing, there are few full-time jobs in the field. Generally, those positions are with animal-protection organizations or government agencies. Most lawyers with an interest in animal law volunteer with animal-related projects.

It can be difficult to make a living in animal law because many states limit awards to no more than the animal's replacement value, disallowing sentimental value or emotional damages.

DO YOU HAVE WHAT IT TAKES?

ATTORNEY

An attorney should have the following characteristics:

○ A logical mind
○ A talent for argumentation
○ Research ability
○ Good mediation skills
○ Excellent written and verbal skills
○ Integrity
○ Perseverance

Many animal-law attorneys are challenging these legal precedents, however. Although there are no statistics on the salaries of animal-law attorneys, law-school graduates in general earn a starting salary of approximately $60,000.

Librarian

Organizations and companies with dog-centric libraries include the American Kennel Club (AKC); the National Sporting Library and Museum (NSL); pet-food companies such as Nestlé Purina, which has a library services department to assist employees with research; and veterinary schools. Even if a dog-loving librarian doesn't seek a job in the rarefied world of specialty, university, or corporate libraries, he or she may oversee a program in which children read to dogs to practice their skills, select books for a library's pet section, or help patrons find the next great dog book to read.

In addition to the AKC and the NSL, several libraries have canine literature and field-sports collections. They include the Cleveland Public Library; the Chapin-Horowitz Collection of Cynogetica, part of the Earl Gregg Swem Library at Virginia's College of William and Mary; and the John S. Best Collection at the Golda Meir Library of the University of Wisconsin.

At the Cleveland Public Library, the collection contains more than 3,000 books on breeds, care and training, canine psychology, breeding, showing, and kennel management. Stud books from the AKC, the Canadian Kennel Club, and The Kennel Club (United Kingdom) are a treasure trove for breeders.

The Chapin-Horowitz collection is one of the largest collections of books about dogs in the country, second only to that of the AKC's library. It contains scholarly works dating to the sixteenth century, plus children's books, breed books, and various AKC publications and records.

The Museum of Hounds and Hunting North America is home to The Memorial Reading Room, which contains books, papers, and magazines; maps; and videos pertaining to hunting with hounds. Open by appointment only, it is located in the mansion on the grounds of historic Morven Park in Leesburg, Virginia.

DO YOU HAVE WHAT IT TAKES?

LIBRARIAN

A librarian should have the following characteristics:

- ○ Research ability
- ○ Curiosity and perseverance
- ○ Excellent written and verbal skills
- ○ Good people skills

Librarians help patrons find the information they need, often using the most advanced electronic resources. Librarians follow trends in publishing, computers, and the media—not to mention dogs, if that's their field—so they can make the best choices when selecting library materials. They develop information programs and systems for their clients, whether they are schoolchildren, vet students, staff members for humane groups, advertising or marketing managers, or dog breeders and exhibitors.

Education and Training

A master of library science (MLS) degree is the ticket to one of these jobs. Most MLS programs take one to two years to complete. Most library science programs also require knowledge of two foreign languages, one of which may be a computer language. A librarian who wants to work at a veterinary school should have a strong knowledge of the sciences. Your undergraduate degree can be in any field of interest, but if your goal is to work in a canine specialty library, you'll need to hone your dog knowledge as well.

Ciara Farrell, The Kennel Club library and collections manager, displays a rare dog book to interested fanciers. She wears special gloves to protect the pages from skin oils.

Employment

This isn't a field with huge growth potential, and it's hard to land one of the rare positions with a dog-related organization. Nonetheless, many librarians will be retiring over the next decade, so the Bureau of Labor Statistics predicts that job opportunities will be favorable.

Salaries of librarians vary according to the individual's qualifications and the type, size, and location of the library. Librarians who are administrators usually earn the highest salaries. Median annual earnings of librarians in May 2008 were $52,530. The lowest 10 percent earned less than $33,190, and the highest 10 percent earned more than $81,130.

Grief Counselors

Many factors influence the decisions people make regarding the care and death of a pet, and each must be weighed against the pet's well-being. A grief counselor can help pet owners ask the right questions and work through difficult concerns such as what quality of life means and whether the owner is equipped to provide the care a sick or dying animal needs.

Betty J. Carmack, EdD, RN, author of *Grieving the Death of a Pet* (Augsburg Books, 2002), has been a professor at the University of San Francisco School of Nursing since 1975 and a pet-loss counselor since 1982. She gives workshops related to pet loss and speaks to veterinary and vet tech students as well as to veterinary professionals. She says there is more acceptance of grieving for pets now and more support groups are being started, both at brick-and-mortar institutions and online.

These counselors may work at pet hospitals, such as Animal Medical Center in New York, which pioneered grief counseling for pet owners. Clients may be facing decisions about a pet's health care involving painful surgery, debilitating chemotherapy, or costs beyond the owner's means. Counselors can help pet owners examine their feelings about treatment, evaluate the

> ## DO YOU HAVE WHAT IT TAKES?
>
> ### GRIEF COUNSELOR/ THERAPIST
>
> A grief counselor and a pet-assisted therapist should have the following characteristics:
>
> - ○ Emotional stability
> - ○ Sensitivity and compassion
> - ○ Good verbal and written communication skills
> - ○ Ability to inspire respect, trust, and confidence
> - ○ Desire to help others

pet's chances with or without treatment, and explore alternatives. The most important benefit is the chance for a pet owner to express grief to someone who cares. Says Carmack, "People come to the pet loss support groups that I lead and talk about how people say things like 'It's been two weeks; aren't you over it?' Or they'll hear people talking about them, saying, 'It was just a dog.' "

Education and Training

There is no licensing for pet loss bereavement counselors, but an ethical counselor of any stripe will have an education in psychology or counseling. Education and training requirements for counselors vary by state and specialty, but at a minimum a master's degree is required to become a licensed or certified counselor. Departments of education, psychology, or human services at universities may offer education programs in counseling. A typical accredited master's degree program includes a period of supervised clinical experience in counseling. Counselors must often take continuing-education courses to maintain their certificates and licenses. Pet grief counselors often have a psychology or counseling practice in other areas as well or teach at college level.

Psychologists or counselors who wish to specialize in grief counseling may complete a program such as the professional certificate in the study of grief and loss, offered by the University of California at Berkeley's extension school, or become certified in thanatology (the study of death and dying) through the Association for Death Education and Counseling. A ten-hour course in pet grief counseling techniques is offered by the Association for Pet Loss and Bereavement (APLB). The APLB also offers an internship program.

Employment

Psychology and counseling are fields in which employment is growing. Psychologists or counselors interested in pet grief therapy may find jobs at large

Barkworthy BITE

A PET'S LEGACY

"As people in my group go around and tell their stories, they give a witness to the place the animal had in their lives and to the relationship they shared. And what we loved when pets were alive with us, we continue to love when they're no longer physically present. People need to be reminded that the relationship does not end. Their presence in your life is in a different form, but that legacy and those lessons can continue in people's lives." —Betty J. Carmack, grief counselor animal hospitals, at humane organizations such as the American Society for the Prevention of Cruelty to Animals, or in private practice. In 2008, approximately 34 percent of psychologists were self-employed. Some also hold faculty positions at colleges and universities.

A pet grief counselor's income usually ranges from $23,000 to $63,000, depending on location and type of practice and whether the counselor also offers counseling or psychological treatment in other areas.

Therapists

Some therapists use canine cotherapists to offer comfort, help clients develop a rapport with the therapist, and even help the therapist determine what a patient's is suffering from. These dogs provide support to people in the aftermath of crisis and can be trusted confidants to children afraid to tell their secrets to adults. Psychologist Lois Abrams refers to her Cavalier King Charles Spaniels, Duke and Romeo, as "Seeing Heart Dogs." Her clients say the presence of the dogs makes them feel welcome and secure and that touching the dogs is calming. Therapy fields incorporating animals include psychotherapy, physical therapy, recreational therapy, and speech therapy.

Pet-Assisted Psychotherapist

Judy Welch, PsyD, a psychologist and family therapist in Thousand Oaks, California, shares her office with a partner. Not the kind of partner you might think, though: Louie is a Dachshund who assists Welch in tending to the emotional needs of her clients. The long-backed dog with the chocolate-brown coat has the ability to sense and respond appropriately to people's emotions. His presence often helps to decrease clients' anxiety, a bonus for people suffering from depression or feeling overwhelmed by problems. Louie also helps patients make emotional connections that help them to cope with fear or resistance to change. Louie even has his own credentials: he's an AKC Canine Good Citizen and a certified therapy dog. Including dogs as part of psychotherapy isn't new. The first book to address the subject was written in 1969, but references date to before the eighteenth century. More recently, many articles have cited the effectiveness of animals in clinical psychological settings.

Education and Training: A master's or doctorate degree in psychology, social work, or therapy is required to enter this field. For more information on training, see the section on grief counselor on the previous page. There are no training programs for psychotherapists who work with dogs, but Abrams believes therapists should take their dogs through basic and intermediate obedience courses, ideally with a trainer who uses positive reinforcement techniques. She says dogs should also have Canine Good Citizen titles, and dog and handler should be trained in animal-assisted therapy through an organization such as the Delta Society and Therapy Dogs International. Therapists should also be familiar with dog behavior so they can interpret canine body language.

Employment: Jobs for psychologists as counselors or therapists are expected to grow by 11 to 14 percent through 2018. Prospects are best for people with doctorates. Approximately 34 percent of psychologists are in private practice. Median annual wages of clinical and counseling psychologists were $64,140 in May 2008. The lowest 10 percent earned less than $37,900, and the highest 10 percent earned more than $106,840.

Pet-Assisted Physical, Occupational, and Speech Therapy

Physical, occupational, and speech therapists who work with people sometimes have pet partners in their practices. A canine assistant in a

Psychotherapist Jane Miller looks on as her Golden Retriever cotherapists, Simcha and Ahava, interact with a client. Miller also trains psychiatric service dogs.

Portrait of a Psychotherapist

Jane Miller (*pictured with Simcha and Ahava*) always had a connection to animals. Her interests led her to obtain a degree in psychology and biology from Oberlin College, a background that she describes as a wonderful intertwining of the human mind and body and the animal mind and body. She became immersed in human and animal behavior.

"I wanted to do something that would make a difference in the world, and I really wanted to work with people," she says. So after Oberlin, she went to graduate school in social work. "Social work gave me incredible flexibility because I could do advocacy work, public policy, teaching. It gave me a lot of realms I could explore."

Miller was working as a psychotherapist in a group practice with terminally and chronically ill clients when her Golden Retriever Umaya was diagnosed with a rare fibrosarcoma. Umaya needed radiation treatments for eighteen consecutive days, so Miller began bringing Umaya with her to the office after each treatment.

The presence of her jovial dog with the bald rear end radically changed the waiting room atmosphere. "You'd hear people laughing and giggling out there because Umaya would be so silly greeting them and so filled with life. They'd come in the office, and Umaya would sit beside them, lie on the floor with them, or get on the couch with them. They'd be patting her, and I can't tell you the stories that would come out. I was seeing severe trauma survivors at that point, and I'd hear these horrible incest stories and it was like my clients weren't even aware they were sharing it because they were petting Umaya. [She] was a big part of their therapeutic process."

Miller, author of *Healing Companions: Ordinary Dogs and Their Extraordinary Power to Transform Lives* (New Page Books, 2010), trains psychiatric service dogs and lectures on the legal, ethical, and practical aspects of working with them. She continues to work with her two dogs as cotherapists. Miller says, "My dogs love going to work with me and greet clients with excitement and affection." She believes the sheer joy, comfort, and calm they bring to the therapeutic milieu is healing and transforming for her clients.

physical-therapy practice may help patients improve their strength, mobility, and balance through therapy sessions that may involve brushing and petting a dog for tactile stimulation or to increase range of motion, standing and tossing a ball for the dog, and reaching down to retrieve the ball. To help clients improve social skills, practice problem-solving, or increase self-confidence and motivation, an occupational therapist may have clients give commands, participate in socialization events, or write about or draw the dog. Not only are the patients working on learning or relearning skills but they also get the enjoyment of being with a dog. A speech therapist may have his or her clients give a dog commands or may ask them to remember information about the dog to improve short-term memory.

Education and Training: Susie Roof is a physical therapist who has worked with pets in her job at Saddleback Memorial Medical Center. In addition to a high level of education—usually a doctorate or at a minimum a master's degree in physical therapy—she says that a physical therapist needs extremely good people skills, including the ability to relate to many different personality types.

Employment: Physical therapy is expected to grow rapidly, by as much as 30 percent, through 2018. As the population ages, increasing the number of senior citizens, the need for physical therapists will increase. Employment for speech therapists has a favorable outlook. The field is expected to grow by 19 percent through 2018. Occupational therapy is another growing field with good prospects. Employment of occupational therapists is expected to grow by 26 percent through 2018.

Median annual wages of physical therapists were $72,790 in May 2008. The lowest 10 percent earned less than $50,350, and the highest 10 percent earned more than $104,350. Salaries for speech therapists range from $41,000 to $99,000. Occupational therapists can earn $42,000 to $98,000.

PET-ORIENTED PROFESSIONAL RESOURCES

- AKC Library, www.akc.org/about/library
- American Library Association, www.ala.org
- American Physical Therapy Association, www.apta.org
- American Veterinary Medical Law Association, www.avmla.org
- *Animal-Assisted Brief Therapy: A Solution-Focused Approach,* by Teri Pichot and Marc Coulter. Routledge, 2007.
- *Animal-Assisted Therapy in Counseling,* by Cynthia K. Chandler. Routledge, 2005.
- Animal Legal Defense Fund, www.aldf.org
- Argus Institute, Colorado State University, www.argusinstitute.colostate.edu
- Association for Pet Loss and Bereavement, www.aplb.org
- Love on a Leash, www.loveonaleash.org
- Seattle Animal Lawyer, www.seattleanimallawyer.com
- Special Libraries Association, www.sla.org
- The Delta Society, www.deltasociety.org
- *The Handbook on Animal-Assisted Therapy: Theoretical Foundations and Guidelines for Practice,* edited by Aubrey H. Fine. 2nd edition. Academic Press, 2006.
- *The Loss of a Pet: A Guide to Coping with the Grieving Process When a Pet Dies,* 3rd ed., by Wallace Sife. Howell Book House, 2005.
- Therapy Dogs Inc., www.therapydogs.com
- Therapy Dogs International, www.tdi-dog.org

CHAPTER 31

Product Developers, Marketers, and Retailers

As dogs have become members of the family, pet owners have begun to look more closely at what their animals eat, what they wear, what they play with, and where they sleep. Pet-food manufacturers and product designers have responded by creating ever more specialty products for dogs, cats, and other companion animals.

To market these pet products, manufacturers turn to marketers and advertisers. Then there are the people who sell the products at retail stores such as PETCO and PetSmart as well as boutiques and other pet-supply places. Working at a pet-supply store is a good way to gain work experience as well as to learn about the pet industry, either in a managerial or a staff position. American Pet Products Association predicted that owners would spend $45.4 billion on pet products in 2010 alone.

Pet-Food Developer

Not everyone is satisfied with commercially available foods. Some people go on to manufacture pet food to their own exacting standards. Lucy Postins, founder and president of The Honest Kitchen, is one of them. Postins, who holds a bachelor's degree in equine business studies from Moreton Morrell College of Agriculture in the United Kingdom, began her education in pet food when she was hired as an equine nutritionist for a U.S. manufacturer. Eventually, she moved into the company's canine and feline

division, acquiring a puppy along the way. The desire to provide him with a top-quality diet led her to experiment with a raw diet prepared at home.

"It was very time-consuming and messy, and I ended up in a kitchen covered in broccoli and all sorts of horrible things," Postins says. The experience sparked the idea to create a dehydrated food that would be simple, convenient, and easy to store while offering nutritional benefits.

Pet-food developer Lucy Postins meets with a canine "consultant."

"It took about eighteen months or so to get the first recipe together. I put together different meal combinations for my dog, and whatever he approved of got short-listed and whatever he didn't approve of got scratched. I put together formulations using spreadsheets and then evaluated everything against the AAFCO nutrient profile and started it from that," Postins says. She started The Honest Kitchen in 2002 with a single formulation.

One of the next hurdles was to find a manufacturing facility capable of meeting the production standards for human food. "I didn't want my food made in a pet-food plant," Postins says. "I wanted it to be made right alongside food made for people." Postins has also made the effort to use high-quality human-grade ingredients, such as free-range chicken and turkey, a goal that was important to her personal ethics.

"I think probably one of the more peculiar things about our business is that it was started not to be a business but to fulfill a need for my own dog and for my friends' dogs, and it was just intended to be a very small business," Postins says. "People are fascinated to hear that we didn't actually just sit down and go 'OK, how are we going to make some money?' There's more of an underlying purpose to what we do." Postins was motivated to create her own company, but that is not the only route to a career in pet-food manufacturing.

Pet-Food Manufacturing Positions

There are several positions in private companies and the government. Here are a few of them.

Ingredient-development scientist: This scientist identifies, evaluates, and develops new ingredients or sources for ingredients; designs feeding or shelf-life studies; follows ingredient trends; evaluates and modifies recipes to meet nutritional adequacy; assesses potential risks of reformulation; and recommends quality-control criteria.

Product-development scientist: This scientist develops and implements new products and processes; identifies new or innovative food technologies; documents factory trials; develops raw material specifications; coordinates feeding trials; and ensures that products meet nutritional requirements.

Food scientist: The food scientists working for government agencies inspect food-processing areas, enforce regulations, and ensure manufacturers meet standards for safety, sanitation, quality, and waste management.

Education and Training

An ingredient-development scientist will likely have a degree in biology, chemistry, animal sciences, or agricultural sciences, or in chemical, mechanical, or food engineering. A product-development scientist may have a master's degree in food science with an emphasis in food engineering. Lucy Postins's degree was unusual in that it combined an education in nutrition, anatomy, and physiology with courses in business, marketing, and finance. She has additional training in some holistic modalities, including homeopathy and herbal medicine.

DO YOU HAVE WHAT IT TAKES?

PET-FOOD DEVELOPER

A pet-food developer should have the following characteristics:

○ An appropriate educational background
○ An interest in animal nutrition
○ Good written and verbal communication skills
○ Knowledge of food-ingredient technology
○ Ability to design and conduct animal-feeding studies
○ Basic statistics and computer skills
○ Good understanding of consumer and market testing

Swedish dog-toy designer Nina Ottosson poses with two of her Bouviers des Flandres product testers.

Employment

The BLS predicts that food-science jobs will grow by 16 percent through 2018. Job opportunities are expected to be good in all fields of food science, including pet food. Consumer demand for improvement in the safety and quality of pet food will be an important factor.

Depending on the position, level of experience, and whether they work for government or industry, food scientists and related professionals may earn salaries of $33,000 to more than $100,000. If you create and successfully market your own brand of dog food, the financial reward could be much higher. The Honest Kitchen had revenue of $3.5 million in 2007.

Pet Product Designer and Manufacturer

When Sonya Sargent brought home her new Jack Russell Terrier puppy, Gidget, a few years ago, she was frustrated because she couldn't find a collar Gidget found comfortable. Her husband suggested that she make Gidget a collar. "You can't make dog collars at home," Sargent replied.

But she sought out a pattern for making a collar, and although the resulting cotton flannel collar was, in Sargent's words, "sad and ugly and crooked," it apparently suited Gidget, who stopped scratching at her neck. A passion to create comfortable, safe, pretty products for pets was born.

"My sewing got better, and I launched a little company called If It Wags with $5 and an old sewing machine," Sargent says. "I happily worked that company for five years, sewing, packing, and shipping everything myself. In 2008, I had matured into a person who was not just concerned with the safety and comfort of pets but also passionate about caring for the environment. From this passion, my current company, Wagging Green, was born." The company makes earth-friendly leashes, collars, identification tags, and T-shirts for pets.

What Product Designers Do

Pet-product designers create collars, leashes, pet clothing, grooming tools, toys, and more, or they use their design skills to improve existing products. They may be employed by large pet-related manufacturing or development corporations, they may design products independently for many different companies, or they may own their own businesses.

In whatever they create, people who design and manufacture pet products are concerned with style, function, quality, and safety. Creation of a new product starts with the design idea. The designer then determines the product's specific characteristics: size, shape, weight, color, materials, cost, ease of use, fit, and safety. Sources for this type of information include clients, market research; design publications; consumer magazines, such as *Dog Fancy* and *Dog World*; pet trade shows; and suppliers and manufacturers.

In the pet-product field, designers also rely on their own knowledge of dogs. Swedish dog-toy designer Nina Ottosson recognized that dogs have different levels of intelligence and varying abilities, so she created toys and games with different levels of difficulty.

DO YOU HAVE WHAT IT TAKES?

PRODUCT DESIGNER

A pet-product designer should have the following characteristics:

- ○ Creativity
- ○ Technical knowledge
- ○ Sketching ability
- ○ Knowledge of computer-aided design software
- ○ An eye for color and detail
- ○ A sense of balance and proportion
- ○ Imagination
- ○ Persistence
- ○ Good verbal and written communication skills
- ○ Problem-solving ability

Tracy Swinea stirs up a batch of natural soaps for her canine customers. She began her career making soap for people but changed focus when her dog developed skin problems.

Next, designers prepare sketches or diagrams of the proposed product, which can allow them to create 3-D digital models and tweak them. They may consult with engineers or accountants to discuss product safety, assembly, and cost of manufacture. They may make prototypes for pet owners and dogs to try out and then make adjustments based on responses.

Once the product has been designed and tested, it is ready for manufacturing. It may be made by the designer or produced by a factory. Sargent doesn't sew Wagging Green's products herself, but she oversees the workroom and trains everyone who sews the products.

Finished products can be sold wholesale to pet-supply stores or boutiques. This entails attending pet-product trade shows, where products can be seen by buyers, and pitching the product directly to retailers. Some pet-product makers sell directly to consumers via the Internet. They may also advertise in magazines or other publications, exhibit and sell their products at dog shows or similar events, or open retail storefronts.

CHECK PATENTS

Check with the U.S. Patent and Trademark Office at www.uspto.gov to make sure your idea hasn't already been patented by someone else. Do this early on in the process, not at the last minute. You don't want to have gone through the hard work only to find at the last minute that you can't make your product because someone else has the rights to it.

Getting Started

Ottosson started Zoo Active Products AB in 1993 when she was looking for a way to entertain, train, and mentally stimulate her two Bouviers des Flandres, large and intelligent herding-breed dogs who needed more work than she could give them after her two daughters were born. She came up with the idea of hiding treats in different ways for the dogs to find, and she now has a line of toys based on the same idea. Today, Ottosson's toys are recommended by behaviorists, trainers, veterinarians, and dog owners, and the company does product development, design, and manufacturing, with sales and distribution to wholesalers and retailers in many countries.

For a pet-product designer who works for him- or herself, simply starting a business is the biggest challenge. "Having the courage to leave a stable

Stephanie Blank displays one of her her dog-themed products, a toy box that can be customed designed for different breeds.

job with vacation time and health care and strike out into the unknown was really hard to do," Sargent says. "It's taking a giant leap of faith that things will work out." She recommends doing market research and writing a business plan to make sure everything is well thought out. A plan will help ensure that you don't forget any important details.

Ask friends, family members, and strangers if they would buy the type of product you have in mind, research where and how you can have your product made, and talk to suppliers before putting a lot of effort into design and production. For instance, Stella Clary, who built a business designing attractive covers for dog crates, spent nearly eight months testing and perfecting her design before going into production.

Cost is always a factor, no matter how well prepared you are or how creative your design. Starting a new product line is expensive. To be successful, Clary says, offer a product or service that fills a need in the marketplace, use only the best materials and craftspeople, inspect products for quality before shipping, and give excellent customer service. It's difficult to compete when price is the only thing that differentiates your product.

Education and Training

People who design products may hold bachelor's or advanced degrees in art, industrial design, engineering, and they may have taken courses in such areas as principles of design, sketching, computer-aided design, industrial materials and processes, and manufacturing methods. Classes in anthropology and psychology are useful as well when it comes to studying what people want or will buy. To round out their education, some designers obtain master's degrees in business administration.

Barkworthy ADVICE

TALK, ASK, CONSIDER
Stephanie Blank, owner of Blankety Blank Designs! Inc., offers good advice to would-be product designers who want to start their own businesses: Talk to as many people in related fields as you can. Visit as many pet-related trade shows as possible. Speak to reps and visit showrooms to find like-minded people with whom you feel comfortable. Ask yourself how much time you are willing to be away from home. For example, will you set up booths and travel to trade shows or would you rather hire a great rep to do it for you? Consider whether you need a creative or financial partner. Realize that you must be ready for all your wishes to come true.

Portrait of a Product Designer

Stephanie Blank (*pictured with Mr. Bigg*) majored in fine art and graphic design in college, but she first found her calling for product design at the sales end of the spectrum. While still in school, she was recruited by some friends to help them sell a giftware line at a trade show.

"I didn't know a purchase order from an invoice or a COD from OCD, but I loved selling and was really good at it," she says. "My friends asked me to stay on and work for them as an in-house sales rep."

After three years, Blank had learned how to run a business and, with her friends' blessing, left to start her own company, Blankety Blank Designs! Inc., relying on her background in art, collage, and a collection of ephemera (paper items) to get started.

"I started small, working from my kitchen table. I made some samples, created a business plan, and right out of the chute hired a sales team with a showroom in Dallas. Almost instantly, I started receiving orders and suddenly the kitchen table was too small! I needed a studio, a nanny, a bookkeeper, packers, shippers, and as much help as I could find—right away!"

In 1996, Blank's line began to evolve into a pet line, thanks to her Bernese Mountain Dog puppy, Homer. She began making frames and boxes with different dog breeds on them. Within two years, the pet designs had become the greater part of her business. Homer became a "spokesdog" and shook hands and gave kisses to all potential customers at trade shows.

Blank's challenges included not being prepared for an onslaught of orders, not having adequate space or help, and not being prepared for the amount of work and time it took to stay on top of filling orders, making samples for reps, and running a household, not to mention having a baby the same year.

Sargent has a bachelor's degree in fashion design with a minor in fashion merchandising. After college, she went into soft-goods buying. Her jobs included working for Bed, Bath & Beyond as a bedding buyer and for April Cornell as an accessories and children's clothing buyer, so she had a good background in design, purchasing, and merchandising.

Ottosson worked in health care for seventeen years and had no design education. What she had was a knowledge of dogs and a persistent nature.

Dogs Take to the Catwalk

"It all started with a little Yorkie named Manfred. Manfred did not like the cold winter weather in Sweden, so we started designing clothes for him to wear during our daily walks in the neighborhood." Ann Gärdsby (*pictured with Manfred*) went from clothing one small dog with style and flair to creating a thriving internationally acclaimed fashion company offering high-end dog apparel and

accessories. Named Manfred of Sweden, the company clothes and accessorizes the canine companions of such celebrities as Robin Williams, Kelly Osbourne, and Amy Tan. Manfred, who travels the world with his people, has promenaded on fashion runways from New York to Tokyo, modeling MoS designs ranging from a bad-boy black leather biker jacket, complete with straps, pockets, and pawcuffs, to a choir-boy white silk jacket sporting pearls and angel wings.

Haute dog fashion is in. New York and Tokyo host Pet Fashion Week shows to display woofwear for pets of the rich and famous—and people who just like their dogs to show a little style. Besides Manfred of Sweden, international couturiers for canines include DoggiDog Paris, Milan's For Pets Only, and MODRuff. The material dogs they dress wear everything from Swarovski crystals and metallic leather to faux fur and stretchy sport fabrics.

If you're a would-be pet clothing designer, study fashion at art school and hone your hand-stitching and custom-fitting skills on items for your own dogs and those of your friends and relatives. The curriculum at New York's Fashion Institute of Technology includes a pet product design and marketing segment. Courses in psychology (for predicting what people will buy), mathematics (for manipulating angles, shapes, and movement), and canine anatomy will also be useful. If you're already confident in your sewing and design prowess, study trends in styles, colors, and fabrics, and start planning your collection.

Clary also did not have any background in product design, art, or manufacturing, but she is a self-taught seamstress with a business-school degree who combined her love of dogs with her enjoyment of working with fabric.

Employment Outlook

The job market for product designers in general is highly competitive and is often outsourced to designers overseas. For salaried positions, it helps to have a strong background in engineering and computer-aided design, but it's not essential for success in independent pet-product design. Employment of commercial and industrial designers as a whole, not solely for pet products, will probably grow as fast as the average for all occupations, thanks to an expected increase in consumer and business demand for products that are new and improved, safe, and high-quality. These types of jobs are frequently affected negatively by economic downturns, however. When companies need to cut costs, spending on research and development for new products is often one of the first things to go.

Commercial and industrial designers who are salaried can earn a median annual income of $57,350. The salary range is $31,000 to nearly $98,000. Income for designers and manufacturers who are self-employed is much more variable, depending on the type of products and their success in marketing them.

Advertisers and Marketers

There are many different positions in the fields of advertising and marketing, and their success can be judged by the size of the market for pet products and pet care—it's a billion-dollar industry. Ad agencies that specialize in the pet field are few, however, and it's unlikely that you will be able to work solely on products in a specific industry, such as pet treats, unless you are hired for an in-house position at a pet-product company.

People who specialize in marketing can work for pet-food companies and other pet-related businesses. They may also work for agencies that specialize in marketing and promotions. Their jobs call for them to estimate the demand for products and services offered by a company and its competitors and to identify potential markets. They develop pricing strategies that help the business maximize profits and market share while ensuring that customers are satisfied with and willing to buy what the company is selling.

Managerial and Nonmanagerial Positions

There are several different types of managerial and nonmanagerial positions in marketing and advertising. Here are a few.

Advertising manager: An advertising manager oversees the company's advertising and promotions staffs. He or she may serve as a liaison between the firm and an advertising or promotion agency or may oversee in-house account-, creative-, and media-services departments at, for instance, a pet-food company. Whatever the product or service advertising managers are selling, their job is to plan and manage print, TV, radio, and Internet ad campaigns by conducting research, devising strategies to get their messages across, doing the concept and pre-production work necessary to create advertisements, and hiring production companies to create props and special effects, do filming, and do editing and other post-production work.

Animal Health Foundation executive director Pam Becker got into sales as a product demonstrator, talking about the nutritious food she gave Bentley, Mia, and Abby.

Marketing manager: Marketing jobs also entail monitoring trends that indicate the need for new products and services and to oversee product development. Marketing managers work with advertising and promotions managers to promote a company's products and services, develop new products or reinvent old ones, conduct consumer research studies, develop attractive packaging, and catch the attention of potential consumers.

The job of a marketing manager may be to direct a field-support marketing group, manage local marketing efforts for the field sales force, and plan and manage special events. Marketing and breeder programs must be developed to fit the requirements of a market. Marketing managers help to plan and manage company-sponsored dog and cat shows and trade shows.

Brand manager: A brand manager at a pet food company may be involved in developing a multimedia advertising campaign or launching a new dog treat. Brand managers talk to consumers to find out their needs and desires when it comes to pet foods and treats, and then meet with retail clients such as Wal-Mart or PetSmart. Sometimes they specialize in targeting a specific market, such as veterinarians or pet owners.

Promotions manager: Promotions managers direct programs that combine advertising with purchase incentives to increase sales. To establish closer contact with purchasers—breeders, distributors, or pet owners— promotions managers may implement programs that use direct mail, telemarketing, television or radio advertising, catalogs, exhibits, inserts in newspapers, Web sites or Internet advertisements, in-store displays, product endorsements, or special events. Purchasing incentives may include discounts, samples, gifts, rebates, coupons, sweepstakes, and contests.

Sales managers: These managers assign territories to salespeople, set goals, establish training programs for sales representatives, and advise sales representatives on ways to improve their sales performance. In large firms with many products, sales managers oversee regional and local sales managers and their staffs. They analyze sales statistics gathered by their staff members to determine sales potential and inventory requirements and to monitor customer preferences.

Sales representative: These representatives specialize in certain types of clients. For example, a salesperson in the veterinary market works to get veterinary clinics to carry or use the company's products, get good placement in the clinics for the products,

Product Demonstrator

If you are personable, enthusiastic, and honest; are knowledgeable about products and the nutritional needs of dogs and cats; are a good listener; and are comfortable approaching and talking to strangers, you may find a job as a product demonstrator for a pet-food company or other pet-product manufacturer. Pam Becker of Lake Forest, California, works part time for Nature's Variety doing just that. She feeds the brand to her own pets and was referred to the company by a friend who is a pet nutrition specialist. She works on weekends and sometimes on Thursdays and Fridays from late afternoon into evening. Becker is paid by the hour, with a four-hour maximum for each demonstration.

Although she enjoys the work, drawbacks include being on her feet for hours and schlepping tables and crates. "And if a store is slow, it's very boring," Becker says.

The best part of the job is sharing information about a pet food she likes with people who are interested in their pets' nutrition and overall well-being.

develop training programs to teach clients about a product's advantages, maintain account information, and attend and participate in veterinary association meetings. Pet experience isn't usually required, but it definitely doesn't hurt.

Advertising sales representative: These representatives sell space in publications, in event programs, and on the Internet, as well as air time on radio and television. They need great verbal and interpersonal skills to persuade clients to buy ad space. When they aren't talking to clients at dog shows, veterinary conferences, or other industry events, they are on the phone or on the road, drumming up business.

Education and Training

Although for those with the right people skills, just about any educational background from anthropology to zoology will suffice to enter the fields of advertising, marketing, promotions, and sales, some areas of study are more useful than others. Psychology, for instance, is helpful in marketing and sales because it helps you understand people and what motivates them. Some employers have definite preferences when it comes to particular fields. For marketing, sales, and promotions management positions, they may look for bachelor's or master's degree in advertising, business administration with an emphasis in marketing, communications, or marketing.

For a job at a pet-food company, a minor or major in animal nutrition can be of practical use. Territory managers for pet-food companies are often veterinarians. Courses in business law, management, economics, accounting, finance, mathematics, and statistics are always helpful. Completing an internship while you are in school is also a good idea.

For advertising management positions, some employers prefer a bachelor's or a master's degree in advertising or journalism. Good courses to take include marketing, consumer behavior, market research, sales, communication methods and technology, visual arts, art history, and photography.

Employment Outlook

Employment of advertising, marketing, promotions, public relations, and sales managers is expected to increase by 13 percent through 2018, which is about as fast as average for all occupations, but there is a lot of competition in these fields. You'll have your best shot at one of these jobs if you have a college degree, great creative and communication skills, and experience in the pet world.

Salary levels vary substantially, depending upon the type of job, level of managerial responsibility, length of service, education, size of company, location, and industry. For sales managers, the size of their sales territories is a factor. According to a survey by the National Association of Colleges and Employers, starting salaries for marketing majors graduating in 2009 averaged $43,325 and those for advertising majors averaged $36,000.

Event Planners

Among the types of pet-related companies and organizations that may need the services of event or meeting planners are professional associations and pet food companies that sponsor events such as dog shows. The volunteer officers of organizations such as the Dog Writers Association of America also serve as event planners for annual conferences and banquets.

An event planner arranges content and entertainment, all with an eye toward effectively presenting information to attendees. He or she scouts prospective meeting sites, such as hotels, convention centers, or conference centers, and contacts event managers at those venues to ask for proposals. Based on the proposals, the event planner can then choose a site. Once the location is selected, meeting and convention planners arrange support services, coordinate with the facility, prepare the site staff for the meeting, get any necessary permits, and set up all forms of electronic communication. Other aspects of a planner's job might involve arranging for speakers, planning parties or other entertainments, and supervising the set-up and tear-down of booths at a trade show.

In large organizations, it's not unusual for event planners to specialize in a particular aspect of conference planning. Conference coordinators handle meeting logistics; registrars are in charge of advance registration and payment, name badges, and on-site registration; and education planners coordinate the meeting content, including speakers and topics.

Education and Training

For event planners, a bachelor's degree in marketing, public relations, communications, business, or hotel and hospitality management can be beneficial. Several universities such as San Jose State University, George Washington University, Indiana University, and University of Massachusetts offer certificates in event or meeting planning or bachelor's or

With the help of her resuce dog, Pebbles, event planner Linday Warren works on the details for an upcoming event. Her many clients include animal shelters and rescues.

Portrait of an Event Planner

Enthusiasm, attention to detail, and a positive attitude are hallmarks of a great event planner. Ask Lindsay Warren (*pictured with Pebbles*) of Royal Oak, Michigan, who has all three in abundance and has used them to create a business that includes managing and promoting large and small events for businesses and nonprofits, including animal shelters and rescue groups.

Event planners help clients find sponsors; get door prizes; arrange details such as location, food, and insurance coverage; and publicize the occasion to ensure a great turnout. They must also be flexible and plan for the unexpected, especially with animals. You never know when a dog fight will break out or a pet will get loose.

A good event planner is also possessed of obsessive attention to detail. Warren learned quickly that every single detail must be written down, preferably on a spreadsheet, so there are no misunderstandings about what needs to be done, when, and by whom. Those organizational skills can be learned on the job, Warren says, but it takes a certain type of person to be successful. "Things can go wrong, and no matter how well you plan you have to be ready to take whatever comes at you," she says. "There are definitely some people who wouldn't be a good match for this job."

Warren has bachelor's and master's degrees in telecommunications and her first jobs were in radio, where her responsibilities included preparing event sponsorship proposals and planning station events. As she moved up in the field, she began managing large sponsored events and interactive online media programs and writing, editing, and distributing national press releases.

Now that she's in business for herself, she applies the skills she learned to her own clients' needs, not only helping them plan and publicize events but also buying advertising and doing social media marketing. She loves the daily variety and the chance to make a difference for pets, serving as public relations director for the Michigan Animal Adoption Network and volunteering for Los Angeles–based A Dog's Life Rescue.

"I've loved animals my whole life, so when I left my job in radio, my first goal was to start volunteering because I never had the opportunity when I worked for a large company. When I started volunteering with the Michigan Animal Adoption Network, I started getting freelance work off the bat from people, after they heard what I did, and that I liked working with animals. It's worked out well enough that I can do my freelance work and the volunteering. I thought 'Well, I'll at least start volunteering and the job will come, and it did.' For me it's a win-win; I get to pay the bills and I get to help animals."

master's degrees with majors in hospitality management that encompass event or meetings management. You can also take certification programs and college courses in meeting and convention planning. These programs vary in length from one semester to two years. Although experience is often just as good as a college degree, more and more employers are looking for planners with degrees because of the complexity of the work.

Employment Outlook

With experience, you may choose to become an independent meeting consultant, take a position as executive director of an association, or start your own meeting-planning firm specializing in pet-related events. According to the Bureau of Labor Statistics, employment of meeting and convention planners is expected to grow by 16 percent through 2018, faster than average for all occupations, and it's likely that opportunities for event planners in the pet industry will experience similar growth. As the great popularity of pets remains steady and even increases, this could be an important field.

Pet-Supply Store Positions

For a person who is knowledgeable about animals and has good organi-

PETCO inventory and pricing manager Jen Harris checks the store's supplies.

zational ability and a knack for getting along with people, managing a pet-supply store can be a rewarding career. Store managers must be familiar with the products they sell and be able to tell customers about them, so good communication skills and a strong knowledge of pets are essential.

Jim Nash of Los Altos, California, found that a position in retail-store management turned out to be a good match for his background. Son of a veterinarian, Nash had and worked in his father's clinic from the time he was a young boy. As an adult, he continued his association with dogs and cats, and after leaving the restaurant business, he decided that he would take a part-time job at a pet-supply store. The job turned into a full-time position, and his familiarity with animals was one of the reasons. "Customers appreciate the manager knowing from firsthand experience how to solve pet-related problems," Nash says.

Managerial and Nonmanagerial Positions

There are managerial and nonmanagerial opportunities at pet-supply stores. Here are a few.

Store manager: A store manager's duties include overseeing the work of salespeople and cashiers. Managers interview, hire, and train employees; prepare work schedules; and may handle purchasing, budgeting, and accounting. They are ultimately responsible for customer satisfaction, and they help answer customer questions and deal with any complaints.

Different types of stores have different types of managers. At a small independent pet-supply store, a manager may do everything, but at chain stores such as PETCO or PetSmart, managers have defined responsibilities. For instance, at PetSmart, a store manager supervises three to five department managers and twenty-five to thirty hourly salespeople. The assistant store manager, also known as the operations manager, is responsible for hiring and training. At PETCO, an inventory and pricing manager is responsible not only for inventory and pricing but also for overseeing shipments and opening and closing the store.

Set-up coordinator: Another type of supervisory job is that of store set-up coordinator. This position involves organizing new store openings and store remodels, training and supervising associates and vendors, ensuring that fixtures and stock are in place, and managing the entire process so that it stays on schedule. Store set-up coordinators travel frequently, often more

Sales associate Lorien Pedenelli fills a bag with goodies from a PETCO Treat Bar. Sales associates are cross-trained in many jobs, including checkout, stocking, and customer service.

than 75 percent of the time, and must have superb organizational and leadership skills, plus at least three years of retail management experience.

Nonmanagerial positions: In pet-supply stores, these positions include sales, cashier, and inventory clerk. Successful salespeople have good verbal communication skills, patience, and people skills. They enjoy talking to customers and helping them find what they need. Cashiers ring up sales, count money, and balance the cash registers at the end of each shift. Inventory clerks keep track of what's in stock and what needs to be reordered. Cashiers and inventory clerks should be organized and good with numbers.

Education and Training

Most store managers learn on the job. Those with high-school diplomas often learn by doing, starting as cashiers or salespeople, where they learn merchandising, customer service, and the basic policies and procedures of the company. Employees with bachelor's degrees—which can be in the liberal arts, social sciences, or business—may be hired and then go through a corporate management training program that can be as brief as one week or as lengthy as a year or more. Training may include instruction in interview techniques, customer-service skills, inventory management, employee relations, scheduling, budgeting, marketing, and purchasing.

A high-school diploma or a GED is generally the minimum requirement for a job at a pet-supply store, although many stores hire high-school students, especially those in business programs. Courses in English, accounting or arithmetic, and computer skills are useful.

Employment Outlook

Currently, positions in general retail-store management are projected to grow slowly, but the pet industry is strong, so there may be more opportunities available in the pet field. Nonetheless, people with retail sales experience have the best chance to land jobs.

Salaries in this field vary depending on level of responsibility, length of employment, the size of the store, and whether it is a corporate or independent establishment. In 2008, median annual earnings, including commissions, were $35,310, with the lowest 10 percent earning $22,000 and the highest 10 percent earning $62,000.

In retail, work hours may be part-or full–time and may require working nights, weekends, or holidays. Job prospects are good in retail sales as a whole. Employment is expected to grow by 8 percent through 2018, about as fast as the average. Jobs are often available because of the high turnover rate and the expansion of big-box pet-supply stores. Retail salespeople and other retail workers are usually paid by the hour. Wages range from minimum wage to $10 or more an hour. These rates may include commissions.

DEVELOPER, MARKETER, AND RETAILER RESOURCES

- American Association of Advertising Agencies, http://careercenter.aaaa.org
- American Advertising Federation, www.aaf.org
- American Marketing Association, www.marketingpower.com
- American Pet Products Association, www.americanpetproducts.org
- Association of American Feed Control Officials, www.aafco.org
- Craft and Fabric Links, www.craftandfabriclinks.com
- Doggidog Paris, www.doggidog.com
- Etsy, www.etsy.com
- Fashion Institute of Technology, www.fitnyc.edu
- Industrial Designers Society of America, www.idsa.org
- Luxury Pet Pavilion, www.luxurypetpavilion.com
- Manfred of Sweden, www.manfredofsweden.com
- Modruff Sculpted Dogwear, www.modruff.com
- National Association of Schools of Art and Design, http://nasad.arts-accredit.org
- National Association of Schools of Art and Design, www.nasad.arts-accredit.org
- PETCO, www.petco.com
- Pet Fashion Week, www.petfashionweek.com
- PetSmart, www.petsmart.com
- SparkFun, www.sparkfun.com
- Techshop, http://techshop.ws

Acknowledgments

M any thanks to Virginia Parker Guidry and Christie Keith for their contributions to the text and to the many sources who made this book what it is: Lois Abrams, PhD; Lowell Ackerman, DVM; Terry Albert; Kat Albrecht; Jennifer Armbruster; Rich Avanzino; Mike Bannasch; Tony Basher, DVM; Ericka Basile; Francis Battista; Richard Beauchamp; Marty Becker, DVM; Pam Becker; John Berg, DVM; Steven Biller; Alysa Binder; Stephanie Blank; Mary Bloom; Mara Bovsun; Sue Bulanda; Linda M. Campbell; Betty J. Carmack; Stella Clary; Richard Crook; Terry Curtis, DVM; Pamela Dennison; Dennis Dolan; Dee Dee Drake; Amanda Eick-Miller; Kate Eldredge; Katherine Feldman, DVM; Nancy Fierer; Jean Fogle; David Frei; Ava Frick, DVM; Lea-Ann Germinder; Bill Given; Randi Golub; Chris Grisell; Carol Gurney; John Hamil, DVM; Amie Lamoreaux Hesbach; Heather Houlahan; Heidi Jeter; Alicia Karas, DVM; John Kerwick; Peter Kraatz; Amy Kramer; Charlene LaBelle; Marion Lane; Julie Levy, DVM; Lynn Lloyd; Cheryl Lopate, DVM; Fred J. Lyman; Laurie McCauley, DVM; Patricia McConnell; Susan McCullough; Barbara Jedda McNab; Jason Merrihew; Shawn Messonnier, DVM; Jane Miller; Sarah Miller, DVM; Dale Moone; Arden Moore; Jim Nash; Joanne Nash; Robert Newman; Pam Nichols, DVM; Glenye Cain Oakford; Nina Ottosson; John C. Pearce; Sally Perea, DVM; Lucy Postins; Susan Rhoades; Jill Richardson, DVM; Susie Roof; Elizabeth Rozanski, DVM; Sonya Ryan; Marta Sanchez, DVM; William Secord; Monica Segal; Bianca Shaw, DVM; Julie K. Shaw; John Sherman, DVM; Amy Shojai; Doyle L. Shugart; Nicole Sipe; Martha Smith, DVM; Gina Spadafori; Jaynie Spector; Janet Steiss, DVM; Rubi Sullivan; Nathan Sutter, PhD; John Tegzes, VMD; Sari Brewster Tietjen; Elizabeth Tobey; Kim Toepfer; Betsy Uhl, DVM; Susan Wagner, DVM; Chris Walkowicz; Lindsay Warren; Judy Welch, PsyD; Barbara Williamson; John Wright, CAAB; and the many other people whose stories inspired me.

Many thanks as well to Tamela Klisura for her insights on opening a retail store and to my very fine editors who did a wonderful job of taming and improving the unruly manuscript: Jarelle Stein, Amy Deputato, and Andrew DePrisco. And finally to my husband, Jerry, and my dogs, Bella, Twyla, and Harper, for patiently living through the writing of another book.

Resources

COLLEGES AND UNIVERSITIES

Below is contact information for colleges and universities in the United States with animal science and pre-veterinary programs. You will also find contact information on veterinary schools in the United States and Canada and a listing of veterinary technology and technician programs.

Animal Science and
Pre-Veterinary Programs
Alabama
Auburn University
College of Veterinary Medicine
Auburn, AL 36849
334-844-4546
www.auburn.edu

Tuskegee University
College of Agricultural, Environmental,
and Natural Sciences
Tuskegee, AL 36088
334-727-8174
www.tuskegee.edu

Arizona
University of Arizona
Education Bldg. 69, Rm 104
Tucson, AZ 85721-0069
520-621-7621
www.arizona.edu

California
California State Polytechnic
University Pomona
3801 W. Temple Ave.
Pomona, CA 91768
909-869-7659
www.csupomona.edu

California State University, Fresno
California Agricultural
Technology Institute
5241 N. Maple Ave.
Fresno, CA 93740
559-278-4240
www.csufresno.edu

University of California, Davis
School of Veterinary Medicine
One Shields Ave.
Davis, CA 95616
530-752-1383
www.ucdavis.edu

Colorado
Colorado State University
Fort Collins, CO 80523
530-752-1383
www.colostate.edu

Connecticut
University of Connecticut
College of Agriculture and
Natural Resources
Stoors, CT 06269
860-486-2000
www.uconn.edu

Delaware
University of Delaware
College of Agriculture and
Natural Resources
113 Townsend Hall
Newark, DE 19717
302-831-2792
www.udel.edu

Florida
University of Florida
Gainesville, FL 32611
352-392-3261
www.ufl.edu

Georgia
Berry College
2277 Martha Berry Hwy. NW
Mount Berry, GA 30149
706-232-5374
www.berry.edu

The University of Georgia
College of Veterinary Medicine
Athens, GA 30602-7371
706-542-5728
www.vet.uga.edu

Illinois
Southern Illinois University
College of Agricultural Sciences
1205 Lincoln Drive [Mail Code 4416]
Carbondale, IL 62901
618-453-2469
www.siu.edu

University of Illinois at Urbana-Champaign
College of Veterinary Medicine
3505 Veterinary Medicine Basic
Sciences Building
2001 South Lincoln Ave.
Urbana, IL 61802
217-265-0380
www.uiuc.edu

Indiana
Purdue University
School of Veterinary Medicine
615 W. State St.
West Lafayette, IN 47907
765-494-7893
www.purdue.edu

Iowa
Iowa State University of
Science and Technology
College of Agriculture and Life Sciences
138 Curtiss Hall, Ames, IA 50011-1050Ð
515-294-2518
www.ag.iastate.edu

Kansas
Kansas State University
College of Agriculture
112 Waters Hall
Manhattan, KS 66506
785-532-6151
www.ag.ksu.edu

Kentucky
Berea College
Berea, KY 40404
859-985-3000
www.berea.edu

Morehead State University
150 University Blvd.
Morehead, KY 40351
800-585-6781
www.moreheadstate.edu

Murray State University
PO Box 9
Murray, KY 42071
800-272-4678
www.murraystate.edu

University of Kentucky
College of Agriculture
Lexington, KY 40506
859-257-9000
www.uky.edu

Louisiana
Louisiana State University
College of Agriculture
104 Agricultural Administration Bldg.
Baton Rouge, LA 70803
225-578-2065
www.lsu.edu

Maine
University of Maine
College of Natural Sciences,
Forestry, and Agriculture
5782 Winslow Hall, Rm 2
Orono, ME 04469
207-581-3206
www.umaine.edu

Maryland
University of Maryland
Institute of Applied
Agriculture
2115 Jull Hall
College Park, MD 20742
301-405-1000
www.umd.edu

Massachusetts
Mount Ida College
777 Dedham St.
Newton Center, MA 02459
617-928-4500
www.mountida.edu

Tufts University
Cummings School of
Veterinary Medicine
200 Westboro Rd.
Grafton, MA 01536
508-839-5302
www.tufts.edu

University of Massachusetts
College of Natural Sciences
Amherst, MA 01003
413-545-0111
www.umass.edu

Michigan
Michigan State University
College of Agriculture and
Natural Resources
102 Agriculture Hall
East Lansing, MI 48824-1039
517-355-8383
www.canr.msu.edu

Mississippi
Mississippi State University
Mississippi State, MS 39762
662-325-2323
www.msstate.edu

Missouri
Southwest Missouri State University
901 S. National Ave.
Springfield, MO 65804
417-836-5000
www.missouristate.edu

Stephens College
1200 E. Broadway
Columbia, MO 65215
800-876-7207
www.stephens.edu

University of Missouri
Columbia, MO 65211
573-882-7786
www.missouri.edu

Montana
Montana State University
PO Box 172860
Bozeman, MT 59717-2860
406-994-0211
www.montana.edu

New Mexico
New Mexico State University
College of Agriculture
and Home Economics
Las Cruces, NM 88003-8001
575-646-0111
www.nmsu.edu

Nevada
University of Nevada
1664 N. Virginia St.
Reno, NV 89557
866-263-8232
www.unr.edu

New York
Cornell University
College of Agriculture
and Life Sciences
274 Roberts Hall
Ithaca, NY 14853
607-255-2036
www.cals.cornell.edu

Mercy College
555 Broadway
Dobbs Ferry, NY 10522
877-637-2946
www.mercy.edu

State University of New York
College of Agriculture
and Technology
Cobleskill, NY 12043
518-255-5700
www.cobleskill.edu

North Carolina
North Carolina State University
College of Agriculture and Life Sciences
115 Patterson Hall
Raleigh, NC 27695
919-515-2011
www.ncsu.edu

St. Andrews Presbyterian College
1700 Dogwood Mile
Laurinburg, NC 28352
800-763-0198
www.sapc.edu

North Dakota
North Dakota State University
College of Agriculture, Food Systems
and Natural Resources
1301 Twelfth Ave.
Fargo, ND 58105
701-231-8011
www.ndsu.edu

Ohio
Lake Erie College
391 W. Washington St.
Painesville, OH 44077-3309
800-533-4996
www.lec.edu

Ohio State University
100 Agricultural Administration Bldg.
2120 Fyffe Rd.
Columbus, OH 43210
614-292-6556
www.osu.edu

Otterbein College
Westerville, OH 43081-2006
614-890-3000
www.otterbein.edu

University of Findlay
1000 Main St.
Findlay, OH 45840
800-472-9502
www.findlay.edu

Oklahoma
Oklahoma State University
324 Student Union
Stillwater, OK 74078
405-744-5000
http://osu.okstate.edu/welcome

Oregon
Oregon State University
Withycombe Hall
Corvallis, OR 97331
541-737-1000
www.oregonstate.edu

Pennsylvania
Delaware Valley College
700 E. Butler Ave.
Doylestown, PA 18901
800-233-5825
www.delval.edu

Pennsylvania State University
College of Agricultural Sciences
University Park, PA 16802
814-865-4700
www.psu.edu

Wilson College
1015 Philadelphia Ave.
Chambersburg, PA 17201
717-264-4141
www.wilson.edu

Rhode Island
University of Rhode Island
Kingston, RI 02881
401-874-1000
www.uri.edu

South Carolina
Clemson University
College of Agriculture, Forestry and
Life Sciences
PO Box 345125
Clemson, SC 29634
864-656-3311
www.clemson.edu

South Dakota
South Dakota State University
PO Box 2207
Brookings, SD 57007
800-952-3541
www.sdstate.edu

Tennessee
Middle Tennessee State University
1301 E. Main St.
Murfreesboro, TN 37132
615-898-2300
www.mtsu.edu

University of Tennessee
Institute of Agriculture
Knoxville, TN 37996
865-974-1000
www.utk.edu

Texas
Sul Ross State University
PO Box C-114
Alpine, TX 79832
432-837-8011
www.sulross.edu

Texas A&M University
2112 TAMU
College Station, TX 77843
979-845-3211
www.tamu.edu

West Texas A&M University
2501 Fourteenth Ave.
Canyon, TX 79016-0001
806-651-0000
www.wtamu.edu

Utah
Brigham Young University
Provo, UT 84602
801-422-4636
www.byu.edu

Utah State University
4800 Old Main Hill
Logan, UT 84322
435-797-1000
www.usu.edu

Vermont
University of Vermont
College of Agriculture
and Life Sciences
Burlington, VT 05405
802-656-3131
www.uvm.edu

Washington
Washington State University
College of Agriculture
and Home Economics
PO Box 646242
Pullman, WA 99164-1067
888-468-6978
www.wsu.edu

Wisconsin
University of Wisconsin
College of Agricultural
and Life Sciences
140 Agricultural Hall
Madison, WI 53706
608-263-2400
www.wisc.edu

Colleges of Veterinary Medicine
Alabama
Auburn University
College of Veterinary Medicine
Auburn University, AL 36849
334-844-4546
www.vetmed.auburn.edu

Tuskegee University
College of Veterinary Medicine,
Nursing and Allied Health
334-727-8174
Tuskegee, AL 36088
www.tuskegee.edu

California
University of California, Davis
School of Veterinary Medicine
Office of the Dean
One Shields Ave.
Davis, CA 95616
530-752-1383
www.vetmed.ucdavis.edu

Western University of
Health Sciences College of
Veterinary Medicine
Admissions Office
309 E. 2nd St.
Pomona, CA 91766
909-623-6116
www.westernu.edu

Colorado
Colorado State University
College of Veterinary Medicine
& Biomedical Sciences
1601 Campus Delivery
Fort Collins, CO 80523-1601
970-491-7051
www.cvmbs.colostate.edu

Florida
University of Florida
The College of Veterinary
Medicine
Campus Box 10012
Gainesville, FL 32610
352-294-4214
www.vetmed.ufl.edu

Georgia
University of Georgia
The College of Veterinary
Medicine
Athens, GA 30602
706-542-3221
www.vet.uga.edu

Illinois
University of Illinois at
Urbana-Champaign
College of Veterinary Medicine
3503 Veterinary Medicine
Basic Sciences Bldg.
2001 S. Lincoln Ave.
Urbana, IL 61801
217-265-0380
www.cvm.uiuc.edu

Indiana
Purdue University
School of Veterinary Medicine
1240 Lynn Hall, Rm. 1176
West Lafayette, IN 47907
765-494-7607
www.vet.purdue.edu

Iowa
Iowa State University
College of Veterinary Medicine
Christensen Dr.
Ames, IA 50011
515-294-1250
www.vetmed.iastate.edu

Kansas
Kansas State University
College of Veterinary Medicine
101 Trotter Hall
Manhattan, KS 66506
785-532-5660
www.vet.ksu.edu

Louisiana
Louisiana State University
School of Veterinary Medicine
Skip Bertman Dr.
Baton Rouge, LA 70803
225-578-9900
www.vetmed.lsu.edu

Massachusetts
Tufts University
Cummings School of Veterinary
Medicine at Tufts University
200 Westboro Rd.
North Grafton, MA 01536
508-839-5302
www.tufts.edu/vet

Michigan
Michigan State University
College of Veterinary Medicine
G100 Vet Med Center
East Lansing, MI 48824
517-355-6510
www.cvm.msu.edu

Minnesota
University of Minnesota
College of Veterinary Medicine
1365 Gortner Ave.
St. Paul, MN 55108
612-625-5255
www.cvm.umn.edu/

Mississippi
Mississippi State University
College of Veterinary Medicine
PO Box 9825
Mississippi State, MS 39762-9825
662-325-3432
www.cvm.msstate.edu

Missouri
University of Missouri-Columbia
College of Veterinary Medicine
W-203 Veterinary Medicine Bldg.
Columbia, MO 65211
573-882-3554
www.cvm.missouri.edu

New York
Cornell University
College of Veterinary Medicine
Ithaca, NY 14853
607-253-3700
www.vet.cornell.edu

North Carolina
North Carolina State University
College of Veterinary Medicine
4700 Hillsborough St.
Raleigh, NC 27606
919-513-6786
www.cvm.ncsu.edu

Ohio
Ohio State University
College of Veterinary Medicine
1900 Coffey Rd.
Columbus, OH 43210
614-292-8831
www.vet.ohio-state.edu

Oklahoma
Oklahoma State University
College of Veterinary Medicine
110 McElroy Hall
Stillwater, OK 74078
405-744-6651
www.cvm.okstate.edu

Oregon
Oregon State University
College of Veterinary Medicine
Oregon State University
200 Magruder Hall
Corvallis, OR 97331-4801
541-737-2098
http://oregonstate.edu/vetmed/

Pennsylvania
University of Pennsylvania
School of Veterinary Medicine
3800 Spruce St.
Philadelphia, PA 19104
215-898-8841
www.vet.upenn.edu

Tennessee
University of Tennessee
College of Veterinary Medicine
2407 River Dr.
Knoxville, TN 37996
865-974-8387
www.vet.utk.edu

Texas
Texas A&M University
College of Veterinary Medicine
Suite 101-VMA
College Station, TX 77843
979-845-4941
www.cvm.tamu.edu

Virginia
Virginia Tech and University of Maryland
Virginia-Maryland Regional College of
Veterinary Medicine
Duck Pond Drive (0442)
Blacksburg, VA 24061
540-231-7666
www.vetmed.vt.edu

Washington
Washington State University
College of Veterinary Medicine
Pullman, WA 99164
509-335-5107
www.vetmed.wsu.edu

Wisconsin
University of Wisconsin
School of Veterinary Medicine
2015 Linden Dr.
Madison, WI 53706
608-263-6716
www.vetmed.wisc.edu

**Canadian Veterinary Schools
with AVMA Accreditation**
Ontario Veterinary College
University of Guelph
Guelph, ON N1G 2W1
Canada
519-824-4120, ext. 54401
www.ovc.uoguelph.ca

University of Montreal
Faculty of Veterinary Medicine
3200 Sicotte St.
Saint-Hyacinthe, QC J2S 7C6
Canada
450-773-8521
www.medvet.umontreal.ca

University of Prince Edward Island
Atlantic Veterinary College
550 University Ave.
Charlottetown, PEI C1A 4P3
Canada
800-606-8734
www.upei.ca/avc

University of Saskatchewan
Western College of
Veterinary Medicine
52 Campus Dr.
Saskatoon, Saskatchewan
Canada S7N 5B4
306-966-7447
www.usask.ca/wcvm

**Veterinary Technology
or Technician Schools
with AVMA Accreditation**
Arizona
Pima County Community College
Veterinary Technology Program
8181 E. Irvington Rd.
Tucson, AZ 85709-4000
520-206-7414
www.pima.edu

California
California State Polytechnic
University Pomona
College of Agriculture
Animal Health Technology Program
3801 W. Temple Ave.
Pomona, CA 91768
909-869-2136
www.csupomona.edu

Cosumnes River College
Veterinary Technology Program
8401 Center Pkwy.
Sacramento, CA 95823
916-691-7355
 www.crc.losrios.edu

Foothill College
Veterinary Technology Program
12345 El Monte Rd.
Los Altos Hills, CA 94022
650-949-7203
www.foothill.edu/bio/programs/vettech

Hartnell College
Animal Health Technology Program
156 Homestead Ave.
Salinas, CA 93901
831-755-6855
www.hartnell.cc.ca.us/

Los Angeles Pierce College
Veterinary Technology Program
6201 Winnetka Ave.
Woodland Hills, CA 91371
818-347-0551
 www.macrohead.com/rvt

Mt. San Antonio College
Animal Health Technology Program
1100 N. Grand Ave.
Walnut, CA 91789
909-594-5611
www.mtsac.edu

Western Career College, Citrus Heights
7301 Greenback Lane, Suite A
Citrus Heights, CA 95621
916-722-8200
www.westerncollege.com/california/
citrus-heights-vocational-career-
college-campus.php

Western Career College, Pleasant Hill
Veterinary Technician Program
380 Civic Drive, #300
Pleasant Hill, CA 94523
888-203-9947
www.westerncollege.com/california/
pleasant-hill-vocational-career-college-
campus.php

Western Career College, Sacramento
Veterinary Technology Program
8909 Folsom Blvd.
Sacramento, CA 95826
916-361-1660
www.westerncollege.com/california/
sacramento-vocational-college-career-
campus.php

Western Career College, San Leandro
Veterinary Technology Program
170 Bayfair Mall
San Leandro, CA 94578
510-276-3888
www.westerncollege.com/california/
san-leandro-vocational-college-career-
training.php

Yuba College
Veterinary Technology Program
2088 N. Beale Rd.
Marysville, CA 95901
530-741-6962
http://yc.yccd.edu

Colorado
Bel-Rea Institute of Animal Technology
1681 S. Dayton St.
Denver, CO 80231
800-950-8001
www.bel-rea.com

Colorado Mountain College
Veterinary Technology Program
Spring Valley Campus
3000 County Rd. 114
Glenwood Springs, CO 81601
970-945-8691
www.coloradomtn.edu

Community College of Denver
Veterinary Technology Program
1070 Alton Way, Bldg. 849
Denver, CO 80230
303-365-8300
www.ccd.edu

Front Range Community College
Veterinary Research
Technology Program
4616 S. Shields
Ft. Collins, CO 80526
970-226-2500
www.frontrange.edu

Pima Medical Institute,
Colorado Springs
3770 North Citadel Drive
Colorado Springs, CO 80910
719-482-7462
http://coloradosprings.pmi.edu

Connecticut
NW Connecticut Community College
Veterinary Technology Program
Park Place East
Winsted, CT 06098
860-738-6490
www.nwctc.commnet.edu

Delaware
Delaware Technical and
Community College
Veterinary Technology Program
PO Box 610, Route 18
Georgetown, DE 19947
302-855-5918
www.dtcc.edu

Florida
Brevard Community College
Veterinary Technology Program
1519 Clearlake Rd.
Cocoa, FL 32922
321-433-7594
www.brevardcc.edu

Miami-Dade College
Veterinary Technology Program
Medical Center Campus
950 NW 20th St.
Miami, FL 33127
305-237-4473
www.mdc.edu

St. Petersburg College
Veterinary Technology Program
Box 13489
St. Petersburg, FL 33733
727-341-3652
www.spcollege.edu

Georgia
Athens Technical College
Veterinary Technology Program
800 US Highway 29N
Athens, GA 30601
706-355-5107
www.athenstech.edu

Fort Valley State University
Veterinary Technology Program
1005 State University Drive
Fort Valley, GA 31030
478-825-6353
www.fvsu.edu

Gwinnett Technical College
Veterinary Technology Program
5150 Sugarloaf Pkwy.
Lawrenceville, GA 30043
770-962-7580
www.gwinnetttech.edu

Idaho
College of Southern Idaho
Veterinary Technology Program
315 Falls Ave.
Twin Falls, ID 83303-1238
208-733-9554, ext. 2408
http://agriculture.csi.edu

Illinois
Joliet Junior College
Agriculture Sciences Department
1215 Houbolt Rd.
Joliet, IL 60431
815-280-2746
www.jjc.edu

Parkland College
Veterinary Technology Program
2400 W. Bradley Ave.
Champaign, IL 61821
217-351-2224
www.parkland.edu

Indiana
Purdue University
School of Veterinary Medicine
Veterinary Technology Program
West Lafayette, IN 47907
765-494-7619
www.vet.purdue.edu

Iowa
Des Moines Area Community College
Veterinary Technology Program
2805 SW Snyder Dr., Suite 505
Ankeny, IA 50023
800-362-2127
www.dmacc.edu

Kirkwood Community College
Animal Health Technology Program
6301 Kirkwood Blvd., SW
Cedar Rapids, IA 52406
319-398-4978
www.kirkwood.edu

Kansas
Colby Community College
Veterinary Technology Program
1255 S. Range
Colby, KS 67701
785-460-5466
www.colbycc.edu

Kentucky
Morehead State University
Veterinary Technology Program
25 MSU Farm Dr.
Morehead, KY 40351
606-783-2326
www.moreheadstate.edu

Murray State University
Breathitt Veterinary Center
100 AHT Center
Murray, KY 42071
270-762-7001
http://breathitt.murraystate.edu

Louisiana
Northwestern State University of Louisiana
Veterinary Technology Program
Department of Life Sciences
225 Bienvenu Hall
Natchitoches, LA 71497
318-357-5323
www.nsula.edu

Maine
University College of Bangor
Veterinary Technology Program
85 Texas Ave., 217 Belfast Hall
Bangor, ME 04401-4367
207-262-7852
www.uma.maine.edu/bangor

Maryland
Essex Campus of the Community College
Of Baltimore County
Veterinary Technology Program
7201 Rossville Blvd.
Baltimore, MD 21237
410-682-6000
www.ccbcmd.edu

Massachusetts
Becker College
Veterinary Technology Program
964 Main St.
Leicester, MA 01524
508-791-9241
www.becker.edu

Holyoke Community College
Veterinary Technician Program
303 Homestead Ave.
Holyoke, MA 01040-1099
413-538-7000
www.hcc.edu

Mount Ida College
Veterinary Technology Program
777 Dedham St.
Newton, MA 02459
617-928-4545
www.mountida.edu

North Shore Community College
Veterinary Technology Program
1 Ferncroft Rd.
Danvers, MA 01923
978-762-4000
www.northshore.edu

Michigan
Baker College of Cadillac
Veterinary Technology Program
9600 East 13th St.
Cadillac, MI 49601
231-775-8458
www.baker.edu

Baker College of Flint
Veterinary Technology Program
1050 W. Bristol Rd.
Flint, MI 48507
800-964-4299 or 810-766-4153
www.baker.edu

Baker College of Muskegon
Veterinary Technology Program
1903 Marquette Ave.
Muskegon, MI 49442
800-937-0337 or 231-777-5275
www.baker.edu

Macomb Community College
Veterinary Technician Program
Center Campus
44575 Garfield Rd.
Clinton Township, MI 48044
586-286-2096
www.macomb.edu

Michigan State University
College of Veterinary Medicine
Veterinary Technology Program
A-10 Veterinary Medical Center
East Lansing, MI 48824
517-353-7267
www.cvm.msu.edu

Wayne County Community
College District
Veterinary Technology Program
c/o Wayne State University
Div. of Laboratory Animal Resources
540 E. Canfield
Detroit, MI 48201
313-577-1156
www.dlar.wayne.edu

Minnesota
Argosy University
Twin Cities
Veterinary Technician Program
1515 Central Parkway
Eagan, MN 55121
888-844-2004
www.argosy.edu

Globe University
Veterinary Technology Program
8089 Globe Drive
Woodbury, MN 55125
800-231-0660
www.msbcollege.edu/campus-
locations/woodbury-mn

Minnesota School of Business,
Plymouth
Veterinary Technology Program
1455 County Rd. 101 North
Plymouth, MN 55447
763-476-2000
plymouth.msbcollege.edu

Ridgewater College
Veterinary Technology Dept.
2101 15th Ave., NW
Willmar, MN 56201
320-222-5200
www.ridgewater.edu

Mississippi
Hinds Community College
Veterinary Technology Program
1100 PMB 11160
Raymond, MS 39154
601-857-3456
www.hindscc.edu

Missouri
Crowder College
601 LaClede Ave.
Neosho, MO 64850
417-455-5772
www.crowder.edu

Jefferson College
Veterinary Technology Program
1000 Viking Dr.
Hillsboro, MO 63050
636-942-3000
www.jeffco.edu/jeffco/

Maple Woods Community College
Veterinary Technology Program
2601 NE Barry Rd.
Kansas City, MO 64156
816-437-3235
www.mcckc.edu

Nebraska
Nebraska College of Technical Agriculture
Veterinary Technology Program
RR3, Box 23A
Curtis, NE 69025
308-367-4124
http://ncta.unl.edu/majors/vettech.html

Northeast Community College
Veterinary Technician Program
801 E. Benjamin Ave.
Norfolk, NE 68702-0469
402-371-2020
www.nemcc.edu

Vatterott College
Veterinary Technician Program
11818 I St.
Omaha, NE 68137-1237
402-392-1300
www.vatterott-college.edu

Nevada
College of Southern Nevada
Veterinary Technology Program
6375 W. Charleston Blvd.
Las Vegas, NV 89146-1164
702-651-5852
www.csn.edu

Truckee Meadows
Community College
Veterinary Technology Program
7000 Dandini Blvd.
Reno, NV 89512
775-850-4005
www.tmcc.edu

New Hampshire
Great Bay Community College
Veterinary Technology Program
320 Corporate Drive
Portsmouth, NH 03801
603-427-7695
www.greatbay.edu

New Jersey
Camden County College
Animal Science Technology Program
P.O. Box 200
Blackwood, NJ 08012
856-227-7200
www.camdencc.edu

New Mexico
Central New Mexico
Community College
Veterinary Technology Program
525 Buena Vista SE
Albuquerque, NM 87106
505-224-5043
www.cnm.edu

San Juan College
Veterinary Technology Distance
Learning Program
4601 College Blvd.
Farmington, NM 87402
505-566-3182
www.sjc.cc.nm.us

New York
Alfred State College
Veterinary Technology Program
Agriculture Science Building
Alfred, NY 14801
607-578-3009
www.alfredstate.edu

La Guardia Community College
The City University of New York
Veterinary Technology Program
31-10 Thomson Ave.
Long Island City, NY 11101
718-482-5470
www.lagcc.cuny.edu

Medaille College
Veterinary Technology Program
18 Agassiz Cr.
Buffalo, NY 14214
716-884-3281
www.medaille.edu

Mercy College
Veterinary Technology Program
555 Broadway
Dobbs Ferry, NY 10522
914-674-7530
www.mercy.edu

State University of New York-Canton
Agricultural & Technical College
Health Sciences & Medical Technologies
Veterinary Science Technology Program
34 Cornell Drive
Canton, NY 13617
315-386-7410
www.canton.edu

State University of New York-Delhi
College of Technology
Veterinary Science Technology Program
156 Farnsworth Hall
Delhi, NY 13753
607-746-4306
www.delhi.edu

State University of New York, Ulster
(Ulster County Community College)
Veterinary Technology Program
Cottekill Road
Stone Ridge, NY 12484
800-724-0833, ext. 5233
www.sunyulster.edu

Suffolk Community College
Veterinary Science Technology Program
Western Campus
Crooked Hill Rd.
Brentwood, NY 11717
631-851-6289
www3.sunysuffolk.edu

North Carolina
Asheville-Buncombe Technical
Community College
Veterinary Medical Technology
Program
340 Victoria Rd.
Asheville, NC 28801
828-254-1921, ext. 273
www.abtech.edu

Central Carolina Community College
Veterinary Medical Technology
Program
1105 Kelly Dr.
Sanford, NC 27330
919-775-5401
www.cccc.edu

Gaston College
Veterinary Medical Technology Program
201 Hwy. 321 South
Dallas, NC 28034-1499
704-922-6200
www.gaston.edu

North Dakota
North Dakota State University
Veterinary Technology Program
NDSU Dept. 2230
PO Box 6050
Fargo, ND 58108
701-231-7511
vettech.ndsu.nodak.edu

Ohio
Columbus State Community College
Veterinary Technology Program
550 E. Spring St.
Columbus, OH 43216
614-287-3685
www.cscc.edu

Cuyahoga Community College
Veterinary Technology Program
11000 Pleasant Valley Rd.
Parma, OH 44130
216-987-5450
www.tri-c.edu

UC Raymond Walters College
Veterinary Technology Program
9555 Plainfield Rd.
Blue Ash, OH 45236
513-936-7173
www.rwc.uc.edu

Stautzenberger College-Brecksville
Veterinary Technology Program
8001 Katherine Blvd.
Brecksville, OH 44141
440-846-1999
www.learnwhatyoulove.com

Stautzenberger College, Maumee
Veterinary Technology Program
1796 Indian Wood Circle
Maumee, OH 43537
419-866-0261
www.learnwhatyoulove.com/

Oklahoma
Murray State College
Veterinary Technology Program
One Murray Campus
Tishomingo, OK 73460
580-371-2371
www.mscok.edu

Oklahoma State University, Oklahoma City
Veterinary Technology Program
900 N. Portland Ave.
Oklahoma City, OK 73107
405-945-9112
www.osuokc.edu/vettech/

Tulsa Community College
Veterinary Technology Program
7505 W. 41st St.
Tulsa, OK 74107
918-595-8212
www.tulsacc.edu

Oregon
Portland Community College
Veterinary Technology Program
P.O. Box 19000
Portland, OR 97219
503-244-6111
www.pcc.edu/programs/vet-tech

Pennsylvania
Harcum College
Veterinary Technology Program
750 Montgomery Ave.
Bryn Mawr, PA 19010-3476
610-526-6055
www.harcum.edu

Johnson College
Veterinary Science Technology Program
3427 N. Main Ave.
Scranton, PA 18508
800-293-9675
www.johnson.edu

Lehigh Carbon & Northampton
Community Colleges
Veterinary Technology Program
3835 Green Pond Rd.
Bethlehem, PA 18020
610-861-5548
www.lccc.edu

Manor College
Veterinary Technology Program
700 Fox Chase Rd.
Jenkintown, PA 19046
215-885-2360
www.manorvettech.com

The Vet Tech Institute
Veterinary Technician Program
125 Seventh St.
Pittsburgh, PA 15222
800-570-0693
www.vettechinstitute.edu

Sanford-Brown Institute
(formerly Western School of Health
and Business Careers
Veterinary Technology Program
421 7th Ave.
Pittsburgh, PA 15219
412-281-2600
www.sanfordbrown.edu

Wilson College
Veterinary Medical Technology
Program
1015 Philadelphia Ave.
Chambersburg, PA 17201
717-264-4141
www.wilson.edu

Puerto Rico
University of Puerto Rico
Veterinary Technology Program
Medical Sciences Campus
P.O. Box 365067
San Juan, PR 00936-5067
787-758-2525, ext. 1051 or 1052
www.cprsweb.rcm.upr.edu

South Carolina
Tri-County Technical College
Veterinary Technology Program
P.O. Box 587
Pendleton, SC 29670
864-646-8361
www.tctc.edu

Trident Technical College
Veterinary Technology Program
1001 South Live Oak Drive
Moncks Corner, SC 29461
843-899-8011
www.tridenttech.edu

South Dakota
National American University
Allied Health Division
Veterinary Technology Program
321 Kansas City St.
Rapid City, SD 57701
800-843-8892
www.national.edu

Tennessee
Columbia State Community College
Veterinary Technology Program
P.O. Box 1315, Health Sciences 105
Columbia, TN 38401
931-540-2722
www.columbiastate.edu

Lincoln Memorial University
Veterinary Technology Program
Cumberland Gap Pkwy.
LMU Box 1659
Harrogate, TN 37752
423-869-6278
www.lmunet.edu

Texas
Cedar Valley College
Veterinary Technology
Program
3030 N. Dallas Ave.
Lancaster, TX 75134
972-860-8127
www.cedarvalleycollege.edu

McLennan Community College
Veterinary Technology
Program
1400 College Drive
Waco, TX 76708
254-299-8750
www.mclennan.edu

Midland College
Veterinary Technology Program
3600 N. Garfield
Midland, TX 79705
432-685-4619
www.midland.edu

Palo Alto College
Veterinary Technology Program
1400 W. Villaret Blvd.
San Antonio, TX 78224-2499
210-486-3355
www.alamo.edu

Lone Star College-Tomball
Veterinary Technology Program
30555 Tomball Pkwy.
Tomball, TX 77375-4036
281-351-3357
http://tomball.lonestar.edu

Vet Tech Institute of Houston
4669 Southwest Freeway, Suite 100
Houston, TX 77027
713-629-1500
www.vettechinstitute.edu

Utah
Utah Career College
Veterinary Technician Program
1902 West 7800 South
West Jordan, UT 84088
801-304-4224
www.utahcollege.edu

Vermont
Vermont Technical College
Veterinary Technology Program
Randolph Center, VT 05061
802-728-3391
www.vtc.edu

Virginia
Blue Ridge Community College
Veterinary Technology Program
Box 80
Weyers Cave, VA 24486
540-234-9261
http://community.brcc.edu

Northern Virginia
Community College
Veterinary Technology Program
Loudoun Campus
1000 Harry Flood Byrd Hwy.
Sterling, VA 20164-8699
703-450-2525
www.nvcc.edu

Washington
Pierce College Ft. Steilacoom
Veterinary Technology Program
9401 Farwest Dr., SW
Lakewood, WA 98498
253-964-6668
www.pierce.ctc.edu

Pima Medical Institute-Seattle
Veterinary Technology Program
9709 Third Ave. NE, Suite 400
Seattle, WA 98115
Carol Mayer, DVM-Program Director
800-477-PIMA
http://pmi.edu

Yakima Valley
Community College
Veterinary Technology Program
P.O. Box 22520
Yakima, WA 98907-1647
509-574-4759
www.yvcc.edu

Wisconsin
Madison Area Technical College
Veterinary Technician Program
3550 Anderson
Madison, WI 53704
608-246-6100
http://matcmadison.edu

Wyoming
Eastern Wyoming College
Veterinary Technology
Program
3200 W. "C" St.
Torrington, WY 82240
800-658-3195, ext. 8268
www.ewc.wy.edu

Photo Credits

The images in this book are reproduced courtesy of/by permission of the following:

Front Cover—Seth Casteel.

Title page—Shutterstock.

Introduction—Mary Bloom.

Section 1—12: Shutterstock. 13 (clockwise from top left): Karen Taylor, Shutterstock, Mary Bloom (2 images), Shutterstock.

Chapter 1—15: Best Friends Pet Care. 16: Karen Taylor. 17: Shutterstock.

Chapter 2—21: Karen Taylor. 22: Jess Eisenhardt. 24: Sarah Carey. 27: CBP, photo by James R. Tourtellotte. 29: NPS, photo by Jim Peaco.

Chapter 3—31, 32, 35, 36, 39, 41, 43: Shutterstock. 33: Kris Parlett. 40: Karen Taylor. 42: AVMA. 44: Amie Lamoreaux Hesbach.

Chapter 4—47, 48: Shutterstock. 51: Gina Cioli and Pamela Hunnicutt/BowTie Inc.

Section 2—54: Shutterstock. 55 (clockwise from top left): Karen Taylor, Gail Miller Bisher, Shutterstock, Pam Marks, Patricia McConnell.

Chapter 5—57, 61, 72: Mary Bloom. 58: Pam Marks. 62: Gail Miller Bisher. 63: The Seeing Eye. 67: Ian Dunbar. 69: Susan McCullough.

Chapter 6—75: Shutterstock. 76: Jon Smith, www.jonsmithphotos.com. 78: APDT. 80: John Wright. 81, 82: Mary Burch.

Section 3—85: Mary Bloom (5 images).

Chapter 7—87: Fiona Green. 88, 94, 95, 97: Mary Bloom. 91, 93: Sally Perea.

Chapter 8—101: U.S. Army, photo by Michael Crescitelli. 102: Mary Bloom. 103: Joel Riner. 106: Stephen Ausmus. 107: Orthopedic Foundation for Animals. 108: U.S. Army, photo by Sadie Bleistein.

Chapter 9—111, 115, 116, 119, 121, 124, 126: Mary Bloom. 112: Alicia Karas. 117: Richard Pitcairn. 123: Juliette de Bairacli Levy Archive. 129: Chris Zink. 130: Karen Taylor.

Chapter 10—135: Amelia Hughes Photography. 136: Stephen Ausmus. 137: Katherine Feldman. 138: CDC/Minnesota Dept. of Health, RN Barr Library, Librarians M. Rethlefsen and M. Jones. 139: Mary Bloom. 140: Eric Kulin Photography.

Chapter 11—143: USDA/ARS, photo by Scott Bauer. 144: NASA. 146: ASPCA. 150: Betsy Uhl. 151: School of Veterinary Medicine/University of Pennsylvania.

Section 4—154: Shutterstock. 155 (clockwise from top left): Fiona Green, Jerry Schinberg, AVMA, Mary Bloom (3 images).

Chapter 12—157, 172: Jess Eisenhardt. 159: Mary Bloom. 160: Karen Taylor. 162, 170: jeanmfogle.com. 164: Arden Moore. 169: Amanda Eick-Miller. 174: Amie Lamoreaux Hesbach.

Chapter 13—177: Fiona Green. 178: Dwayne King. 179: Andre Petkus. 182, 189, 192: Karen Taylor. 186: Teri DiMarino. 187: jeanmfogle.com. 190, 191: Barkleigh.com.

Section 5—194: Shutterstock. 195 (clockwise from top left): NHGRI, photo by Maggie Bartlett; NPS, photo by Jim Peaco; Mary Bloom; NPS, photo by Jim Peaco; USGS, photo by Dean Cluff.

Chapter 14—197: Nathan Sutter. 198: Mary Bloom. 201: Elaine Ostrander. 202: Uppsala Universitet, photo by Denny Lorentzen. 204: School of Veterinary Medicine/University of Pennsylvania.

Chapter 15—207: NPS, photo by Jim Peaco. 208: USGS, photo by David Mech. 209: Christophe Lepetit. 210, 215: Bill Given. 212: NPS, photo by Barry O'Neill. 216: Cheetah Conservation Fund, www.cheetah.org.

Section 6—218: Shutterstock. 219 (clockwise from top left): Mary Bloom; William Secord Gallery, New York; photo by Lisa Croft-Elliott, courtesy James P. Taylor; BowTie Press; Mary Bloom.

Chapter 16—221: Karen Taylor. 222, 230: William Secord Gallery, New York. 224, 225: Buck Jones. 226: Barbara Beck. 227, 228, 234: Mary Bloom. 236: Barbara Jedda McNab. 237: Jaynie Milligan Spector.

Chapter 17—241, 246, 248 (bottom): Mary Bloom. 242, 248 (top): jeanmfogle.com. 244: Kerrin Winter Churchill. 245: Gay Glazbrook. 250: James P. Taylor.

Chapter 18—253: Tom Barthel. 254, 256: Mary Bloom. 255: Tom Eldredge. 261: Marion Lane. 263: Gina Cioli and Pamela Hunnicutt/BowTie Inc. 265: Mara Bovsun. 266, 269, 271: BowTie Press. 273: Ericka Basile. 274: Kim Booth.

Chapter 19—277, 280: Mary Bloom. 278: AKC. 283: Jason Merrihew. 284: Jenn Armbruster. 285: Lea-Ann Germinder. 287: Pet Life Radio. 289: Steve Dale. 290: Arden Moore.

Section 7—294: Shutterstock. 219 (clockwise from top left): Pam Marks, Howard Gold/Pawprint Productions, Pam Marks, Karen Taylor, Pam Marks.

Chapter 20—297: jeanmfogle.com. 298: Francis Battista. 300: 304: Karen Taylor. 302: Mary Bloom. 305: Nicholas Mazzucco. 306: Pam Marks.

Chapter 21—309, 312, 314, 316: Howard Gold/Pawprint Productions. 311: Richard Crook.

Section 8—318: Shutterstock. 319 (clockwise from top left): Amy Stevens, Tom LaBriola, Fiona Green, jeanmfogle.com (2 images).

Chapter 22—321: Amy Stevens. 322: Carol Gurney. 325: Fiona Green. 328: Melanie Snowhite. 330: jeanmfogle.com. 332: Dawn Celapino.

Chapter 23—335, 340: Fiona Green. 336: Heidi Ganahl. 338: Best Friends Pet Care. 339: jeanmfogle.com. 342: Joseph Sporn.

Chapter 24—345: Karen Taylor. 346, 349: Kat Albrecht. 347: Shutterstock. 350, 352, 354: jeanmfogle.com. 357: Tom LaBriola.

Section 9—360: Shutterstock. 361 (clockwise from top left): Mary Bloom, Karen Taylor, Julie Poole, Mary Bloom, Lynn Lloyd.

Chapter 25—363: Steve Surfman. 364: Joanne Nash. 367 (top): Frank Photography. 367 (bottom): Missy Yuhl. 368: Claudia Orlandi. 370: Julie Poole. 372: Dagmar Kenis. 374: Mary Bloom.

Chapter 26—377: Mary Bloom. 378: Luke Allen Photography. 379: Joan Ludwig. 381, 382: Sara Tietjan. 383: Mary Bloom. 385: jeanmfogle.com.

Chapter 27—389, 395: Karen Taylor. 390, 393: Lynn Lloyd. 392: Shutterstock. 397: NPS, photo by Jared Withers.

Section 10—398: Shutterstock. 361 (clockwise from top left): FEMA, photo by Andrea Booher; CBP, photo by Gerald Nino; SDF; FEMA, photo by Andrea Booher; Kat Albrecht

Chapter 28—401: Karen Taylor. 402: Dale Moone. 405: John Kerwick. 406: John C. Pearce. 407, 408, 412: Tara Darling. 410: jeanmfogle.com.

Chapter 29—415: FEMA, photo by Andrea Booher. 416, 423, 424, 425: Susan Bulanda. 418: FEMA, photo by Amanda Bicknell. 419: SDF. 422: FEMA, photo by Leif Skoogfors.

Section 11—426: Shutterstock. 427 (clockwise from top left): Shutterstock, Stephan Otto, Mary Bloom, Karen Taylor.

Chapter 30—429: Shutterstock. 430: Meg Callea. 433: Heidi Hudson/The Kennel Club Picture Library. 437, 438: Jerry Mann.

Chapter 31—441: America's Top Dog Model®. 442: Lucy Postins. 444: Nina Ottosson. 446, 456, 457, 458, 460: Karen Taylor. 447, 449: Michael Garland Photo. 450: MoS/Björn Gärdsby. 452: Pam Becker.

Acknowledgments—Cindy Kassebaum.

Index—Shutterstock.

Back Flap—Jerry M. Thornton.

Back Cover—Jess Eisenhardt.

Abbreviations
AKC—American Kennel Club; APDT—Association of Pet Dog Trainers; ASPCA—American Society for the Prevention of Cruelty to Animals; AVMA—American Veterinary Medical Association; CARE—California Animal Rehabilitation; CBP—U.S. Customs and Border Protection; CDC—Centers for Disease Control; FEMA—Federal Emergency Management Agency; NASA—National Aeronautics and Space Administration; NHGRI—National Human Genome Research Institute; NPS—National Park Service; USGS—U.S. Geological Survey; SDF—National Disaster Search Dog Foundation; SPCA—Society for the Prevention of Cruelty to Animals; USDA/ARS—U.S. Dept. of Agriculture/Agricultural Research Service.

Index